THE LIVES OF THE
TWELVE CAESARS

THE MODERN LIBRARY
OF THE WORLD'S BEST BOOKS

The publishers will be pleased to send, upon request, an illustrated folder setting forth the purpose and scope of THE MODERN LIBRARY, *and listing each volume in the series. Every reader of books will find titles he has been looking for, handsomely printed, in unabridged editions, and at an unusually low price.*

THE LIVES
OF THE
TWELVE
CAESARS

BY
SUETONIUS

An unexpurgated English version
Edited with notes and an introduction

BY JOSEPH GAVORSE

MODERN LIBRARY · NEW YORK

CONTENTS

THE TWELVE CAESARS

	Birth and Death		*Reign*
Julius Caesar	102 or 100 B.C.–44 B.C.	Dictator	44 B.C.
Augustus	63 B.C.–14 A.D.	Emperor	27 B.C.–14 A.D.
Tiberius	42 B.C.–37 A.D.	"	14–37 A.D.
Caligula	12–41 A.D.	"	37–41 A.D.
Claudius	10 B.C.–54 A.D.	"	41–54 A.D.
Nero	37–68 A.D.	"	54–68 A.D.
Galba	3 B.C.–69 A.D.	"	68 (June)–69 (January) A.D.
Otho	32–69 A.D.	"	69 A.D. (January 15 to April 16)
Vitellius	15–69 A.D.	"	69 A.D. (January 2 to December 22)
Vespasian	9–79 A.D	"	69–79 A.D.
Titus	39 or 41–81 A.D.	"	79–81 A.D.
Domitian	51–96 A.D.	"	81–96 A.D.

THE TWELVE CAESARS

INTRODUCTION

I

GAIUS SUETONIUS TRANQUILLUS lived at a time of particular significance for western civilization. The political and cultural greatness of Rome had reached its climax and begun its long decline. The Apostles Paul and Peter had been martyred and Christianity had begun the long ascent of its influence.

Of the manifold ramifications of effect that the events of his century were to have on later life Suetonius was completely oblivious. Even the mind of his time most gifted with historical perspective, that of Tacitus, could not accurately envisage the implications of history of 1st Century Rome. This, of course, is peculiarly true in regard to the influence which Christianity was to have, true not only of Suetonius, but of all contemporary with its beginnings. The greatness of this influence was to surpass even the most consolatory dreams of the most fanatical Christian zealot writhing in the arena for his cause. To our Roman authors the Christians of the 1st Century were a pitiable lot. And they give us never a clue as to whether a man Christ actually lived and was crucified, or whether he was a fiction Rome herself pieced together in an effort to create a religious tool by which further to unite the diverse peoples under her dominion.

That Suetonius was utterly unsuspecting of the focal strength of Christianity is readily understood. But he appears, as well, not even to have been conscious of the effects which would issue from many of the acts of the Caesars whose lives interested him so minutely. Important historical events he often dismisses in a paragraph, as the Gallic conquests of Julius, or with a casual allusion, as the defeat of Varus. Though he was aware the age was degenerate he did not realize its abasement was not a valley between two hills but an incline leading inexorably toward the sea of ineffectuality into which Rome was to descend. He was not concerned with political ideals or with ethics, as was Tacitus. He had little appreciation of the significance of events, and less historical perspective. He presents no composite picture of the manners or society in which his characters moved. He produced neither history nor biography, though he handled the materials of both. Nor is he a literary artist, though he wrote Latin with the clarity of the conscientious grammarian.

II

If the defects of Suetonius are so considerable it may well be asked in what way his work is valuable to us. For, the *Lives of the Twelve Caesars* remains a peculiarly valuable and interesting work.

Unlike the *Annals* of Tacitus, which covers much of the same period of Roman history, the *Lives* has always been popular.

Suetonius' keynote is the personal. And detail of person, especially the persons of the powerful Caesars, had a particular fascination for the Romans of his time and that immediately following. Its popularity in the Middle Ages is shown by the hundreds of manuscript copies which have come down to us. There exist three Incunabula of the *Lives*. And between 1470 and 1820 more than forty editions appeared, some under the editorship of such eminent scholars as Erasmus, Stephanus, and Casaulon. Between 1606 and 1796 three English translations appeared.

Unlike Tacitus, Suetonius has had many imitators.

Until Suetonius Roman biography was restricted to meager, one-sided forms. They were mostly of a laudatory character. They arose from three sources: (1) funeral eulogies spoken from the rostrum by a son or other near relative of the deceased; (2) eulogies of ancestors by magistrates on entering office; (3) the recitation at banquets of narratives dealing with the valorous deeds and great virtues of illustrious men.

That biography among the Romans had developed no farther by Suetonius' day is due largely to the rigidity of the forms of biography they had inherited from the Greeks, among whom this branch of writing had always been subordinate to other forms of philosophic teaching. For the essence of the "philosophic type" of Greek biography was that it should have a moral and didactic purpose, should present idealized pictures of the art of living as models for imitation. The "grammatical type" of Greek biography was perhaps even more restricted in scope. This type developed from outlines of the lives of authors to whose works they served as introductions, drawing their material largely from these works themselves.

Suetonius' work, therefore, though seemingly modeled on the "grammatical type" of his time, differed so radically in conception, scope, and form from earlier biography that he may be taken as a starting point for subsequent Roman biography. He gave a biographical turn to historical writing that endured for centuries. This is seen by the number of later writers, among them Marius Maximus, and the authors of the Augustan History *Scriptores Historiae Augustae,* who used the *Lives* as model. His influence extended to the Greek and Byzantine writers, and even to Christian, as appears from the biography of Ambrosius by his Secretary Paulinus.

Nor were the other works of Suetonius without influence on succeeding writers.

The lexicographer Suidas of the 10th Century has given us a list of eighteen titles, though doubtless some of these are sub-headings of larger works rather than separate titles. The titles show a vast field of interest. Among them is one "on the origin and early import of imprecations and words of abuse." Another treats "of those courtesans who were celebrated for their beauty or accomplishments," of which Apuleius made use. Hieronymus wrote of the "Illustrious Men" of the Church in imitation of Suetonius' work of the same title, while the ecclesiastical chronographers, such as Julius Africanus, drew on his treatise "On the Kings." Tertullian based his *De Spectaculis* on a similar work of Suetonius. Censorinus, Solinus, Macrobius, Isidore, the learned bishop of Seville, were all indebted to him.

But of all these works only the *Lives of the Twelve Caesars* has come down to us practically entire.

III

Though Suetonius does not compare favorably with many authors more eminent, the reason for the anomaly of his popularity and influence is, however, quite apparent.

Suetonius is inveterately human. While Tacitus soars and views the horizons Suetonius grubs like a naturalist for every minute act, private or public, every particular trait, habit, or idiosyncrasy of the man under the miscroscope of his indefatigable curiosity for realistic detail. He permits himself the omission of no minute item, good, bad or indifferent. He feels himself bound to report not only all his subject did but all that was said about him, after he has sifted its authenticity according to his criterions. They are high. Suetonius was critical of his sources. One may smile at his painstaking attention to detail, but the human interests of the reader are all the more engaged.

The result is that we are given a vivid picture of the external man. In not one of the twelve portraits do we perceive the inner man. Either Suetonius had no interest in portraying the growth of a soul in the welter of human circumstance, or he realized he had no gift for such portrayal, chose a method of narration which precluded it, and followed his plan with rigor, wisely limiting himself to the marshaling of external facts.

These he presents with business-like brevity, stripped of comment, but so grouped as to produce his effect without the use of rhetoric, with no studied climaxes, no bursts of declamatory eloquence, no verbal pictures set in frames of rhetorical richness, with utter absence of attempt to sway the emotions of the reader, with no personal bias either in enthusiasm for virtue or repugnance before vice. From this indifference the reader comes to feel he is truly impartial, that he is merely telling what he believes to be true, and leaving each to his own conclusion. The impressiveness of the facts detain and interest the reader. Suetonius is, despite the disadvantages of his method, never colorless or dull, even in the parts devoted to genealogy. And at times his clear, terse record of events reaches heights of power in their very sobriety and simplicity, as in the scene of Caesar's death, or Nero's.

Such records are undoubtedly very valuable supplements to the more formal historical sources. Suetonius is one of our guides closest to that remarkable period of transition in the history of Rome, the two centuries on either side of the birth of Christ. Sometimes he is our most direct and only source, for there are lacunae in the works of Tacitus and Dion Cassius, as they have come down to us.

Because of the seeming sensationalism of some parts of his work, the reliability of Suetonius as a guide and even his honesty have been attacked. He certainly does tell a prodigious number of scandalous anecdotes about the Caesars. But there was doubtless more of that than any man could tell. He had access to a vast amount of public and, as secretary to Hadrian, private records now lost to us. And that he depended on such sources more than, as some assert, on hearsay and gossip, is shown not only by a critical reading of his text but by the fact that as his narrative approaches and overlaps the period of his own life the detail becomes meager, and the biographies consequently shorter.

Thus, while we have in Suetonius no tracing of the connection of events or of the effects of circumstance in developing character we have a great vividness of presentation of the external personality. Thanks to him men know still intimately indeed the flesh and blood of the Caesars. It is to such work that men still grant popularity.

IV

No biography of Suetonius has come down to us. The biographical data we have is not extensive, though good. It consists in: (1) references to himself in the *Lives* (five in number, though only one gives us direct information); (2) six letters of Pliny the Younger, four addressed to Suetonius, and two concerning him; (3) a letter from Trajan to Pliny about Suetonius; (4) a sentence concerning him in Spartianus' *Life of Hadrian;* which is further elucidated by a bit of information given us by the Byzantine antiquarian Johannes Lydus (circa 550).

From this material we cannot reconstruct his life in detail, but we can, fortunately, sketch its general outlines.

He himself tells us in *Otho*, X: "My father Suetonius Laetus took part in that war [Otho against Vitellius] as a Tribune of the equestrian order in the 13th legion." This was in 69 A.D., which year Macé argues is the date of Tranquillus' birth, an event he places in Rome. To fix either exactly will very likely remain impossible. But from two other references of Suetonius to himself we set it around the beginning of the reign of Vespasian, which was from 70 to 79.

Where, how, or by whom he was educated we do not know. For our next glimpse of him is as a lawyer in Rome, in a letter from Pliny, which reads:

"Your letter informs me, that you are extremely alarmed by a dream; apprehending that it forebodes some ill success to you in the cause you have undertaken to defend; and, therefore, you desire that I get it adjourned for a few days, or, at least to the next. This is a favor, you realize, not very easily obtained, but I will use all my influence for that purpose: 'For dreams descend from Jupiter.' In the meanwhile, it is very material for you to recollect, whether your dreams generally represent things as they afterwards fall out, or quite the reverse. But if I may judge of yours by one that happened to myself, you have nothing to fear; for it portends you will acquit yourself with great success. . . . But, after all, perhaps you will think it more safe to pursue this cautious maxim: 'never do a thing concerning the rectitude of which you are in doubt.' If so, write me. In the interval, I will consider some expedient, and endeavor that your cause shall be heard any day you like best. In this respect, you are in a better situation than I was: the court of the *centumviri*, where I was to plead, admits of no adjournment; whereas, in that where your cause is to be heard, though it is not easy to procure one, still, however, it is possible." (Letter 18 of Book I.)

That Suetonius was not interested in military life can be inferred from a second letter of Pliny addressed to him:

"The obliging way in which you request me to confer the military Tribuneship upon your relation, which I had obtained of the honorable Neratius Marcellus for yourself, is consistent with that respect with which you always treat me. As it would have given me great pleasure to have seen you in that post, so it will not be less acceptable to me to see another there through your means. For it would hardly, I think, be consistent to wish the advancement of a friend's honors and yet envy him the noblest of all distinctions, that of a generous and affectionate relation. To deserve preferment and to bestow it is glorious, and the praise of both will be yours if you resign to another what is your own due. In this glory I too shall share, when the world shall learn from the present instance that my friends can not only fill Tribuneships but confer them as well. I therefore readily comply with your generous request; and as your name is not yet entered upon the roll, I can without difficulty insert that of Silvanus in its stead. May he accept this good office at your hands in as grateful a spirit as I am sure you will receive it at mine." (Letter 8 of Book III.)

Pliny's third letter to Suetonius merely concerns his desire to have his friend's advice on how he shall present his verses to a company of friends, and gives us no further information of Suetonius. But in the fourth we see the character of our author more plainly:

"It is time you should acquit the promise my verses gave of your works to our common friends. The world is every day impatiently inquiring after them, and there is some danger of their publication being forced upon you by legal proceedings. I myself am backward in publishing. But you quite get the better of even me in slowness and procrastination. You must rouse yourself, then, otherwise the severity of my satire may perhaps extort from you what the blandishments of my gentler muse could not obtain. Your work is already arrived to that degree of perfection that the file can only weaken, not polish it. Allow me, then, the pleasure of seeing your name on the title-page of a book, and suffer the works of my dear Tranquillus to be recited and transcribed, to be bought and read. It is but fair, and suitable to our mutual friendship, that you should give me in return the same pleasure you receive from me." (Letter 11 of Book V.)

Pliny's petition to Trajan asking a privilege for Suetonius, and Trajan's reply add further information:

"Suetonius Tranquillus, Sir, is a most excellent, honorable, and learned man. I was so much pleased with his tastes and disposition that I have long since invited him into my family, as my constant guest and domestic friend; and my affection for him increased the more I knew of him. Two reasons concur to render the privilege which the law grants to those who have three children particularly necessary to him; I mean the bounty of his friends, and the ill-success of his marriage. Those advantages, therefore, which nature has denied to him, he hopes to obtain from your goodness, by my intercession. I am thoroughly sensible, Sir, of the value of the privilege I am asking. But I know, too, I am asking it from one whose gracious compliance with all my desires I have amply experienced. How passionately I wish to do so in the present instance, you will judge by my thus requesting it in my absence; which I would not do had it not been a favor which I am more than ordinarily anxious to obtain." (Letter 95 of Book X.)

"You cannot but be sensible, my dearest Secundus, how reserved I am in granting favors of the kind you desire; having frequently declared in the Senate that I had not exceeded the number of which I assured that illustrious body I would be contented with. I have yielded, however, to your request, and have directed an article to be inserted in my register, that I have conferred upon Tranquillus, on my usual conditions, the privilege which the law grants to those who have three children." (Trajan to Pliny, Letter 96 of Book X.)

The picture we have of Suetonius in Pliny's *Letters* is completed by a sixth letter, to one Bebius:

"My friend and guest, Tranquillus, has an inclination to purchase a small farm, of which, as I am informed, an acquaintance of yours intends to dispose. I beg you would endeavor he may get it upon reasonable terms, which will add to his satisfaction in the purchase. A dear bargain is always a disagreeable thing, particularly as it reflects upon the judgment of the buyer. There are several circumstances attending this little villa, which (supposing my friend has no objection to the price) are extremely suitable to his taste and desires: the convenient distance from Rome, the goodness of the roads, the smallness of the building, and the very few acres of land around it, which are just enough to amuse him, without taking up his time. To a man of Tranquillus' studious turn, it is sufficient if he have but a small spot to relieve the mind and divert the eye, where he may saunter round his grounds, traverse his single walk, grow familiar with all his little vines, and count the trees in his shrubbery. I mention these particulars to let you see how much he will be obliged to me, as I shall be to you, if you can help him to this convenient little nest, at a price which he shall have no occasion to repent." (Letter 24 of Book I.)

These letters cover the period between A.D. 96 and 112, according to the dates assigned to them by Mommsen.

Our final bit of information is important though it comes from a man who lived around 300, Aelianus Spartianus. In Chapter X of his *Life of the Emperor Hadrian* we read:

"Although he [Hadrian] often complained of his wife Sabina's difficult and cross-grained humor and said if he had been a private person he would have divorced her, he dismissed Septicius Clarus, Praefect of the Guard, and Suetonius Tranquillus, his Secretary, also several others, who had behaved towards her with less ceremony than was required by court etiquette."

We thus learn that Suetonius was associated at court. But we do not know how he obtained his post as Secretary to Hadrian. Lydus speaks of a manuscript of the *Lives of the Twelve Caesars* which he states contained a dedication to C. Septicius Clarus, the same, presumably, who was dismissed by Hadrian at the same time as our author. It has, therefore, been inferred Suetonius obtained his post as Secretary through the patronage of Clarus. Nor do we know how long he held the post. The dismissal Macé dates during Hadrian's sojourn in Britain, 121-122, when Suetonius would have been around fifty years of age.

This is our last reference to him. But, that he was slow to publish considered with the fact that he was a voluminous writer would seem to indicate that he lived to a good, old age, including a part of the reign of Antoninus Pius (138-161).

V

Thus, in spite of the paucity of information concerning the external detail of Suetonius' life we have after all a rather definite picture of Suetonius the man. "A most excellent, honorable, and learned man" the gentle Pliny undoubtedly believed him to be. A tranquil, peace-loving man of scholarly tastes and habits he most probably was; rather disdainful of the ordinary ambitions of men's lives, leisurely intent on living up to his ideals of authorship. Though he did not rise above the superstition of his age, we have some basis for inferring that he did rise above the baseness of flattery and the venality of the age. A man who enjoyed the intimate friendship of a number of the more distinguished men of his age, and who from his connection with them and his position under Hadrian led a life not unsuitable to the purposes to which he had set his desire.

For the rest, those deeper purposes and intents of Suetonius' life, they are clearly enough reflected in his writings. He undoubtedly had a high conception of the function of the author. Though he did not attain the heights of artistry, he was a conscientious scholar who loved study for herself, and whose love was fruitful. Scrupulously impartial, he was possessed with a zeal to tell the whole truth as he saw it. One feels, at least, that his picture of Imperial Rome is less distorted than that of men who cannot look on evil and putrescence with so calm a face. And not for any amount of description of conquest, battle, data of election, march of external event, would men give up such glimpses as that of the great Augustus clad in four robes playing at dice all of a holiday, or three servants carrying home the murdered Caesar on a litter, "with one arm hanging down."

—JOSEPH GAVORSE.

TENTREES.
May, 1931.

BOOK I
JULIUS CAESAR

THE DEIFIED JULIUS

[1] In his sixteenth year Caesar lost his father. During the next consulate, having been nominated high-priest of Jupiter,[2] he broke his engagement with Cossutia, a lady of only equestrian rank but very wealthy, engaged to him since his childhood, and married Cornelia, the daughter of Cinna, four times Consul, by whom he afterwards had a daughter, Julia. In resisting the efforts of Sulla, the Dictator, to force him to divorce Cornelia, he suffered the loss of his sacerdotal office, his wife's dowry, all his family inheritances, and was held to be of the opposition. He was accordingly forced to leave Rome, and although suffering from a quartan ague, to shift from one hiding-place to another almost every night. He saved himself from Sulla's detectives by bribes, until by the mediation of the Vestal Virgins and of his near kinsmen, Aemilius Mamercus and Aurelius Cotta, he obtained a pardon. Every one knows that Sulla, after he had long denied the requests of the most devoted and eminent men of his own party who interceded for Caesar, and they obstinately persisted, at last yielded and cried out, either through divine inspiration or shrewd conjecture: "Have your way and take him. But, bear this in mind: the man you are so eager to save will one day be the ruin of the nobles, whose side you have upheld with me; for in this Caesar there is more than one Marius."[3]

He first served in the wars in Asia on the personal staff of Marcus Thermus, Governor of the province, by whom he was sent to Bithynia[4] to bring out a fleet. He loitered there so

---

[1] The opening chapters of this life are missing.

[2] *Flamen Dialis,* an office of great dignity, political rather than religious.

[3] Marius (Consul with Cinna in 86 B.C.) was leader of the party of the people, Sulla of the nobles. Sulla suspected Caesar of belonging to Marius' party because Marius' wife, Julia, was Caesar's aunt.

[4] South of the Black Sea.

long at the court of Nicomedes as to give occasion to rumors that he prostituted his body to the use of the King. He augmented this rumor by a hasty return to Bithynia under the pretext of collecting a debt for a freedman, one of his dependents. The rest of the campaign was more favorable to his reputation, and, after the successful assault of Mytilene, Thermus honored him with a civic garland.[1]

He also served in Cilicia [2] under Servilius Isauricus, but only for a short time. For, upon learning of the death of Sulla, and at the same time with the hope of profiting by the new dissensions which Marcus Lepidus was instigating, he hastily returned to Rome. But, although he was offered highly favorable terms, he did not join up with Lepidus, through lack of confidence in that leader's capacity and in the outlook, which he found much less favorable than he had expected.

After this civil discord had been composed, he preferred a charge of extortion against Cornelius Dolabella, an ex-Consul who had been honored with a triumph. On the acquittal of the accused, Caesar determined to retire to Rhodes,[3] as well to escape the ill-will he had incurred, as to rest and have leisure to study under Apollonius Molo, the most renowned teacher of oratory in those days.

On his voyage there, the winter season having already begun, he was taken by pirates near the island of Pharmacussa, and, burning with indignation, held captive by them for nearly forty days, accompanied only by a physician and two body-servants. For his traveling companions and the rest of his attendants he had sent off at the outset, to procure money for his ransom. Once they released him on shore, upon payment of fifty talents,[4] he did not delay but at once collected some ships, put to sea again, and did not cease pursuing them till he had overtaken them. No sooner were they in his

---

[1] A crown of oak leaves usually given for having saved the life of a fellow-citizen, although officers in the army were sometimes honored with it.

[2] Southern Asia Minor, Syria to the east, the Mediterranean to the south.

[3] Famous then as a center of learning. The Colossus, a huge statue dedicated to the sun, was there.

[4] $56,600!

power than he inflicted on them the punishment with which he had often threatened them in jest.[1] He then proceeded to Rhodes.

At that time Mithridates was ravaging the adjoining regions. Because he would not be thought to sit still and do nothing when the confederate nations and allies of Rome were in this dangerous situation, he crossed over into Asia, gathered a power of auxiliaries, drove the King's Governor from the province, and so held the wavering and irresolute states to their allegiance.

While serving as Military Tribune,[2] the first office conferred on him by the vote of the people after his return to Rome, he zealously supported those leaders who stood out for the restitution of the authority of the Tribunes of the Commons,[3] the extent of which Sulla had curtailed. Furthermore, through a bill proposed by one Plotius, he effected the recall of Lucius Cinna, his wife's brother, as well as that of the others who had been adherents of Lepidus in his insurrection and who, after that Consul's death, had fled to Sertorius. He himself supported the measure in a speech.

When Quaestor,[4] he pronounced the customary orations from the rostra in praise of his aunt Julia and his wife Cornelia, both deceased. And in the eulogy of his aunt he spoke in the following terms of her paternal and maternal ancestry and that of his own father: "My aunt Julia is descended on her mother's side from the Kings, and on her father's side is akin to the immortal Gods: for the Marcii Reges, from whom comes the name of her mother's family, are derived from Ancus Marcius, and the Julii, the family of which ours is a branch, from Venus.[5] Our stock therefore has at once the sanctity of Kings, who among men are most powerful, and the

---

[1] Suetonius says later that he was merciful. He cut their throats before crucifying them.

[2] Colonel. A legion had six, each commanding for two months in the year.

[3] A magistrate charged with the protection of the commons against the patricians.

[4] Originally two deputies of the Consuls, to investigate and try capital crimes.

[5] Through Aeneas, fabled prince of Troy, and his son Julius.

claim to reverence which attaches to the Gods, to whom Kings themselves are subject."

In place of Cornelia he then wedded Pompeia, daughter of Quintus Pompeius and granddaughter of Lucius Sulla. But he afterward divorced her, suspecting her of adultery with Publius Clodius. As a matter of fact the report was so persistent that Clodius, disguised in woman's apparel, had secretly gained access to her at the celebration of a public religious ceremony the Senate by decree directed that this pollution of sacred rites be judicially investigated.[1]

While he was Quaestor it fell to him by lot to serve in Farther Spain. While there, as he rode his circuit of the assize-towns to hold court under order of the Praetor,[2] he came to Gades, where he noticed a statue of Alexander the Great in the temple of Hercules. At the sight of it he drew a deep sigh, as one displeased with his own shortcomings, in that he had as yet performed no memorable act, whereas at his age Alexander had already conquered the whole world.[3]

He soon after made earnest suit for his discharge, in order to seize the first opportunity to compass greater enterprises at home within the city. The following night he was much disquieted by a dream in which he imagined he had carnal company with his own mother. But hopes of most glorious achievement were kindled in him by the soothsayers, who interpreted the dream to mean that he was destined to have sovereignty over all the world, his mother whom he saw under him signifying none other than the earth, which is counted the mother of all things.

Leaving Spain, therefore, before the expiration of the accustomed term, he went to the Latin colonies, which were then in a state of unrest and meditating a demand for citizenship. He might have excited them to some rash act, but that the Consuls,[4] anticipating this very danger, detained there the

---

[1] From the rites of Bona Dea, which were performed at night, all men were excluded.

[2] Governor of the province.

[3] Alexander, it will be remembered, was only 33 at the time of his death.

[4] The highest magistracy of the Roman republic was vested in two Consuls, chosen by vote annually. About 367 B.C. plebeians were admitted to the office.

legions which had been enrolled for service in Cilicia.

And yet, for all that, he soon after entertained more daring designs in Rome. For only a few days before he entered upon his aedileship,[1] he was suspected of having conspired with Marcus Crassus, an ex-consul, together with Publius Sulla and Lucius Autronius, who, after they had been elected Consuls, had been convicted of bribery. The plan of the conspirators was to fall upon the Senate at the opening of the new year and, after they had massacred as many as they thought necessary, Crassus was to usurp the Dictatorship and appoint Caesar Master of Horse.[2] When they had re-organized the state to their wishes, the consulship was to be restored to Autronius. Mention is made of this conspiracy by Tanusius Geminus in his History, by Marcus Bibulus [3] in his edicts, and by Gaius Curio the elder in his speeches. Cicero, too, seems to imply as much in a letter to Axius, where he says that Caesar in his consulship secured for himself that arbitrary power which he had contemplated when Aedile. Tanusius adds that Crassus, either from remorse or from fear, did not appear on the day appointed for the massacre, and that therefore Caesar did not give the signal, which it had been agreed he should give. This signal, Curio says, was that Caesar should let his toga fall from his shoulder. We have the authority of the same Curio, as well as that of Marcus Actorius Naso, that Caesar also conspired with Gnaeus Piso, a youth to whom the province of Spain was assigned unsought and out of regular order,[4] because he was suspected of conspiring in the city; that they had agreed to stir up insurrection simultaneously, Piso abroad and Caesar at Rome, using as their instruments the Ambrani and the tribes beyond the Po; but that the death of Piso frustrated both their designs.

When Caesar was Aedile, he decorated not only the Comitium [5] and the Forum with its adjacent halls but also the

---

[1] Aedile, commissioner of buildings.

[2] The Master of Horse commanded the Knights, and executed the orders of the Dictator.

[3] Caesar's colleague, both as Aedile and Consul.

[4] An honorable banishment.

[5] A covered building in which the assemblies of the people were held.

Capitol, building temporary galleries for the purpose of displaying some part of the abundant paraphernalia he had collected for the amusement of the people. He exhibited combats with wild beasts, and stage-plays, too, both jointly with his companion in office and independently. The result was that, although the charges were borne in common by them both, Caesar alone obtained all the credit. Nor did his colleague, Marcus Bibulus, dissemble the matter, but openly said that he served in the manner of Pollux; that just as the temple erected in the Forum to both the twin brothers bore the name of Castor alone, even so the joint munificence of Caesar and himself was credited to Caesar alone. Caesar gave a gladiatorial show besides, but not with so many pairs of combatants as he had intended.[1] He had assembled from all quarters such a huge band his enemies became alarmed, and a decree was made restricting the number of gladiators which any one was permitted to retain in Rome.

Having won the favor of the populace, Caesar endeavored, through his association with some of the Tribunes, to obtain, by a decree of the Commons, Egypt assigned him as a province. The opportunity he seized for asking so irregular an appointment was that the Alexandrians had deposed their King [2] whom the Senate had named an ally and friend of the Roman people, and this was generally resented. Nevertheless, there was so much opposition from the party of the nobles, he failed to carry his point. Wishing, therefore, to impair their influence by every means in his power he restored the trophies erected to commemorate the victories of Gaius Marius over Jugurtha, the Cimbri, and Teutoni, which had long before been demolished by Sulla. Furthermore, when sitting in judgment upon murders he treated as assassins even those who, in the late proscription,[3] had received money from the public treasury for bringing in the heads of Roman citizens, although they were expressly excepted by the Cornelian laws.

He likewise bribed some one to prefer a charge of treason

---

[1] And yet with 320 pairs according to Plutarch.

[2] Ptolemy Auletes, father of Cleopatra.

[3] That of Sulla, who had outlawed the opposing faction led by C. Marius, and had given a reward of $2,264 for the head of any of its partisans brought in.

against Caius Rabirius, who, a few years before, had rendered conspicuous service to the Senate in repressing the seditious designs of the Tribune Lucius Saturninus, and being drawn by lot a judge on the trial, he condemned the man with such eagerness that when Rabirius appealed to the people, nothing did him so much good as the extraordinary bitterness of his judge.

After renouncing all hope of obtaining Egypt for his province, he announced himself candidate for the office of Chief Priest, having recourse to the most profuse bribery. Thinking about the enormous debts he had thus contracted, he is reported to have said to his mother, when she kissed him as he was going out in the morning to the assembly for the election, that he would never return home except as Pontiff. And indeed, he so decisively defeated his two most powerful competitors, both his superiors in age and rank, that he had more votes in their tribes than were cast for both of them in all the tribes together.

After he was chosen Praetor,[1] the conspiracy of Catiline was discovered. And while every other member of the Senate voted for inflicting capital punishment on the accomplices in the plot, he alone proposed that their property be confiscated, and that each be imprisoned in a separate town. He even struck such terror into those who advocated greater severity, by representing to them what universal odium would be attached to their memories by the Roman people, that Decius Silanus, Consul-elect, was not ashamed to mollify his proposal, since it would have been humiliating to change it, alleging it had been understood in a harsher sense than he had intended. Caesar would certainly have carried his point, for many had already gone over to his side, among them Cicero, the Consul's brother, had not a speech by Marcus Cato kept the wavering Senate in line.

Yet not even then did he cease from obstructing the measure until a body of the Roman Knights, who stood under arms as a guard, threatened him with instant death, if he continued his headstrong opposition. They even made such passes at

---

[1] At Rome the Praetor's function was judicial. After 264 B.C. there were two, one the judge over citizens' cases, one over those of strangers.

him with their drawn swords that those who sat next him moved away, while a few friends with difficulty protected him by throwing their arms or togas about him. At last, in evident fear, he not only yielded the point but, for the rest of the year, absented himself from the senate-house.

On the first day of his praetorship, he called upon Quintus Catulus to render an account to the people respecting the restoration of the Capitol, proposing a bill for transferring the office of curator to another. But he withdrew the measure, since he could not cope with the united opposition of the aristocrats, who he perceived had at once dropped attendance on the newly elected Consuls,[1] and hastily gathered in throngs resolved on obstinate resistance.

Nevertheless, when Caecilius Metellus, Tribune of the Commons, brought forward some bills of a highly seditious nature [2] in spite of all the opposition of his colleagues, Caesar abetted him and espoused his cause in the most stubborn manner, until at last both were suspended from the exercise of their public functions by a decree of the Senate. Yet in spite of this, Caesar had the audacity to continue in office and to hold court. But when he learned that some were ready to stop him by force of arms, he dismissed his Lictors,[3] laid aside his robe of office, and slipped off privily to his house, intending to remain in retirement because of the state of the times. Indeed, when the populace on the following day flocked to him quite of their own accord, and with riotous demonstrations offered him their aid in recovering his position, he held them in check. Since this action of his was wholly unexpected, the Senate, which had been hurriedly convoked to take action about that very gathering, publicly thanked him through its leading men. Then, summoning him to the House and lauding him in the strongest terms, they rescinded their former decree and restored him to his office.

---

[1] When Consuls-elect went to the Capitol to offer sacrifice at the beginning of their term of office, January 1, it was the custom for their friends to escort them to the temple and back to their homes.

[2] One of these proposed that Pompey be recalled from Asia, on the pretext the commonwealth was in danger. Cato was one of the colleagues who saw through the design and opposed the decree.

[3] Official attendants on a magistrate.

He again fell into danger by being named among the accomplices of Catiline, both before the commissioner Novius Niger by an informer called Lucius Vettius and in the Senate by Quintus Curius, who had been voted a sum of money from the public funds for having first discovered the designs of the conspirators. Curius alleged that his information came directly from Catiline, while Vettius actually offered to produce a letter to Catiline in Caesar's handwriting. As this was an indignity Caesar knew intolerable, he showed by appealing to Cicero's testimony that he had of his own accord reported to the Consul certain details of the plot, and thus prevented Curius from getting the reward. As for Vettius, after his bond was declared forfeit and his goods seized, he was roughly handled by the populace assembled before the rostra, and all but torn to pieces. Caesar then put him in prison, and Novius the commissioner went there, too, for allowing an official of superior rank to be arraigned before his tribunal.

Being allotted the province of Farther Spain after his praetorship, Caesar got rid of his creditors, who tried to detain him, by means of sureties,[1] and, contrary to both law and precedent, was on his way before his appointment was confirmed by the Senate and funds and equipment provided. It is uncertain whether this precipitancy arose through fear of some judicial proceeding against him as a private person, or that he might the more promptly respond to the entreaties of our allies for help. After restoring order in his province, he made as great haste to leave it, not waiting for the arrival of his successor, and to sue at the same time for a triumph and the consulship. But inasmuch as the day for the elections had already been announced and no account could be taken of Caesar's candidacy unless he entered the city as a private citizen, and since his intrigues to gain exemption from the laws met with general protest, he was forced to forego the triumph, to avoid losing the consulship.

Of the two competing candidates for this office, Lucius Lucceius and Marcus Bibulus, Caesar joined forces with the former, making a bargain with him that since Lucceius had less

---

[1] Plutarch asserts that Caesar, when he came into office, owed $1,471,600. From then until he departed for Spain his debts increased.

influence but more funds, he should in their common name promise largess to the electors from his own pocket. When this became known, the aristocracy authorized Bibulus to promise the same amount, being seized with fear that Caesar would stick at nothing when he became chief magistrate, if he had a colleague who was heart and soul with him. Many of them contributed to the fund, and even Cato did not deny that bribery under such circumstances was for the good of the commonwealth.[1]

So Caesar was chosen Consul with Bibulus. With the same motives the aristocracy took care that provinces of the smallest importance should be assigned to the newly elected Consuls, that is, mere woods and pastures.[2] Thereupon Caesar, especially incensed by this slight, by every possible attention courted the goodwill of Gnaeus Pompeius, who was at odds with the Senate because of its tardiness in ratifying his acts after his victory over King Mithridates. He also patched up a peace between Pompeius and Marcus Crassus, who had been enemies since their consulship, which had been one of constant wrangling. Then he made an agreement[3] with them, that no step should be taken in public affairs which did not suit any one of the three.

Caesar's very first enactment after becoming Consul was, that the proceedings both of the Senate and of the people should day by day be compiled and published. He also revived a by-gone custom, that during the months when he did not have the fasces an orderly should walk before him, while the Lictors followed him. He brought forward an agrarian law, too, and when his colleague announced adverse omens,[4] he resorted to arms and drove him from the Forum; and when

---

[1] Yet there were strict laws against bribery at electons. Sallust (*Jugurth.* VIII, 20, 3) says that, were one rich enough, Rome itself might be bought.

[2] The Senate would not run the risk of letting Caesar secure a province involving the command of an army.

[3] This compact bred the civil war that ensued between Caesar and Pompey.

[4] Business could be interrupted or postponed by the announcement of an auger or a magistrate that he had seen a flash of lightning or some other adverse sign; sometimes an opponent merely announced that he would "watch the skies" for such omens.

next day Bibulus made complaint in the Senate and no one could be found who ventured to make a motion, or even to express an opinion about so high-handed a proceeding (although decrees had often been passed touching less serious breaches of the peace), Caesar's conduct drove him to such a pitch of desperation, that from that time until the end of his term he did not leave his house, but merely issued proclamations announcing adverse omens.

From that time on Caesar managed all the affairs of state alone and according to his own pleasure; so that sundry witty fellows, pretending by way of jest to sign and seal testamentary documents, wrote "Done in the consulship of Julius and Caesar," instead of "Bibulus and Caesar," writing down the same man twice, by name and by surname. Presently too the following verses were on every one's lips:—

"Caesar of late did many things, but Bibulus not one;
For naught by Consul Bibulus can I remember done."

The plain called Stellas, which had been devoted to the Gods by the men of by-gone days, and the Campanian territory, which had been reserved to pay revenues for the aid of the government, he divided [1] without casting lots among twenty thousand citizens who had three or more children each. When the publicans asked for relief, he freed them from a third part of their obligation, and openly warned them in contracting for taxes in the future not to bid too recklessly. He freely granted everything else that any one took it into his head to ask, either without opposition or by intimidating any one who tried to object. Marcus Cato, who tried to delay proceedings,[2] was dragged from the House by a Lictor at Caesar's command and taken off to prison. When Lucius Lucullus was somewhat too outspoken in his opposition, he filled him with such fear of malicious prosecution,[3] that Lucullus actually fell on his knees before him. Because Cicero, while pleading in court, deplored the state of the times, Caesar transferred the orator's enemy Publius Clodius that very same

---

[1] Through a special commission of twenty men.
[2] By making a speech of several hours' duration.
[3] For his conduct during the war with Mithridates.

day from the patricians to the plebeians, a thing for which Clodius had for a long time been vainly striving; [1] and that too at the ninth hour.[2] Finally taking action against all the opposition in a body, he bribed an informer to declare that he had been egged on by certain men to murder Pompey, and to come out upon the rostrum and name the guilty parties according to a prearranged plot. But when the informer had named one or two to no purpose and not without suspicion of double-dealing, Caesar, hopeless of the success of his over-hasty attempt, is supposed to have had him taken off by poison.

At about the same time he took to wife Calpurnia, daughter of Lucius Piso, who was to succeed him in the consulship, and affianced his own daughter Julia to Gnaeus Pompeius, breaking a previous engagement with Servilius Caepio, although the latter had shortly before rendered him conspicuous service in his contest with Bibulus. After this new alliance he began to call upon Pompey first to give his opinion in the Senate, although it had been his habit to begin with Crassus, and it was the rule for the Consul in calling for opinions to continue throughout the year the order which he had established on the Kalends of January.

Backed therefore by his father-in-law and son-in-law, out of all the numerous provinces he made the Gauls his choice, as the most likely to enrich him and furnish suitable material for triumphs. At first, it is true, by the bill of Vatinius he received only Cisalpine Gaul with the addition of Illyricum. But presently he was assigned Gallia Comata as well by the Senate, since the members feared that even if they should refuse it, the people would give him this also. Transported with joy at this success, he could not keep from boasting a few days later before a crowded house, that having gained his heart's desire to the grief and lamentation of his opponents, he would therefore from that time mount on their heads.[3] And when some one insultingly remarked that that would be no easy matter for any woman, he replied in the same vein that Semi-

---

[1] That he might be a candidate for the tribuneship of the people.

[2] At 3 P.M. when the business day ended.

[3] Used in a double sense, the second implying fellatio.

his enterprises prospered, supplication days[1] were appointed in his honor oftener and for longer periods than for any one before his time.

During the nine years of his command this is in substance what he did. All that part of Gaul which is bounded by the Pyrenees, the Alps and the Cévennes, and by the Rhine and Rhone rivers, a circuit of some 3,200[2] miles, not counting some allied states which had rendered him good service, he reduced to the form of a province; and imposed upon it a yearly tribute of 40,000,000 sesterces.[3] He was the first Roman to build a bridge and attack the Germans beyond the Rhine; and he inflicted heavy losses upon them. He invaded the Britons too, a people unknown before, vanquished them, and exacted moneys and hostages. Amid all these successes he met with adverse fortune but three times in all: in Britain, where his fleet narrowly escaped destruction in a violent storm; in Gaul, when one of his legions was routed at Gergovia; and in the land of Germany, when his lieutenants Titurius and Aurunculeius were ambushed and slain.

Within this same space of time he lost first his mother, then his daughter,[4] and soon afterwards his grandson. Meanwhile, as the community was aghast at the murder of Publius Clodius, the Senate had voted that only one Consul should be chosen, and expressly named Gnaeus Pompeius. When the Tribunes planned to make him Pompey's colleague, Caesar urged them rather to propose to the people that he be permitted to stand for a second consulship without coming to Rome, when the term of his governorship drew near its end, to prevent his being forced for the sake of the office to leave his province prematurely and without finishing the war. On the granting of this, aiming still higher and flushed with hope, he neglected nothing in the way of lavish expenditure or of favors to any one, either in his public capacity or privately. He

---

[1] Thanksgiving days in which honor was done to a victorious general. At first the solemnities continued but one day, but in time to twelve. At length Caesar obtained it for fifteen and even twenty days together, as he himself proudly asserts in his *Commentaries*, II, 35 and VII, 80.

[2] Roman measure A Roman mile was 1,000 paces.

[3] $2,040,000.00.

[4] Julia died in childbirth.

ramis too had been Queen in Syria and the Amazons in of
old had held sway over a great part of Asia.

When, at the close of his consulship, the Praetors C
Memmius and Lucius Domitius moved an inquiry into
conduct during the previous year, Caesar laid the matter
fore the Senate. When they failed to take it up, and three da
had been wasted in fruitless wrangling, he went off to h
province. Whereupon his Quaestor was at once arraigned or
several counts, as a preliminary to his own impeachment.
Presently he himself too was prosecuted by Lucius Antistius,
Tribune of the Commons, and it was only by appealing to the
whole college that he contrived not to be brought to trial, on
the ground that he was absent on public service. Then to secure himself for the future, he took great pains always to put
the magistrates for the year under personal obligation, and
not to aid any candidates or suffer any to be elected, save such
as guaranteed to defend him in his absence. And he did not
hesitate in some cases to exact an oath to keep this pledge or
even a written contract.

When, however, Lucius Domitius, candidate for the consulship, openly threatened to effect as Consul what he had been
unable to do as Praetor, and to take his armies from him,
Caesar compelled Pompeius and Crassus to come to Luca, a
city in his province, where he prevailed on them to stand for a
second consulship, to defeat Domitius; and he also succeeded
through their influence in having his term as Governor of
Gaul made five years longer. Encouraged by this, he added to
the legions which he had received from the state others at his
own cost, one actually composed of men of Transalpine Gaul
and bearing a Gallic name too (for it was called Alauda),
which he trained in the Roman tactics and equipped with
Roman arms; and later on he gave every man of it citizenship.
After that he did not let slip any pretext for war, however
unjust and dangerous it might be, picking quarrels as well
with allied, as with hostile and barbarous nations; so that
once the Senate decreed that a commission be sent to inquire
into the condition of the Gallic provinces, and some even recommended that Caesar be handed over to the enemy. But a

began a Forum with the proceeds of his spoils, the ground for which cost more than a hundred million sesterces.[1] He announced a combat of gladiators and a feast for the people in memory of his daughter, a thing quite without precedent. To raise the expectation of these events to the highest possible pitch, he had the material for the banquet prepared in part by his own household, although he had let contracts to the markets as well. He issued an order too that whenever famous gladiators fought without winning the favor of the people, they should be rescued by force and kept for him.[2] He had the novices trained, not in a gladiatorial school by professionals, but in private houses by Roman Knights and even by Senators who were skilled in arms, earnestly beseeching them, as is shown by his own letters, to give the recruits individual attention and personally direct their exercises. He doubled the pay of the legions for all time. Whenever grain was plentiful, he distributed it to them without stint or measure, and now and then gave each man a slave from among the captives.

Moreover, to retain his relationship and friendship with Pompey, Caesar offered him his sister's granddaughter Octavia in marriage, although she was already the wife of Gaius Marcellus, and asked for the hand of Pompey's daughter, who was promised to Faustus Sulla. When he had put all Pompey's friends under obligation, as well as the great part of the Senate, through loans made without interest or at a low rate, he lavished gifts on men of all other classes, both those whom he invited to accept his bounty and those who applied to him unasked, including even freedmen and slaves who were special favorites of their masters or patrons. In short, he was the sole and ever ready help of all who were in legal difficulties or in debt and of young spendthrifts, excepting only those whose burden of guilt or of poverty was so heavy, or who were so given up to riotous living, that even he could not save them. And to these he declared in the plainest terms that what they needed was a civil war.

He took no less pains to win the devotion of princes and

---

[1] $4,400,000.00. Conquest had so multiplied business at Rome, the Forum had become too small for transacting it. It could not be enlarged without razing adjoining buildings.

[2] Ordinarily they would be put to death.

provinces all over the world, offering prisoners to some by the thousand as a gift, and sending auxiliary troops to the aid of others whenever they wished, and as often as they wished, without the sanction of the Senate or people, besides adorning the principal cities of Asia and Greece with magnificent public works, as well as those of Italy and the provinces of Gaul and Spain. At last, when all were thunder-struck at his actions and wondered what their purpose could be, the Consul Marcus Claudius Marcellus, after first making proclamation that he purposed to bring before the Senate a matter of the highest public moment, proposed that a successor to Caesar be appointed before the end of his term, on the ground that the war was ended, peace was established, and the victorious army ought to be disbanded. He further proposed that no account be taken of Caesar at the elections, unless he were present, as Pompey himself had afterwards not annulled the decree of the people. And it was true that when Pompey proposed a bill touching the privileges of officials, in the clause where he debarred absentees from candidacy for office he forgot to make a special exception in Caesar's case, and did not correct the oversight until the law had been inscribed on a tablet of bronze and deposited in the treasury. Not content with depriving Caesar of his provinces and his privilege, Marcellus also moved that the colonists whom Caesar had settled in Novum Comum by the bill of Vatinius should lose their citizenship, on the ground that it had been given from political motives and was not authorized by the law.

Aroused by these measures, and thinking, as they say he was often heard to remark, that now that he was the leading man of the state, it would be harder to push him down from the first place to the second than from the second to the lowest, Caesar stoutly resisted Marcellus, partly through vetoes of the Tribunes and partly through the other Consul, Servius Sulpicius. When next year Gaius Marcellus, who had succeeded his cousin Marcus as Consul, tried the same thing, Caesar by means of an immense bribe secured the support of the other Consul, Aemilius Paulus, and of Gaius Curio, the most reckless of the Tribunes. But seeing that everything against him was being pushed most persistently, and that even the Consuls-elect were among the opposition, he sent a written

appeal to the Senate, not to take from him the privilege which
the people had granted, or else to compel the others in command of armies to resign also; feeling sure, it was thought,
that he could more readily muster his veterans as soon as he
wished, than Pompey his newly levied troops. He further
proposed a compromise to his opponents, that after giving up
eight legions and Transalpine Gaul, he be allowed to keep
two legions and Cisalpine Gaul, or at least one legion [1] and
Illyricum, until he was elected Consul.

But when the Senate declined to interfere, and his opponents declared that they would accept no compromise in a
matter affecting the public welfare, he crossed to Hither Gaul,
and after holding all the assizes, halted at Ravenna, intending to resort to war if the Senate took any drastic action
against the Tribunes of the Commons who interposed vetoes
in his behalf.[2] Now this was his excuse for the civil war, but
it is believed that he had other motives. Gnaeus Pompeius
used to declare that since Caesar's own means were not sufficient to complete the works which he had planned, nor to do
all that he had led the people to expect on his return, he desired a state of general unrest and turmoil. Others say that
he dreaded the necessity of rendering an account for what he
had done in his first consulship contrary to the auspices and
the laws, and regardless of vetoes. For Marcus Cato often declared, and took oath too, that he would impeach Caesar the
moment he had disbanded his army. It was openly said too
that if he was out of office on his return, he would be obliged,
like Milo,[3] to make his defense in a court hedged about by
armed men. The latter opinion is the more credible one in
view of the assertion of Asinius Pollio, that when Caesar at
the battle of Pharsalus [4] saw his enemies slain or in flight, he
said, word for word: "They would have it so. Even I, Gaius
Caesar, after so many great deeds, should have been found

---

[1] A legion was a force of 3,600 foot-soldiers and 300 cavalry.

[2] The Senate did pass a decree that Caesar should disband his army
before a given date. The Tribunes Mark Antony and Quintus Cassius
exercised their privilege and vetoed it. The Senate disregarded the veto,
and the Tribunes were obliged to seek safety in flight.

[3] Milo had murdered Publius Clodius.

[4] Where he defeated Pompey in 48 B.C.

guilty, if I had not turned to my army for help." Some think habit had given him a love of power, and that weighing the strength of his adversaries against his own, he grasped the opportunity of usurping the despotism which had been his heart's desire from early youth. Cicero too was seemingly of this opinion, when he wrote in the third book of his *De Officiis* that Caesar ever had upon his lips these lines of Euripides,[1] of which Cicero himself adds a version:

> "Be just, unless a kingdom tempts to break the laws,
> For sovereign power alone can justify the cause."

Accordingly, when word came that the veto of the Tribunes had been set aside and they themselves had left the city, he at once sent on a few cohorts with all secrecy, and then, to disarm suspicion, concealed his purpose by appearing at a public show, inspecting the plans of a gladiatorial school which he intended building, and joining as usual in a banquet with a large company. It was not until after sunset that he set out very privily with a small company, taking the mules from a bakeshop hard by and harnessing them to a carriage. When his lights went out and he lost his way, he was astray for some time, but at last found a guide at dawn and got back to the road on foot by narrow bypaths. Then, overtaking his cohorts at the river Rubicon,[2] which was the boundary of his province, he paused for a while, and realizing what a step he was taking, he turned to those about him and said: "Even yet we may turn back; but once cross yon little bridge, and the whole issue is with the sword."

As he stood in doubt, this sign was given him. On a sudden there appeared hard by a being of wondrous stature and beauty, who sat and played upon a reed. And when not only the shepherds flocked to hear him, but many of the soldiers left their posts, and among them some of the trumpeters, the apparition snatched a trumpet from one of them, rushed to the river, and sounding the warnote with mighty blast, strode to the opposite bank. Then Caesar cried: "Take we the course

---

[1] In *Phoenissae*, 524.
[2] It was near Rimini. There was a very old law of the republic to the effect that no general, returning from the wars, should cross the Rubicon with his troops under arms.

which the signs of the Gods and the false dealing of our foes point out. The die is cast," said he.

Accordingly, crossing with his army, and welcoming the Tribunes of the Commons, who had come to him after being driven from Rome, he harangued the soldiers with tears, and rending his robe from his breast besought their faithful service. It is even thought that he promised every man a Knight's estate, but that came of a misunderstanding. For, since he often pointed to the finger of his left hand as he addressed them and urged them on, declaring that to satisfy all those who helped him to defend his honor he would gladly tear his very ring from his hand, those on the edge of the assembly, who could see him better than they could hear his words, assumed that he said what his gesture seemed to mean; and so the report went about that he had promised them the right of the ring and four hundred thousand sesterces [1] as well.

The sum total of his movements after that is, in their order, as follows: He overran Umbria, Picenum, and Etruria, took prisoner Lucius Domitius, who had been irregularly named his successor and was holding Corfinium with a garrison, let him go free, and then proceeded along the Adriatic to Brundisium, where Pompey and the Consuls had taken refuge, intending to cross the sea as soon as might be. After vainly trying by every kind of hindrance to prevent their sailing, he marched off to Rome, and after calling the Senate together to discuss public business, went to attack Pompey's strongest forces, which were in Spain under command of three of his lieutenants—Marcus Petreius, Lucius Afranius, and Marcus Varro—saying to his friends before he left: "I go to meet an army without a leader, and I shall return to meet a leader without an army." And in fact, though his advance was delayed by the siege of Massilia, which had shut its gates against him, and by extreme scarcity of supplies, he nevertheless quickly gained a complete victory.

Returning thence to Rome, he crossed into Macedonia, and after blockading Pompey for almost four months behind

---

[1] Knights, as well as Senators, had the privilege of wearing a gold ring, and must possess an estate of 400,000 sesterces ($16,400). Liberal as Caesar was to his legionaries, such imagined largess was beyond all reasonable expectation.

mighty ramparts, finally routed him in the battle of Pharsalus, followed him in his flight to Alexandria, and when he
learned that his rival had been slain, made war on King
Ptolemy, who he perceived had treacherous designs upon
his own life as well; a war in truth of great difficulty, convenient neither in time nor place, but carried on during the
winter season, within the walls of a well-provisioned and crafty
foeman, while Caesar himself was without supplies of any
kind and ill-prepared. Victor in spite of all, he turned over the
rule of Egypt to Cleopatra and her younger brother, fearing
that if he made a province of it, it might one day under a
headstrong Governor be a source of revolution. From Alexandria he crossed to Syria, and from there went to Pontus,
spurred on by the news that Pharnaces, son of Mithridates
the Great, had taken advantage of the situation to make war,
and was already flushed with numerous successes. But Caesar
vanquished him in a single battle within five days after his
arrival and four hours after getting sight of him, often re-
marking on Pompey's good luck in gaining his principal fame
as a general by victories over such feeble foemen. Then he
overcame Scipio and Juba, who were patching up the remnants
of their party in Africa, and the sons of Pompey in Spain.

In all the civil wars he suffered not a single disaster except
among his lieutenants, of whom Gaius Curio perished in
Africa, Gaius Antonius fell into the hands of the enemy in
Illyricum, Publius Dolabella lost a fleet also off Illyricum, and
Gnaeus Domitius Calvinus an army in Pontus. Personally he
always fought with the utmost success, and the issue was
never even in doubt save twice: once at Dyrrachium, where he
was put to flight, and said of Pompey, who failed to follow up
his success, that he did not know how to use a victory; again
in Spain, in the final struggle, when, believing the battle lost,
he actually thought of suicide.

Having ended the wars, he celebrated five triumphs, four
in a single month, but at intervals of a few days, after vanquishing Scipio; and another on defeating Pompey's sons.
The first and most splendid was the Gallic triumph, the next
the Alexandrian, then the Pontic, after that the African, and
finally the Spanish, each differing from the rest in its equipment and display of spoils. As he rode through the Velabrum

on the day of his Gallic triumph, the axle of his chariot broke, and he was all but thrown out; and he mounted the Capitol by torchlight, with forty elephants bearing lamps on his right and his left. In his Pontic triumph he displayed among the show-pieces of the procession an inscription of but three words, "I came, I saw, I conquered," not indicating the events of the war, as the others did, but the speed with which it was finished.

To each and every foot-soldier of his veteran legions he gave twenty-four thousand sesterces [1] by way of booty, over and above the two thousand [2] apiece which he had paid them at the beginning of the civil strife. He also assigned them lands, but not side by side, to avoid dispossessing any of the former owners. To every man of the people, besides ten pecks of grain and the same number of pounds of oil, he distributed the three hundred sesterces which he had promised at first, and one hundred apiece to boot because of the delay.[3] He also remitted a year's rent in Rome to tenants who paid two thousand sesterces [4] or less, and in Italy up to five hundred sesterces.[5] He added a banquet and a dole of meat, and after his Spanish victory two dinners. For, deeming that the former of these had not been served with a liberality creditable to his generosity, he gave another five days later on a most lavish scale.

He gave entertainments of divers kinds: a combat of gladiators [6] and also stage-plays in every ward all over the city, performed too by actors of all languages, as well as races in the circus, athletic contests, and a sham sea-fight. In the gladiatorial contest in the Forum Furius Leptinus, a man of praetorian stock, and Quintus Calpenus, a former Senator and pleader at the bar, fought to a finish. A Pyrrhic dance was performed by the sons of the princes of Asia and Bithynia. During the plays Decimus Laberius, a Roman Knight, acted

---

[1] $984.00.

[2] $82.00.

[3] $16.40 altogether.

[4] $82.00.

[5] $20.50.

[6] Gladiators were first publicly exhibited at Rome by two brothers called Bruti, at the funeral of their father, 263 B.C., and for some time were exhibited only on such occasions. They were prohibited by Constantine, but not entirely suppressed until the time of Honorius.

a farce of his own composition, and having been presented with five hundred thousand sesterces and a gold ring,[1] passed from the stage through the orchestra and took his place in the fourteen rows.[2] For the races the circus was lengthened at either end and a broad canal was dug all about it; then young men of the highest rank drove four-horse and two-horse chariots and rode pairs of horses, vaulting from one to the other. The game called Troy was performed by two troops, of younger and older boys. Combats with wild beasts were presented on five successive days, and last of all there was a battle between two opposing armies, in which five hundred foot-soldiers, twenty elephants, and thirty horsemen engaged on each side. To make room for this, the goals were taken down and in their place two camps were pitched over against each other. The athletic competitions lasted for three days in a temporary stadium built for the purpose in the region of the Campus Martius. For the naval battle a pool was dug in the lesser Codeta and there was a contest of ships of two, three, and four banks of oars, belonging to the Tyrian and Egyptian fleets, manned by a large force of fighting men. Such a throng flocked to all these shows from every quarter, that many strangers had to lodge in tents pitched in the streets or along the roads, and the press was often such that many were crushed to death, including two Senators.

Then turning his attention to the reorganization of the state, he reformed the calendar, which the negligence of the pontiffs had long since so disordered, through their privilege of adding months or days at pleasure, that the harvest festivals did not come in summer nor those of the vintage in the autumn. And he adjusted the year to the sun's course by making it consist of three hundred and sixty-five days, abolishing the intercalary month,[3] and adding one day every fourth year.

---

[1] In token of his restoration to the rank of Knight, which he forfeited by appearing on the stage.

[2] The first fourteen rows above the orchestra were reserved for the Knights by a law of 67 B.C.

[3] The year had previously consisted of 355 days, and the deficiency of about 11 days was made up by inserting an intercalary month of 22 or 23 days after February. Caesar was assisted in this reform by Sosigenes, an Egyptian philosopher. The Julian calendar was in use till 1582 when Pope Gregory XIII further corrected it.

Furthermore, that the correct reckoning of time might begin with the next Kalends of January, he inserted two other months between those of November and December. Hence the year in which these arrangements were made was one of fifteen months, including the intercalary month, which belonged to that year according to the former custom.

He filled the vacancies in the Senate, enrolled additional patricians, and increased the number of Praetors, Aediles, and Quaestors, as well as of the minor officials. He reinstated those who had been degraded by official action of the Censors [1] or found guilty of bribery by verdict of the jurors. He shared the elections with the people on this basis: that except in the case of the consulship, half of the magistrates should be appointed by the people's choice, while the rest should be those whom he had personally nominated. And these he announced in brief notes like the following, circulated in each tribe: "Caesar the Dictator to this or that tribe. I commend to you so and so, to hold their positions by your votes." He admitted to office even the sons of those who had been proscribed. He limited the right of serving as jurors to two classes, the equestrian and senatorial orders, disqualifying the third class, the Tribunes of the treasury.

He made the enumeration of the people neither in the usual manner nor place, but from street to street aided by the owners of blocks of houses, and reduced the number of those who received grain at public expense from three hundred and twenty thousand to one hundred and fifty thousand. And to prevent the calling of additional meetings at any future time for purposes of enrollment, he provided that the places of such as died should be filled each year by the Praetors from those who were not on the list.

Moreover, to keep up the population of the city, depleted as it was by the assignment of eighty thousand citizens to colonies [2] across the sea, he made a law that no citizen older than twenty or younger than forty, unless detained by service in the army, should be absent from Italy for more than three

---

[1] There were two Censors, usually patricians of high rank, elected originally every five years.

[2] Principally Carthage and Corinth.

successive years; that no Senator's son should go abroad except as the companion of a magistrate or on his staff; and that those who made a business of grazing should have among their herdsmen at least one-third who were men of free birth. He conferred citizenship on all who practiced medicine at Rome, and on all teachers of the liberal arts, to make them more desirous of living in the city and to induce others to resort to it.

As to debts, he disappointed those who looked for their cancellation, which was often agitated, but finally decreed that the debtors should satisfy their creditors according to a valuation of their possessions at the price which they had paid for them before the civil war, deducting from the principal whatever interest had been paid in cash or pledged through bankers; an arrangement which wiped out about a fourth part of their indebtedness. He dissolved all guilds, except those of ancient foundation. He increased the penalties for crimes; and inasmuch as the rich involved themselves in guilt with less hesitation because they merely suffered exile, without any loss of property, he punished murderers of freemen by the confiscation of all their goods, as Cicero writes, and others by the loss of one-half.

He administered justice with the utmost conscientiousness and strictness. Those convicted of extortion he even dismissed from the senatorial order. He annulled the marriage of an ex-praetor, who had married a woman the very day after her divorce, although there was no suspicion of adultery. He imposed duties on foreign wares. He denied the use of litters and the wearing of scarlet robes or pearls to all except to those of a designated position and age, and on set days. In particular he enforced the law against extravagance,[1] setting watchmen in various parts of the market, to seize and bring to him dainties which were exposed for sale in violation of the law; and sometimes he sent his Lictors and soldiers to take from a dining-room any articles which had escaped the vigilance of his watchmen, even after they had been served.

In particular, for the beautification and convenience of the

---

[1] There were many such laws. Their number grew with the growing extravagance of the Emperors.

city, as well as for guarding and extending the bounds of the empire, he formed more projects and more extensive ones every day: first of all, to rear a temple to Mars, greater than any in existence, filling up and leveling the pool in which he had exhibited the sea-fight, and to build a theater of vast size, sloping down from the Tarpeian rock; to reduce the civil code to fixed limits, and of the vast and prolix mass of statutes to include only the best and most essential in a limited number of volumes; to open to the public the greatest possible libraries of Greek and Latin books, assigning to Marcus Varro the charge of procuring and classifying them; to drain the Pomptine marshes; to let out the water from Lake Fucinus; to make a highway from the Adriatic across the summit of the Apennines as far as the Tiber; to cut a canal through the Isthmus; [1] to check the Dacians, who had poured into Pontus and Thrace; then to make war on the Parthians by way of Lesser Armenia, but not to risk a battle with them until he had first tested their mettle.

All these enterprises and plans were cut short by his death. But before I speak of that, it will not be amiss to describe briefly his personal appearance, his dress, his mode of life, and his character, as well as his conduct in civil and military life.

He is said to have been tall of stature, with a fair complexion, shapely limbs, a somewhat full face, and keen black eyes; sound of health, except that towards the end he was subject to sudden fainting fits and to nightmare as well. He was twice attacked by the falling sickness [2] during his campaigns. He was somewhat overnice in the care of his person, not only keeping the hair of his head closely cut and his face smoothly shaved, but, as some have charged even having superfluous hair plucked out. His baldness was a disfigurement which troubled him greatly, since he found that it was often the subject of the gibes of his detractors. Because of it he used to comb forward his scanty locks from the crown of his head, and of all the honors voted him by the Senate and people there was none which he received or made use of more

---

[1] The Isthmus of Corinth, lying between the Ionian and the Aegean seas. This work Demetrius had before attempted, as later, Caligula and Nero, without success.

[2] Epilepsy. Sometimes a seizure was feigned for political purposes.

gladly than the privilege of wearing a laurel wreath at all times. They say, too, that he was fantastic in his dress; that he wore a Senator's tunic with fringed sleeves reaching to the wrist, and always had a girdle over it, though rather a loose one; and this, they say, was the occasion of Sulla's *mot*, when he often warned the nobles to keep an eye on the ill-girt boy.[1]

He lived at first in the Subura in a modest house, but after he became Chief Priest, in the official residence on the Sacred Way. Many have written that he was very fond of elegance and luxury; that having laid the foundations of a country-house on his estate at Nemi[2] and finished it at great cost, he tore it all down because it did not suit him in every particular, although at the time he was still poor and heavily in debt; and that he carried tesselated and mosaic floors about with him on his campaigns.

They say that he was led to invade Britain by the hope of getting pearls, and that in comparing their size he sometimes weighed them with his own hand; that he was always a most enthusiastic collector of gems, carvings, statues, and pictures by early artists; also of slaves of exceptional figure and train-ing at enormous prices, of which he himself was so ashamed that he forbade their entry in his accounts.

It is further reported that in the provinces he gave banquets constantly in two dining-halls, in one of which his officers or Greek companions, in the other Roman civilians and the more distinguished of the provincials reclined at table. He was so punctilious and strict in the management of his household, in small matters as well as in those of greater importance, that he put his baker in irons for serving him with one kind of bread and his guests with another; and he inflicted capital punishment on a favorite freedman for adultery with the wife of a Roman Knight, although no complaint was made against him.

There was no stain on his reputation for chastity except his

---

[1] His manner of dress undoubtedly impressed people as effeminate. Macrobius relates (*Sat.* II, 3, 10) that Cicero, questioned as to why he had been deceived in siding with Pompey rather than Caesar, seeing that Caesar was victorious, replied: "I was deceived by that loose girdling of his."

[2] Sixteen miles from Rome.

intimacy with King Nicomedes, but that was a deep and lasting reproach, which laid him open to insults from every quarter. I say nothing of the notorious lines of Licinius Calvus:

"Whatever Bithynia had, and Caesar's paramour."

I pass over, too, the invectives of Dolabella and the elder
Curio, in which Dolabella calls him "the Queen's rival, the
inner partner of the royal couch," and Curio, "the brothel of
Nicomedes and the stew of Bithynia." I take no account of
the edicts of Bibulus, in which he posted his colleague as "the
Queen of Bithynia," saying that "of yore he was enamoured
of a King, but now of a King's estate." At this same time, so
Marcus Brutus declares, one Octavius, a man whose disordered mind made him somewhat free with his tongue, after
saluting Pompey as "King" in a crowded assembly, greeted
Caesar as "Queen." But Gaius Memmius makes the direct
charge that he acted as cup-bearer to Nicomedes with the
rest of his wantons at a large dinner-party, and that among
the guests were some merchants from Rome, whose names
Memmius gives. Cicero, indeed, is not content with having
written in sundry letters that Caesar was led by the King's
attendants to the royal apartments, that he lay on a golden
couch arrayed in purple, and that the virginity of this scion
of Venus was lost in Bithynia; but when Caesar was once
addressing the Senate in defense of Nysa, daughter of Nicomedes, and was recounting the King's kindness to him,
Cicero cried: "No more of that, pray, for it is well known
what he gave you, and what you gave him in turn." Finally,
in his Gallic triumph his soldiers, among the bantering songs
which are usually sung by those who follow the chariot,
shouted these lines, which became a by-word:

"Gaul to Caesar yielded, Caesar to Nicomedes.
Lo! Caesar triumphs for his glorious deed,
But Caesar's conqueror gains no victor's meed."

It is admitted by all that he was much addicted to women,
as well as very extravagant in his intrigues with them, and
that he seduced many illustrious women, among them Pos-

tumia, wife of Servius Sulpicius, Lollia, wife of Aulus Gabinius, Tertulla, wife of Marcus Crassus, and even Gnaeus Pompey's wife Mucia. At all events there is no doubt that Pompey was taken to task by the elder and the younger Curio, as well as by many others, because through a desire for power he had afterwards married the daughter of a man on whose account he divorced a wife who had borne him three children, and whom he had often referred to with a groan as an Aegisthus.[1] But beyond all others Caesar loved Servilia, the mother of Marcus Brutus, for whom in his first consulship he bought a pearl costing six million sesterces.[2] During the civil war, too, besides other presents, he knocked down some fine estates to her in a public auction at a nominal price, and when some expressed their surprise at the low figure, Cicero wittily remarked: "To let you know the real value of the purchase, between ourselves, Tertia was deducted."[3] And in fact it was thought that Servilia was prostituting her own daughter Tertia to Caesar.

That he did not refrain from intrigues with married women in the provinces is shown in particular by this distich, which was also shouted by the soldiers in his Gallic triumph:

> "Watch well your wives, O citizens
> A lecher bald we bring.
> In Gaul adultery cost thee gold,
> Here 'tis but borrowing."[4]

He had love affairs with Queens, too, including Eunoe the Moor, wife of Bogudes, on whom, as well as on her husband, he bestowed many splendid presents, as Naso writes. But his greatest favorite was Cleopatra, with whom he often feasted

---

[1] That is, adulterer; for Aegisthus, who, like Caesar, was a pontiff, committed adultery with Clytemnestra while Agamemnon was off at the Trojan war, as did Caesar with Mucia, when Pompey was absent in the war against Mithridates.

[2] $246,000.

[3] *Double-entendre* in the Latin *tertia deducta;* Tertia signifying a third off (the value of the farm) as well as being the name of the girl for whose favors the reduction was made.

[4] Implying that as he borrowed of other men, so he lent as much in return, for, as was said, his own wife Pompeia was kept by P. Clodius.

until daybreak, and he would have gone through Egypt with her in her state-barge almost to Aethiopia, had not his soldiers refused to follow him. Finally he called her to Rome and did not let her leave until he had laden her with high honors and rich gifts, and he allowed her to give his name to the child which she bore. In fact, according to certain Greek writers, this child was very like Caesar in looks and carriage. Mark Antony declared to the Senate that Caesar had really acknowledged the boy, and that Gaius Matius, Gaius Oppius, and other friends of Caesar knew this. Of these Gaius Oppius, as if admitting that the situation required apology and defense, published a book, to prove that the child whom Cleopatra fathered on Caesar was not his. Helvius Cinna, Tribune of the Commons, admitted to several that he had a bill drawn up in due form, which Caesar had ordered him to propose to the people in his absence, making it lawful for Caesar to marry what wives he wished, and as many as he wished, "for the purpose of begetting children." To leave no room for doubt of his evil reputation both for sodomy and adultery, Curio the elder, in one of his speeches, calls him "every woman's man and every man's woman."

That he drank very little wine not even his enemies denied. There is a saying of Marcus Cato that Caesar was the only man who undertook to overthrow the state when sober. Even in the matter of food Gaius Oppius tells us that he was so indifferent, that once when his host served stale oil instead of fresh, and the other guests would have none of it, Caesar partook even more plentifully than usual, that he might not seem to charge his host with carelessness or lack of manners.

But his abstinence did not extend to pecuniary advantages, either when in command of armies or when in civil office For we have the testimony of some writers that when he was Proconsul in Spain, he not only begged money from the allies, to help pay his debts, but also attacked and sacked some towns of the Lusitanians, although they did not refuse his terms and opened their gates to him on his arrival. In Gaul he pillaged shrines and temples of the Gods filled with offerings, and oftener sacked towns for the sake of plunder than for any fault. In consequence he had more gold than he knew what to do with, and offered it for sale throughout Italy and the provinces at the rate of three thousand sesterces the pound.[1] In his first consulship he stole three thousand pounds of gold from the Capitol, replacing it with the same weight of gilded bronze. He made alliances and thrones a matter of barter, for he extorted from Ptolemy alone in his own name and that of Pompey nearly six thousand talents,[2] while later on he met the heavy expenses of the civil wars and of his triumphs and entertainments by the most bare-faced pillage and sacrilege.

In eloquence and in the art of war he either equaled or excelled the glory of the very best. After his prosecution of Dolabella, he was indisputably reckoned one of the most distinguished advocates. Cicero, at all events, in reviewing the orators in his *Brutus* says that he does not see that Caesar was inferior to any one of them, maintaining that his style is elegant as well as brilliant, even grand and in a sense noble. Again in a letter to Cornelius Nepos he writes thus of Caesar: "Come now, what orator would you rank above him of those who have devoted themselves to nothing else? Who has more clever or more frequent epigrams? Who is more polished or more elegant in diction?" He appears, at least in his youth, to have imitated the manner of Caesar Strabo, from whose speech entitled "For the Sardinians" he actually transferred some passages word for word to a trial address [3] of his own. He is said to have delivered himself in a high-pitched voice with impassioned action and gestures, which were not without grace. He left several speeches, including some which are attributed to him on insufficient evidence. Augustus had good reason to think that the speech "For Quintus Metellus" was rather taken down by shorthand writers who could not keep pace with his delivery, than published by Caesar himself. For in some copies I find that even the title is not "For Metellus," but, "Which he wrote for Metellus," although the discourse purports to be from Caesar's lips, defending Metellus and himself against the charges of their common detractors. Augustus also questions the authenticity of the address "To his Soldiers in Spain," although there are two versions

---

[1] Apparently about two-thirds less than the usual price.

[2] $6,792,000.00.

[3] That is, a speech in which he competed with other lawyers for the right to conduct a prosecution.

of it: one purporting to have been spoken at the first battle, the other at the second, when Asinius Pollio writes that be- cause of the sudden onslaught of the enemy he actually did not have time to make an harangue.

He left memoirs too of his deeds in the Gallic war and in the civil strife with Pompey; for the author of the Alexan- drian, African, and Spanish Wars is unknown; some think it was Oppius, others Hirtius, who also supplied the final book of the Gallic War, which Caesar left unwritten. With regard to Caesar's memoirs Cicero, also in the *Brutus,* speaks in the following terms: "He wrote memoirs which deserve the high- est praise; they are naked in their simplicity, straightforward, yet graceful, stripped of all rhetorical adornment, as of a garment. While his purpose was to supply material to others, on which those who wished to write history might draw, he perhaps gratified silly folk, who will try to use the curling-irons, on his narrative, yet he has kept men of any sense from touch- ing the subject." Of these same memoirs Hirtius uses this emphatic language: "They are so highly rated in the judg- ment of all men, that he seems to have deprived writers of an opportunity, rather than given them one. Yet our admira- tion for this feat is greater than that of others. For they know how well and faultlessly he wrote, while we know be- sides how easily and rapidly he finished his task." Asinius Pollio thinks that they were put together somewhat carelessly and without strict regard for truth; since in many cases Caesar was too ready to believe the accounts which others gave of their actions, and gave a perverted account of his own, either designedly or perhaps through defect of memory; and he thinks that he intended to revise and rewrite them. He left besides a work in two volumes "On Analogy," the same num- ber of "Speeches in Reply to Cato," in addition to a poem, entitled "The Journey." He wrote the first of these works while crossing the Alps and returning to his army from Hither Gaul, where he had held the assizes, the second about the time of the battle of Munda, and the third in the course of a twenty-four days' journey from Rome to Farther Spain. Some letters of his to the Senate are also preserved, and he seems to have been the first to reduce such documents to pages and the form of a memorial volume, whereas previously Consuls and Generals sent their reports written right across the sheet. There are also letters of his to Cicero, as well as to his intimates on private affairs. In the latter, if he had anything confidential to say, he wrote it in cipher, that is, by so changing the order of the letters of the alphabet, that not a word could be made out. If any one wishes to decipher these, and get at their meaning, he must substitute the fourth letter of the alphabet, namely D, for A, and so with the others. We also have mention of certain writings of his boyhood and early youth, such as the "Praises of Hercules," a tragedy "Oedipus," and a "Collection of Apophthegms"; but Augustus forbade the publication of all these minor works in a very brief and frank letter sent to Pompeius Macer, whom he had selected to set his libraries in order.

He was highly skilled in arms and horsemanship, and of incredible powers of endurance. On the march he headed his army, sometimes on horseback, but oftener on foot, bareheaded both in the heat of the sun and in rain. He covered great distances with incredible speed, making a hundred miles a day in a hired carriage and with little baggage, swimming the rivers which barred his path or crossing them on inflated skins, and very often arriving before the messengers sent to announce his coming.

In the conduct of his campaigns it is a question whether he was more cautious or more daring, for he never led his army where ambuscades were possible without carefully reconnoitering the country, and he did not cross to Britain without making personal inquiries about the harbors, the course, and the approach to the island. But on the other hand, when news came that his camp in Germany was besieged, he made his way to his men through the enemies' pickets, disguised as a Gaul. He crossed from Brundisium to Dyrrachium in winter time, running the blockade of the enemy's fleets; and when the troops which he had ordered to follow him delayed to do so, and he had sent to fetch them many times in vain, at last in secret and alone he boarded a small boat at night with his head muffled up; and he did not reveal who he was, or suffer the helmsman to give way to the gale blowing in their teeth, until he was all but overwhelmed by the waves.

No regard for religion ever turned him from any undertaking or even delayed him. Though the victim escaped as he was offering sacrifice, he did not put off his expedition against Scipio and Juba. Even when he had a fall as he disembarked, he gave the omen a favorable turn by crying: "I hold thee fast, Africa." Furthermore, to make the prophecies ridiculous which declared that the stock of the Scipios was fated to be fortunate and invincible in that province, he kept with him in camp a contemptible fellow belonging to the Cornelian family, to whom the nickname Salvito had been given as a reproach for his manner of life.

He joined battle, not only after planning his movements in advance but on a sudden opportunity, often immediately at the end of a march, and sometimes in the foulest weather, when one would least expect him to make a move. It was not until his later years that he became slower to engage, through a conviction that the oftener he had been victor, the less he ought to tempt fate, and that he could not possibly gain as much by success as he might lose by a defeat. He never put his enemy to flight without also driving him from his camp, thus giving him no respite in his panic. When the issue was doubtful, he used to send away the horses, and his own among the first, to impose upon his troops the greater necessity of standing their ground by taking away that aid to flight.

He rode a remarkable horse, too, with feet that were almost human, for its hoofs were cloven in such a way as to look like toes. This horse was foaled on his own place, and since the soothsayers had declared that it foretold the rule of the world for its master, he reared it with the greatest care, and was the first to mount it, for it would endure no other rider. Afterwards, too, he dedicated a statue of it before the temple of Venus Genetrix.

When his army gave way, he often rallied it single-handed, planting himself in the way of the fleeing men, laying hold of them one by one, even seizing them by the throat and turning them to face the enemy; that, too, when they were in such a panic that an eagle-bearer made a pass at him with the point [1]

---

[1] The principal standard of the Roman legion was a silver eagle with outspread wings and clutching a golden thunder bolt in its claw. It was mounted on a pole sharp at one end so that it could be set firmly in the ground. In camp it stood in a little shrine.

as he tried to stop him, while another left the standard in Caesar's hand when he would hold him back.

His presence of mind was no less renowned and the instances of it will appear even more striking. After the battle of Pharsalus, when he had sent on his troops and was crossing the strait of the Hellespont in a small passenger boat, he met Lucius Cassius, of the hostile party, with ten armored ships, and made no attempt to escape, but went to meet Cassius and actually exhorted him to surrender. Cassius sued for mercy and was taken on board.

At Alexandria, while assaulting a bridge, he was forced by a sudden sally of the enemy to take to a small skiff. When many others threw themselves into the same boat, he plunged into the sea, and after swimming for two hundred paces, got away to the nearest ship, holding up his left hand all the way, so as not to wet some papers which he was carrying, and dragging his cloak after him with his teeth, to keep the enemy from getting it as a trophy.

He valued his soldiers neither for their personal character nor their fortune, but solely for their prowess, and he treated them with equal strictness and indulgence. For he did not curb them everywhere and at all times, but only in the presence of the enemy. Then he required the strictest discipline, not announcing the time of a march or a battle, but keeping them ready and alert to be led on a sudden at any moment wheresoever he might wish. He often called them out even when there was no occasion for it, especially on rainy days and holidays. Sometimes, giving them orders not to lose sight of him, he would steal away suddenly by day or night and make a longer march than usual, to tire out those who were tardy in following.

When they were in a panic through reports about the enemy's numbers, he used to rouse their courage not by denying or discounting the rumors, but by falsely exaggerating the true danger. For instance, when the anticipation of Juba's coming filled them with terror, he called the soldiers together and said: "Let me tell you that within the next few days the king will be here with ten legions, thirty thousand horsemen a hundred thousand light-armed troops, and three hundred elephants. Let none of you, therefore, presume to make fur ther inquiry or to indulge in conjectures, but take my word for what I tell you, which I have on good information. Other wise, I shall surely have them shipped on some worn out craft and carried off to whatever lands the wind may blow them."

He did not take notice of all their offenses or punish them by rule, but he kept a sharp lookout for deserters and mutineers, and chastised them most severely, shutting his eyes to other faults. Sometimes, too, after a great victory he relieved them of all duties and gave them full license to revel, being in the habit of boasting that his soldiers could fight well even when reeking of perfumes. In the assembly he addressed them not as "soldiers," but by the more flattering term "comrades," and he kept them in fine trim, furnishing them with arms inlaid with silver and gold, both for show and to make them hold the faster to them in battle, through fear of the greatness of the loss. Such was his love for them that when he heard of the disaster to Titurius,[1] he let his hair and beard grow long, and would not cut them until he had taken vengeance. In this way he made them most devoted to his interests as well as most valiant.

When he began the civil war,[2] every Centurion [3] of each legion proposed to supply a horseman from his own allowance, and the soldiers one and all offered their service without pay and without rations, the richer assuming the care of the poorer. Throughout the long struggle not one deserted and many of them, on being taken prisoner, refused to accept their lives, when offered them on the condition of consenting to serve against Caesar. They bore hunger and other hardships, both when in a state of siege and when besieging others, with such fortitude, that when Pompey saw in the works at Dyrrachium a kind of bread made of herbs, on which they were living, he said that he was fighting wild beasts, and gave or-

---

[1] 54 B.C. The legions under Titurius Sabinus and L. Cotta while wintering in the territory of the Eburones. in Gaul, were attacked and cut to pieces by Ambiorix, their chief.

[2] The war against Pompey.

[3] Captain of a hundred men; appointed by the commander-in-chief; next in rank to the Military Tribunes.

ders that it be put out of sight quickly and shown to none of his men for fear that the endurance and resolution of the foe would break their spirit.

How valiantly they fought is shown by the fact that when they suffered their sole defeat before Dyrrachium, they insisted on being punished, and their commander felt called upon rather to console than to chastise them. In the other battles they overcame with ease countless forces of the enemy, though decidedly fewer in number themselves. Indeed one cohort [1] of the sixth legion, when set to defend a redoubt, kept four legions of Pompey at bay for several hours, though almost all were wounded by the enemy's showers of arrows, of which a hundred and thirty thousand were picked up within the ramparts. And no wonder, when one thinks of the deeds of individual soldiers, either of Cassius Scaeva the Centurion, or of Gaius Acilius of the rank and file, not to mention others. Scaeva, with one eye gone, his thigh and shoulder wounded, and his shield bored through in a hundred and twenty places, continued to guard the gate of a fortress put in his charge. Acilius in the sea-fight at Massilia grasped the stern of one of the enemy's ships, and when his right hand was lopped off, rivaling the famous exploit of the Greek hero Cynegirus,[2] boarded the ship and drove the enemy before him with the boss of his shield.

They did not mutiny once during the ten years of the Gallic war; in the civil wars they did so now and then, but quickly resumed their duty, not so much owing to any indulgence of their General as to his authority. For he never gave way to them when they were insubordinate, but always boldly faced them, discharging the entire ninth legion in disgrace before Placentia, though Pompey was still in the field, reinstating them unwillingly and only after many abject entreaties, and insisting on punishing the ringleaders.

Again at Rome, when the men of the tenth legion clamored for their discharge and rewards with terrible threats and no little peril to the city, though the war in Africa was then raging, he did not hesitate to appear before them, against the ad-

---

[1] A tenth part of a legion, about 400 men.
[2] At the battle of Marathon.

vice of his friends, and to disband them. But with a single word, calling them "citizens," [1] instead of "soldiers," he easily brought them round and bent them to his will. For they at once replied that they were his "soldiers" and insisted on following him to Africa, although he refused their service. Even then he punished the most insubordinate by the loss of a third part of the booty and of the land intended for them.

Even when a young man he showed no lack of devotion and fidelity to his dependents. He defended the cause of a noble youth, Masintha, against King Hiempsal with such spirit, that in the dispute he caught the King's son Juba by the beard. [2] On Masintha's being declared subject to the King, he at once rescued him from those who were carrying him off, and kept him hidden for some time in his own house. When presently he left for Spain after his praetorship, he carried the young man off in his own litter, unnoticed amid the crowd that came to see him off and the Lictors with their fasces.

His friends he treated with invariable kindness and consideration. When Gaius Oppius was his companion on a journey through a wild, woody country and was suddenly taken ill, Caesar gave up to him the only shelter there was, while he himself slept on the ground out-of-doors. Moreover, when he came to power, he advanced some of his friends to the highest positions, even though they were of the humblest origin, and when taken to task for it, flatly declared that if he had been helped in defending his honor by brigands and cutthroats, he would have requited even such men in the same way.

On the other hand he never formed such bitter enmities that he was not glad to lay them aside when opportunity offered. Although Gaius Memmius had made highly caustic speeches against him, to which he had replied with equal bitterness, he went so far as to support Memmius afterwards in his suit for the consulship. When Gaius Calvus, after some scurrilous epigrams took steps through his friends towards a reconciliation, Caesar wrote to him first and of his own free

---

[1] As though freed from the allegiance to which they were bound by the military oath.

[2] A great insult to barbarians, who set great store by their beards, which they wore long.

will. Valerius Catullus, as Caesar himself did not hesitate to
say, inflicted a lasting stain on his name by the verses about
Mamurra. Yet when he apologized, Caesar invited the poet to
dinner that very same day, and continued his usual friendly
relations with Catullus's father.

Even in avenging wrongs he was by nature most merciful.
When he got hold of the pirates who had captured him, having sworn that he would crucify them, he did so indeed, but
ordered that their throats be cut first. He could never make
up his mind to harm Cornelius Phagites, although when he
was sick and in hiding, the man had waylaid him night after
night, and even a bribe had barely saved him from being
handed over to Sulla.[1] The slave Philemon, his amanuensis,
who had promised Caesar's enemies that he would poison him,
he merely punished by death, without torture. When summoned as a witness against Publius Clodius, the paramour of
his wife Pompeia, who was being prosecuted for desecration
of sacred rights,[2] Caesar declared that he had no evidence, although both his mother Aurelia and his sister Julia had given
the same jurors a faithful account of the whole affair. When
he was then asked why after all he had divorced Pompeia, he
replied: "Because I maintain that the members of my family
should be free not only from guilt, but from even the suspicion of guilt."

He certainly showed admirable self-restraint and mercy,
both in his conduct of the civil war and in the hour of victory.
While Pompey threatened to treat as enemies those who did
not take up arms for the government, Caesar gave out that
those who were neutral and of neither party should be numbered with his friends. He freely allowed all those whom he
had made Centurions on Pompey's recommendation to go
over to his rival. When conditions of surrender were under
discussion at Ilerda, and friendly intercourse between the two
parties was constant, Afranius and Petreius, with a sudden
change of purpose, put to death all of Caesar's soldiers whom
they found in their camp, but Caesar could not bring himself

---

[1] Phagites, a freedman of Sulla, and one of those delegated to appre-
hend Caesar when he was under the disfavor of Sulla. Plutarch, in his
Life of Caesar, says the amount of this bribe was $2,264.00.

[2] Those of Bona Dea.

to retaliate in kind. At the battle of Pharsalus he cried out, "Spare your fellow citizens," and afterwards allowed each of his men to save any one man he pleased of the opposite party. None on Pompey's side, so far as appears, lost their lives but in battle, save only Afranius and Faustus, and the young Lucius Caesar. And it is believed that not even these men were slain by his wish, even though the two former had taken up arms again after being pardoned, and the latter had not only cruelly put to death the Dictator's slaves and freedmen with fire and sword, but had even butchered the wild beasts which he had procured for the entertainment of the people. At last, in his later years, he went so far as to allow all those whom he had not yet pardoned to return to Italy, and to hold offices both civil and military; and he actually set up the statues of Lucius Sulla and Pompey, which had been broken to pieces by the populace. After this, if any dangerous plots were formed against him, or slanders uttered, he chose rather to check than to punish them. Accordingly, he took no further notice of the conspiracies which were detected, and of meetings by night, than to make known by proclamation that he was aware of them. To those who spoke ill of him he thought it enough to give public warning not to persist in their offense, bearing with good nature the attacks on his reputation made by the scurrilous volume of Aulus Caecina and the abusive lampoons of Pitholaus.

Yet after all, his other actions and words so far outweigh all his good qualities that it is thought he abused his power and was justly slain. For not only did he accept excessive honors, such as an uninterrupted consulship, the dictatorship for life, and the censorship of public morals, as well as the forename Imperator,[1] the surname of Father of his Country, a statue among those of the Kings,[2] and a raised couch in the orchestra of the theater. He also allowed honors to be bestowed

---

[1] The title *Imperator*, synonymous with conqueror, was that by which troops would hail a victorious commander. It first assumed a permanent and royal character through Caesar's use of it as a prenomen.

[2] Statues of each of the seven Kings of Rome were in the Capitol, to which an eighth was added in honor of Brutus, who expelled the last. The statue of Julius was afterwards raised near them.

on him which were too great for mortal man: a golden throne in the House and on the judgment seat; a chariot and litter [1] in the procession at the circus; temples, altars, and statues beside those of the Gods; a special priest, an additional college of the Luperci, and the calling of one of the months by his name. In fact, there were no honors which he did not receive or confer at pleasure.

He held his third and fourth consulships in name only, content with the power of the dictatorship conferred on him at the same time as the consulships. Moreover, in both years he substituted two Consuls for himself for the last three months, in the meantime holding no elections except for Tribunes and plebeian Aediles, and appointing Praefects instead of the Praetors, to manage the affairs of the city during his absence. When one of the Consuls suddenly died the day before the Kalends of January, he gave the vacant office for a few hours to a man who asked for it. With the same disregard of law and precedent he named magistrates for several years to come, bestowed the emblems of consular rank on ten ex-Praetors, and admitted to the House men who had been given citizenship, and in some cases even half-civilized Gauls. He assigned the charge of the mint and of the public revenues to his own slaves, and gave the oversight and command of the three legions which he had left at Alexandria to a favorite boy of his called Rufio, son of one of his freedmen.

No less arrogant were his public utterances, which Titus Ampius [2] records: that the Republic was a name only, without substance or reality; that Sulla did not know his A. B. C. when he laid down his dictatorship; that men ought now to be more circumspect in addressing him, and to regard his word as law. So far did he go in his presumption, that when a soothsayer once announced to him the direful omen that a victim offered for sacrifice was without a heart, he said: "The entrails will be more favorable when I please. It ought not to be taken as a miracle if a beast have no heart."

But it was the following action in particular that roused deadly hatred against him. When the Senate approached him

---

[1] For carrying an image of him among those of the Gods.
[2] Titus Ampius Balbus, the friend of Cicero and one of the supporters of Pompey whom Caesar pardoned after the civil war.

in a body with many highly honorary decrees, he received them before the temple of Venus Genetrix without rising. Some think that when he attempted to get up, he was held back by Cornelius Balbus; others, that he made no such move at all, but on the contrary frowned angrily on Gaius Trebatius when he suggested that he should rise. This action of his seemed the more intolerable, because when he himself in one of his triumphal processions rode past the benches of the Tribunes, he was so incensed because one of their number, Pontius Aquila by name, did not rise, that he cried: "Come then, Aquila, mighty Tribune, and take from me the Republic," and for several days afterwards, he would promise a favor to no one without adding, "That is, if Pontius Aquila will give me leave."

To an insult which so plainly showed his contempt for the Senate he added an act of even greater insolence. After the sacred rites of the Latin Festival, as he was returning to the city, amid the extravagant and unprecedented demonstrations of the populace, some one in the press placed on his statue a laurel wreath with a white fillet [1] tied to it. When Epidius Marullus and Caesetius Flavus, Tribunes of the Commons, gave orders that the ribbon be removed from the crown and the man taken off to prison, Caesar sharply rebuked and deposed them, either offended that the hint at regal power had been received with so little favor, or, as was said, that he had been robbed of the glory of refusing it. But from that time on he could not rid himself of the odium of having aspired to the title of monarch, although he replied to the Commons, when they hailed him as King, "I am Caesar and not King." At the Lupercalia,[2] when the Consul Antony several times attempted to place a crown upon his head as he spoke from the rostra, he put it aside and at last sent it to the Capitol, to be offered to Jupiter Optimus Maximus. Nay, more, the

---

[1] Emblematic of royalty.

[2] An orgiastic festival in February in honor of the Lycaen Pan, identified by the Romans with Faunus. During the solemnity, the Luperci, priests of that god, ran naked in the streets, striking those they met with goat-skin thongs, particularly married women, who were thereby supposed to be rendered fecund.

report had spread in various quarters that he intended to move to Ilium [1] or Alexandria, taking with him the resource of the state, draining Italy by levies, and leaving it and the charge of the city to his friends; also that at the next meeting of the Senate Lucius Cotta would announce as the decision of the Fifteen,[2] that inasmuch as it was written in the books of fate that the Parthians could be conquered only by a King, Caesar should be given that title.

In order to avoid giving assent to this proposal the conspirators hastened the execution of their designs. Therefore the plots which had previously been formed separately, often by groups of two or three, were united in a general conspiracy, since even the populace no longer were pleased with present conditions, but both secretly and openly rebelled at his tyranny and cried out for defenders of their liberty. On the admission of foreigners to the Senate, a placard was posted: "God bless the Commonwealth! Let no one consent to point out the House to a newly made Senator." The following verses too were repeated everywhere:—

> "The Gauls he dragged in triumph through the town
> Caesar has brought into the Senate house
> And changed their breeches for the purple gown."

When Quintus Maximus, whom he had appointed Consul in his place for three months, was entering the theater, and his Lictor in the usual manner called attention to his arrival, a general shout was raised: "He's no Consul!" After the removal of Caesetius and Marullus from office as Tribunes, they were bound to have not a few votes at the next elections of Consuls. Some wrote on the base of Lucius Brutus's statue, "Oh, that you were still alive"; and on that of Caesar himself:

> "Because he drove from Rome the royal race
> Brutus was first made Consul in their place.
> This man, because he put the Consuls down,
> Has been rewarded with a royal crown."

---

[1] A city where Troy stood.
[2] The college of fifteen priests who inspected and expounded the Sybilline books.

More than sixty joined the conspiracy against him, led by Gaius Cassius and Marcus and Decimus Brutus. At first they hesitated whether to form two divisions at the elections in the Campus Martius, so that while some hurled him from the bridge [1] as he summoned the tribes to vote, the rest might wait below and slay him; or to set upon him in the Sacred Way or at the entrance to the theater. When, however, a meeting of the Senate was called for the Ides [2] of March in the Hall of Pompey, they readily gave that time and place the preference.

Now Caesar's approaching murder was foretold to him by unmistakable signs. A few months before, when the settlers assigned to the colony at Capua by the Julian Law were demolishing some tombs of great antiquity, to build country houses, and plied their work with the greater vigor because as they rummaged about they found a quantity of vases of ancient workmanship, there was discovered in a tomb, which was said to be that of Capys, the founder of Capua, a bronze tablet, inscribed with Greek words and characters to this effect: "Whenever the bones of Capys shall be discovered, it will come to pass that a descendant of his shall be slain at the hands of his kindred, and presently avenged at heavy cost to Italy." And let no one think this tale a myth or a lie, for it is vouched for by Cornelius Balbus, an intimate friend of Caesar. Shortly before his death, as he was told, the herds of horses which he had dedicated to the river Rubicon when he crossed it, and had let loose without a keeper, stubbornly refused to graze and wept copiously. Again, when he was offering sacrifice, the soothsayer Spurinna warned him to beware of danger, which would come not later than the Ides of March. On the day before the Ides of that month a little bird called the king-bird flew into the Hall of Pompey with a sprig of laurel, pursued by others of various kinds from the grove hard by, which tore it to pieces in the hall. In fact the very night before his murder he dreamt now that he was flying above the clouds, and now that he was clasping the

---

[1] A temporary bridge of planks over which the voters passed one by one to cast their ballots.

[2] The 15th of March, May, July, and October; the 13th of every other month.

hand of Jupiter; and his wife Calpurnia thought that the pediment of their house fell, and that her husband was stabbed in her arms; and on a sudden the door of the room flew open of its own accord.

Both for these reasons and because of poor health he hesitated for a long time whether to stay at home and put off what he had planned to do in the Senate. But at last, urged by Decimus Brutus not to disappoint the full meeting, which had for some time been waiting for him, he went forth almost at the end of the fifth hour.[1] When a note revealing the plot was handed him by some one on the way, he put it with others which he held in his left hand, intending to read them presently. Then, after many victims had been slain, and he could not get favorable omens, he entered the House in defiance of portents, laughing at Spurinna and calling him a false prophet, because the Ides of March were come without bringing him harm. Spurinna replied that they had of a truth come, but they had not gone.

As he took his seat, the conspirators gathered about him as if to pay their respects, and straightway Tillius Cimber, who had assumed the lead, came nearer as though to ask something. When Caesar with a gesture put him off to another time, Cimber caught his toga by both shoulders. As Caesar cried, "Why, this is violence!" one of the Cascas stabbed him from one side just below the throat. Caesar caught Casca's arm and ran it through with his stylus,[2] but as he tried to leap to his feet, he was stopped by another wound. When he saw that he was beset on every side by drawn daggers, he muffled his head in his robe, and at the same time drew down its lap [3] to his feet with his left hand, in order to fall more decently, with the lower part of his body also covered. And in this wise he was stabbed with three and twenty wounds, uttering not a word, but merely a groan at the first stroke, though some have written that when Marcus Brutus rushed at him, he

---

[1] Eleven in the morning.

[2] Used for writing on wax tablets. The Romans also wrote on parchment with pens of sharpened reed split at the point. For ink they used the black liquid emitted by the cuttle fish.

[3] The part worn over the shoulder or tucked up slack above the waist.

said in Greek, "You too, my child?" All the conspirators made off, and he lay there lifeless for some time, until finally three common slaves put him on a litter and carried him home, with one arm hanging down. And of so many wounds none, in the opinion of the physician Antistius, would have proved mortal except the second one in the breast.

The conspirators had intended after slaying him to drag his body to the Tiber, confiscate his property, and revoke his decrees. But they forebore through fear of Marcus Antonius, the Consul, and Lepidus, the master of horse.

At the request of his father-in-law, Lucius Piso, his will was opened and read in Antony's house. He had made it on the Ides of the preceding September at his villa near Lavicum, and committed it to the care of the chief Vestal Virgin. Quintus Tubero states that from his first consulship until the beginning of the civil war it was his wont to write down Gnaeus Pompeius as his heir, and to read this to the assembled soldiers. In his last will, however, he named three heirs, the grandsons of his sisters, namely: Gaius Octavius,[1] to three-fourths of his estate, and Lucius Pinarius and Quintus Pedius to share the remainder. At the end of the will, too, he adopted Gaius Octavius into his family and gave him his name. Several of his assassins were named among the guardians of his son, in case one should be born to him, and Decimus Brutus even among his heirs in the second degree.[2] To the people he left his gardens near the Tiber for their common use and three hundred sesterces to each man.[3]

When the funeral was announced, a pyre was erected in the Campus Martius near the tomb of Julia. On the rostra was placed a gilded shrine, made after the model of the temple of Venus Genetrix. Within was a bier of ivory with coverlets of purple and gold, and at its head a pillar hung with the robe in which he was slain. Since it was clear that the day would not be long enough for those who offered gifts, they were directed

---

[1] Who became Augustus.

[2] To inherit a share of his estate in the event of the death of the heirs in the first degree or their refusal to accept the inheritance. It was often no more than a final courtesy.

[3] $12.30.

to bring them to the Campus by whatsoever streets of the city they wished, regardless of any order of precedence.[1] At the funeral games, to rouse pity and indignation at his death, these words from the "Contest for the Arms" of Pacuvius were sung:—

"Saved I these men that they might murder me?"

and words of a like purport from the "Electra" of Atilius. Instead of a eulogy the Consul Antonius caused a herald to recite the decree of the Senate in which it had voted Caesar all divine and human honors at once, and likewise the oath with which they had all pledged themselves to watch over his personal safety; to which he added a very few words of his own. The bier on the rostra was carried to the Forum by magistrates and ex-magistrates. While some were urging that it be burned in the temple of Jupiter of the Capitol, and others in the Hall of Pompey, on a sudden two beings with swords by their sides and brandishing a pair of darts set fire to it with blazing torches, and at once the throng of bystanders heaped upon it dry branches, the judgment seats with the benches, and whatever else could serve as an offering. Then the musicians and actors tore off their robes, which they had taken from the equipment of his triumphs and put on for the occasion, rent them to bits and threw them into the flames, and the veterans of the legions the arms with which they had adorned themselves for the funeral. Many of the women, too, offered up the jewels which they wore and the amulets and robes of their children.

At the height of the public grief a throng of foreigners went about lamenting each after the fashion of his country, above all the Jews,[2] who even flocked to the place for several successive nights.

The populace, with torches in their hands, ran from the

---

[1] The usual order on such occasions was: Magistrates and Senators without their badges and robes of dignity; Knights in mourning; soldiers carrying the points of their weapons downwards; commons, marshaled according to tribe.

[2] Caesar was beloved by the Jews, not only because he had overthrown Pompey, who had violated their Holy of Holies, but because of many acts of kindness besides.

funeral to the houses of Brutus and Cassius and after being repelled with difficulty, they slew Helvius Cinna when they met him, through a mistake in the name, supposing that he was Cornelius Cinna, who had the day before made a bitter indictment of Caesar and for whom they were looking; and they set his head upon a spear and paraded it about the streets. Afterwards they set up in the Forum a solid column of Numidian marble almost twenty feet high, and inscribed upon it, "To the Father of his Country." At the foot of this they continued for a long time to sacrifice, make vows, and settle some of their disputes by an oath in the name of Caesar.

Caesar left in the minds of some of his friends the suspicion that he did not wish to live any longer and had taken no precautions, because of his failing health; and that therefore he neglected the warnings which came to him from portents and from the reports of his friends. Some think that it was because he had full trust in that last decree of the Senators and their oath that he dismissed even the armed bodyguard of Spanish soldiers that formerly attended him. Others, on the contrary, believe that he elected to expose himself once for all to the plots that threatened him on every hand, rather than to be always anxious and on his guard. Some, too, say that he was wont to declare that it was not so much to his own interest as to that of his country that he remain alive. He had long since had his fill of power and glory. But if aught befell him, the commonwealth would have no peace, and, involved in another civil war, would be in a worse state than before.

About one thing almost all are fully agreed, that his death was in many respects such as he would have chosen. For once when he read in Xenophon how Cyrus in his last illness gave directions for his funeral, he expressed his horror of such a lingering kind of end and his wish for one which was swift and sudden. And the day before his murder, in a conversation which arose at a dinner at the house of Marcus Lepidus, as to what manner of death was most to be desired, he had given his preference to one which was sudden and unexpected.

He died in the fifty-sixth year of his age, and was numbered among the Gods, not only by a formal decree, but also in the conviction of the vulgar. For at the first of the games which his heir Augustus gave in honor of his apotheosis, a comet shone for seven successive days, rising about the eleventh hour,[1] and was believed to be the soul of Caesar, who had been taken to heaven. This is why a star is set upon the crown of his head in his statue.

It was voted that the hall in which he was slain be walled up, that the Ides of March be called the Day of Parricide, and that a meeting of the Senate should never be called on that day.

Hardly any of his assassins survived him for more than three years, or died a natural death. They were all condemned. and they perished in various ways—some by shipwreck, some in battle; and some took their own lives with the self-same dagger with which they had impiously slain Caesar.

---

[1] About an hour before sunset.

BOOK II

OCTAVIUS AUGUSTUS

THE DEIFIED AUGUSTUS

There are many indications that the Octavian family was from early days a distinguished one at Velitrae.[1] For in the most frequented part of the town there was not only a street long called Octavian, but an altar consecrated by an Octavius was also to be seen there. This man, leader in a war with a neighboring people, happening once to be sacrificing to Mars when a messenger brought news of an unexpected attack, snatched the entrails of the victim off the fire, offered them up half raw, marched off to battle, and returned victorious. There was, besides, a decree of the people on record, providing that for all future time the entrails should be offered to Mars in the same manner, and the rest of the victim be handed over to the Octavii.

This family was admitted to the Senate by King Tarquinius Priscus among the lesser clans; [2] was later enrolled by Servius Tullius among the patricians; in course of time returned to the ranks of the plebeians; and after a long interval was restored to patrician rank by the Deified Julius. The first of the house to be elected by the people to a magistracy was Gaius Rufus, who became Quaestor. He begot Gnaeus and Gaius, from whom the two branches of the Octavian family were descended, which have had very different fortunes. For Gnaeus and all his scions in turn held the highest offices, but Gaius and his progeny, whether from chance or choice, remained in the equestrian order down to the father of Augustus.

Augustus's great-grandfather served in Sicily in the second Punic war [3] as Tribune of the Soldiers under the command of Aemilius Papus. His grandfather, content with the offices of

---

[1] An ancient Volscian town, now Veletri on the road to Naples.

[2] A term applied to the plebeian families in the Senate enrolled in addition to the patricians.

[3] Against Hannibal and the Carthaginians.

a municipal town and possessing an abundant income, lived to a peaceful old age. This is the account given by others. Augustus himself merely writes [1] that he came of an old and wealthy equestrian family, in which his own father was the first to become a Senator. Marcus Antonius taunts him with his great-grandfather, saying that he was a freedman and a rope-maker from the country about Thurii, while his grand-father was a money-changer. This is all that I have been able to learn about the paternal ancestors of Augustus.

His father, Gaius Octavius, was from the beginning of his life a man of wealth and repute, and I cannot but wonder that some have said that he too was a money-changer, and was even employed to distribute bribes at the elections and perform other services in the Campus. For, as a matter of fact, having been brought up in affluence, he readily attained to high positions and filled them with distinction. Macedonia fell to his lot at the end of his praetorship. On his way to the province, executing a special commission from the Senate, he wiped out a band of runaway slaves, refugees from the armies of Spartacus and Catiline, who held possession of the country about Thurii. In governing his province he showed equal justice and courage. Besides routing the Bessi and the other Thracians in a great battle, his treatment of our allies was such, that Marcus Cicero, in letters which are still in existence, urges and admonishes his brother Quintus, who at the time was serving as Proconsular Governor [2] of Asia with no great credit to himself, to imitate his neighbor Octavius in winning the favor of our allies.

While returning from Macedonia, before he could declare himself a candidate for the consulship, he died suddenly, sur-vived by three children, an elder Octavia by Ancharia, and by Atia a younger Octavia and Augustus. Atia was the daugh-ter of Marcus Atius Balbus and Julia, sister of Gaius Caesar. Balbus, a native of Aricia on his father's side, and of a family displaying many senatorial portraits, [3] was closely connected

---

[1] In his Memoirs.

[2] Quintus Cicero was really *Propraetor*, i.e. he had been Praetor and not Consul before he had been sent out as Governor of Asia.

[3] These were waxen masks of ancestors of senatorial rank, kept in the hall of the homes of their descendants.

on his mother's side with Pompey the Great. After holding the office of Praetor, he was one of the commission of twenty appointed by the Julian law to distribute lands in Campania to the Commons. But Antonius [1] again, trying to disparage the maternal ancestors of Augustus as well, twits him with having a great-grandfather of African birth, who kept first a perfumery shop and then a bakery at Aricia. Cassius of Parma also taunts Augustus with being the grandson both of a baker and of a money-changer, saying in one of his letters: "Your mother's meal came from a vulgar bakeshop of Aricia; this a money-changer from Nerulum kneaded into shape with hands stained with filthy lucre."

Augustus was born just before sunrise on the ninth day before the Kalends of October in the consulship of Marcus Tullius Cicero and Gaius Antonius, at the Ox-Heads in the Palatine quarter, where he now has a shrine, built shortly after his death. For it is recorded in the proceedings of the Senate, that when Gaius Laetorius, a young man of patrician family, was pleading for a milder punishment for adultery because of his youth and position, he further urged upon the Senators that he was the possessor and as it were the warden of the spot which the Deified Augustus first touched at his birth, and begged that he be pardoned for the sake of what might be called his own special God. Whereupon it was decreed that that part of his house should be consecrated.

A small room like a pantry is shown to this day as the Emperor's nursery in his grandfather's country-house near Velitrae, and the opinion prevails in the neighborhood that he was also born there. No one ventures to enter this room except of necessity and after purification, since there is a conviction of long standing that those who approach it without ceremony are seized with shuddering and terror; and what is more, this has recently been shown to be true. For when a new owner, either by chance or to test the matter, went to bed in that room, it came to pass that, after a very few hours of the night, he was thrown out by a sudden mysterious force, and was found bedclothes and all half-dead before the door.

---

[1] Mark Antony.

In his infancy he was given the surname Thurinus in memory of the home of his ancestors, or else because it was near Thurii that his father, Octavius, shortly before the birth of his son, had gained his victory over the runaway slaves. That he was surnamed Thurinus I may assert on very truthworthy evidence, since I once owned a little bronze bust, representing him as a boy and inscribed with that name in letters of iron almost illegible from age. This I presented to the Emperor,[1] who cherishes it among the Lares of his bedchamber. Furthermore, he is often called Thurinus in Mark Antony's letters by way of insult. To this Augustus merely replied he was surprised that his former name was thrown in his face as a reproach. Later he took the name of Gaius Caesar and then the surname Augustus, the former by the will of his great-uncle, the latter on the motion of Munatius Plancus. For when some expressed the opinion that he ought to be called Romulus as a second founder of the city, Plancus carried the proposal that he should rather be named Augustus, on the ground that this was not merely a new title but a more honorable one, inasmuch as sacred places too, and those in which anything is consecrated by augural rites are called "august" (*augusta*), from the increase (*auctus*) in dignity, or from the movements or feeding of the birds (*avium gestus gustusve*), as Ennius also shows when he writes:

"After by august augury illustrious Rome was built."

At the age of four he lost his father. In his twelfth year he delivered a funeral oration to the assembled people in honor of his grandmother Julia. Four years later, after assuming the gown of manhood,[2] he received military prizes at Caesar's African triumph, although he had taken no part in the war on account of his youth. When his uncle presently went to Spain to engage the sons of Pompey, although Augustus had hardly yet recovered his strength after a severe illness, he followed over roads beset by the enemy with only a very few companions, and that too after suffering shipwreck, and

---

[1] That is, to Hadrian.

[2] The ordinary Roman toga, all white, usually first worn at sixteen years of age.

thereby greatly endeared himself to Caesar, who soon formed a high opinion of his character over and above the energy with vhich he had made the journey.

When Caesar, after recovering the Spanish provinces, planned an expedition against the Dacians and then against the Parthians, Augustus, who had been sent on in advance to Apollonia, devoted his leisure to study. As soon as he learned that his uncle had been slain and that he was his heir, he was in doubt for some time whether to appeal to the nearest legions, but gave up the idea as hasty and premature. He did, however, return to the city and enter upon his inheritance, in spite of the doubts of his mother and the strong opposition of his stepfather, the ex-Consul Marcius Philippus. Then he levied armies and henceforth ruled the State, at first with Marcus Antonius and Marcus Lepidus, then with Antony alone for nearly twelve years, and finally by himself for forty-four.

Having given as it were a summary of his life, I shall now take up its various phases one by one, not in chronological order, but by classes, to make the account clearer and more intelligible.

The civil wars which he waged were five, called by the names of Mutina, Philippi, Perusia, Sicily, and Actium. The first and last of these were against Marcus Antonius, the second against Brutus and Cassius, the third against Lucius Antonius, brother of the Triumvir, and the fourth against Sextus Pompeius, son of Gnaeus.

The initial reason for all these wars was this: he considered nothing more incumbent on him than to avenge his uncle's death and maintain the validity of his enactments. He resolved, therefore, immediately on his return from Apollonia to surprise Brutus and Cassius by taking up arms against them. When they foresaw the danger and fled, he resolved to proceed against them by an appeal to the laws in their absence and impeach them for the murder. In the meantime, since those who had been appointed to celebrate Caesar's last victory by games did not dare to do so, he gave them himself. To be able to carry out his other plans with more authority, he announced himself candidate for the office of one of the Tribunes of the people, who happened to die at that time, though he was a patrician, and not yet a Senator.[1] But when his designs were opposed by Marcus Antonius, who was then Consul, and on whose help he had especially counted, and Antony would not allow him even common and ordinary justice without the promise of a heavy bribe, he went over to the aristocrats, who he knew detested Antony, especially because he was besieging Decimus Brutus at Mutina, and trying to drive him by force of arms from the province given him by Caesar and ratified by the Senate. Accordingly at the advice of certain men he hired assassins to kill Antony, and when the plot was discovered, fearing retaliation he mustered veterans, by the use of all the money he could command, both for his own protection and that of the State. Put in command of the army which he had raised, with the rank of Propraetor, and bidden to join with Hirtius and Pansa, who had become Consuls, in lending aid to Decimus Brutus, he finished the war which had been entrusted to him within three months in two battles. In the former of these, so Antony writes, he took flight and was not seen again until the next day, when he returned without his cloak and his horse. But in that which followed all agree he played the part not only of a leader, but of a soldier as well, and that, in the thick of the fight, when the eagle-bearer of his legion was severely wounded, he shouldered the eagle and carried it for some time.

As Hirtius lost his life in battle during this war, and Pansa shortly afterwards from a wound, the rumor spread that he had caused the death of both, in order that after Antony had been put to flight and the state bereft of its Consuls, he might gain sole control of the victorious armies. The circumstances of Pansa's death in particular were so suspicious, that the physician Glyco was imprisoned on the charge of having applied poison to his wound. Aquilius Niger adds to this that Augustus himself slew the other Consul Hirtius amid the confusion of the battle.

But when he learned that Antony after his flight had found a protector in Marcus Lepidus, and that the rest of the leaders and armies were coming to terms with them, he abandoned the cause of the nobles without hesitation, alleging as

---

[1] Since the time of Sulla only Senators had been eligible for the position of Tribune.

a pretext for his change of allegiance the words and acts of certain of their number, asserting that some had called him a boy, while others had openly said that he ought to be honored and got rid of, to escape the necessity of making suitable recompense to him or to his veterans. To show more plainly that he regretted his connection with the former party, he imposed a heavy fine on the people of Nursia and banished them from their city when they were unable to pay it, because they had at public expense erected a monument to their citizens who were slain in the battles at Mutina and inscribed upon it: "They fell for liberty."

Then, forming a league with Antony and Lepidus, he finished the war of Philippi also in two battles, although, weakened by illness, he was in the first battle driven from his camp and barely made his escape by fleeing to Antony's division. He did not use his victory with moderation, but after sending Brutus's head to Rome,[1] to be cast at the feet of Caesar's statue, he vented his spleen upon the most distinguished of his captives, not even sparing them insulting language. For instance, to one man who begged humbly for burial, he is said to have replied: "The birds will soon settle that question." When two others, father and son, begged for their lives, he is said to have bidden them cast lots or play mora,[2] to decide which should be spared, and then to have looked on while both died, since the father was executed because he offered to die for his son, and the latter thereupon took his own life. Because of this the rest, including Marcus Favonius, the well-known imitator of Cato, saluted Antony respectfully as Imperator,[3] when they were led out in chains, but lashed Augustus to his face with the foulest abuse.

When the duties of administration were divided after the victory, Antony undertaking to restore order in the East, and Augustus to lead the veterans back to Italy and assign them

---

[1] Defeated in the second engagement, Brutus retired to a hill, and slew himself in the night.

[2] A game still common in Italy, in which the players suddenly thrust out their fingers, the winner being the one who names correctly the number of fingers held out by his opponent.

[3] That is, victorious general, implying that he and not Octavius was their conqueror.

lands in the municipalities, he could neither satisfy the veterans nor the landowners,[1] since the latter complained that they were driven from their homes, and the former that they were not being treated as their services had led them to hope.

When Lucius Antonius at this juncture attempted a revolution, relying on his position as Consul and his brother's power, he forced him to take refuge in Perusia, and starved him into surrender, not, however, without great personal danger both before and during the war. For at an exhibition of games, when he had given orders that a common soldier who was sitting within the fourteen reserved rows be put out by an attendant, a report was spread by his detractors that he had afterwards tortured the man and put him to death, and the soldiers flocked together so enraged that he narrowly escaped with his life. The only thing that saved him was the sudden reappearance of the man, safe and sound, no violence having been offered him. Again, when he was sacrificing near the walls of Perusia, he was well nigh cut off by a band of gladiators, who had made a sally from the town.

After the capture of Perusia he took vengeance on many, meeting all attempts to beg for pardon or to make excuses with the one reply, "You must die." Some write that three hundred men of both orders were selected from the prisoners of war and sacrifices[2] on the Ides of March like so many victims at the altar raised to the Deified Julius. Some have written that he took up arms of a set purpose, to unmask his secret opponents and those whom fear rather than good-will kept faithful to him, by giving them the chance to follow the lead of Lucius Antonius; and then by vanquishing them and confiscating their estates to pay the rewards promised to his veterans.

The Sicilian war was among the first that he began, but it was long drawn out by many interruptions, now for the purpose of rebuilding his fleets, which he twice lost by shipwreck and storms, and that, too, in the summer; and again by patching up a peace to which he was forced by the clamors of the people when supplies were cut off and there was a severe

---

[1] Vergil was one of the landowners ejected from his farm. He narrowly escaped being killed by the Centurion Ario.

[2] Brained with an axe and not beheaded.

famine. Finally, after new ships had been built and twenty thousand slaves set free and trained as oarsmen,[1] he made the Julian harbor at Baiae by letting the sea into the Lucrine lake and lake Avernus. After drilling his forces there all winter, he defeated Pompey between Mylae and Naulochus, though just before the battle he was suddenly overcome by so deep a sleep that his friends had to awaken him to give the signal. And it was this, I think, that gave Antony opportunity for the taunt: "He could not even look with steady eyes at the fleet when it was ready for battle, but lay in a stupor on his back, looking up at the sky, and did not rise or appear before the soldiers until the enemy's ships had been put to flight by Marcus Agrippa." Some censured another act and saying of his, declaring that when his fleets were lost in the storm, he cried out, "I will have the victory spite of Neptune," and that on the next day on which there were games in the Circus, he removed the statue of that god from the sacred procession. And it is safe to say that in none of his wars did he encounter more dangers or greater ones. For when he had transported an army to Sicily and was on his way back to the rest of his forces on the mainland, he was surprised by Pompey's admirals Demochares and Apollophanes and barely escaped with but a single ship. Again, as he was going on foot to Regium by way of Locri, he saw some of Pompey's galleys coasting along the shore, and taking them for his own ships and going down to the beach, narrowly escaped capture. At that same time, too, as he was making his escape by narrow bypaths, a slave of his companion Aemilius Paulus, nursing a grudge because Augustus had outlawed his master's father some time before, and thinking that he had an opportunity for revenge, attempted to slay him.

After the flight of Pompey, Marcus Lepidus, his other colleague, whom he had summoned from Africa to help him, was puffed up by confidence in his twenty legions and claimed the first place with terrible threats. But Augustus stripped him of his army, and though he granted him his life when he sued for it, he banished him for all time to Circei.

---

[1] The Romans employed slaves in their wars only in cases of great emergency, and with much reluctance. Augustus was the first who manumitted them and used them as rowers in his galleys.

At last he broke off his alliance with Marcus Antonius, which was always doubtful and uncertain, and with difficulty kept alive by various reconcilations. The better to show that his rival had fallen away from conduct becoming a citizen, he had the will which Antony had left in Rome, naming his children by Cleopatra among his heirs, opened and read before the people. But when Antony was declared a public enemy, he sent back to him all his kinsfolk and friends, among others Gaius Sosius and Titus Domitius, who were still Consuls at the time. He also excused the community of Bononia from joining in the rally of all Italy to his standards, since they had been from ancient days dependents of the Antonii. Not long afterwards he won the sea-fight at Actium, where the contest continued to so late an hour that the victor passed the night on board. From Actium he went to the Island of Samos to winter. But being alarmed by news of a mutiny of the troops that he had selected from every division of his army and sent on to Brundisium [1] after the victory, who demanded their rewards and discharge, he returned to Italy. On this passage he twice encountered storms at sea, first between the headlands of the Peloponnesus and Aetolia, and again off the Ceraunian mountains. In both places a part of his galleys were sunk, while the rigging of the ship in which he was sailing was carried away and its rudder broken. He delayed at Brundisium only twenty-seven days—just long enough to satisfy all the demands of the soldiers—and then went to Egypt by a roundabout way through Asia and Syria, laid siege to Alexandria, where Antony had taken refuge with Cleopatra, and soon took the city. Although Antony tried to make terms at the eleventh hour, Augustus forced him to commit suicide, and viewed his corpse.[2] He greatly desired to save Cleopatra alive for his triumph, and even had Psylli [3] brought to her, to suck the poison from her wound, since it was thought that

---

[1] The usual port of embarkation for the East, now Brindisi. Vergil died there.

[2] We have no other authority that Octavius viewed Antony's corpse. Plutarch says that when he heard of Antony's death he sought the interior of his tent and wept over the fate of his colleague and friend.

[3] These people were supposed to have especial skill in saving those bitten by snakes.

she died from the bite of an asp. He allowed them both the honor of burial, and in the same tomb, giving orders that the mausoleum which they had begun should be finished. The young Antony, the elder of Fulvia's two sons, he dragged from the image of the Deified Julius, to which he had fled after many vain entreaties, and slew him. Caesarion, too, whom Cleopatra fathered on Caesar, he overtook in his flight, brought back, and put to death. But he spared the rest of the offspring of Antony and Cleopatra, and afterwards maintained and reared them according to their several positions, as carefully as if they were his own kin.

About this time he had the sarcophagus and body of Alexander the Great brought forth from its shrine, and after gazing on it, showed his respect by placing upon it a golden crown and strewing it with flowers. When he was then asked if he wished to see the tomb of the Ptolemies as well, he replied, "My wish was to see a King, not corpses."

He reduced Egypt to the form of a province, and then to make it more fruitful and better adapted to supply the city with grain, he set his soldiers at work cleaning out all the canals into which the Nile overflows, which in the course of many years had become choked with mud. To extend the fame of his victory at Actium and perpetuate its memory, he founded a city called Nicopolis near Actium, and provided for the celebration of games there every five years; enlarged the ancient temple of Apollo; and after adorning the site of the camp which he had occupied with naval trophies,* consecrated it to Neptune and Mars.

After this he nipped in the bud at various times several outbreaks, insurrections, and conspiracies, which were betrayed before they became formidable. The ringleaders were, first the young Lepidus, then Varro Murena and Fannius Caepio, later Marcus Egnatius, next Plautius Rufus and Lucius Paulus, husband of the Emperor's granddaughter, and besides these Lucius Audasius, who had been charged with forgery, and was moreover old and feeble; also Asinius Epicadus, a half-breed of Parthian descent, and finally Telephus,

---

* Formed of the prows of ships.

slave and page [1] of a woman, for even men of the lowest condition conspired against him and imperiled his safety. Audasius and Epicadus had formed the design of forcibly carrying
off to the armies his daughter Julia, and his grandson Agrippa,
from the islands where they were confined. Telephus, under
the delusion that he himself was destined for empire, proposed
to fall upon both Octavius and the Senate. Even a soldier's
servant from the army in Illyricum, who had escaped the vigilance of the door-keepers, was caught at night near the Emperor's bedroom, armed with a hunting knife. But whether
this fellow was crazy or only feigned madness is uncertain,
since nothing could be wrung from him by torture.

He conducted in person only two foreign wars: the Dal-
matian, when he was but a youth; and after Antony's final
defeat, the Cantabrian. He was wounded, too, in the former
campaign, being struck on the right knee with a stone in one
battle, and in another having a leg and both arms severely injured by the collapse of a bridge. His other wars he carried
on through his generals, although he was either present at
some of those in Pannonia and Germany, or was not far from
the front, since he went from Rome as far as Ravenna, Medio-
lanum, or Aquileia.

In part as leader, and in part with armies serving under his
auspices, he subdued Cantabria, Aquitania, Pannonia, Dalmatia, and all Illyricum, as well as Raetia and the Vindelici
and Salassi, which are Alpine tribes. He also put a stop to
the inroads of the Dacians, slaying great numbers of them,
together with three of their leaders, and forced the Germans
back to the farther side of the river Albis, with the exception
of the Suebi and Sigambri, who submitted to him and were
taken into Gaul and settled in lands near the Rhine. He reduced to submission other peoples, too, that were in a state
of unrest.

But he never made war on any nation without just and due
cause, and he was so far from desiring to increase his dominion or his military glory at any cost, that he forced the
chiefs of certain barbarians to take oath in the temple of

---

[1] *Nomenculator:* a name-prompter, used most often by candidates
electioneering, when it was of course most necessary to address by his
right name one whose vote was being solicited.

Mars the Avenger that they would faithfully keep the peace for which they asked. Of some he demanded a new kind of hostages, their women, having found from experience that they cared little for pledges secured by males. But he always afforded them the privilege of reclaiming their hostages whenever they wished. On those who rebelled often or under circumstances of especial treachery he never inflicted any severer punishment than that of selling the prisoners, with the condition that they should not pass their term of slavery in a country near their own, nor be set free within thirty years. The reputation for virtue and moderation which he thus gained led even the Indians and the Scythians, nations known to us only by hearsay, to send envoys of their own free will and sue for his friendship and that of the Roman people. The Parthians, too, readily yielded to him, when he laid claim to Armenia, and at his demand surrendered the standards which they had taken from Marcus Crassus and Marcus Antonius. They offered him hostages besides, and once when there were several claimants of their throne, they would accept only the one whom he selected.

The temple of Janus Quirinus, which had been closed but twice before his time since the founding of the city,[1] he closed three times in a far shorter period, having won peace on land and sea. He twice entered the city in an ovation, after the war of Philippi, and again after that in Sicily, and he celebrated three regular triumphs [2] for his victories in Dalmatia, at Actium, and at Alexandria, all on three successive days.

He suffered but two severe and ignominious defeats, those of Lollius and Varus, both of which were in Germany. Of these the former was more humiliating than serious, but the latter was almost fatal, since three legions were cut to pieces with their general, his lieutenants, and all the auxiliaries. When the news of this came, he ordered that watch be kept by night throughout the city, to prevent any outbreak, and

---

[1] In the reign of Numa, and in 235 B.C., after the first Punic war. It was Numa, successor of Romulus, founder of Rome, who was said to have ordained the temple be open when Rome was at war, closed when at peace.

[2] The ovation was a lesser triumph, in which the general entered the city on foot or horseback, instead of a chariot. He received the myrtle crown in an ovation, in a triumph the laurel.

he prolonged the terms of the Governors of the provinces, that the allies might be held to their allegiance by experienced men with whom they were acquaintd. He also made a vow to celebrate great games in honor of Jupiter Optimus Maximus, a thing which had been done in the Cimbric and Marsic wars, if the condition of the commonwealth were restored to greater prosperity. In fact, they say that he was so greatly affected that for several months in succession he cut neither his beard nor his hair, and sometimes he would dash his head against a door,[1] crying: "Quintilius Varus, give me back my legions!" And he observed the day of the disaster each year as one of sorrow and mourning.

He made many changes and innovations in the army, besides reviving some usages of former times. He exacted the strictest discipline. It was with great reluctance that he allowed even his generals to visit their wives, and then only in the winter season. He sold a Roman knight and his property at public auction, because he had cut off the thumbs of his two young sons to make them unfit for military service; but when he saw that some tax-gatherers were intent upon buying him, he knocked him down to a freeman of his own, with the understanding that he should be banished to the country districts, but allowed to live in freedom. He dismissed the entire tenth legion in disgrace, because they were insubordinate, and others, too, that demanded their discharge in an insolent fashion, he disbanded without the rewards which would have been due for faithful service. If any cohorts gave way in battle, he decimated them,[2] and fed the rest on barley. When Centurions left their posts, he punished them with death, just as he did the rank and file; for faults of other kinds he imposed various ignominious penalties, such as ordering them to stand all day long before the general's tent, sometimes in their tunics without their sword-belts, or again holding ten-foot poles or even a clod of earth.[3]

---

[1] In the belief that by doing injury to one's own body the Gods would be sooner pacified.

[2] That is, executed every tenth man, selected by lot.

[3] Carrying the pole to measure off the camp, or clods for building the rampart, was the work of common soldiers, hence degrading for officers.

After the civil wars he never called any of the troops "comrades," either in the assembly or in an edict, but always "soldiers"; and he would not allow them to be addressed otherwise, even by those of his sons or stepsons who held military commands, thinking the former term too flattering for the requirements of discipline, the peaceful state of the times, and his own dignity and that of his household. Except as a fire-brigade at Rome, and when there was fear of riots in times of scarcity, he employed freedmen as soldiers only twice: once as a guard for the colonies in the vicinity of Illyricum, and again to defend the bank of the river Rhine. These he conscripted from men and women of wealth, and at once gave them their freedom. But he kept them under a standard of their own, not mingling them with the soldiers of free birth or arming them in the same fashion.

As military prizes he was somewhat more ready to give trappings or collars, valuable for their gold and silver, than crowns for scaling ramparts or walls, which conferred high honor. The latter he gave as sparingly as possible and without favoritism, often even to the common soldiers. He presented Marcus Agrippa with a blue banner in Sicily after his naval victory. Those who had celebrated triumphs were the only ones whom he thought ineligible for prizes, even though they had been the companions of his campaigns and shared in his victories, on the ground that they themselves had the privilege of bestowing such honors wherever they wished. He thought nothing less becoming in a well-trained leader than haste and rashness, and, accordingly, favorite sayings of his were: "More haste, less speed"; "Better a safe commander than a bold" [1]; and "That is done quickly enough which is done well enough." He used to say that a war or a battle should not be begun under any circumstances unless the hope of gain was clearly greater than the fear of loss; for he likened such as grasped at slight gains with no slight risk to those who fished with a golden hook, the loss of which, if it were carried off, could not be made good by any catch.

He received offices and honors before the usual age, and some of a new kind and for life. He usurped the consulship in

---

[1] From Euripides' *Phoenicians.*

the twentieth year of his age,[1] leading his legions against the city as if it were that of an enemy, and sending messengers to demand the office for him in the name of his army. When the Senate hesitated, his Centurion, Cornelius, leader of the deputation, throwing back his cloak and showing the hilt of his sword, did not hesitate to say in the House, "This will make him Consul, if you do not." He held his second consulship nine years later, a third after a year's interval, and the rest up to the eleventh were in successive years. Then after declining a number of terms that were offered him, he asked of his own accord for a twelfth after a long interval, no less than seventeen years, and two years later for a thirteenth, wishing to hold the highest magistracy at the time when he introduced each of his sons, Gaius and Lucius, to public life upon their coming of age. The five consulships from the sixth to the tenth he held for the full year, the rest for nine, six, four, or three months, except the second, which lasted only a few hours; for after sitting for a short time on the curule[2] chair in front of the temple of Jupiter Capitolinus in the early morning, he resigned the honor on the Kalends of January and appointed another in his place. He did not begin all his consulships in Rome, but the fourth in Asia, the fifth on the Isle of Samos, the eighth and ninth at Tarraco.

He was for ten years a member of the Triumvirate[3] for restoring the State to order, and though he opposed his colleagues for some time and tried to prevent a proscription, yet when it was begun, he carried it through with greater severity than either of them. For while they could oftentimes be moved by personal influence and entreaties, he alone was most insistent that no one should be spared, even adding to the list his guardian, Gaius Toranius, who had also been the colleague of his father, Octavius, in the aedileship. Julius Saturninus adds that after the proscription was over Marcus Lepidus made an apology in the Senate for their past proceedings, and gave them hopes of a more mild administration for the

---

[1] The law called *Annalis* required Consuls to be at least 43.

[2] Used by a principal magistrate. Constructed of wood, inlaid with ivory, the seat of leather. It could be folded for convenience in carrying, and had no back.

[3] The other two being Antony and Lepidus.

future, since enough punishment had been inflicted; but that Augustus on the contrary declared that he had consented to end the proscription only on condition that he was allowed a free hand for the future. However, to show his regret for this inflexibility, he later honored Titus Vinius Philopoemen with equestrian rank, because it was said that he had hidden his patron, who was on the proscription list.

While he was Triumvir, Augustus incurred general detestation by many of his acts. For example, when he was addressing the soldiers and a throng of civilians had been admitted to the assembly, noticing that Pinarius, a Roman Knight, was taking notes, he ordered that he be stabbed on the spot, thinking him an eavesdropper and a spy. Because Tedius Afer, Consul-elect, railed at some act of his in spiteful terms, he uttered such terrible threats that Afer committed suicide. Again, when Quintus Gallius, a Praetor, held some folded tablets under his robe as he was paying his respects, Augustus, suspecting that he had a sword concealed there, did not dare to make a search on the spot for fear it should turn out to be something else; but a little later he had Gallius hustled from the tribunal by some Centurions, tortured him as if he were a slave, and though he made no confession, ordered his execution, first tearing out the man's eyes with his own hand. He himself writes, however, that Gallius made a treacherous attack on him after asking for an audience, and was haled to prison; and that after he was dismissed under sentence of banishment, he either lost his life by shipwreck or was waylaid by brigands.

He received the tribunician power for life, and once or twice chose a colleague in the office for periods of five years each. He was also given the supervision of morals and of the laws for all time, and by the virtue of this position, although without the title of Censor, he nevertheless took the census thrice, the first and last time with a colleague, the second time alone.

He twice thought of restoring the republic; first immediately after the overthrow of Antony, remembering that his rival had often made the charge that it was his fault that it was not restored; and again in the weariness of a lingering illness, when he went so far as to summon the magistrates and the Senate to his house, and submit an account of the general condition of the empire. Reflecting, however, that as he himself would not be free from danger if he should retire, so too it would be hazardous to trust the State to the control of the populace, he continued to keep it in his hands; and it is not easy to say whether his intentions or their results were the better. His good intentions he not only expressed from time to time, but put them on record as well in an edict in the following words: "May it be my privilege to establish the State in a firm and secure position, and enjoy therefrom the rewards of which I am ambitious, that of being called the author of the best possible government, and of carrying with me when I die the hope that the foundations which I have laid for the State will remain unshaken." And he realized his hope by making every effort to prevent any dissatisfaction with the new régime.

The city, which was not built in a manner suitable to the grandeur of the Empire, and was liable to inundations as well as to fires, was so improved and beautified under his administration that he boasted, not without reason, that he had found it built of brick and left it in marble. He made it secure for the future against such disasters as far as human foresight could effect this.

He built many public works, in particular the following: his Forum with the temple of Mars the Avenger, the temple of Apollo on the Palatine, and the fane of Jupiter the Thunderer on the Capitol. His reason for building the Forum was the increase in the number of the people and of cases at law, which seemed to call for a third Forum, since two were no longer adequate. Therefore it was opened to the public with some haste, before the temple of Mars was finished, and it was provided that the public prosecutions be held there apart from the rest, as well as the selection of jurors by lot. He had made a vow to build the temple of Mars in the war of Philippi, which he undertook to avenge his father. Accordingly he decreed that in it the Senate should consider wars and claims for triumphs, from it those who were on their way to the provinces with military commands should be escorted, and to it victors on their return should bear the tokens of their triumphs. He reared the temple of Apollo in that part of his house on the Palatine for which the sooth-sayers declared that the God had shown his desire by striking it with lightning. He joined to it colonnades with Latin and Greek libraries, and when he was getting to be an old man he often held meetings of the Senate there as well, and revised the lists of jurors. He dedicated the shrine to Jupiter the Thunderer because of a narrow escape. For, on his Cantabrian expedition during a march by night, a flash of lightning grazed his litter and struck the slave dead who was carrying a torch before him. He constructed some works, too, in the name of others, his grandsons to wit, his wife and his sister, such as the colonnade and basilica of Gaius and Lucius; also the colonnades of Livia and Octavia, and the theater of Marcellus. More than that, he often urged other prominent men to adorn the city with new monuments or to restore and embellish old ones, each according to his means. And many such works were built at that time by many men; for example, the temple of Hercules of the Muses by Marcius Philippus, the temple of Diana by Lucius Cornificius, the Hall of Liberty by Asinius Pollio, the temple of Saturn by Munatius Plancus, a theater by Cornelius Balbus, an amphitheater by Statilius Taurus, and by Marcus Agrippa in particular many magnificent structures.

He divided the area of the city into regions and wards, arranging that the former should be under the charge of magistrates selected each year by lot, and the latter under wardens elected by the inhabitants of the respective neighborhoods. To guard against fires he devised a system of stations of night watchmen, and to control the floods, he widened and cleared out the channel of the Tiber, which had for some time been filled with rubbish and narrowed by jutting buildings. Further, to make the approach to the city easier from every direction, he personally undertook to rebuild the Flaminian Road all the way to Ariminum, and assigned the rest of the highways to others who had been honored with triumphs, asking them to use their prize-money in paving them.

He restored sacred edifices which had gone to ruin through lapse of time or had been destroyed by fire, and adorned both these and the other temples with most lavish gifts, depositing in the shrine of Jupiter Capitolinus as a single offering sixteen thousand pounds of gold, besides pearls and other precious stones to the value of fifty million sesterces.[1]

The office of High Priest, of which he could not decently deprive Lepidus as long as he lived, he assumed as soon as he was dead.[2] He then collected whatever prophetic writings of Greek or Latin origin were in circulation anonymously or under the names of authors of little repute, and burned more than two thousand of them, preserving only the Sibylline books, and even among those he made a choice. These he deposited in two gilded cases under the pedestal of the Palatine Apollo. Inasmuch as the calendar, which had been set in order by the Deified Julius, had later been confused and disordered through negligence, he restored it to its former system. In making this arrangement he called the month Sextilis by his own surname, rather than his birth-month September, because in the former he had won his first consulship and his most brilliant victories. He increased the number and importance of the priests, and also their allowances and privileges, in particular those of the Vestal Virgins. Moreover, when there was occasion to choose another Vestal in place of one who had died, and many used all their influence to avoid submitting their daughters to the hazard of the lot, he solemnly swore that if any one of his granddaughters were of eligible age, he would have proposed her name. He also revived some of the ancient rites which had gradually fallen into disuse, such as the augury of Public Health,[3] the office of Flamen Dialis, the ceremonies of the Lupercalia, the Secular Games, and the festival of the Compitalia. At the Lupercalia he forbade beardless youths to join in the running, and at the Secular Games he would not allow young people of either sex to attend any entertainment by night except in company with some adult relative. He provided that the Guardian Gods

---

[1] $2,050,000.00.

[2] This office, *Pontifex Maximus,* was of importance from the sanctity attached to it and the influence which could be wielded from it over the whole system of religion. In this case it served as a sort of honorable retirement in which Lepidus had been shelved when Augustus got rid of him quietly from the Triumvirate.

[3] "As if even that could not be implored from the gods, unless the signs were propitious." Dio xxxvii, 24.

of the Crossroads be crowned twice a year, with spring and summer flowers.

Next to the immortal Gods he honored the memory of the leaders who had raised the estate of the Roman people from obscurity to greatness. Accordingly he restored the works of such men with their original inscriptions, and in the two colonnades of his Forum dedicated statues of all of them in triumphal garb, declaring besides in a proclamation: "I have contrived this to lead the citizens to require me, while I live, and the rulers of later times as well, to attain the standard set by those worthies of old." He also moved the statue of Pompey from the hall in which Gaius Caesar had been slain and placed it on a marble arch opposite the grand door of Pompey's theater.

Many pernicious practices militating against public security had survived as a result of the lawless habits of the civil wars, or had even arisen in time of peace. Gangs of footpads openly went about with swords by their sides, ostensibly to protect themselves, and travelers in the country, freemen and slaves alike, were seized and kept in confinement in the slave-prisons [1] of the landowners. Numerous leagues, too, were formed for the commission of crimes of every kind, assuming the title of some new guild. Therefore to put a stop to brigandage, he stationed guards of soldiers wherever it seemed advisable, inspected the workhouses, and disbanded all guilds, except such as were of long standing and formed for legitimate purposes. He burned the records of old debts to the treasury, which were by far the most frequent source of blackmail. He made over to their holders places in the city to which the claim of the state was uncertain. He struck off the lists the names of those who had long been under accusation, from whose humiliation nothing was to be gained except the gratification of their enemies, with the stipulation that if any one was minded to renew the charge, he should be liable to the same penalty. [2] To prevent any action for damages or

---

[1] These were underground strong rooms, in country houses, where unruly slaves were confined in fetters.

[2] That is, if he failed to win his suit, he should suffer the penalty that would have been inflicted on the defendant, if he had been convicted.

a disputed claim from falling through or being put off, he ordered the courts to sit during the thirty days which were spent
in celebrating honorary games. To the three divisions of jurors he added a fourth of a lower estate, to be called *ducenarii* [1]
and to sit on cases involving trifling amounts. He enrolled as
jurors men of thirty years or more, that is five years younger
than usual. But when many strove to escape court duty, he
reluctantly consented that each division in turn should have
a year's exemption, and that the custom of holding court
during the months of November and December should be
given up. [2]

He himself administered justice regularly and sometimes
up to nightfall, having a litter placed upon the tribunal, if he
was indisposed, or even lying down at home. In his administration of justice he was both highly conscientious and very
lenient; for to save a man clearly guilty of parricide from being sewn up in the sack, [3] a punishment which was inflicted
only on those who pleaded guilty, he is said to have put the
question to him in this form: "You surely did not kill your
father, did you?" Again, in a case touching a forged will, in
which all the signers were liable to punishment by the Cornelian Law, he distributed to the jury not merely the two tablets
for condemnation or acquittal, but a third as well, for the
pardon of those who were shown to have been induced to sign
by misrepresentation or misunderstanding. Each year he referred appeals of cases involving citizens to the city Praetor,
but those between foreigners to ex-Consuls, of whom he had
put one in charge of the business affairs of each province.

He revised existing laws and enacted some new ones, for
example, on extravagance, on adultery and chastity, on bribery, and on the encouragement of marriage among the various classes of citizens. Having made somewhat more stringent
changes in the last of these than in the others, he was unable

---

[1] Men whose property amounted to 200,000 sesterces ($8,200.00),
half of a Knight's estate.

[2] During these months there were a great number of holidays, including those of the gay *Saturnalia*. There was consequently a general relaxation and cessation of business in Rome at this time.

[3] Parricides were beaten with rods, sewn up in a leather sack, with
a dog, a cock, a monkey, and a snake, and thrown into the sea or a
river.

to carry it out because of an open revolt against its provisions, until he had abolished or mitigated a part of the penalties, besides increasing the rewards and allowing a three years' exemption from the obligation to marry after the death of a husband or wife. When the Knights even then persistently called for its repeal at a public show, he sent for the children of Germanicus and exhibited them, some in his own lap and some in their father's, intimating by his gestures and expression that they should not refuse to follow that young man's example. And on finding that the spirit of the law was being evaded by betrothal with immature girls and by frequent changes of wives, he shortened the duration of betrothals and set a limit on divorce.

The number of the Senators was swelled by a low-born and ill-assorted rabble. That body, in fact, now numbered more than a thousand, some of whom, called by the vulgar Orcivi,[1] were wholly unworthy, and had been admitted after Caesar's death [2] through favor or bribery. He therefore restored it to its former limits and distinction by two enrolments, one according to the choice of the members themselves, each man naming one other, and a second made by Agrippa and himself. On the latter occasion it is thought that he wore a coat of mail under his tunic as he presided, and a sword by his side, while ten of the most robust of his friends among the Senators stood by his chair. Cremutius Cordus [3] writes that even then the Senators were not allowed to approach except one by one, and after the folds of their robes had been carefully searched. Some he shamed into resigning, but he allowed even these to retain their distinctive dress, as well as the privilege of viewing the games from the orchestra and taking part in the public banquets of the order. Furthermore, that those who were chosen and approved might perform their duties more conscientiously, and also with less inconvenience, he provided that before taking his seat each member should

---

[1] The *Orcivi* "men freed by the grace of Orcus" (God of the dead) were slaves set free in the wills of their masters.

[2] By Mark Antony under the pretense they had been so named in papers left by Caesar.

[3] Who lived at the time of Augustus and Tiberius and wrote a History of the Civil Wars and the times of Augustus, as Dio (VI, 52) informs us.

offer incense and wine at the altar of the god in whose temple the meeting was held; that regular meetings of the Senate should be held not oftener than twice a month, on the Kalends [1] and the Ides; and that in the months of September and October [2] only those should be obliged to attend who were drawn by lot, to a number sufficient for the passing of decrees. He also adopted the plan of privy councils chosen by lot for terms of six months, with which to discuss in advance matters which were to come before the entire body. On questions of special importance he called upon the Senators to give their opinions, not according to the order established by precedent, but just as he fancied, to induce each man to keep his mind on the alert, to induce every one to hold himself ready to give his opinion rather than a mere vote of assent.

He introduced other innovations too, among them these: that the proceedings of the Senate should not be published; that magistrates should not be sent to the provinces immediately after laying down their office; that a fixed sum should be allowed the Proconsuls for mules and tents, which it was the custom to contract for and charge to the State; that the management of the public treasury should be transferred from the city Quaestors to ex-Praetors or Praetors; and that the centumviral court, which it was usual for ex-Quaestors to convoke, should be summoned by the Board of Ten.

To enable more men to take part in the administration of the State, he devised new offices: the charge of public buildings, of the roads, of the aqueducts, of the channel of the Tiber, of the distribution of grain to the people, as well as the prefecture of the city, a board of three for choosing Senators, and another for reviewing the companies of the knights whenever it should be necessary. He appointed Censors, [3] an office which had long been discontinued. He increased the number of Praetors. He also demanded that whenever the consulship

---

[1] 1st of every month.

[2] Doubtless to allow of their absence during the vintage.

[3] The office of Censor was first established in 441 B.C. with duties to take a census of the people and make an account of the value of their estates. Power as arbiter of morals was afterwards given them. The office then became one of great importance. Under most of the Emperors the office was dispensed with, the Emperor himself exercising its functions, frequently with both caprice and severity.

was conferred on him, he should have two colleagues instead of one; but this was not granted, since all cried out that it was a sufficient offense to his supreme dignity that he held the office with another and not alone.

He was not less geneorus in honoring martial prowess, for he had regular triumphs voted to above thirty generals, and the triumphal regalia to somewhat more than that number.

To enable Senators' sons to gain an earlier acquaintance with public affairs, he allowed them to assume the broad purple stripe immediately after the gown of manhood and to attend meetings of the Senate; and when they began their military career, he gave them not merely a tribunate in a legion, but the command of a division of cavalry as well; and to furnish all of them with experience in camp life, he usually appointed two Senators' sons to command each division.

He reviewed the companies of Knights at frequent intervals, reviving the custom of the procession [1] after long disuse. But he would not allow an accuser to force any one to dismount as he rode by, as was often done in the past; and he permitted those who were conspicuous because of old age or any bodily infirmity to send on their horses in the review, and come on foot to answer to their names whenever they were summoned. Later, those who were over thirty-five years of age and desired to keep their horses no longer he excused from formally surrendering them.

Having obtained ten assistants from the Senate, he compelled each Knight to render an account of his life, punishing some of those whose conduct was scandalous and degrading others; but the greater part he reprimanded with varying degrees of severity. The mildest form of reprimand was to hand them a pair of tablets publicly, which they were to read in silence on the spot.[2] He censured some because they had borrowed money at low interest and invested it at a higher rate.

At the elections for Tribunes if there were not candidates

---

[1] A splendid parade on July 15 of the Knights of the equestrian order. Dressed in scarlet, wearing their decorations and olive wreaths, they rode their horses through the city to the Capitol. There each dismounted, and, leading his horse, passed in review before the Censor. If he were corrupt in his morals, or had diminished his fortunes below the prescribed standard for Knights, the Censor deprived him of his rank.

[2] And learn the faults they should amend.

enough of senatorial rank, he made appointments from among the Knights, with the understanding that after their term they might remain in whichever order they wished. Moreover, since many Knights whose property was diminished during the civil wars did not venture to view the games from the fourteen rows through fear of the penalty of the law regarding seating of the theaters, he declared that none were liable to its provisions, if they themselves or their parents had ever possessed a Knight's estate.

He revised the lists of the people street by street, and to prevent the Commons from being called away from their occupations too often because of the distributions of grain, he determined to give out tickets for four months' supply three times a year; but at their urgent request he allowed a return to the old custom of receiving a share every month. He also revived the old time election privileges, endeavoring, by numerous penalties, to suppress the practice of bribery, and distributing to his fellow members of the Fabian and Scaptian tribes [1] a thousand sesterces [2] a man from his own purse on the day of the elections, to keep them from looking for anything from any of the candidates.

Considering it also of great importance to keep the people pure and unsullied by any taint of foreign or servile blood, he was most chary of conferring Roman citizenship and set a limit to manumission. When Tiberius requested citizenship for a Grecian dependent of his, Augustus wrote in reply that he would not grant it unless the man appeared in person and convinced him that he had reasonable grounds for the request. When Livia asked it for a Gaul from a tributary province, he refused, offering instead freedom from tribute, and declaring that he would more willingly suffer a loss to his privy purse than the prostitution of the honor of Roman citizenship. Not content with making it difficult for slaves to acquire freedom, and still more so for them to attain full rights, by making careful provision as to the number, condition, and status of those who were manumitted, he added the proviso

---

[1] Augustus was a member of the Fabian tribe through his adoption into the Julian family, and a member of the Scaptian tribe because of his connection with the Octavian family.

[2] $41.00.

that any one who had ever been put in irons or tortured should never, by any grade of freedom, acquire citizenship.

He desired also to revive the ancient fashion of dress, and once when he saw in an assembly a throng of men in dark cloaks, he cried out indignantly, "Behold them

Romans, lords of the world, the nation clad in the toga," [1]

and he directed the Aediles never again to allow any one to appear in the Forum or its neighborhood except in the toga and without a cloak.

He often showed generosity to all classes when occasion offered. For example, by bringing the royal treasures to Rome in his Alexandrian triumph he made ready money so abundant, that the rate of interest fell, and the value of real estate rose greatly. And after that, whenever there was an excess of funds from the property of those who had been condemned, he loaned it without interest for fixed periods to any who could give security for double the amount. He increased the property qualification for Senators, requiring one million two hundred thousand sesterces, instead of eight hundred thousand,[2] and making up the amount for those who did not possess it. He often gave largess to the people, but usually of different sums: now four hundred, now three hundred, now two hundred and fifty sesterces a man; and he did not even exclude young boys, though it had been usual for them to receive a share only after the age of eleven. In times of scarcity too he often distributed grain to each man at a very low figure, sometimes for nothing, and he doubled the money tickets.[3]

But to show that he was a prince who desired the public welfare rather than popularity, when the people complained of the scarcity and high price of wine, he sharply rebuked them by saying: "My son-in-law Agrippa has taken good care, by building several aqueducts, that men shall not go thirsty."

---

[1] *Aeneid* I, 282.

[2] $49,200.00 instead of $32,800.00.

[3] These were small tablets or round, hollow balls of wood marked with numbers, sometimes distributed to the people instead of money, and entitling the holder to receive the amount inscribed on them. Grain, oil, and various other commodities were thus distributed.

Again, when the people demanded largess which he had in fact promised, he replied: "I am a man of my word"; but when they called for one which had not been promised, he rebuked them in a proclamation for their shameless impudence, and declared that he would not give it, even though he was intending to do so. With equal dignity and firmness, when he had announced a distribution of money and found that many had been manumitted and added to the list of citizens, he declared that those to whom no promise had been made should receive nothing, and gave the rest less than he had promised, to make the appointed sum suffice. Once indeed in a season of great scarcity, which it was difficult to remedy, he expelled from the city the slaves that were for sale, as well as the schools of gladiators, all foreigners with the exception of physicians and teachers, and a part of the household slaves; and when grain at last became more plentiful, he writes: "I was strongly inclined to abolish forever the custom of distributing grain to the people at the public expense, because they depend so much on it that agriculture has been neglected. But I did not carry out my purpose, feeling sure that the practice would one day be renewed by some one ambitious of popular favor." But from that time on he regulated the practice with no less regard for the interests of the farmers and grain-dealers than for those of the populace.

He surpassed all his predecessors in the frequency, variety, and magnificence of his public shows. He says that he gave games four times in his own name and twenty-three times for other magistrates, who were either away from Rome or lacked means. He gave them sometimes in all the wards and on many stages with actors in all languages, and combats of gladiators not only in the Forum or the amphitheater, but in the Circus and in the Saepta. Sometimes, however, he gave nothing except a fight with wild beasts. He gave athletic contests too in the Campus Martius, erecting wooden seats; also a sea-fight, constructing an artificial lake near the Tiber, where the grove of the Caesars now stands. On such occasions he stationed guards in various parts of the city, to prevent it from falling a prey to footpads because of the few people who remained at home. In the Circus he exhibited charioteers, runners, and slayers of wild animals, who were sometimes young men of the highest rank. Besides he gave frequent performances of the game of Troy by older and younger boys, thinking it a time-honored and worthy custom for the flower of the nobility to become known in this way. When Nonius Asprenas was lamed by a fall while taking part in this game, he presented him with a golden necklace and allowed him and his descendants to bear the surname Torquatus. But soon afterwards he gave up that form of entertainment, because Asinius Pollio the orator complained bitterly and angrily in the Senate of an accident to his grandson Aeserninus, who also had broken his leg.

He sometimes employed even Roman Knights in scenic and gladiatorial performance, but only before it was forbidden by decree of the Senate. After that he exhibited no one of respectable parentage, with the exception of a young man named Lycius, whom he showed merely as a curiosity; for he was less than two feet tall, weighed but seventeen pounds, yet had a stentorian voice. He did however on the day of one of the shows make a display of the first Parthian hostages that had ever been sent to Rome, by leading them through the middle of the arena and placing them in the second row above his own seat. Furthermore, if anything rare and worth seeing was ever brought to the city, it was his habit to make a special exhibit of it in any convenient place on days when no shows were appointed. For example a rhinoceros in the Saepta, a tiger on the stage and a snake of fifty cubits in the Comitium.

It chanced that at the time of the games which he had vowed to give in the circus, he was taken ill and headed the sacred procession lying in a litter. Again, at the opening of the games with which he dedicated the theater of Marcellus, it happened that the joints of his curule chair gave way and he fell on his back. At the games for his grandsons, when the people were in a panic for fear the theater should fall, and he could not calm them or encourage them in any way, he left his own place and took his seat in the part which appeared most dangerous.

He put a stop by special regulations to the disorderly and indiscriminate fashion of viewing the games, through exasperation at the insult to a Senator, to whom no one offered a seat in a crowded house at some largely attended games in

Puteoli. In consequence of this the Senate decreed that, whenever any public show was given anywhere, the first row of seats should be reserved for Senators. At Rome he would not allow the envoys of the free and allied nations to sit in the orchestra, since he was informed that even freedmen were sometimes appointed. He separated the soldiery from the people. He assigned special seats to the married men of the Commons, to boys under age their own section and the adjoining one to their tutors; and he decreed that no one wearing a dark cloak should sit in the middle rows of the house. He would not allow women to view even the gladiators except from the upper seats, though it had been the custom for men and women to sit together at such shows. Only the Vestal Virgins were assigned a place to themselves, opposite the Praetor's tribunal. As for the contests of the athletes, he excluded women from them so strictly, that when a contest between a pair of boxers had been called for at the games in honor of his appointment as High Priest, he postponed it until early the following day, making proclamation that it was his desire that women should not come to the theater before the fifth hour.[1]

He himself usually watched the games in the Circus from the upper rooms of his friends and freedmen, but sometimes from the imperial box, and even in company with his wife and children. He was sometimes absent for several hours, and now and then for whole days, making his excuses and appointing presiding officers to take his place. But whenever he was present, he gave his entire attention to the performance, either to avoid the censure to which he realized that his father Caesar had been generally exposed, because he spent his time in reading or answering letters and petitions; or from his interest and pleasure in the spectacle, which he never denied but often frankly confessed. Because of this he used to offer special prizes and numerous valuable gifts from his own purse at games given by others, and he appeared at no contest given in the Greek language and dress without making a present to each of the participants according to his deserts. He took especial pleasure in watching boxers, particularly those of Latin birth, not merely such as were recognized and classed as pro-

---

[1] II A.M.

fessionals, whom he was wont to match even with Greeks, but the common untrained townspeople that fought rough and tumble and without skill in the narrow streets. In fine, he honored with his interest all classes of performers who took part in the public shows; maintained the privileges of the athletes and even increased them; forbade the matching of gladiators without the right of appeal for quarter; and deprived the magistrates of the power allowed them by an ancient law of punishing actors anywhere and everywhere, restricting it to the time of games and to the theater. Nevertheless he exacted the severest discipline in the contests in the wrestling halls and the combats of the gladiators. In particular he was so strict in curbing the lawlessness of the actors, that when he learned that Stephanio, an actor of Roman plays, was waited on by a matron with hair cut short to look like a boy, he had him whipped with rods through the three theaters and then banished him. Hylas, a pantomimic actor, was publicly scourged in the atrium of his own house, on complaint of a Praetor, and Pylades was expelled from the city and from Italy as well, because by pointing at him with his finger he turned all eyes upon a spectator who was hissing him.

After having thus set the city and its affairs in order, he added to the population of Italy by personally establishing twenty-eight colonies; furnished many parts of it with public buildings and revenues; and even gave it, at least to some degree, equal rights and dignity with the city of Rome, by devising a kind of votes which the members of the local Senate were to cast in each colony for candidates for the city offices and send under seal to Rome against the day of the elections. To keep up the supply of men of rank and induce the Commons to increase and multiply, he admitted to the equestrian military career those who were recommended by any town, while to those of the Commons who could lay claim to worthy sons and daughters when he made his rounds of the city he distributed a thousand sesterces for each child.[1]

The stronger provinces, which could neither easily nor safely be governed by annual magistrates, he took to himself; the others he assigned to proconsular Governors selected by

[1] $41.00.

lot. But he changed some of them at times from one class to the other, and often visited many of both sorts. Certain of the cities which had treaties with Rome, but were on the road to ruin through their lawlessness, he deprived of their independence; he relieved others that were overwhelmed with debt, rebuilt some which had been destroyed by earthquakes, and gave Latin rights[1] or full citizenship to such as could point to services rendered the Roman people. I believe there is no province, excepting only Africa and Sardinia, which he did not visit; and he was planning to cross to these from Sicily after his defeat of Sextus Pompeius, but was prevented by a series of violent storms, and later had neither opportunity nor occasion to make the voyage.

Except in a few instances he restored the kingdoms of which he gained possession by the right of conquest to those from whom he had taken them or joined them with other foreign nations. He also united the Kings with whom he was in alliance by mutual ties, and was very ready to propose or favor intermarriages or friendships among them. He never failed to treat them all with consideration as integral parts of the Empire, regularly appointing a guardian for such as were too young to rule or whose minds were affected, until they grew up or recovered; and he brought up the children of many of them and educated them with his own.

Of his military forces he assigned legions and auxiliaries to the various provinces, stationed a fleet at Misenum and another at Ravenna, to defend the Upper and Lower seas, and employed the remainder partly in the defense of the city and partly in that of his own person, disbanding a troop of Calagurritani which had formed a part of his body-guard until the overthrow of Antony, and also one of Germans, which he had retained until the defeat of Varus. However, he never allowed more than three cohorts to remain in the city and even those were without a permanent camp. The rest he regularly sent to winter or summer quarters in the towns near Rome. Furthermore, he restricted all the soldiery everywhere to a fixed scale of pay and allowances, designating the duration of their service and the rewards on its completion according

---

[1] A limited citizenship, the rights of which varied.

to each man's rank, in order to keep them from being tempted to revolution after their discharge either by age or poverty. To have funds ready at all times without difficulty for maintaining the soldiers and paying the rewards due to them, he established a military treasury, supported by new taxes.

To enable what was going on in each of the provinces to be reported and known more speedily and promptly, he at first stationed young men at short intervals along the military roads, and afterwards post-chaises. The latter has seemed the more convenient arrangement, since the same men who bring the dispatches from any place can, if occasion demands, be questioned as well.

In passports, dispatches, and private letters he used as his seal at first a sphinx, later an image of Alexander the Great, and finally his own, carved by the hand of Dioscurides; and this his successors continued to use as their seal. He always attached to all letters the exact hour, not only of the day, but even of the night, to indicate precisely when they were written.

Of his clemency and moderation there were abundant and signal instances. Not to give the full list of the men of the opposite factions whom he not only pardoned and spared, but allowed to hold high positions in the state, I may say that he thought it enough to punish two plebeians, Junius Novatus and Cassius Patavinus, with a fine and with a mild form of banishment respectively, although the former had circulated a most scathing letter about him under the name of the young Agrippa, while the latter had openly declared at a large dinner party that he lacked neither the earnest desire nor the courage to stab him. Again, when he was hearing a case against Aemilius Aelianus of Corduba and it was made the chief offense, amongst other charges, that he was in the habit of expressing a bad opinion of Caesar, Augustus turned to the accuser with assumed anger and said: "I wish you could prove the truth of that. I'll let Aelianus know that I have a tongue as well as he, for I'll say even more about him"; and he made no further inquiry either at the time or afterwards. When Tiberius complained to him of the same thing in a letter, but in more forcible language, he replied as follows: "My dear Tiberius, do not be carried away by the ardor of youth in this matter, or take it too much to heart that any one speak evil of me; we must be content if we can stop any one from doing evil to us."

Although well aware that it was usual to vote temples even to Proconsuls, yet he would not accept that honor even in a province save jointly in his own name and that of Rome. In the city itself he refused this honor most emphatically, even melting down the silver statues which had been erected to him in former times and with the money coined from them dedicating golden tripods to Apollo of the Palatine.

When the people did their best to force the Dictatorship upon him, he knelt down, threw off his toga from his shoulders and with bare breast begged them not to insist.

He always shrank from the title of Lord [1] as reproachful and insulting. When the words

"O just and gracious Lord!"

were uttered in a farce at which he was a spectator and all the people sprang to their feet and applauded as if they were said of him, he at once checked their unseemly flattery by look and gesture, and on the following day sharply reproved them in an edict. After that he would not suffer himself to be addressed by that term even by his children or his grandchildren either in jest or earnest, and he forbade them to use such flattering terms even among themselves. He did not if he could help it leave or enter any city or town except in the evening or at night, to avoid disturbing any one by the obligations of ceremony. In his consulship he commonly went through the streets on foot, and when he was not Consul, generally in a closed litter. His morning receptions were open to all, including even the Commons, and he met the requests of those who approached him with great affability, jocosely reproving one man because he presented a petition to him with as much hesitation "as he would a penny to an elephant." On the day of a meeting of the Senate he always greeted the members in the House as they sat, addressing each by name

---

[1] *Dominus*, "master," in the time of the Republic indicated the relation between master and slave. Tiberius also shrank from it, and it was first adopted by Caligula and Domitian. From the time of Trajan it was usual in the sense of "lord" or "sire."

without a prompter; and when he left the House, he used to bid them farewell in the same manner, while they remained seated. He exchanged social calls with many, and did not cease to attend all their anniversaries, until he was well on in years and was once incommoded by the crowd on the day of a betrothal. When Gallus Cerrinius, a Senator with whom he was not at all intimate, had become blind and had therefore resolved to end his life by starvation, Augustus called on him and by his consoling words induced him to live.

As he was delivering a speech in the Senate some one said to him: "I did not understand," and another: "I would contradict you if I had an opportunity." Several times when he was rushing from the House in anger at the excessive bickering of the disputants, some shouted after him: "Senators ought to have the right of speaking their mind on public affairs." At the selection of Senators when each member chose another, Antistius Labeo nominated Marcus Lepidus, an old enemy of the Emperor's who was at the time in banishment; and when Augustus asked him whether there were not others more deserving of the honor, Labeo replied that every man had his own opinion. Yet for all that no one suffered for his freedom of speech or insolence.

Even when some infamous libels against him were scattered in the Senate house he was neither disturbed nor gave himself great trouble to refute them. Without trying to discover the authors, he merely proposed that henceforth those who under a false name published notes or verses defamatory of any one should be called to account.

When he was assailed with scurrilous or spiteful jests by certain men, he made reply in a public proclamation; yet he vetoed a law to check freedom of speech in wills.[1] Whenever he took part in the election of magistrates, he went the round of the tribes with his candidates and appealed for them in the traditional manner. He also cast his own vote in his tribe, as one of the people. When he gave testimony in court, he was most patient in submitting to questions and even to contradiction. He made his Forum narrower than he had planned,

---

[1] The Romans in their wills often expressed their opinions freely about public men and affairs.

because he did not venture to eject the owners of the neighboring houses. He never recommended his sons for office without adding "If they be worthy of it." When they were still under age and the audience at the theater rose as one man in their honor, and stood up and applauded them, he expressed strong disapproval. He wished his friends to be prominent and influential in the state, but to be bound by the same laws as the rest and equally liable to prosecution. When Nonius Asprenas, a close friend of his, was meeting a charge of poisoning made by Cassius Severus,[1] Augustus asked the Senate what they thought he ought to do; for he hesitated, he said for fear that if he should support him, it might be thought that he was shielding a guilty man, but if he failed to do so, that he was proving false to a friend and prejudicing his case. Then, since all approved of his appearing in the case, he sat on the benches for several hours, but in silence and without even speaking in praise of the defendant.[2] He did however defend some of his clients, for instance a certain Scutarius, one of his former officers, who was accused of slander. But he secured the acquittal of no more than one single man, and then only by entreaty, making a successful appeal to the accuser in the presence of the jurors. This was Castricius, through whom he had learned of Murena's conspiracy.

How much he was beloved for his admirable conduct in all these respects it is easy to imagine. I say nothing of decrees of the Senate, which might seem to have been dictated by necessity or by awe. The Roman Knights celebrated his birthday of their own accord by common consent, and always for two successive days. All sorts and conditions of men, in fulfillment of a vow for his welfare, each year threw a small coin into the Lacus Curtius,[3] and also brought a New Year's gift to the Capitol on the Kalends of January, even when he was away from Rome. With this sum he bought and dedicated in each of the city wards costly statues of the gods, such as

---

[1] Cassius' charge was that Nonius had with one platter of poisoned meat killed a hundred and thirty guests.

[2] It was customary in defending an accused person to make a general eulogy of his character.

[3] An altar in the Forum, restored by Augustus.

Apollo Sandaliarius, Jupiter Tragoedus, and others. To re-build his house on the Palatine, which had been destroyed by fire, the veterans, the guilds, the tribes, and even individuals of other conditions gladly contributed money, each according to his means. But he merely took a little from each sum collected as a matter of form, not more than a denarius [1] from any of them. On his return from a province they received him not only with prayers and good wishes, but with songs. It was the rule, too, that whenever he entered the city, no one that day should suffer punishment.

The whole body of citizens with a sudden unanimous impulse proffered him the title of Father of his Country: first the Commons, by a deputation sent to Antium, and then, because he declined it, again at Rome as he entered the theater, which they attended in throngs, all wearing laurel wreaths; the Senate afterwards in the House, not by a decree or by acclamation, but through Valerius Messala. He, speaking for the whole body, said: "Good fortune and divine favor attend thee and thy house, Caesar Augustus; for thus we feel that we are praying for lasting prosperity for our country and happiness for our city. The Senate in accord with the people of Rome hails thee Father of thy Country." Then Augustus, with tears in his eyes, replied as follows (and I have given his exact words, as I did those of Messala): "Having attained my highest hopes, Fathers of the Senate, what more have I to ask of the immortal gods than that I may retain this same unanimous approval of yours to the very end of my life."

In honor of his physician, Antonius Musa, through whose care he had recovered from a dangerous illness, a sum of money was raised and Musa's statue set up beside that of Aesculapius. Some householders provided in their wills that their heirs should drive victims to the Capitol and pay a thank-offering in their behalf, because Augustus had survived them, and that a placard to this effect should be carried before them. Some of the Italian cities made the day on which he first visited them the beginning of their year. Many of the provinces in almost every one of their towns, besides erecting

---

[1] About $0.15.

temples and altars to his honor, instituted games to be celebrated every fifth year.

Kings who were his friends and allies, built cities in their respective kingdoms, to which they gave the name of Caesarea; and all with one consent resolved to finish, at their common expense, the temple of Jupiter Olympius, which was begun at Athens in ancient days, and to consecrate it to his genius.[1] They also would frequently leave their kingdoms and show him the attentions usual in dependents, clad in the toga and without the emblems of royalty, not only at Rome, but even when he was traveling through the provinces.

Now that I have shown how he conducted himself in civil and military positions, and in ruling the State in all parts of the world in peace and in war, I shall next give an account of his private and domestic life, describing his character and his fortune at home and in his household from his youth until the last day of his life.

He lost his mother during his first consulship and his sister Octavia in his fifty-fourth year. To both he showed marked devotion during their lifetime, and also paid them the highest honors after their death.

In his youth he was betrothed to the daughter of Publius Servilius Isauricus, but when he became reconciled with Antony after their first quarrel, and their troops begged that the rivals be further united by some tie of kinship, he took to wife Antony's stepdaughter Claudia, daughter of Fulvia by Publius Clodius, although she was barely of marriageable age; but because of a falling out with his mother-in-law Fulvia, he divorced her before they had begun to live together. Shortly after that he married Scribonia, who had been wedded before to two ex-Consuls, and was a mother by one of them. He divorced her also, "unable to put up with her shrewish disposition," as he himself writes, and at once took Livia Drusilla from her husband Tiberius Nero, although she was with child at the time. Her he loved and esteemed to the end without a rival.

---

[1] His tutelary God, or protecting spirit, analogous to the *daemon* of the Greeks and the guardian angels of the Catholic Church. To the Romans every living being, animal as well as man, and every place, had its genius.

By Scribonia he had a daughter Julia, by Livia no children at all, although he earnestly desired issue. One baby was conceived, but was prematurely born. He gave Julia in marriage first to Marcellus, son of his sister Octavia and hardly more than a boy, and then after his death to Marcus Agrippa, prevailing upon his sister to yield her son-in-law to his wishes; for at that time Agrippa had to wife one of the Marcellas and had chcildren from her. When Agrippa also died, Augustus, after considering various alliances for a long time, even in the equestrian order, finally chose for her his stepson Tiberius,[1] obliging him to divorce his wife, who was with child and by whom he was already a father. Mark Antony writes that Augustus first betrothed his daughter to his son Antonius and then to Cotiso, King of the Getae, at the same time asking for the hand of the King's daughter for himself in turn.

From Agrippa and Julia he had three grandsons, Gaius, Lucius, and Agrippa, and two granddaughters, Julia and Agrippina. He married Julia to Lucius Paulus, the Censor's son, and Agrippina to Germanicus [1] his sister's grandson. Gaius and Lucius he adopted at home, privately buying them from their father by a symbolic sale,[2] and initiated them into administrative life when they were still young, sending them to the provinces and the armies as Consuls-elect. In bringing up his daughter and his granddaughters he even had them taught spinning and weaving, and he forbade them to say or do anything except openly and such as might be recorded in the household diary. He so strictly prohibited them from all converse with strangers that he once wrote to Lucius Vinicius, a young man of good position and character: "You have acted presumptuously in coming to Baiae to call on my daughter." He taught his grandsons reading, swimming, and the other elements of education, for the most part himself, taking special pains to train them to imitate his own handwriting. He never dined in their company unless they sat beside him on the lowest couch, or made a journey unless they preceded his carriage or rode close by it on either side.

But at the height of his happiness and his confidence in his

---

[1] The same who afterwards became Emperor.

[2] The form of purchase consisted in touching a pair of scales three times with a penny in the presence of the Praetor.

famil*y* and its training, Fortune proved fickle. He found the two Julias, his daughter and granddaughter, guilty of every form of vice, and banished them. He lost Gaius and Lucius within the span of eighteen months, for the former died in Lycia and the latter at Massilia. He then publicly adopted his third grandson Agrippa and at the same time his stepson Tiberius by a bill passed in the assembly of the *curiae;* [1] but he soon disowned Agrippa because of his low tastes and violent temper, and sent him off to Surrentum.

He bore the death of his kin with far more resignation than their misconduct. For he was not greatly broken by the fate of Gaius and Lucius, but he informed the Senate of his daughter's fall through a letter read in his absence by a Quaestor, and for very shame would meet no one for a long time, and even thought of putting her to death. At all events, when one of her confidantes, a freedwoman called Phoebe, hanged herself at about that same time, he said: "I would rather have been Phoebe's father." In her banishment he denied Julia the use of wine, and every form of luxury, and would not allow any man, bond or free, to come near her without his permission, and then not without being informed of his stature, complexion, and even of any marks or scars upon his body. It was not until five years later that he moved her from the island to the mainland [2] and treated her with somewhat less severity. But he could not by any means be prevailed on to recall her altogether, and when the Roman people several times interceded for her and urgently pressed their suit, he in open assembly called upon the gods to curse them with like daughters and like wives. He would not allow the child born to his granddaughter Julia after her sentence to be recognized or reared. As Agrippa grew no more manageable, but on the contrary became madder from day to day, he transferred him to an island [3] and set a guard of soldiers over him besides. He also provided by a decree of the Senate that he

---

[1] Romulus was supposed to have divided the people of Rome into three Tribes and each Tribe into ten Curiae. The number of Tribes was gradually increased to thirty-five, but that of the Curiae always remained the same.

[2] From Pandataria to Reggio in Calabria.

[3] Planasia, a little desolate island between Elba and Corsica.

should be confined there for all time, and at every mention of him and of the Julias he would sigh deeply and even cry out:

"Would God I never had wedded bride
Or else that I had childless died." [1]

and he never alluded to them except as his three boils and his three ulcers.

He was cautious in forming friendships, but he clung to them with the utmost constancy, not only suitably rewarding their virtues and deserts but even condoning their faults, provided they were not too great. In fact one cannot readily name any of his numerous friends who fell into disgrace, except Salvidienus Rufus, whom he had advanced to a Consul's rank, and Cornelius Gallus, whom he had raised to the Prefecture of Egypt, both from the lowest estate. The former he handed over to the Senate that it might condemn him to death, because he was plotting revolution; the latter he forbade his house and the privilege of residence in the imperial provinces, because of his ungrateful and envious spirit. But when Gallus died by his own hand, driven to it by the menaces of his accusers and the decrees of the Senate, though commending their loyalty and their indignation on his account, Augustus yet shed tears and bewailed his lot, because he alone could not set what limits he chose to his anger with his friends. All the rest of his friends continued to enjoy power and wealth to the end of their lives, each holding a leading place in his own class, although sometimes differences arose. Not to mention the others, he occasionally found Agrippa lacking in patience and Maecenas in the gift of silence; for the former because of a slight suspicion of coolness and of a preference shown for Marcellus, threw up everything and went off to Mytilene, while the latter betrayed to his wife Terentia the secret of the discovery of the conspiracy of Murena.

He demanded of his friends proofs of reciprocal attachment at their deaths as well as during their lives. For though he was in no sense a legacy-hunter, and in fact could never bring

---

[1] An adaptation of line 40 Book III of the *Iliad* in a passage in which Hector is cursing Paris.

himself to accept anything from the will of a stranger, yet he was highly sensitive in weighing the death-bed utterances of his friends, concealing neither his chagrin if he was left a niggardly bequest or one unaccompanied with compliments, nor his satisfaction, if he was praised in terms of gratitude and affection. Whenever legacies or shares in inheritances were left him by men of any station who had offspring, he either turned them over to the children at once, or if the latter were in their minority, paid the money back with interest on the day when they assumed the gown of manhood or married.

As patron and master he was no less strict than gracious and merciful, while he held many of his freedmen in high honor and close intimacy, such as Licinus, Celadus, and others. His slave Cosmus, who spoke of him most insultingly, he merely put in irons. When he was walking with his steward Diomedes, and the latter in a panic got behind him when they were suddenly charged by a wild boar, he preferred to tax the man with timorousness rather than with anything more serious, and turned a matter of grave danger into a jest, because after all there was no evil intent. But he forced Polus, a favorite freedman of his, to take his own life, because he was convicted of adultery with Roman matrons, and broke the legs of his secretary Thallus for taking five hundred denarii [1] to betray the contents of a letter. Because the tutor and attendants of his son Gaius took advantage of their master's illness and death to commit acts of arrogance and greed in his province, he had them thrown into a river with heavy weights about their necks.

In early youth he incurred the reproach of sundry shameless acts. Sextus Pompey taunted him with effeminacy; Mark Antony with having earned adoption by his uncle through unnatural relations; and Lucius, brother of Mark Antony, that after sacrificing his honor to Caesar he had given himself to Aulus Hirtius in Spain for three hundred thousand sesterces,[2] and that he used to singe his legs with red-hot nutshells, to make the hair grow softer. What is more, one day when there were plays in the theater, all the people took as

---

[1] About $75.00.
[2] $12,300.00.

directed against him and loudly applauded the following line, spoken on the stage and referring to a priest of the Mother of the Gods, as he beat his drum:

"See'st how a wanton's finger sways the world?" [1]

That he was given to adultery not even his friends deny, although it is true that they excuse it as committed not from passion but from policy, in order to discover more easily the designs of his adversaries through the women of their households. Mark Antony charged him, besides his hasty marriage with Livia, with taking the wife of an ex-Consul from her husband's dining room before his very eyes into a bed-chamber, and bringing her back to the table with her hair in disorder and her ears glowing; that he divorced Scribonia because she expressed her resentment too freely at the excessive influence of a rival; that his friends acted as his panders, and stripped and inspected matrons and well-grown girls, as if Toranius the slave-dealer were putting them up for sale. Antony also writes to Augustus himself in the following familiar terms, when he had not yet wholly broken with him privately or publicly: "What has made such a change in you? Because I lie with the Queen? She is my wife. Am I just beginning this, or was it nine years ago? What then of you—do you lie only with Drusilla? Good luck to you if when you read this letter you have not been with Tertulla or Terentilla or Rufilla or Salvia Titisenia, or all of them. Does it matter where or with whom you take your pleasure?"

There was besides a private entertainment which he gave, commonly called the Supper of the Twelve Gods, which was the subject of gossip. At this the guests appeared in the guise of Gods and Goddesses, while he himself was made up to represent Apollo, as was charged not merely in letters of Antony, who spitefully gives the names of all the guests, but also in these anonymous verses, which every one knows:

---

[1] There is a double play on words: "Sways the world" might also be rendered "tops the orb." The allusion is to a priest of Cybele ("Mother of the Gods") beating a drum in the orgiastic rites of that Goddess.

"When Mallia late beheld, in mingled train,
  Twelve mortals ape twelve deities in vain;
  Caesar assumed what was Apollo's due,
  And wine and lust inflamed the motley crew.
  At the foul sight the Gods avert their eyes,
  And from his throne great Jove indignant flies."

The scandal of this banquet was the greater because of dearth
and famine in the land at the time, and on the following
day there was an outcry that the Gods had eaten all the grain
and that Caesar was in truth Apollo, but Apollo the Tormen-
tor, a surname under which the God was worshiped in one
part of the city. He was also charged with being excessively
fond of costly furniture and Corinthian bronzes as well as
with being addicted to gambling. Indeed, as early as the time
of the proscriptions there was written on his statue—

"In silver once my father dealt, now in Corinthians I,"

since it was believed that he caused some men to be entered
in the list of the proscribed only because he coveted their
Corinthian vases. Later, during the Sicilian war, this epigram
was current:

"Twice having lost a fleet in luckless flight,
  To win at last, he games both day and night."

Of these charges or slanders (whichever we may call them)
he easily refuted that for unnatural vice by the purity of his
life at the time and afterwards; so, too, the odium of extravagance by the fact that when he took Alexandria, he kept none
of the furniture of the palace for himself except a single agate
cup, and presently melted down all the golden vessels intended for everyday use. He could not dispose of the charge
of lustfulness and they say that even in his later years he was
fond of deflowering maidens, who were brought together for
him from all quarters, even by his own wife. He did not in the
least shrink from a reputation for gaming, and played frankly
and openly for recreation, even when he was well on in years,
not only in the month of December,[1] but on other holidays

---

[1] When freedom to gamble, feast, and revel was granted by the spirit
of the *Saturnalia*.

as well, and on working days too. There is no question about this, for in a letter in his own handwriting he says: "I dined, dear Tiberius, with the same company; we had besides as guests Vinicius and the elder Silius. We gambled like old men during the meal both yesterday and to-day; for when the dice were thrown, whoever turned up the 'dog' or the six, put a denarius in the pool for each one of the dice, and the whole was taken by any one who threw the 'Venus.' " [1] Again in an-other letter: "We spent the Quinquatria [2] very merrily, my dear Tiberius, for we played all day long and kept the gaming-board warm. Your brother made a great outcry about his luck, but after all did not come out far behind in the long run; for after losing heavily, he unexpectedly and little by little got back a good deal. For my part, I lost twenty thou-sand sesterces,[3] but because I was extravagantly generous in my play, as usual. If I had demanded of every one the stakes which I let go, or had kept all that I gave away, I should have won fully fifty thousand. But I like that better, for my generosity will exalt me to immortal glory." To his daughter he writes: "I send you two hundred and fifty denarii,[4] the sum which I gave each of my guests, in case they wished to play at dice or at odd and even during the dinner."

In the other details of his life it is generally agreed that he was most temperate and without even the suspicion of any vice. He lived at first near the Forum Romanum, above the Stairs of the Ringmakers, in a house which had belonged to the orator Calvus; afterwards, on the Palatine, but in the no less modest dwelling of Hortensius, no way remarkable either for size or elegance, having but a short colonnade with col-umns of Alban stone,[5] and rooms without any marble decora-tions or handsome pavements. For more than forty years too he used the same bedroom in winter and summer; for al-though he found the city unfavorable to his health in the win-ter, yet he nevertheless continued to winter there. If ever he

---

[1] When only aces appeared, the throw was called the "dog"; when all the dice turned up different numbers, "Venus."

[2] A five-day festival in March in honor of Minerva.

[3] $820.00.

[4] $37.50.

[5] A gray, volcanic stone, cheaply procured and easily worked.

planned to do anything in private or without interruption, he had a retired place at the top of the house, which he called "Syracuse" and "little workshop." In this he used to take refuge, or else in the villa of one of his freedmen in the suburbs. But whenever he was not well, he slept at Maecenas's house. For retirement he went most frequently to places by the sea and the islands of Campania, or to the towns near Rome, such as Lanuvium, Praeneste or Tibur, where he very often sat for the administration of justice in the colonnades of the Temple of Hercules. He disliked large and sumptuous country palaces, actually razing to the ground one which his granddaughter Julia built on a lavish scale. His own villas, which were modest enough, he decorated not so much with handsome statues and pictures as with terraces, groves, and objects noteworthy for their antiquity and rarity; for example, at Capreae the monstrous bones of huge sea monsters and wild beasts, called the "bones of the giants," and the weapons of ancient heroes.

The simplicity of his furniture and household goods may be seen from couches and tables still in existence, many of which are scarcely fine enough for a private citizen. They say that he always slept on a low and plainly furnished bed. Except on special occasions he wore common clothes for the house, made by his sister, wife, daughter or granddaughters. His togas were neither close nor full, his purple stripe neither narrow nor broad, and his shoes somewhat high-soled, to make him look taller than he really was. But he always kept shoes and clothing to wear in public ready in his room for sudden and unexpected occasions.

He gave dinner parties constantly and always formally, with great regard to the rank and personality of his guests. Valerius Messala writes that he never invited a freedman to dinner with the exception of Menas, and then only when he had been enrolled among the freeborn after betraying the fleet of Sextus Pompey. Augustus himself writes that he once entertained a man at whose villa he used to stop, who had been one of his body-guard. He would sometimes come to table late on these occasions and leave early, allowing his guests to begin to dine before he took his place and keep their places after he went out. He served a dinner of three courses or of six when he was most lavish, without needless extravagance but with the greatest goodfellowship. For he drew into the general conversation those who were silent or chatted under their breath, and introduced music and actors, or even strolling players from the circus, and especially story-tellers.

Festivals and holidays he celebrated lavishly as a rule, but sometimes only with merrymaking. In the Saturnalia, or at any other time when the fancy took him, he distributed to his company clothes, gold, or silver; sometimes coins of all sorts, even of the ancient Kings of Rome and of foreign nations; sometimes nothing but hair cloth, sponges, pokers and tongs, and other such things under names that were enigmatical and had a double meaning. He used also at a dinner party to put up for auction lottery-tickets for articles of most unequal value, and paintings of which only the back was shown, and so, by the unknown quality of the lot disappoint or fully gratify the expectations of the purchasers. He required, however, that all the guests take part in the bidding and share the loss or gain.

He was a light eater (for I would not omit even this detail) and as a rule ate plain food. He particularly liked coarse bread, small fishes, handmade moist cheese, and green figs of the second crop; and he would eat even before dinner, wherever and whenever he felt hungry. I quote word for word from some of his letters: "I ate a little bread and some dates in my carriage." And again: "As I was returning home from the palace in my litter, I devoured an ounce of bread and a few hard-pulped grapes." Once more: "Not even a Jew, my dear Tiberius, fasts so scrupulously on his sabbaths as I have to-day; for it was not until after the first hour of the night that I ate two mouthfuls of bread in the bath before I began to be anointed." Because of this irregularity he sometimes ate alone either before a dinner party began or after it was over, touching nothing while it was in progress.

He was by nature most sparing also in his use of wine. Cornelius Nepos writes that in camp before Mutina it was his habit to drink not more than three times at dinner. Afterwards, when he indulged most freely he never exceeded a pint; or if he did, he used to throw it up. He liked Raetian wine [1] best, but rarely drank before dinner. Instead he would take a bit of bread soaked in cold water, a slice of cucumber, a sprig of young lettuce, or an apple with a tart flavor, either fresh or dried.

After his midday meal he used to rest for a while just as he was, without taking off his clothes or his shoes, with his feet uncovered and his hand to his eyes. After dinner he went to a couch in his study, where he remained to late at night, until he had attended to what was left of the day's business, either wholly or in great part. Then he went to bed and slept not more than seven hours at most, and not even that length of time without a break, but waking three or four times. If he could not resume his sleep when it was interrupted, as would happen, he sent for readers or story-tellers, and when sleep came to him he often prolonged it until after daylight. He would never lie awake in the dark without having some one sit by his side. He detested early rising and when he had to get up earlier than usual because of some official or religious duty, to avoid inconveniencing himself he spent the night in the room of one of his friends near the appointed place. Even so, he often suffered from want of sleep, and he would drop off while he was being carried through the streets and when his litter was set down because of some delay.

In person he was unusually handsome and exceedingly graceful at all periods of his life, though he cared nothing for personal adornment. He was so far from being particular about the dressing of his hair, that he would have several barbers working in a hurry at the same time, and as for his beard he now had it clipped and now shaved, while at the very same time he would either be reading or writing something. His expression, whether in conversation or when he was silent, was so calm and mild, that one of the leading men of the Gallic provinces admitted to his countrymen that it had softened his heart, and kept him from carrying out his design of pushing the Emperor over a cliff, when he had been allowed to approach him under the pretense of a conference, as he was crossing the Alps. He had clear, bright eyes, in which he liked to have it thought that there was a kind of di-

---

[1] A wine of great reputation from the foot of the Rhaetian Alps.

vine power, and it greatly pleased him, whenever he looked keenly at any one, if he let his face fall as if before the radiance of the sun. But in his old age he could not see very well with his left eye. His teeth were wide apart, small and ill-kept. His hair was slightly curly and inclining to golden. His eyebrows met. His ears were of moderate size, and his nose projected a little at the top and then bent slightly inward.[1] His complexion was between dark and fair. He was short of stature (although Julius Marathus, his freedman and keeper of his records, says that he was five feet and nine inches in height [2]), but this was concealed by the fine proportion and symmetry of his figure, and was noticeable only by comparison with some taller person standing beside him.

It is said that his body was covered with spots and that he had birthmarks scattered over his breast and belly, corresponding in form, order and number with the stars of the Bear in the heavens; [3] also numerous callous places resembling ringworm, caused by a constant itching of his body and a vigorous use of the strigil.[4] He was not very strong in his left hip, thigh, and leg, and even limped slightly at times; but he strengthened them by treatment with sand and reeds.[5] He sometimes found the forefinger of his right hand so weak, when it was numb and shrunken with the cold, that he could hardly use it for writing even with the aid of a finger-stall of horn. He complained of his bladder too, and was relieved of the pain only after passing stones in his urine.

In the course of his life he suffered from several severe and dangerous illnesses, especially after the subjugation of Cantabria, when he was in such a desperate plight from abscesses of the liver, that he was forced to submit to an unprecedented and hazardous course of treatment. Since hot fomentations gave him no relief, he was led by the advice of his physician Antonius Musa to try cold ones.

He experienced also some disorders which recurred every

---

[1] The so-called "Roman nose."
[2] Roman measure. A little less than five feet seven inches English.
[3] The Great Dipper.
[4] An instrument of metal not unlike a curry-comb used in the baths for scraping the body.
[5] Apparently in a sort of poultice.

year at definite times; for he was commonly ailing just before his birthday; and at the beginning of spring he was troubled with an enlargement of the diaphragm, and when the wind was in the south, with catarrh. Hence his constitution was so weakened that he could not readily endure either cold or heat.

In the winter he protected himself with four tunics and a heavy toga, besides an undershirt, a woolen chest-protector and wraps for his thighs and shins, while in summer he slept with the doors of his bedroom open, oftentimes in the open court near a fountain, besides having some one to fan him. Yet he could not endure the sun even in winter, and never walked in the open air without wearing a broad-brimmed hat, even at home. He traveled in a litter, usually at night, and by such slow and easy stages that he took two days to go to Praeneste or Tibur. If he could reach his destination by sea, he preferred to sail. Yet in spite of all he made good his weakness by great care, especially by moderation in bathing; for as a rule he was anointed or took a sweat by a fire, after which he was doused with water either lukewarm or tepid from long exposure to the sun. When however he had to use hot salt water and sulphur baths for rheumatism, he contented himself with sitting on a wooden bath-seat, which he called by the Spanish name *dureta,* and plunging his hands and feet in the water one after the other.

Immediately after the civil war he gave up exercise with horses and arms in the Campus Martius, at first turning to pass-ball and balloon-ball, but soon confining himself to riding or taking a walk, ending the latter by running and leaping, wrapped in a mantle or a blanket. To divert his mind he sometimes angled and sometimes played at dice, marbles and nuts [1] with little boys, searching everywhere for such as were attractive for their pretty faces or their prattle, especially Syrians and Moors; for he abhorred dwarfs, cripples, and everything of that sort, as freaks of nature and of ill omen.

From early youth he devoted himself eagerly and with the utmost diligence to oratory and liberal studies. During the war at Mutina, amid such a press of affairs, he is said to have read, written and declaimed every day. In fact he never after-

---

[1] The Romans had many games that were played with nuts.

wards spoke in the Senate, or to the people or the soldiers, except in a studied and written address, although he did not lack the gift of speaking offhand without preparation. Moreover, to avoid the danger of forgetting what he was to say, or wasting time in committing it to memory, he adopted the practice of reading everything from a manuscript. Even his conversations with individuals and the more important of those with his own wife Livia, he always wrote out and read from a notebook, for fear of saying too much or too little if he spoke offhand. He had an agreeable and rather characteristic enunciation, and he practiced constantly with a teacher of elocution; but sometimes because of weakness of the throat he addressed the people through a herald.

He wrote numerous works of various kinds in prose, some of which he read to a group of his intimate friends, as one might in a lecture-room; for example, his "Reply to Brutus on Cato." At the reading of these volumes he had all but come to the end, when he grew tired and handed them to Tiberius to finish, for he was well on in years. He also wrote "Exhortations to Philosophy" and some volumes of an Autobiography, giving an account of his life in thirteen books up to the time of the Cantabrian war, but no farther. His essays in poetry were but slight. One book has come down to us written in hexameter verse, of which the subject and the title is "Sicily." There is another, equally brief, of "Epigrams," which he composed for the most part while he was in his bath. Though he began a tragedy with much enthusiasm, he destroyed it because his style did not satisfy him, and when some of his friends asked him what in the world had become of Ajax, he answered that "his Ajax had fallen on his sponge." [1]

He cultivated a style of speaking that was chaste and elegant, avoiding the vanity of attempts at epigram and an artificial order, and as he himself expresses it, "the noisomeness of far-fetched words," making it his chief aim to express his thought as clearly as possible. With this end in view, to avoid confusing and checking his reader or hearer at any point, he did not hesitate to use prepositions with names of cities, nor to repeat conjunctions several times, the omission

---

[1] Ajax is said to have perished by falling upon his sword.

of which causes some obscurity, though it adds grace. He looked on innovators and archaizers with equal contempt, as faulty in opposite directions, and he sometimes had a fling at them, in particular his friend Maecenas, whose "unguent-dripping curls," as he calls them, he loses no opportunity of belaboring and pokes fun at them by parody. He did not spare even Tiberius, who sometimes hunted up obsolete and pedantic expressions; and as for Mark Antony, he calls him a madman, for writing rather to be admired than to be understood. Then going on to ridicule his perverse and inconsistent taste in choosing an oratorical style, he adds the following: "Can you doubt whether you ought to imitate Annius Cimber or Veranius Flaccus, that you use the words which Sallustis Crispus gleaned from Cato's *Origines*? Or would you rather introduce into our tongue the verbose and unmeaning fluency of the Asiatic orators?" And in a letter praising the talent of his granddaughter Agrippina he writes: "But you must take great care not to write and talk affectedly."

That in his everyday conversation he used certain favorite and peculiar expressions appears from letters in his own hand, in which he says every now and then, when he wishes to indicate that certain men will never pay, that "they will pay on the Greek Kalends."[1] Urging his correspondent to put up with present circumstances, such as they are, he says: "Let's be satisfied with the Cato we have"; and to express the speed of a hasty action, "Quicker than you can cook asparagus." He continually used *baceolus* (dolt) for *stultus* (fool), for *pullus* (dark) *pulleiaceus* (darkish), and for *cerritus* (mad) *vacerrosus* (blockhead); also *vapide se habere* (feel flat) for *male se habere* (feel badly), and *betizare* (be like a beet) for *languere* (be weak), for which the vulgar term is *lachanizare*.[2] Besides he used *simus* for *sumus* and *domos* in the genitive singular instead of *domuos*. The last two forms he wrote invariably, for fear they should be thought errors rather than a habit.

I have also observed this special peculiarity in his manner

---

[1] That is, never, for the Greeks had nothing corresponding to the Roman Kalends.

[2] All these words which Augustus is said to have used are colloquialisms or slang of his day.

of writing: he does not divide words or carry superfluous letters from the end of one line to the beginning of the next,
but writes them just below the rest of the word and draws a
loop around them.

He does not strictly comply with orthography, that is to
say the theoretical rules of spelling laid down by the grammarians, seeming to be rather of the mind of those who believe that we should spell exactly as we pronounce. Of course
his frequent transposition or omission of syllables as well as
of letters are slips common to all mankind. I should not have
noted this, did it not seem to me surprising that some have
written that he cashiered a consular Governor, as an uncul-
tivated and ignorant fellow, because he observed that he had
written *ixi* for *ipsi*. Whenever he wrote in cipher, he wrote
B for A, C for B, and the rest of the letters on the same prin-
ciple, using AA for X.

He was equally interested in Greek studies, and in these,
too, he greatly excelled. His teacher of declamation was Apollodorus of Pergamon, whom he even took with him in his
youthful days from Rome to Apollonia, though Apollodorus
was an old man at the time. Later he became versed in various
forms of learning through association with the philosopher
Areus and his sons Dionysius and Nicanor. Yet he never
acquired the ability to speak Greek fluently or to compose
anything in it; for if he had occasion to use the language,
he wrote what he had to say in Latin and gave it to some
one else to translate. Still he was far from being ignorant
of Greek poetry, even taking great pleasure in the Old
Comedy and frequently staging it at his public entertainments. In reading the writers of both tongues there was nothing for which he looked so carefully as precepts and examples
instructive to the public or to individuals. These he would
often copy word for word, and send to the members of his
household, or to his Generals and provincial Governors, whenever any of them required admonition. He even read entire
volumes to the Senate and called the attention of the people
to them by proclamations; for example, the speeches of
Quintus Metellus "On Increasing the Family," and of Ru-
tilius "On the Height of Buildings"; to convince them that

he was not the first to give attention to such matters, but that they aroused the interest even of their forefathers.

He gave every encouragement to the men of talent of his own age, listening with courtesy and patience to their readings, not only of poetry and history, but of speeches and dialogues as well. But he took offense at being made the subject of any composition except in serious earnest and by the most eminent writers, often charging the Praetors not to let his name be cheapened in prize declamations.

This is what we are told of his attitude towards matters of religion.[1] He was somewhat weak in his fear of thunder and lightning, for he always carried a seal-skin about with him everywhere as a protection, and at any sign of a violent storm took refuge in an underground vaulted room; [2] for as I have said [3] he was once badly frightened by a narrow escape from lightning during a journey by night.

He was not indifferent to his own dreams or to those which others dreamed about him. At the battle of Philippi, though he had made up his mind not to leave his tent because of illness, he did so after all when warned by a friend's dream; fortunately, as it turned out, for his camp was taken and when the enemy rushed in, his litter was stabbed through and through and torn to pieces, in the belief that he was still lying there ill. All through the spring his own dreams were very numerous and fearful, but idle and unfulfilled; during the rest of the year they were less frequent and more reliable. Being in the habit of making constant visits to the temple of Jupiter the Thunderer, which he had founded on the Capitol, he dreamed that Jupiter Capitolinus complained that his worshipers were being taken from him, and that he answered that he had placed the Thunderer hard by to be his doorkeeper. He therefore soon after festooned the gable of the temple with bells, because these commonly hung at house-doors. It was likewise because of a dream that every

---

[1] *Religiones*: which for the Roman included religious belief as we still know it, and especially regard for omens and portents.

[2] Pliny (*Natural History* II, 55) says that lightning never goes more than five feet below the ground, and also that the laurel tree and the seal are never struck by it.

[3] See *Gaius Caligula*.

year on an appointed day he begged alms of the people, holding out his open hand to have pennies dropped in it.

Certain auspices and omens he regarded as infallible. If his shoes were put on in the wrong way in the morning, the left instead of the right, he considered it a bad sign. If there chanced to be a drizzle of rain when he was starting on a long journey by land or sea, he thought it a good omen, betokening a speedy and prosperous return. But he was especially affected by prodigies. When a palm tree [1] sprang up between the crevices of the pavement before his house, he transplanted it to the inner court beside his household Gods and took great pains to make it grow. He was so pleased that the branches of an old oak, which had already drooped to the ground and were withering, became vigorous again on his arrival in the island of Capri, that he arranged with the city of Naples to give him the island in exchange for Aenaria. He also had regard to certain days, refusing ever to begin a journey on the day after a market day,[2] or to take up any important business on the Nones; [3] though in the latter case, as he writes to Tiberius, he merely dreaded the unlucky sound of the name.

He treated with great respect such foreign rites as were ancient and well established, but held the rest in contempt For example, having been initiated at Athens [4] and afterwards sitting in judgment of a case at Rome involving the privileges of the priests of Ceres, in which certain matters of secrecy were brought up, he dismissed his councilors and the throng of bystanders and heard the disputants in private. But on the other hand he not only omitted to make a slight detour to visit Apis, when he was traveling through Egypt, but

----

[1] If this is true, winters in Rome in Augustus' time must have been much milder than they now are.

[2] The Roman month was divided into periods of eight days, lettered in the calendar A to H. On the last of these, every ninth day according to the Roman reckoning, a market and fair was held at Rome, and many people came in from the country. It was not till near the reign of Severus that the Romans began to divide their time into weeks, as we do, in imitation of the Jews.

[3] Ninth day before the *Ides*.

[4] Into the Eleusinian Mysteries of Ceres.

highly commended his grandson Gaius for not offering prayers at Jerusalem as he passed by Judaea.[1]

Having reached this point, it will not be out of place to add an account of the omens which occurred before he was born, on the very day of his birth, and afterwards, from which it was possible to anticipate and perceive his future greatness and uninterrupted good fortune.

In ancient days, when a part of the wall of Velitrae had been struck by lightning, the prediction was made that a citizen of that town would one day rule the world. Through their confidence in this the people of Velitrae had at once made war on the Roman people and fought with them many times after that almost to their utter destruction; but at last long afterward the event proved that the omen had foretold the rule of Augustus.

According to Julius Marathus, a few months before Augustus was born a portent was generally observed at Rome, which gave warning that nature was pregnant with a King for the Roman people. Thereupon the Senate in consternation decreed that no male child born that year should be reared. But those whose wives were with child saw to it that the decree was not filed in the treasury,[2] since each one appropriated the prediction to his own family.

I have read the following story in the books of Asclepias of Mendes entitled "Discourses about the Gods." When Atia[3] had come in the middle of the night to the solemn service of Apollo, she had her litter set down in the temple and fell asleep, while the rest of the matrons also slept. On a sudden a serpent[4] glided up to her and shortly went away. When she awoke, she purified herself, as if after the embraces of her husband, and at once there appeared on her body a mark in the form and colors of a serpent, which she never after could efface, and which obliged her, during the subsequent part of her life, to forego the use of the public baths. In the

---

[1] Augustus' attitude toward the Jews was favorable.

[2] The decree was not complete until this was done.

[3] The mother of Augustus.

[4] The *familiar spirit* or *genius* was often represented by a serpent, and those of husband and wife by two serpents, as we may see in Pompeian frescoes.

tenth month after that Augustus was born and was therefore
regarded as the son of Apollo. Atia too, before she gave him
birth, dreamed that her vitals were borne up to the stars
and spread over the whole extent of land and sea, while
Octavius, his father, dreamed that the sun rose from Atia's
womb.

The day he was born the conspiracy of Catiline was before
the House, and Octavius came late because of his wife's confinement. Whereupon Publius Nigidius, as every one knows,
learning the reason for his tardiness and being informed also
of the hour of the birth, declared that the ruler of the world
had been born. Later, when Octavius was leading an army
through remote parts of Thrace, and in the grove of Father
Bacchus consulted the priests about his son according to the
barbarians' rites, they made the same prediction; since such
a pillar of flame sprang forth from the wine that was poured
over the altar, that it rose above the temple roof and mounted
to the very sky. Such an omen had befallen no one save
Alexander the Great, when he offered sacrifice at the same
altar. Moreover, the very next night he dreamt that his son
appeared to him in a guise more majestic than that of mortal
man, with the thunderbolt, scepter, and insignia of Jupiter
Optimus Maximus, wearing a crown begirt with rays and
mounted upon a laurel-wreathed chariot drawn by twelve
horses of surpassing whiteness.

When Augustus was still an infant, as is recorded by the
hand of Gaius Drusus, he was placed by his nurse at evening
in his cradle on the ground floor and the next morning had
disappeared. After long search he was at last discovered on
a lofty tower, lying with his face towards the rising sun
As soon as he began to talk, it chanced that the frogs were
making a great noise at his grandfather's country place. He
bade them be silent, and they say that since then no frog has
ever croaked there. As he was breakfasting in a grove at the
fourth milestone on the Campanian road, an eagle surprised
him by snatching his bread from his hand, and after flying
to a great height, equally to his surprise dropped gently down
again and gave it back to him.

Quintus Catulus, after he had dedicated the Capitol,
dreamed two nights in succession. The first night he dreamed

that Jupiter Optimus Maximus, out of a group of boys of good family who were playing about his altar, called aside one and put the public seal of the commonwealth which he carried in his hand in the lap of the boy's toga. The next night he dreamt that he saw this same boy in the lap of Jupiter of the Capitol, and that when he ordered that he be removed, the God warned him to desist, declaring that the boy was being reared to be the savior of his country. When Catulus next day met Augustus, whom he had never seen before, he looked at him in great surprise and said that he was very like the boy of whom he had dreamed. Some give a different account of Catulus's first dream, namely, that Jupiter, when a group of well-born children requested him for a tutor, pointed out one of their number, to whom they were to submit all their requests, and then, after lightly touching the boy's mouth with his fingers, laid them on his own lips.

As Marcus Cicero was once attending Gaius Caesar to the Capitol, he happened to tell his friends a dream which he had had the night before, in which a boy of noble countenance was let down from heaven on a golden chain and, standing at the door of the temple, was given a whip by Jupiter. Just then suddenly catching sight of Augustus, who was still unknown to the greater number of those present and had been brought to the ceremony by his uncle Caesar, he declared that he was the very one whose form had appeared to him in his dream.

When Augustus was assuming the gown of manhood, his senatorial tunic [1] becoming loose in the seam on each side, fell at his feet, which some interpreted as a sure sign that the order of which the tunic was the badge [2] would one day be brought to his feet.

As the Deified Julius was cutting down a wood at Munda and preparing a place for his camp, coming across a palm tree, he caused it to be spared as an omen of victory. From this a shoot at once sprang forth and in a few days grew so great that it not only equalled the parent tree, but even over-

[1] Augustus was not yet a Senator, but the privilege of wearing the broad purple stripe, which distinguished the gown of the Senators, was doubtless one of the honors conferred on him by Caesar.

[2] That is, the Senate.

shadowed it. Many doves, moreover, built their nests there, although that kind of bird especially avoids hard and rough foliage. Indeed, it was that omen in particular, they say, that led Caesar to wish that none other than his sister's grandson should be his successor.

While in retirement at Apollonia, Augustus mounted with Agrippa to the studio of the astrologer Theogenes. Agrippa was the first to try his fortune, and when a great and almost incredible career was predicted for him, Augustus chose not to disclose the time of his own birth, and persisted for some time in the refusal, from a mixture of shame and fear lest he be predicted less eminent. When he at last gave it unwillingly and hesitatingly, and only after many urgent requests, Theogenes sprang up and threw himself at his feet. From that time on Augustus had such faith in his destiny, that he made his horoscope public and issued a silver coin stamped with the sign of the constellation Capricornus, under which he was born.

As he was entering the city on his return from Apollonia after Caesar's death, though the heaven was clear and cloudless, a circle like a rainbow suddenly formed around the sun's disc, and straightway the tomb of Caesar's daughter Julia was struck by lightning. Again, as he was taking the auspices in his first consulship, twelve vultures appeared to him, as to Romulus, and when he slew the victims, the livers within all of them were found to be double at the lower end, which all those who were skilled in such matters unanimously declared to be an omen of a great and happy future.

He even divined beforehand the outcome of all his wars. When the forces of the Triumvirs were assembled at Bononia, an eagle that had perched upon his tent made a dash at two ravens, which attacked it on either side, and struck them to the ground. From this the whole army inferred that there would one day be discord among the colleagues, as actually came to pass, and divined its result. As he was on his way to Philippi, a Thessalian gave him notice of his coming victory on the authority of the deified Caesar, whose shade had met him on a lonely road. When he was sacrificing at Perusia without getting a favorable omen, and so had ordered more victims to be brought, the enemy made a sudden sally and carried off all the equipment of the sacrifice. Whereupon the soothsayers agreed that all the dangers and disasters with which the sacrificer had been threatened would recoil on the heads of those who were in possession of the entrails. And so it turned out. As he was walking on the shore the day before the sea-fight off Sicily, a fish sprang from the sea and fell at his feet. At Actium, as he was going down to begin the battle, he met an ass with his driver, the man having the name Eutychus [1] and the beast that of Nicon.[2] And after the victory he set up bronze images of the two in the sacred enclosure into which he converted the side of his camp.

His death, too, of which I shall speak next, and his deification after death, were known in advance by unmistakable signs. As he was bringing the lustrum [3] to an end in the Campus Martius before a great throng of people, an eagle flew several times about him and then going across to the temple hard by, perched above the first letter of Agrippa's name. On noticing this, Augustus bade his colleague Tiberius recite the vows which it is usual to make for the next five years; for although he had them prepared and written out on a tablet, he declared that he would not be responsible for vows which he should never accomplish. At about the same time the first letter of his name was melted from the inscription on one of his statues by a flash of lightning. This was interpreted to mean that he would live only a hundred days from that time, the number indicated by the letter C, and that he would be numbered with the gods, since *aesar* (that is, the part of the name Caesar which was left) is the word for god in the Etruscan tongue.

Then, too, when he was on the point of sending Tiberius to Illyricum and was proposing to escort him as far as Beneventum, and litigants detained him on the judgment seat by bringing forward case after case, he cried out that he would stay no longer in Rome, even if everything conspired to delay him—and this too was afterwards looked upon as one

---

[1] Prosper.

[2] Victor.

[3] The sacrifice of purification made every five years by one of the Censors after the taking of the census. A pig, a sheep, and a bull were sacrificed.

of the omens of his death. So entered upon his journey, he went on as far as Astura [1] and from there, contrary to his custom, took ship by night since it chanced that there was a favorable breeze, and thus contracted an illness beginning with diarrhoea.

Then after skirting the coast of Campania and the neighboring islands, he spent four more days at his villa in Capri, where he gave himself up wholly to rest and social diversions. As he sailed by the gulf of Puteoli, it happened that from an Alexandrian ship which had just arrived there, the passengers and crew, clad in white, crowned with garlands, and burning incense, lavished upon him good wishes and the highest praise, saying that it was through him they lived, through him that they sailed the seas, and through him that they enjoyed their liberty and their fortunes. Exceedingly pleased at this, he gave forty gold pieces to each of his companions, exacting from every one of them a pledge under oath not to spend the sum that had been given them in any other way than in buying wares from Alexandria. More than that, for the several remaining days of his stay, among little presents of various kinds, he distributed togas and pallia [2] as well, stipulating that the Romans should use the Greek dress and language and the Greeks the Romans. He continually watched the exercises of the ephebi,[3] of whom there was still a goodly number at Capri, according to the ancient usage. He also gave these youths a banquet at which he himself was present, and not only allowed, but even required perfect freedom in jesting and in scrambling for tickets for fruit, dainties and all kinds of things, which he threw to them. In short, there was no form of gayety in which he did not indulge.

The neighboring part of the island of Capri he called "City of Do-littles," from the indolent life which some of his party led there. Besides he used to call one of his favorites,

---

[1] On the road to Naples.

[2] The *pallium* corresponded to the *himation,* the distinctive garment of the Greeks, as the *toga* of the Romans.

[3] Greek youths between the ages of 18 and that of full citizenship, who had regular gymnastic training as a part of their education.

Masgaba by name, Ktistes,[1] as if he were the founder of the island. Noticing from his dining-room that the tomb of this Masgaba, who had died the year before, was visited by a large crowd with many torches, he uttered aloud this verse, composed offhand: [2]

"I see the founder's tomb alight with fire";

and turning to Thrasyllus, one of the suite of Tiberius who was reclining opposite him and knew nothing about the matter, he asked of what poet he thought it was the work. When Thrasyllus hesitated, he added another verse:

"See you with lights Masgaba honored now?"

and asked his opinion of this one also. When Thrasyllus could say nothing except that they were very good, whoever made them, he burst into a laugh and fell a joking about it.

Presently he crossed over to Naples, although his bowels were still weak from intermittent attacks. In spite of this he witnessed an exhibition of the gymnastic games which were performed in his honor every five years, and then started with Tiberius for his destination. But as he was returning his illness increased and he at last took to his bed at Nola, calling back Tiberius, who was on his way to Illyricum, and keeping him for a long time in private conversation, after which he gave attention to no business of importance.

On the last day of his life he asked every now and then whether there was any disturbance without on his account. He then called for a mirror and had his hair combed and his falling jaws set straight.[3] After that, calling in his friends and asking whether it seemed to them that he had played the comedy of life fitly, he added the tag:

"Since I've played well, with joy your voices raise
And from the stage dismiss me with your praise." [4]

---

[1] Greek name for the founder of a city or colony.
[2] In Greek, as also the next verse.
[3] As though from weakness he could not keep his mouth closed.
[4] It was customary at the end of comedies to call for applause.

Then he sent them all off, and while he was asking some new-comers from the city about the daughter of Drusus, who was ill, suddenly, amidst the kisses of Livia, he passed away, uttering these last words: "Live mindful of our wedlock, Livia, and farewell." Thus was he blessed with an easy death and such a one as he had always longed for. For almost always on hearing that any one had died swiftly and painlessly, he prayed that he and his might have a like *euthanasia,* for that was the term he was wont to use. He gave but one single sign of wandering before he breathed his last, calling out in sudden terror that forty young men were carrying him off. And even this was rather a premonition than a delusion, since it was that very number of soldiers of the pretorian guard that carried him forth to lie in state.

He died in the same room as his father Octavius had died when the two Sextuses, Pompeius and Appuleius, were Consuls, on the fourteenth day before the Kalends of September at the ninth hour, just thirty-five days before his seventy-sixth birthday.

His body was carried by the Senators of the municipalities and colonies from Nola all the way to Bovillae, in the night time because of the season of the year, being placed by day in the basilica of the town at which they arrived or in its principal temple.[1] At Bovillae the members of the equestrian order [2] met it and bore it to the city, where they placed it in the vestibule of his house.

The Senate proceeded with so much zeal in the arrangement of his funeral, and paying honor to his memory, that, among many other suggestions, some proposed that his cortège pass through the triumphal gate, preceded by the statue of Victory which stands in the House, while a dirge was sung by children of both sexes belonging to the leading families. Others proposed that on the day of the obsequies golden rings be laid aside and iron ones worn; and others, that his ashes be collected by the priests of the highest colleges. One man proposed that the name of the month of August be transferred to September, because Augustus was born in the lat-

---

[1] An especial honor, for it was against Roman custom and law to bring a dead body into a sacred place for fear of polluting it.

[2] See *The Deified Claudius.*

ter, but died in the former; another, that all the period from the day of his birth until his demise be called the Augustan Age, and so entered in the Calendar. But though a limit was set to the honors paid him, his eulogy was twice delivered: before the temple of the Deified Julius by Tiberius, and from the old rostra by Drusus, son of Tiberius. The body was then carried on the shoulders of Senators to the Campus Martius and there cremated. There was even an ex-praetor who took oath that he had seen the form of the Emperor, after he had been reduced to ashes, on its way to heaven. His remains were gathered up by the leading men of the equestrian order, bare-footed and in ungirt tunics, and placed in the Mausoleum. This structure he had built in his sixth consulship between the Via Flaminia and the bank of the Tiber, and at the same time opened to the public the groves and walks by which it was surrounded.

He had made a will in the consulship of Lucius Plancus and Gaius Silius on the third day before the Nones of April, a year and four months before he died, in two note-books, written in part in his own hand and in part in that of his freedmen Polybius and Hilarion. These the Vestal Virgins, with whom they had been deposited, now produced, together with three rolls, which were sealed in the same way. All these were opened and read in the Senate. He appointed as his chief heirs Tiberius, to receive two-thirds of the estate, and Livia, one-third; these he also bade assume his name. His heirs in the second degree were Drusus, son of Tiberius, for one-third, and Germanicus and his three sons for the rest. In the third grade he mentioned many of his relatives and friends. He left to the Roman people forty million sesterces; [1] to the tribes three million five hundred thousand each; to the soldiers of the pretorian guard a thousand each; and to the legionaries three hundred. This sum he ordered to be paid at once, for he had always kept the amount at hand and ready for the purpose. He gave other legacies to various individuals, some amounting to as much as twenty thousand sesterces, and provided for the payment of these a year later, giving as his excuse for the delay the small amount of his property,

---

[1] $1,640,000.00, taking .04 1-10 as equivalent to the *sestertius*.

and declaring that not more than a hundred and fifty millions would come to his heirs. For, though he had received
fourteen hundred millions during the last twenty years from
the wills of his friends, he said that he had spent nearly all
of it, as well as his two paternal estates [1] and his other inheritances, for the benefit of the State. He gave orders that
his daughter and his granddaughter Julia should not be put
in his Mausoleum, if anything befell them.[2] In one of the
three rolls he included directions for his funeral; in the second, an account of what he had accomplished, which he desired to have cut upon bronze tablets and set up at the
entrance to the Mausoleum; [3] in the third, a summary of the
condition of the whole empire; how many soldiers there were
in active service in all parts of it, how much money there was
in the public treasury and in the privy-purse, and what revenues were in arrears. He added, besides, the names of the
freedmen and slaves from whom the details could be demanded.

---

[1] Those of his father Octavius, and his father by adoption, Julius
Caesar.

[2] The common euphemism for, when they died.

[3] The original of this inscription is lost, but the greater part of a
copy inscribed in Greek and Latin on marble is preserved at Ancyra
in Asia Minor and is known as the *Monumentum Ancyranum*.

BOOK III

TIBERIUS

TIBERIUS

THE patrician branch of the Claudian family (for there was, besides, a plebeian branch of no less influence and prestige) came originally from Regilli, a town of the Sabines. From there it moved to Rome shortly after the founding of the city with a large band of dependents, through the influence of Titus Tatius, who shared the kingly power with Romulus; or, perhaps, according to better authority, under Atta Claudius, the head of the family, about six years after the expulsion of the Kings.[1] It was admitted among the patrician families, receiving, besides, from the State a piece of land beyond the river Anio for its dependents, and a burial-site for the family at the foot of the Capitoline hill. After this period, as time went on it was honored with twenty-eight consulships, five dictatorships, seven censorships, six triumphs, and two ovations. While the members of the family were known by various forenames and surnames, [2] they by common consent discarded the forename Lucius after two of the family who bore it had been found guilty, the one of highway robbery, and the other of murder. To their surnames, on the other hand, they added that of Nero, which in the Sabine tongue means "strong and valiant."

There are on record many distinguished services of the Claudii to their country, as well as many deeds of the opposite character. But to mention only the principal instances, Appius Claudius advised against forming an alliance with King Pyrrhus as not at all expedient. Claudius Caudex was the

---

[1] The Tarquins.

[2] The Romans had commonly three names: (1) the *praenomen* designated the individual; (2) the *nomen* marked the *gens;* (3) the *cognomen* came last and marked the *familia.* Sometimes there was a fourth name, properly called the *agnomen,* but sometimes likewise *cognomen,* which was added on account of some illustrious action.

first to cross the straits with a fleet, and drove the Carthaginians from Sicily. Tiberius Nero crushed Hasdrubal, on his arrival from Spain with a vast army, before he could unite with
his brother Hannibal. On the other hand, Claudius Regil-
lianus, Decemvir for codifying the laws, through his lawless attempt to enslave a freeborn maid, to gratify his passion for her,
was the cause of the second secession of the plebeians from the
patricians. Claudius Russus, having set up his statue at
Forum Appi [1] with a crown upon its head, tried to take possession of Italy through his dependents. Claudius Pulcher began
a sea-fight off Sicily, though the sacred chickens would not
eat when he took the auspices, throwing them into the sea in
defiance of the omen, and saying that they might drink, since
they would not eat. He was defeated, and on being bidden by
the Senate to appoint a Dictator, he appointed his messenger
Glycias, as if again making a jest of his country's peril.

The women also have records equally diverse, since both
the famous Claudias belonged to that family: the one who
drew the ship freighted with things sacred to the Idaean
Mother of the Gods [2] from the shoal in the Tiber on which it
was stranded, after first publicly praying that it might yield
to her efforts only if her chastity were beyond question; and
the one who was convicted by the people of treason, an unprecedented thing in the case of a woman, because when her
carriage made but slow progress through the throng, she
openly gave vent to the wish that her brother Pulcher might
come to life and lose another fleet, to make less of a crowd
in Rome. It is notorious besides that all the Claudii were aristocrats and staunch upholders of the prestige and influence
of the patricians, with the sole exception of Publius Clodius,
who for the sake of driving Cicero from the city had himself
adopted by a plebeian and one too who was younger than
himself.[3] Their attitude towards the commons was so headstrong and stubborn that not even when on trial for his life
before the people did any one of them deign to put on mourn-

---

[1] An ancient Latin town in the Via Appia, the present road to Naples.
[2] Cybele, a Phrygian goddess worshiped near Mount Ida. In 204
B.C. her cult was introduced into Rome where she was worshiped as
Magna Mater, "Mother of the Gods."
[3] Mentioned also in *Julius.*

ing or beg for mercy; and some of them during bickerings
and disputes struck the Tribunes of the Commons. A Vestal
Virgin likewise of the family, when her brother was resolved
to have the honor of a triumph contrary to the will of the
people, mounted the chariot with him, and attended him into
the Capitol, in order to make it an act of sacrilege for any one
of the Tribunes to forbid him or interpose his veto.

Such was the stock from which Tiberius Caesar derived his
origin, and that too on both sides: on his father's from Tiberius
Nero; on his mother's from Appius Pulcher, both of whom
were sons of Appius Caecus. He was a member also of the
family of the Livii, through the adoption into it of his maternal grandfather. This family too, though of plebeian origin,
was yet of great prominence and had been honored with eight
consulships, two censorships, and three triumphs, as well as
with the offices of Dictator and Master of the Horse. It was
made illustrious too by distinguished members, in particular
Salinator and the Drusi. The former in his censorship branded
all the tribes [1] for their inconstancy because having convicted
and fined him after a previous consulship, they made him
Consul a second time and Censor as well. Drusus gained a
surname for himself and his descendants by slaying Drausus,
leader of the enemy, in single combat. It is also said that
when Propraetor he brought back from his province of Gaul
the gold which was paid long before to the Senones, when they
beleaguered the Capitol, and that this had not been wrested
from them by Camillus, as tradition has it. His grandson's
grandson, called "Patron of the Senate" because of his distinguished services against the Gracchi, left a son who was
treacherously slain by the party of his opponents, while he
was busily agitating many plans during a similar dissension.

Nero, the father of Tiberius, as Quaestor of Julius Caesar
during the Alexandrian war and commander of a fleet, contributed materially to the victory. For this he was made Pontiff in place of Publius Scipio and sent to conduct colonies to
Gaul, among them Narbonne and Arles. Yet after the murder
of Caesar, when all the others voted for an amnesty through
fear of mob violence, he even favored a proposal for reward-

---

[1] That is, affixed the mark of ignominy to their names on the census
roll.

ing those who had killed a tyrant. Later on, having held the praetorship, since a dispute arose among the Triumvirs at the close of his term, he retained the badges of his rank beyond the legitimate time and followed Lucius Antonius, Consul and brother of the Triumvir, to Perusia. When the others capitulated, he alone held to his allegiance and got away first to Praeneste and then to Naples; and after vainly trying to enlist the slaves by a promise of freedom, he took refuge in Sicily. Piqued however because he was not at once given an audience with Sextus Pompeius, and was denied the use of the fasces, he crossed to Achaia and joined Mark Antony. With him he shortly returned to Rome, on the conclusion of a general peace, and gave up to Augustus at his request his wife Livia Drusilla, who was pregnant at the time and had already borne him a son.[1] Not long afterward he died, survived by both his sons, Tiberius Nero and Drusus Nero.

Some have supposed that Tiberius was born at Fundi, on no better evidence than that his maternal grandmother was a native of that place, and that later a statue of Good Fortune was set up there by decree of the Senate. But according to the most numerous and trustworthy authorities, he was born at Rome, on the Palatine, the sixteenth day before the Kalends of December, in the consulship of Marcus Aemilius Lepidus and Lucius Munatius Plancus (the former for the second time) while the war of Philippi was going on. In fact it is so recorded both in the calendar and in the public registers. Yet in spite of this some write that he was born in the preceding year, that of Hirtius and Pansa, and others in the following year, in the consulate of Servilius Isauricus and Lucius Antonius.

He passed his infancy and his youth amid hardship and tribulation, since he was everywhere the companion of his parents in their flight. At Naples indeed he all but betrayed them twice by his crying, as they were secretly on their way to a ship, just as the enemy burst into the town; once when he was snatched from his nurse's breast, and again from his mother's arms, by some of the company, who in the sudden danger tried to relieve the women of their burden. After being

---

[1] For further detail see *Augustus*.

taken all over Sicily also and Achaia, and consigned to the public care of the Lacedaemonians, because they were dependents of the Claudii, he almost lost his life as he was leaving there by night, when the woods suddenly took fire all about them, and the flames so encircled the whole company that part of Livia's robe and her hair were scorched. The gifts which were given him in Sicily by Pompeia, sister of Sextus Pompeius, a cloak and clasp, as well as studs of gold, are still kept and exhibited at Baiae. Being adopted, after his return to the city, in the will of Marcus Gallius, a Senator, he accepted the inheritance, but soon gave up the name, because Gallius had been a member of the party opposed to Augustus.

At the age of nine he delivered a eulogy of his dead father from the rostra. Then, just as he was arriving at puberty, he accompanied the chariot of Augustus in his triumph after Actium, riding the left trace-horse, while Marcellus, son of Octavia, rode the one on the right. He presided, too, at the city festival, and took part in the game of Troy during the performances in the circus, leading the band of older boys.

The principal events of his youth and later life, from the time he assumed the gown of manhood to the beginning of his reign, were these. He gave a gladiatorial show in memory of his father, and a second in honor of his grandfather Drusus, at different times and in different places, the former in the Forum and the latter in the amphitheater, inducing some retired gladiators to appear with the rest by the payment of a hundred thousand sesterces to each.[1] He also gave stage-plays, but without being present in person. All these were on a grand scale, at the expense of his mother and his stepfather.[2]

He married Agrippina, daughter of Marcus Agrippa, and granddaughter of Caecilius Atticus, the Roman Knight to whom Cicero's letters are addressed; but after he had acknowledged[3] a son from her, Drusus, although she was thoroughly congenial and was a second time with child, he was

---

[1] $4,100.00.

[2] Livia and Augustus.

[3] A child at birth was laid at his father's feet. He then acknowledged the infant by taking it in his arms. Otherwise he assumed no responsibility for it.

forced to divorce her and to contract a hurried marriage with Julia,[1] daughter of Augustus. This caused him no little distress of mind, for he was living happily with Agrippina, and disapproved of Julia's character, having perceived that she had a passion for him even during the lifetime of her former husband, as was in fact the general opinion. But even after the divorce he regretted his separation from Agrippina, and the only time that he chanced to see her, he followed her with such an intent and tearful gaze that care was taken that she should never again come before his eyes. With Julia he lived in harmony at first, and returned her love; but he soon grew cold, and went so far as to cease to live with her at all, after the severing of the tie formed by a child which was born to them, but died at Aquileia in infancy. He lost his brother Drusus in Germany and brought his body to Rome, going before it on foot all the way.

He began his civil career by defending King Archelaus, the people of Tralles, and those of Thessaly, before the judgment seat of Augustus, the charge in each case being different. He made a plea to the Senate in behalf of the citizens of Laodicea, Thyatira, and Chios, who had suffered loss from an earthquake and begged for help. Fannius Caepio, who had conspired with Varro Murena against Augustus, he arraigned for high treason and secured his condemnation. In the meantime he undertook two public charges: that of the grain supply, which, as it happened, was deficient; and the investigation of the slave-prisons [2] throughout Italy, the owners of which had gained a bad reputation; for they were charged with holding in durance not only travelers, but also those whom dread of military service had driven to such places of concealment.

His first military service was as Tribune of the soldiers in the campaign against the Cantabrians. He then led an army to the Orient and restored the throne of Armenia to Tigranes, crowning him on the tribunal. He besides recovered the standards which the Parthians had taken from Marcus Crassus.[3]

---

[1] See *Augustus*.

[2] See also *Augustus*.

[3] But see *Augustus*.

Then for about a year he was governor of Gallia Comata,[1] which was in a state of unrest through the inroads of the barbarians and the dissensions of its chiefs. Next he carried on war with the Raeti and Vindelici, then in Pannonia, and finally in Germany. In the first of these wars he subdued the Alpine tribes, in the second the Breuci and Dalmatians, and in the third he brought forty thousand prisoners of war over into Gaul and assigned them homes near the bank of the Rhine. Because of these exploits he entered the city both in an ovation and in a triumph having previously, as some think, been honored with the triumphal regalia, a new kind of distinction never before conferred upon any one.

He entered upon the offices of Quaestor, Praetor, and Consul before the usual age, and held them almost successively. After an interval he was made Consul again, at the same time receiving the tribunicial power for five years.

At the flood-tide of success, though in the prime of life and health, he suddenly decided to go into retirement and to withdraw as far as possible from the center of the stage. It is uncertain whether this was from disgust at his wife, whom he dared neither accuse nor put away, though he could no longer endure her; or from hope by avoiding the contempt born of familiarity to support and augment his prestige by absence, in case his country should ever need him. Some think that, since the children of Augustus were now of age, he voluntarily gave up the position and the virtual assumption of the second rank which he had long held, thus following the example of Marcus Agrippa, who withdrew to Mytilene when Marcellus began his public career, so that he might not seem either to oppose or belittle him by his presence. This was, in fact, the reason which Tiberius himself gave, but afterwards. At the time he asked for leave of absence on the ground of weariness of office and a desire to rest. Neither his mother's urgent entreaties nor the complaint which his stepfather openly made in the Senate, could alter his resolution. On the contrary, when they made more strenuous efforts to detain him, he refused to take food for four days. Being at last al-

---

[1] Transalpine Gaul was called *Comata*, "long-haired"; the southern part, *Braccata*, "breeches-wearing," and Cisalpine Gaul, *Togata*, "toga-wearing."

lowed to depart, he left his wife and son in Rome and went down to Ostia [1] in haste, without saying a single word to any of those who saw him off, and kissing only a very few when he left.

From Ostia he coasted along the shore of Campania, and learning of an indisposition of Augustus, he stopped for a while. But since gossip was rife that he was lingering on the chance of realizing his highest hopes, although the wind was all but dead ahead, he sailed directly to Rhodes, for he had been attracted by the charm and healthfulness of that island ever since the time when he put in there on his return from Armenia. Content there with a modest house and a villa in the suburbs not much more spacious, he adopted a most unassuming manner of life, at times walking in the gymnasium without a Lictor or a messenger, and exchanging courtesies with the good people of Greece almost as though he were one of them.

It chanced one morning in arranging his program for the day, that he had announced his wish to visit whatever sick folk there were in the city. This was misunderstood by his attendants, and orders were given that all the sick should be taken to a public portico and arranged according to the nature of their complaints. Whereupon Tiberius, shocked at this unexpected sight, and in doubt for some time what to do, at last went about to each one, apologizing for what had happened even to the humblest and most obscure of them.

One instance only was noticed in which he appeared to exercise his tribunicial authority. He was a constant attendant at the schools and lecture-rooms of the professors of philosophy, and once when a hot dispute had arisen among rival sophists, a fellow had the audacity to ply him with abuse when he took part and appeared to favor one side. Thereupon he gradually backed away to his house, and then suddenly coming out with his Lictors and attendants, and bidding his crier to summon the foul-mouthed fellow before his tribunal, he ordered them to take him off to prison.

Shortly after this he learned that his wife Julia had been banished because of her immorality and adulteries, and that

---

[1] Ostia, the port of Rome, about 13 miles from the city.

a bill of divorce had been sent her in his name by authority of
Augustus. Welcome as this news was, he yet considered it his
duty to make every possible effort in numerous letters to
reconcile the father to his daughter; and, regardless of her
deserts, to allow her to keep any gifts which he had himself
made her at any time. Moreover, when the term of his tribunicial power was at an end, at last admitting that the sole
object of his retirement had been to avoid the suspicion of
rivalry with Gaius and Lucius, he asked that inasmuch as
he was free from care in that regard, since they were now
grown up and had an undisputed claim on the succession, he
be allowed to visit his relatives, whom he sorely missed. But
his request was denied and he was besides admonished to
give up all thought of his kindred, whom he had so eagerly
abandoned.

Accordingly he remained in Rhodes against his will, having with difficulty through his mother's aid secured permission that, while away from Rome, he should have the title of
envoy of Augustus, so as to conceal his disgrace.

Then in very truth he lived not only in private, but even
in danger and fear, secluded in the country away from the
sea, and shunning the attentions of those who sailed that way.
These, however, were constantly thrust on him, since no general or magistrate who was on his way to any province failed
to put in at Rhodes. He had besides reasons for still greater
anxiety. For when he had crossed the Samos to visit his
stepson Gaius, who had been made Governor of the Orient,
he found him somewhat estranged through the slanders of
Marcus Lollius, a member of Gaius' staff and his guardian. He
also incurred the suspicion of having through some centurions
of his appointment, who were returning to camp after a fur-
lough, sent messages to several persons which were of an ambiguous character and apparently designed to incite them to
revolution. On being informed by Augustus of this suspicion,
he unceasingly demanded the appointment of some one, of
any rank whatsoever, to keep watch over his actions and
words.

He also gave up his usual exercises with horses and arms,
and laying aside the garb of his country, took to the Greek
dress. In this state he continued for upwards of two years

becoming daily an object of greater contempt and aversion. This went so far that the citizens of Nemausus [1] threw down his statues and busts, and when mention was once made of him at a private dinner party, a man got up and assured Gaius that if he would say the word, he would at once take ship for Rhodes and bring back the head of "the exile," as he was commonly called. It was this act especially, which made his position no longer one of mere fear but of actual peril, that drove Tiberius to sue for his recall with most urgent prayers, in which he was joined by his mother. And he obtained it, although partly owing to a fortunate chance. Augustus had resolved to come to no decision on the question which was not agreeable to his elder son,[2] who, as it happened, was at the time somewhat at odds with Marcus Lollius, and accordingly ready to lend an ear to his stepfather's prayers. With his consent therefore Tiberius was recalled, but on the understanding that he should take no part or active interest in public affairs.

So he returned in the eighth year after his retirement, with that strong and unwavering confidence in his destiny, which he had conceived from his early years because of omens and predictions.

When Livia was with child with him, and was trying to divine by various omens whether she would bring forth a male, she took an egg from under a setting-hen, and when she had warmed it in her own hand and those of her attendants in turn, a cock with a fine crest was hatched. In his infancy the astrologer Scribonius promised him an illustrious career and even that he would one day be King, but without the crown of royalty, for at that time of course the rule of the Caesars was as yet unheard of. Again, on his first campaign, when he was leading an army through Macedonia into Syria, it chanced that at Philippi the altars consecrated in bygone days by the victorious legions gleamed of their own accord with sudden fires. When later, on his way to Illyricum, he visited the oracle of Geryon near Patavium, and drew a lot which advised him to seek an answer to his inquiries by throwing golden dice into the fount of Aponus, it came to pass

---

[1] In *Gallia Comata*, where Tiberius had been governor. Now Nîmes.
[2] His grandson Gaius, the same mentioned just above, eldest son of his daughter Julia by Agrippa.

that the dice which he threw showed the highest possible number and even to-day those very dice may be seen under the
water. A few days before his recall an eagle, a bird never before seen in Rhodes, perched upon the roof of his house and
the day before he was notified that he might return, as he was
changing his clothes, his tunic appeared to be all on fire.
It was just at this time that he was convinced of the powers of
the astrologer Thrasyllus, whom he had attached to his household as an adept in the art. For, as soon as he caught sight
of the ship, Thrasyllus declared that it brought good news.
This happened at the very moment when Tiberius had made
up his mind to push the man off into the sea as they were
strolling together, believing him a false prophet and too hastily
made the confidant of his secrets, because things were turning out adversely and contrary to his predictions.

On his return to Rome, after introducing his son Drusus
to public life, he at once moved from Pompey's house in the
Carinae district to the gardens of Maecenas on the Esquiline,
where he led a very retired life, merely attending to his personal affairs and exercising no public functions.

When Gaius and Lucius died within three years, he, along
with their brother Marcus Agrippa, was adopted by Augustus,
being himself first compelled to adopt his nephew Germanicus.
From that time on he ceased to act as the head of a family,
or to retain in any particular the privileges which he had given
up. For he neither made gifts nor freed slaves, and he did not
even receive any estate left him by will, or any legacy without
reckoning it as part of his property held under his father.
From this time on nothing was left undone which could add
to his prestige, especially after the disowning and banishment
of Agrippa made it clear that the hope of the succession lay in
him alone.

He was given the tribunicial power for a second term of
three years, the duty of subjugating Germany was assigned
him, and the envoys of the Parthians, after presenting their
instructions to Augustus in Rome, were bidden to appear also
before him in his province. But when the revolt of Illyricum
was reported, he was transferred to the charge of a new war,
the most serious of all foreign wars since those with Carthage,
which he carried on for three years with fifteen legions and a

corresponding force of auxiliaries, amid great difficulties of every kind and the utmost scarcity of supplies. But though he was often recalled, he none the less kept on, for fear that the enemy, who were close at hand and very strong, might assume the offensive if the Romans gave ground. He reaped an ample reward for his perseverance, for he completely subdued and reduced to submission the whole of Illyricum, which is bounded by Italy and the kingdom of Noricum, by Thrace and Macedonia, by the Danube, and by the Adriatic sea.

Circumstances gave this exploit a larger and crowning glory; for it was at just about that time that Quintilius Varus perished with three legions in Germany, and no one doubted that the victorious Germans would have united with the Pannonians, had not Illyricum been subdued first. Consequently a triumph was voted him and many high honors. Some also recommended that he be given the surname of Pannonicus, others of Invictus, others of Pius. Augustus, however, vetoed the surname, reiterating the promise that Tiberius would be satisfied with the one which he would receive at his father's death. Tiberius himself put off the triumph, because the country was in mourning for the disaster to Varus. But he entered the city clad in the purple-bordered toga and crowned with laurel, and mounting a tribunal which had been set up in the Saepta, while the Senate stood alongside, he took his seat beside Augustus between the two Consuls. Having greeted the people from this position, he was escorted to the various temples.

The next year he returned to Germany, and realizing that the disaster to Varus was due to that general's rashness and lack of care, he took no step without the approval of a council. Whereas he had always before been a man of independent judgment and self-reliance, at this time, contrary to his habit, he consulted with many advisers about the conduct of the campaign. He also observed more scrupulous care than usual. When on the point of crossing the Rhine, he reduced all the baggage to a prescribed limit, and would not start without standing on the bank and inspecting the loads of the wagons, to make sure that nothing was taken except what was allowed or necessary. Once on the other side, he adopted the following manner of life: he took his meals sitting on the bare turf,

often passed the night without a tent, and gave all his orders
for the following day, as well as notice of any sudden emergency, in writing; adding the injunction that if any one was
in doubt about any matter, he was to consult him personally
at any hour whatsoever, even of the night.

He required the strictest discipline, reviving bygone meth-
ods of punishment and ignominy, and even degrading the
commander of a legion for sending a few soldiers across the
river to accompany one of his freedmen on a hunting expedition. Although he left very little to fortune and chance he
entered battles with considerably greater confidence whenever
it happened that, as he was working at night, his lamp suddenly and without human agency died down and went out;
trusting, as he used to say, to an omen in which he had great
confidence, since both he and his ancestors had found it trustworthy in all of their campaigns. Yet in the very hour of
victory he narrowly escaped assassination by one of the Bruc-
teri, who got access to him among his attendants, but was detected through his nervousness; whereupon a confession of
his intended crime was wrung from him by torture.

After two years he returned to the city from Germany and
celebrated the triumph which he had postponed, accompanied
also by his generals, for whom he had obtained the triumphal
regalia. And before turning to enter the Capitol, he dismounted from his chariot and fell at the knees of his father,
who was presiding over the ceremonies. He sent Bato, the
leader of the Pannonians, to Ravenna,[1] after presenting him
with rich gifts; thus showing his gratitude to him for allowing
him to escape when he was trapped with his army in a dangerous place. Then he gave a banquet to the people at a thousand
tables, and a largess of three hundred sesterces [2] to every man.
With the proceeds of his spoils he restored and dedicated the
temple of Concord, as well as that of Pollux and Castor, in his
own name and that of his brother.

Since the Consuls caused a law to be passed soon after this
that he should govern the provinces jointly with Augustus and
hold the census with him, he set out for Illyricum on the con-

---

[1] Ordinarily the leaders of the enemy were strangled in the dungeon
at the foot of the Capitoline Hill.

[2] $12.30.

clusion of the lustral ceremonies.[1] But he was at once recalled, and finding Augustus in his last illness but still alive, he spent an entire day with him in private.

I know that it is commonly believed, that when Tiberius left the room after this confidential talk, Augustus was overheard by his chamberlains to say: "Alas for the Roman people, to be ground by jaws that crunch so slowly!" I also am aware that some have written that Augustus so openly and unreservedly disapproved of the sourness of his manner that he sometimes broke off his freer and lighter conversation when Tiberius appeared; but that overcome by his wife's entreaties he did not reject his adoption, or perhaps was even led by selfish considerations, that with such a successor he himself might one day be more regretted. But after all I cannot be led to believe that an Emperor of the utmost prudence and foresight acted without consideration, especially in a matter of so great moment. It is my opinion that after weighing the faults and the merits of Tiberius, he decided that the latter preponderated, especially since he took oath before the people that he was adopting Tiberius for the good of the country, and alludes to him in several letters as a most able general and the sole defense of the Roman people. In illustration of both these points, I append a few extracts from these letters.

"Fare thee well, Tiberius, most charming of men, and success go with you, as you war for me and for the Muses. Fare thee well, most charming and valiant of men and most conscientious of generals, or may I never know happiness."

"I have only praise for the conduct of your summer campaigns, dear Tiberius, and I am sure that no one could have acted with better judgment than you did amid so many difficulties and such apathy of your army. All who were with you agree that the well-known verses could be applied to you:

"One man alone by watchful sight
Our tottering state hath set upright." [2]

---

[1] See *Augustus*.
[2] From Ennius' *Annalium* V, 370, with one word changed by Augustus to make it more applicable in this case.

"It anything comes up that calls for careful thought, or if I am vexed at anything, so help me the God of Truth, I long mightily for my dear Tiberius, and the lines of Homer come to my mind:

> "Let him but bear me company,
>   So prudent, he, and sage,
> And home we'll come, both he and I
>   Though flames about us rage." [1]

"When I hear and read that you are worn out by constant hardships, may the Gods confound me if my own body does not wince in sympathy. So I beseech you to spare yourself, that the news of your illness may not kill your mother and me, and endanger the Roman people in the person of their future ruler."

"It matters not whether I am well or not, if you are not well."

"I pray the Gods to preserve you to us and to grant you good health now and forever, if they do not utterly hate the people of Rome."

Tiberius did not make the death of Augustus public until the young Agrippa had been disposed of. The latter was slain by a Tribune of the soldiers appointed to guard him, who received a letter in which he was bidden to do the deed. But it is not known whether Augustus left this letter when he died, to remove a future source of discord, or whether Livia wrote it herself in the name of her husband; and in the latter case, whether it was with or without the connivance of Tiberius. At all events, when the Tribune reported that he had done his bidding, Tiberius replied that he had given no such order, and that the man must render an account to the Senate. Apparently he was trying to avoid odium at the time, for later his silence consigned the matter to oblivion.

When, however, by virtue of his tribunicial power, he had convened the Senate and had begun to address it, he suddenly groaned aloud, as if overcome by grief, and with the wish that not only his voice, but his life as well might leave him

---

[1] *Iliad*, X, 246. Diomede is speaking of Ulysses, where he asks that he may accompany him as a spy into the Trojan camp.

handed the written speech to his son Drusus to finish. Then bringing in the will of Augustus, he had it read by a freedman, admitting of the signers only such as were of the senatorial order, while the others acknowledged their seals outside the House. The will began thus: "Since a cruel fate has bereft me of my sons Gaius and Lucius, be Tiberius Caesar heir to two-thirds of my estate." These words in themselves added to the suspicion of those who believed that he had named Tiberius his successor from necessity rather than from choice, since he allowed himself to write such a preamble.

Though Tiberius did not hesitate at once to assume and to exercise the imperial authority, surrounding himself with a guard of soldiers, that is, with the actual power and the out-ward sign of sovereignty, yet he long refused the title, at one time with barefaced hypocrisy upbraiding his friends who urged him to accept it, saying that they did not realize what a monster the empire was, at another by evasive answers and calculating hesitancy keeping the Senators in suspense when they implored him to yield, and fell at his feet. Finally, some lost patience, and one man cried out in the confusion: "Let him take it or leave it." Another openly voiced the taunt that others were slow in doing what they promised, but that he was slow to promise what he was already doing. At last, as though on compulsion, and complaining that a wretched and burdensome slavery was being forced upon him, he accepted the empire, but in such fashion as to suggest the hope that he would one day lay it down. His own words are: "Until I come to the time when it may seem right to you to grant an old man some repose."

The cause of his hesitation was fear of the dangers which threatened him on every hand, and often led him to say that he was "holding a wolf by the ears." [1] For a slave of Agrippa, Clemens by name, had collected a band of no mean size to avenge his master; Lucius Scribonius Libo, one of the nobles, was secretly plotting a revolution; and a mutiny of the sol-diers broke out in two places, Illyricum and Germany. Both armies demanded numerous special privileges, particularly, that they should receive the same pay as the praetorian sol-

---

[1] A Greek proverb.

diers. The army in Germany was, besides, reluctant to accept
an Emperor who was not its own choice, and with the greatest
urgency besought Germanicus, their commander at the time,
to assume the purple, in spite of his positive refusal. It was
fear of this possibility in particular which led him to request
the Senate to assign him any part in the administration that
it might please them, saying that no one man could bear the
whole burden without a colleague, or even several colleagues.
He also feigned ill-health, to induce Germanicus to wait with
more patience for a speedy succession, or at least for a share
in the sovereignty. The mutinies were put down, and he also
got Clemens into his power, outwitting him by stratagem.
Not until his second year did he finally arraign Libo in the
Senate, fearing to take any severe measures before his power
was secure, being content in the meantime with taking precautions for his own security. Thus when Libo was offering
sacrifice with him among the Pontiffs, instead of the usual
knife he ordered one of lead to be given him; and when he
asked for a private interview, Tiberius would not grant it
except with his son Drusus present, and as long as the conference lasted he held fast to Libo's right arm, under pre-
tence of leaning on it as they walked together.

Once relieved of fear, he at first played a most unassuming part, almost humbler than that of a private citizen. Of
many high honors he accepted only a few of the more modest.
He barely consented to allow his birthday, which came at
the time of the Plebeian games in the Circus, to be recognized
by the addition of a single two-horse chariot. He forbade the
voting of temples, flamens, and priests in his honor, and even
the setting up of statues and busts without his permission;
and this he gave only with the understanding that they were
not to be placed among the likenesses of the Gods, but among
the adornments of the temples. He would not allow an oath
to be taken ratifying his acts, nor the name Tiberius to be
given to the month of September, or that of Livia to October.
He also declined the forename Imperator, the surname of
Father of his Country, and the placing of the civic crown [1]
at his door. He did not even use the title of Augustus in any

---

[1] See *Julius*.

letters except those to Kings and potentates, although it was
his by inheritance. He held but three consulships after becoming Emperor: one for a few days, a second for three
months, and a third, during his absence from the city, until
the Ides of May.

He so loathed flattery that he would not allow any Senator
to approach his litter, either to pay his respects or on business,
and when an ex-consul in apologizing to him attempted to embrace his knees, he drew back in such haste that he fell over
backward. In fact, if any one in conversation or in a set speech
spoke of him in too flattering terms, he did not hesitate to
interrupt him, to take him to task, and to correct his language
on the spot. Being once called "Lord," [1] he warned the speaker
not to address him again in an insulting fashion. When another
spoke of his "sacred duties," and still another said that he
appeared before the Senate "by the Emperor's authority,"
he forced them to change their language, substituting "advice" for "authority" and "laborious" for "sacred."

More than that, he was self-contained and patient in the
face of abuse and slander, and of lampoons on himself and his
family, often asserting that in a free country there should be
free speech and free thought. When the Senate on one occasion demanded that cognizance be taken of such offenses and
those guilty of them, he said: "We have not enough spare
time to warrant involving ourselves in more affairs. If you
open this loophole you will find no time for any other business. It will be an excuse for laying everybody's quarrels before you." A most unassuming remark of his in the Senate
is also a matter of record: "If so and so criticizes me I shall
take care to render an account of my acts and words; if he
persist, I shall return him in kind."

All this was the more noteworthy, because in addressing
and in paying his respects to the Senators individually and
as a body he himself almost exceeded the requirements of
courtesy. In a disagreement with Quintius Haterius in the
House, he said: "I crave your pardon, if in my capacity as
Senator I use too free language in opposing you." Then addressing the whole body: "I say now and have often said

---

[1] See *Augustus*.

before, Fathers of the Senate, that a well-disposed and helpful prince, to whom you have given such great and unrestrained power, ought to be the servant of the Senate, often of the citizens as a whole, and sometimes of individuals. I do not regret my words, but I have looked upon you as kind, just, and indulgent masters,[1] and still so regard you."

He even introduced a semblance of free government by maintaining the ancient dignity and powers of the Senate and the magistrates. For there was no matter of public or private business so small or so great that he did not lay it before the Senators, consulting them about revenues and monopolies,[2] constructing and restoring public buildings, even about levying and disbanding the soldiers, and the disposal of the legionaries and auxiliaries; finally about the extension of military commands and appointments to the conduct of wars, and the form and content of his replies to the letters of Kings. He forced the commander of a troop of horse, when charged with violence and robbery, to plead his cause before the Senate. He always entered the House alone. Once when he was taken there in a litter because of illness he dismissed his attendants at the door.

When certain decrees were passed contrary to his expressed opinion, he did not even remonstrate. Although he declared that those who were elected to office ought to remain in the city and give personal attention to their duties, a Praetor-elect obtained permission to travel abroad with the privileges of an Ambassador. On another occasion when he recommended that the people of Trebia be allowed to use, in making a road, a sum of money which had been left them for the construction of a new theater, he could not prevent the wish of the testator from being carried out. Once, when the Senate was divided and the act might pass by the difference of a few votes he went over to the side of the minority, but not a man followed him.

Other business as well was done solely through the magistrates and the ordinary process of law, while the importance of the Consuls was so great that certain envoys from Africa

---

[1] Using the term by which a slave addressed his owner.
[2] Grants to an individual or a company of an exclusive right to sell certain commodities.

presented themselves before them with the complaint that they could not have their affairs attended to by Caesar, to whom they had been sent. And no wonder: since it was observed that he himself actually arose in the presence of the Consuls, and made way for them on the street.

He rebuked some ex-consuls in command of armies, because they did not write their reports to the Senate, and for referring to him the award of some military prizes,[1] as if they had not themselves the right to bestow everything of the kind. He highly complimented a Praetor, because on entering upon his office he had revived the custom of eulogizing his ancestors before the people. He attended the obsequies of certain distinguished men, even going to the funeral-pyre.

He showed equal modesty towards persons of lower rank and in matters of less moment. When he had summoned the magistrates of Rhodes, because they had written him letters on public business without the concluding formula,[2] he uttered not a word of censure, but merely dismissed them with orders to supply the omission. The grammarian Diogenes, who used to lecture every Sabbath,[3] at Rhodes, would not admit Tiberius when he came to hear him on a different day, but sent a message by a common slave of his, putting him off to the seventh day. When this man waited before the Emperor's door at Rome to pay his respects, Tiberius took no further revenge than to bid him return seven years later. To the governors who recommended burdensome taxes for his provinces, he wrote in answer that it was the part of a good shepherd to shear his flock, not skin it.

Little by little he unmasked the ruler, and although for some time his conduct was variable, yet he more often showed himself kindly and devoted to the public weal. His intervention too was at first limited to the prevention of abuses. Thus he revoked some regulations of the Senate and sometimes offered the magistrates his services as adviser, when they sat in judgment on the tribunal, taking his place beside them or

---

[1] Compare with Augustus' chary bestowal of military prizes.

[2] Which consisted of prayers for the Emperor's welfare.

[3] Calling the seventh day of the week (Saturday) by the Jewish term "Sabbath" seems to have been common.

opposite them at one end of the platform; and if it was ru-
mored that any of the accused were being acquitted through
influence, he would suddenly appear, and either from the floor
or from the judge's tribunal remind the jurors of the laws and
of their oath, as well as of the nature of the crime on which
they were sitting in judgment. Moreover, if the public morals
were in any way affected by laziness or bad habits he undertook to reform them.

He reduced the cost of the games and shows by cutting
down the pay of the actors and limiting the pairs of gladiators
to a fixed number. Complaining bitterly that the prices of
Corinthian bronze vessels had risen to an immense figure and
that three mullets [1] had been sold for thirty thousand sesterces [2] he proposed that a limit be set to household furniture
and that the prices in the market should be regulated each
year at the discretion of the Senate. And the Aediles were
instructed to put such restrictions on cook-shops and eating-
houses as not to allow even pastry to be exposed for sale.
Furthermore, to encourage general frugality by his personal
example, he often served at formal dinners meats left over
from the day before and partly consumed, or the half of a
boar, declaring that it had all the qualities of a whole one.

He issued an edict forbidding general kissing, as well as the
exchange of New Year's gifts [3] after the Kalends of January.
It was his custom to return a gift four times the value of the
one received, and in person; but annoyed at being interrupted
all through the month by those who did not have access to
him on the holiday, he did not continue it.

He revived the custom of our forefathers, that in the absence of a public prosecutor wives of ill-repute be punished
according to the decision of a council of their relatives. He
absolved a Roman Knight from his oath and allowed him to
put away his wife, who was taken in adultery with her son-
in-law, even though he had previously sworn that he would
never divorce her. Notorious women had begun to make an
open profession of prostitution, to avoid the punishment of

---

[1] A fish much esteemed as food.
[2] $1,230.00.
[3] Given for good luck.

the laws by giving up the privileges and rank of matrons.[1] while the most profligate young men of both orders voluntarily incurred degradation from their rank, so as not to be prevented by the decree of the Senate from appearing on the stage and in the arena. All such men and women he punished with exile, to prevent any one from shielding himself by such a device. He deprived a Senator of his broad stripe on learning that he had moved into his gardens just before the Kalends of July,[2] with the design of renting a house in the city at a lower figure after that date. He deposed another from his quaestorship, because he had taken a wife the day before casting lots and divorced her the day after.

He abolished foreign cults, especially the Egyptian and the Jewish rites, compelling all who were addicted to such superstitions to burn their religious vestments and all their para· phernalia. Those of the Jews who were of military age he assigned to provinces of less healthy climate, ostensibly to serve in the army. Others of the same race or of similar beliefs he banished from the city, on pain of slavery for life if they did not obey. He banished the astrologers as well, but pardoned such as begged for indulgence and promised to give up their art.

He gave special attention to securing the public peace against lawless persons, prowling brigands, and those who were disaffected to the government. He stationed garrisons of soldiers nearer together than before throughout Italy, while at Rome he established a camp for the barracks of the praetorian cohorts, which before that time had been quartered in isolated groups in divers lodging houses.

He took great pains to prevent outbreaks of the populace and punished such as occurred with the utmost severity. When a quarrel in the theater ended in bloodshed, he banished the leaders of the factions, as well as the actors who were the cause of the dissension; and no entreaties of the people could ever induce him to recall them. When the populace of Pollentia would not allow the body of a Chief-Cen-

---

[1] Augustus had made the punishments for adultery very severe. To escape these some matrons sacrificed their rights and responsibilities by registering with the Aediles as prostitutes.

[2] July 1st was the day for renewing rents; "moving-day."

turion to be taken from the Forum until their violence had
extorted money from his heirs for a gladiatorial show, he dispatched one cohort from the city and another from the kingdom of Cottius, concealing the reason for the move, sent them
into the city by different gates, suddenly revealing their arms
and sounding their trumpets, and consigned the greater part
of the populace and of the Decurions [1] to life imprisonment.
He abolished the customary right of asylum [2] in all parts of
the empire. Because the people of Cyzicus ventured to commit
acts of special lawlessness against Roman citizens, he took
from them the freedom which they had earned in the war
with Mithridates.

He undertook no campaign after his accession, but quelled
outbreaks of the enemy through his generals; and even this
he did only reluctantly and of necessity. Such Kings as
disaffected and objects of his suspicion he held in check
rather by threats and remonstrances than by force; some he
lured to Rome by flattering promises and detained there,
such as Marobodus the German, Rhascuporis the Thracian,
and Archelaus of Cappadocia, whose realm he also reduced
to the form of a province.

For two whole years after becoming Emperor he did not
set foot outside the gates. After that he went nowhere except
to the neighboring towns, at farthest to Antium,[3] and even
that very seldom and for a few days at a time. Yet he often
gave out that he would visit the provinces too and the armies,
and nearly every year he made preparations for a journey by
chartering carriages and arranging for supplies in the free
towns and colonies. Finally he allowed vows to be put up
for his voyage and return, so that at last everybody jokingly
gave him the name of Callippides, who was proverbial among
the Greeks for running without getting ahead a cubit's
length.[4]

---

[1] Members of the local Senate.

[2] Criminals frequently took refuge in temples or other holy places
where all were immune from arrest.

[3] A favorite resort of the Emperors on the coast about 30 miles from
Rome. The statue known as the Apollo Belvedere was found in its
ruins.

[4] This reference is to an Athenian clown who imitated the movements
of running but remained in the same spot.

But after being bereft of both his sons,—Germanicus [1] had died in Syria and Drusus [2] at Rome,—he retired to Campania, and almost every one firmly believed and openly declared that he would never come back, but would soon die there. And both predictions were all but fulfilled; for he did not return again to Rome, and it chanced a few days later that as he was dining near Tarracina in a villa called the Grotto, many huge rocks fell from the ceiling and crushed a number of the guests and servants, while the Emperor himself had a narrow escape.

After traversing Campania and dedicating the Capitolium at Capua and a temple to Augustus at Nola, which was the pretext he had given for his journey, he went to Capri, particularly attracted to that island because it was accessible by only one small beach, being everywhere else girt with sheer cliffs of great height and by deep water. But he was at once recalled by the constant entreaties of the people, because of a disaster at Fidenae, where more than twenty thousand spectators had perished through the collapse of the amphitheater during a gladiatorial show. So he crossed to the mainland and made himself accessible to all, the more willingly because he had given orders on leaving the city that no one was to disturb him, and during the whole trip had repulsed those who tried to approach him.

Then returning to the island, he utterly neglected the conduct of state affairs, from that time on never filling the vacancies in the Decuries of the Knights, nor changing the Tribunes of the soldiers and Prefects or the Governors of any of his provinces. He left Spain and Syria without consular Governors for several years, suffered Armenia to be overrun by the Parthians, Moesia to be laid waste by the Dacians and Sarmatians, and the Gallic provinces by the Germans, to the great dishonor of the empire and no less to its danger.

---

[1] Adopted son of Tiberius, natural son of Drusus, Tiberius' brother. Tiberius was suspected of having caused Germanicus, a general greatly loved by the people, to be poisoned. For more of Germanicus see below and *Caligula*.

[2] Drusus (Tiberius' own son by his first wife Vipsania) was also poisoned, by his own wife and her paramour Sejanus, Tiberius' minister, who aspired to supreme power.

Moreover, having gained the license of privacy, and being as it were out of sight of the citizens, he at last gave free rein at once to all the vices which he had for a long time ill concealed. Of these I shall give a detailed account from the beginning. Even at the outset of his military career his excessive love of wine gave him the name of Biberius, instead of Tiberius, Caldius for Claudius, and Mero for Nero.[1] Later, when Emperor and at the very time that he was busy correcting the public morals, he spent a night and two whole days feasting and drinking with Pomponius Flaccus and Lucius Piso, immediately afterward making the one Governor of the province of Syria and the other Prefect of the city, and even declaring in their commissions that they were the most agreeable of friends, who could always be counted on. He had a dinner given him by Cestius Gallus, a lustful and prodigal old man, who had once been degraded by Augustus and whom he had himself rebuked a few days before in the Senate, making the condition that Cestius should change or omit none of his usual customs, and that nude girls should wait upon them at table. He gave a very obscure candidate for the quaestorship preference over men of the noblest families, because at the Emperor's challenge he had drained an amphora [2] of wine at a banquet. He paid Asellius Sabinus two hundred thousand sesterces [3] for a dialogue, in which he had introduced a contest of a mushroom, a fig-pecker, an oyster and a thrush. He established a new office, Master of the Imperial Pleasures, assigning it to Titus Caesonius Priscus, a Roman Knight.

In his retreat at Capri there was a room devised by him dedicated to the most arcane lusts. Here he had assembled from all quarters girls and perverts, whom he called *Spintriae*, who invented monstrous feats of lubricity, and defiled one another before him, interlaced in series of threes, in order to inflame his feeble appetite. He also had several other rooms variously adapted to his lusts, decorated with paintings and bas-reliefs depicting scenes of the most lascivious

---

[1] Coined from *bibo*, to drink, *calidus*, hot, and *merum*, strong wine
[2] An *amphora* held about seven gallons!
[3] $8,200.00.

character, and supplied with the books of Elephantis,[1] that no one should lack a model for the execution of any lustful act he was ordered to perform. Different places in the groves and woods he also consecrated to venery, so that young people like Pans and Nymphs lay strewn over hill and valley. People, punning on the name of the island, openly and commonly called him *capret*.

Still more flagrant and brazen was another sort of infamy which he practiced, one that may scarce be told, much less believed. He taught children of the most tender years, whom he called his *little fishes*, to play between his legs while he was in his bath. Those which had not yet been weaned, but were strong and hearty, he set at fellatio, the sort of sport best adapted to his inclination and age. When a painting by Parrhasius in which Atalanta was represented as doing as much to Meleager was willed him with the provision that if the subject was offensive to him he was to receive a million sesterces[2] instead, he not only chose the picture, but hung it in his bedroom as though it were a sacred object. It is also said that one day during a sacrifice he was so smitten by the beauty of a boy who swung a censer that he was hardly able to wait till the rites were over before taking him aside and abusing him as well as his brother who was playing the flute; and that soon afterwards he had the legs of both of them broken because they were reproaching each other with the disgrace.

How grossly he was in the habit of abusing women even of high birth is very clearly shown by the death of a certain Mallonia. When she was brought to his bed and most resolutely refused to submit to his unnatural lust, he turned her over to the informers. Even when she was on trial he did not cease to call out and ask her "whether she was not sorry," until she left the court, hastened home and stabbed herself, having openly upbraided the vile old lecher with his filthy and beastly mouth. Hence a stigma put upon him at the next plays in an Atellan farce was received with great applause and became current, that "the old goat lapped the caprets."

---

[1] A Greek poetess of amatory verse, cited by Martial. She is supposed to have written a book on postures.

[2] $41,000.00.

He was so niggardly and covetous that he never allowed the companions of his foreign tours and campaigns a salary, but merely their keep. Only once did he treat them liberally, and then through the generosity of his stepfather, when he formed three classes according to each man's rank and gave to the first six hundred thousand sesterces, to the second four hundred thousand, and to the third, two hundred thousand, which last class he called not friends, but his Greeks.[1]

While Emperor he constructed no magnificent public works, for the only ones which he undertook, the temple of Augustus and the restoration of Pompey's theater, he left, after so many years, unfinished. He gave no public shows at all, and very seldom attended those given by others, for fear that some request would be made of him, especially after he was forced to buy the freedom of a comic actor named Actius. Having relieved the poverty of a few Senators, he avoided the necessity of further aid by declaring that he would help no others unless they proved to the Senate that there were legitimate causes for their condition. Therefore diffidence and a sense of shame kept many from applying, among them Hortalus, grandson of Quintus Hortensius the orator, who though of very limited means had begotten four children with the encouragement of Augustus.

He showed generosity to the public in but two instances, once when he offered to lend a hundred million sesterces without interest for a period of three years, and again when he made good the losses of some owners of blocks of houses on the Caelian Mount, which had burned down. The first was forced upon him by the clamor of the people for help in a time of great financial stress, after he had failed to relieve the situation by a decree of the Senate, providing that the money-lenders should advance two-thirds of their capital on land, and that debtors should pay at once the same proportion of their indebtedness; and yet the thing was not put through. The second also was to relieve a condition of great hardship. Yet he made so much of his liberality in the latter case, that he had the name of the Caelian changed to the

---

[1] There is more about them later in this section.

Augustan Mount.[1] After he had doubled the legacies provided for in the will of Augustus, he never gave largess to the soldiers, with the exception of a thousand denarii [2] to each of the praetorians, for not taking sides with Sejanus, and some presents to the legions in Syria, because they alone had consecrated no image of Sejanus among their standards. He also very rarely allowed veteran soldiers their discharge, having an eye to their death from years, and a saving of money through their death. Nor did he ever relieve the provinces by any act of liberality, except Asia, when some cities had been destroyed by an earthquake.

Presently, as time went on, he even resorted to plunder. It is certain that he drove Gnaeus Lentulus Augur, a man of great wealth, to take his own life through fear and mental anxiety, and to make the Emperor his sole heir; and that Lepida, too, a woman of high birth, was condemned to death to gratify Quirinius, an opulent and childless ex-consul, who had divorced her after twenty years of wedded life, accusing her of an attempt to poison him many years before. Besides, as is well known, leading men of the Spanish and Gallic provinces, as well as of Syria and Greece, had their estates confiscated upon such despicably trifling and shameless pretenses, that against some of them no other charge was preferred, than that they had a part of their personal property in ready money; [3] also that many states and individuals were deprived of immunities of long standing, and of the right of working mines and collecting revenues; and that Vonones, King of the Parthians, who on being dethroned by his subjects had taken refuge at Antioch with a vast treasure, in the belief that he was putting himself under the protection of the Roman people, was treacherously despoiled and put to death.

He first showed his hatred of his kindred in the case of his

---

[1] Tacitus (*Annals* IV, 64) states this was done by the Senate, because the statue of Tiberius remained uninjured in the midst of the burned district.

[2] About $150.00.

[3] Possibly under pretense that they were hoarding money for revolutionary purposes. Caesar had limited the cash to be held by any one person in Italy to 60,000 sesterces, ($2,460.00).

brother Drusus, producing a letter of his, in which Drusus
discussed with him the question of compelling Augustus to
restore the Republic. And then he turned against the rest.
So far from showing any courtesy or kindness to his wife
Julia, after her banishment, which is the least that one might
expect,[1] although her father's order had merely confined her
to one town, he would not allow her even to leave her house
or enjoy the society of mankind. Nay more, he even deprived
her of the allowance granted her by her father and of her
yearly income, under color of observance of the common law,
because in his will Augustus had made no provision for these
on her behalf. Being harassed by his mother Livia, who
claimed an equal share of power with him, he shunned frequent meetings with her and long and confidential conversations, to avoid the appearance of being guided by her advice; though in point of fact he was wont every now and
then to need and to follow it. He was greatly offended too
by a decree of the Senate, providing that "son of Livia,"
as well as "son of Augustus" should be written in his honorary
inscriptions. For this reason he would not suffer her to be
named "Parent of her Country," nor to receive any conspicuous public honor. More than that, he often warned her
not to meddle with affairs of importance and unbecoming a
woman, especially after he learned that at a fire near the
temple of Vesta she had been present in person, and urged
the people and soldiers to greater efforts, as had been her
way while her husband was alive.

Afterwards he reached the point of open enmity, and the
reason, they say, was this. On her urging him again and
again to appoint among the jurors a man who had been made
a citizen, he declared that he would do it only on condition
that she would allow an entry to be made in the official list
that it was forced upon him by his mother. Then Livia, in a
rage, drew from a secret place and read some old letters
written to her by Augustus with regard to the moroseness
and stubbornness of Tiberius' disposition. He in turn was so
put out that these had been preserved so long and were
thrown up at him in such a spiteful spirit, that some think

---

[1] His earlier conduct to Julia is not so unkind.

this was the very strongest of the reasons for his retirement. At all events, during all the three years that she lived after he left Rome he saw her but once, and then only one day, for a very few hours; and when shortly after that she fell ill, he took no trouble to visit her. When she died, and after a delay of several days, during which he held out hope of his coming, had at last been buried because the condition of the corpse made it necessary, he forbade her deification, alleging that he was acting according to her own instructions. He further disregarded the provisions of her will, and within a short time caused the downfall of all her friends and intimates, even of those to whom she had on her deathbed intrusted the care of her obsequies, actually condemning one of them, and that a man of equestrian rank, to the treadmill.

He had a father's affection neither for his own son Drusus nor his adopted son Germanicus, being exasperated at the former's vices. Drusus did, in fact, lead a somewhat loose and dissolute life. Therefore, even when he died, Tiberius was not greatly affected, but almost immediately after the funeral returned to his usual routine, forbidding a longer period of mourning. Nay, more, when a deputation from Ilium offered him somewhat belated condolences, he replied with a smile, as if the memory of his bereavement had faded from his mind, that they, too, had his sympathy for the loss of their eminent fellow-citizen Hector. As to Germanicus, he was so far from appreciating him that he made light of his illustrious deeds as unimportant, and railed at his brilliant victories as ruinous to his country. He even made complaint in the Senate when Germanicus, on the occasion of a sudden and terrible famine, went to Alexandria without consulting him. It is even believed that he caused his death at the hands of Gnaeus Piso, Governor of Syria, and some think that when Piso was tried on that charge, he would have produced his instructions, had not Tiberius caused them to be taken from him when Piso privately showed them, and the man himself to be put to death. Because of this the words, "Give us back Germanicus," were posted in many places, and shouted at night all over the city. And Tiberius afterwards strengthened this suspicion by cruelly abusing the wife and children of Germanicus as well.

When his daughter-in-law Agrippina was somewhat outspoken in her complaints after her husband's death, he took
her by the hand and quoted a Greek verse, meaning "Because you are not Empress, dear daughter, do you think a
wrong is done you?" After that he never deigned to hold
any conversation with her. Upon her refusing once at dinner
to taste an apple which he handed her, he ceased inviting
her to his table, pretending that she had charged him with a
design to poison her, whereas the whole was a contrivance of
his own: he was to offer the fruit, and she be privately cau-
tioned against eating what contained certain death. At last,
falsely charging her with a desire to take refuge, now at the
statue of Augustus and now with the armies, he exiled her
to Pandateria, and when she loaded him with reproaches, he
had her beaten by a Centurion until one of her eyes was
destroyed. Again, when she resolved to die of starvation, he
had her mouth pried open and food crammed into it. Worst
of all, when she persisted in her resolution and so perished,
he assailed her memory with the basest slanders, persuading
the Senate to add her birthday to the days of ill omen, and
actually taking credit to himself for not having had her
strangled and her body cast out on the Stairs of Mourning.
He even allowed a decree to be passed in recognition of this
remarkable clemency, in which thanks were offered him and
a golden gift was consecrated to Jupiter of the Capitol.

By Germanicus he had three grandsons, Nero, Drusus, and
Gaius, and by Drusus one, called Tiberius. Bereft of his
own children, he recommended Nero and Drusus, the elder
sons of Germanicus, to the Senate, and celebrated the day
when each of them came to his majority by giving largess
to the Commons. But as soon as he learned that at the beginning of the year vows were being put up for their safety also,
he referred the matter to the Senate, saying that such honors
ought to be conferred only on those of tried character and
mature years. By revealing his true feelings towards them
from that time on, he exposed them to accusations from all
quarters, and after resorting to various tricks to rouse them
to rail at him, and seeing to it that they were betrayed when
they did so, he brought most bitter charges against them
both in writing. And when they had in consequence been

pronounced public enemies, he starved them to death, Nero on the island of Pontia and Drusus in a lower room of the Palace. It is thought that Nero was forced to take his own life, since an executioner, who pretended that he came by authority of the Senate, showed him the noose and hooks. It is also thought that Drusus was so tortured by hunger that he tried to eat the stuffing of his mattress. The remains of both were so scattered that it was with difficulty that they could ever be collected.

In addition to his old friends and intimates, he had asked for twenty of the leading men of the State as advisers on public affairs. Of all these he spared hardly two or three; the others he destroyed on one pretext or another, including Aelius Sejanus, whose downfall involved the death of many others. This man he had advanced to the highest power, not so much from regard for him, as that he might through his services and wiles destroy the children of Germanicus and secure the succession for his own grandson, the child of his son Drusus.

He was not a whit milder towards his Greek companions, in whose society he took special pleasure. When one Xeno was holding forth in somewhat far-fetched phrases, he asked him what dialect that was which was so affected, and on Xeno's replying that it was Doric, he banished him to Cinaria, believing that he was being taunted with his old-time exile inasmuch as the Rhodians spoke Doric. He had the habit too, of putting questions at dinner suggested by his daily reading, and learning that the grammarian Seleucus inquired of the imperial attendants what authors Tiberius was reading and so came primed, he at first banished the offender from his society, and later even forced him to commit suicide.

His cruel, and cold-blooded character was not completely hidden even in his boyhood. His teacher of rhetoric, Theodorus of Gadara, seems first to have had the insight to detect it, and to have characterized it very aptly, since in taking him to task he would now and then call him "mud mixed with blood." But it grew still more noticeable after he became Emperor, even at the beginning, when he was still courting popularity by a show of moderation. When a funeral was passing by and a jester called aloud to the corpse to let Augustus know that the legacies which he had left to the people were not yet being paid, Tiberius had the man haled before him, ordered that he receive what was due him and then be put to death, and bade him go tell the truth to his father. Shortly afterwards, when a Roman knight called Pompeius stoutly opposed some action in the Senate, Tiberius threatened him with imprisonment, declaring that from a Pompeius he would make of him a Pompeian, punning cruelly on the man's name and the fate of the old party.

It was at about this time that a Praetor asked him whether he should have the courts convened to consider cases of treason. To this he replied that the laws must be enforced, and he did enforce them most rigorously. One man had removed the head from a statue of Augustus, to substitute that of another. The case was tried in the Senate, and since the evidence was conflicting, the witnesses were examined by torture. After the defendant had been condemned, this kind of accusation gradually went so far that even such acts as these were regarded as capital crimes: to beat a slave near a statue of Augustus, or to change one's clothes there; to carry a ring or coin stamped with his image into a privy or a brothel, or to criticize any word or act of his. Finally, a man was put to death merely for allowing an honor to be voted him in his native town on the same day that honors had previously been voted to Augustus.

He did so many other cruel and savage deeds under the guise of strictness and improvement of the public morals, but in reality rather to gratify his natural instincts, that some resorted to verses to express their detestation of the present ills and a warning against those to come:

"Obdurate wretch! too fierce, too fell to move
The least kind yearnings of a mother's love!

No Knight are you, as having no estate;
Will you hear all? Yours is an exile's fate.

No more the happy Golden Age we see;
The Iron's come, and sure to last with thee.

Instead of wine he thirsted for before
He wallows now in floods of human gore.

Reflect, ye Romans, on the dreadful times,
Made such by Marius, and by Sulla's crimes.

Reflect how Antony's ambitious rage
Twice scarred with horror a distracted age.

And say, Alas! Rome's blood in streams will flow
When banished miscreants rule this world below."

These at first he wished to be taken as the work of those who
were impatient of his reforms, voicing not so much their real
feelings as their anger and vexation. And he used to say from
time to time: "Let them hate me, provided they respect my
conduct." Later he himself proved them only too true and un‑
erring.

A few days after he reached Capri and was by himself, a
fisherman appeared unexpectedly and offered him a huge mul‑
let; whereupon in his alarm that the man had clambered up
to him from the back of the island over rough and pathless
rocks, he had the poor fellow's face scrubbed with the fish.
And because in the midst of his torture the man thanked his
stars that he had not given the Emperor an enormous crab
that he had caught, Tiberius had his face torn with the crab
also. He punished a soldier of the praetorian guard with death
for having stolen a peacock from his preserves. When the litter
in which he was making a trip was stopped by brambles, he
had the man who went ahead to clear the way, a Centurion
of the first cohorts, stretched out on the ground and flogged
half to death.

Presently he broke out into every form of cruelty, for which
he never lacked occasion, venting it on the friends and even
the acquaintances, first of his mother, then of his grandsons
and granddaughter, and finally of Sejanus. After the death of
Sejanus he was more cruel than ever, which showed that his
favorite was not wont to egg him on, but on the contrary gave
him the opportunities which he himself desired. Yet in a brief
and sketchy autobiography which he composed he had the

audacity to write that he had punished Sejanus because he found him venting his hatred on the children of his son Germanicus. Whereas in fact he had himself put one of them to death after he had begun to suspect Sejanus, and another after the latter's downfall.

It is a long story to run through his acts of cruelty in detail. It will be enough to mention the forms which they took, as samples of his barbarity. Not a day passed without an execution, not even days that were sacred and holy, for he put some to death even on New Year's day. Many were accused and condemned with their children and even by their children. The relatives of the victims were forbidden to mourn for them. Special rewards were voted the accusers and sometimes even the witnesses. The word of no informer was doubted. Every crime was treated as capital, even the utterance of a few simple words. A poet was charged with having slandered Agamemnon in a tragedy, and a writer of history of having called Brutus and Cassius the last of the Romans. The writers were at once put to death and their works destroyed, although they had been read with approval in public some years before in the presence of Augustus himself. Some of those who were consigned to prison were denied not only the consolation of reading, but even the privilege of conversing and talking together. Of those who were cited to plead their causes some opened their veins at home, feeling sure of being condemned and wishing to avoid annoyance and humiliation, while others drank poison in full view of the Senate. Yet the wounds of the former were bandaged and they were hurried half-dead, but still quivering, to the prison. Every one of those who were executed was thrown out upon the Stairs of Mourning and dragged to the Tiber with hooks, as many as twenty being so treated in a single day, including women and children. Since ancient usage made it impious to strangle maidens, young girls were first violated by the executioner and then strangled. Those who wished to die were forced to live; for he thought death so light a punishment that when he heard that one of the accused, Carnulus by name, had anticipated his execution, he cried: "Carnulus has given me the slip"; and when he was inspecting the prisons and a man begged for a speedy death, he replied: "I have not yet become your friend." An ex-consul has recorded in his Annals that once at a large dinner-party, at which the writer himself was present, Tiberius was suddenly asked in a loud voice by one of the dwarfs that stood beside the table among the jesters why Paconius, who was charged with treason, remained so long alive; and that the Emperor at the time chided him for his saucy tongue, but a few days later wrote to the Senate to decide as soon as possible about the execution of Paconius.

He increased his cruelty and carried it to greater lengths, exasperated by what he learned about the death of his son Drusus. At first supposing that he had died of disease, due to his bad habits, on finally learning that he had been poisoned by the treachery of his wife Livilla and Sejanus, there was no one whom Tiberius spared from torment and death. Indeed, he gave himself up so utterly for whole days to the investigation of this affair and was so wrapped up in it, that when he was told of the arrival of a host of his from Rhodes, whom he had invited to Rome in a friendly letter, he had him put to the torture at once, supposing that some one had come whose testimony was important for the case. On discovering his mistake, he even had the man put to death, to keep him from giving publicity to the wrong done him.

At Capri they still point out the scene of his executions, from which he used to order that those who had been condemned after long and exquisite tortures be cast headlong into the sea before his eyes, while a band of marines waited below for the bodies and broke their bones with boathooks and oars, to prevent any breath of life from remaining in them. Among various forms of torture he had devised this one: he would trick men into loading themselves with copious draughts of wine, and then on a sudden tying up their private parts, would torment them at the same time by the torture of the cords and of the stoppage of their water. And had not death prevented him, and Thrasyllus, purposely it is said, induced him to put off some things through hope of a longer life, it is believed that still more would have perished, and that he would not even have spared the rest of his grandsons; for he had his suspicions of Gaius and detested Tiberius as the fruit of adultery. And this is highly probable, for he used at times to call Priam happy, because he had outlived all his kindred.

Many things go to show, not only how hated and execrable he was all this time, but also that he lived a life of extreme fear and was even exposed to insult. He forbade any one to consult soothsayers secretly and without witnesses. Indeed, he even attempted to do away with the oracles near the city, but forbore through terror at the divine power of the Praenestine Lots; for though he had them sealed up in a chest and brought to Rome, yet they were not to be found in it until the box was taken back to the temple. Not daring to lose sight of one or two ex-consuls to whom he had assigned provinces he detained them at Rome so long he finally appointed their successors several years later without their having left the city. In the meantime they retained their titles, and he even continued to assign them numerous commissions, to execute through their deputies and assistants.

After the exile of his daughter-in-law and grandchildren he never moved them anywhere except in fetters and in a tightly closed litter, while a guard of soldiers kept any who met them on the road from looking at them or even from stopping as they went by.

When Sejanus was plotting revolution, although he saw the man's birthday publicly celebrated and his golden statues honored everywhere, yet it was with difficulty that he at last overthrew him, rather by craft and deceit than by his imperial authority. First of all, to remove him from his person under color of showing him honor, he chose him as his colleague in a fifth consulship, which, with this very end in view, he assumed after a long interval while absent from the city. Then beguiling him with hope of marriage into the imperial family and of the tribunicial power, he accused him when he least expected it in a shameful and pitiable speech, begging the Senators among other things to send one of the Consuls [1] to bring him, a lonely old man, into their presence under military protection. Even then distrustful and fearful of an outbreak, he had given orders that his grandson Drusus, whom he still kept imprisoned in Rome, should be set free, if occasion demanded, and made commander-in-chief. He even got ships ready and thought of flight to some of the legions, constantly

---

[1] This must mean one of the substitute consuls who assumed the honor for part of the year.

watching from a high cliff for the signals which he had ordered to be raised afar off as each step was taken, for fear the messengers should be delayed. But even when the conspiracy of Sejanus was crushed, he was no whit more confident or courageous, but for the next nine months he did not leave the villa which is called Io's.

His anxiety of mind became torture because of reproaches of all kinds from every quarter, since every single one of those who were condemned to death heaped all kinds of abuse upon him, either to his face or by hand-bills placed in the Senator's seats at the shows. By these, however, he was most diversely affected, now through a sense of shame desiring that they all be concealed and kept secret, sometimes scorning them and producing them of his own accord and giving them publicity. Why, he was even attacked by Artabanus, King of the Parthians, who charged him in a letter with the murder of his kindred, with other bloody deeds, and with shameless and dissolute living, counseling him to gratify the intense and just hatred of the citizens as soon as possible by a voluntary death.

At last in utter self-disgust he all but admitted the extremity of his wretchedness in a letter [1] which began thus: "If I know what to write to you, Fathers of the Senate, or how to write it, or what to leave unwritten at present, may all Gods and Goddesses visit me with more utter destruction than I feel that I am daily suffering." Some think that through his skill in divining the future he had foreknowledge of this situation, and knew long beforehand what detestation and ill-repute one day awaited him; and that therefore when he became Emperor, he positively refused the title of "Father of his Country" and to allow the Senate to take oath to support his acts, for fear that he might presently be found undeserving of such honors and thus be the more shamed. In fact, this may be gathered from the speech which he made regarding these two matters; for example, when he says: "I shall always be consistent and never change my ways so long as I am in my senses. But for the sake of precedent the Senate should beware of binding itself to support the acts of any man, since he might through some mischance suffer a change." Again: "If you ever

---

[1] Quoted also by Tacitus in *Annals* VI, 6.

come to feel any doubt," he says, "of my character or of my heartfelt devotion to you (and before that happens, I pray that my last day may save me from this altered opinion of me), the title of Father of my Country will give me no additional honor, but will be a reproach to you, either for your hasty action in conferring the appellation upon me, or for your inconsistency in changing your estimate of my character."

He was large and strong of frame, and of a stature above the average;[1] broad of shoulders and chest; well proportioned and symmetrical from head to foot. His left hand was the more nimble and stronger, and its joints were so powerful that he could bore through a fresh, sound apple with his finger, and break the head of a boy, or even a young man, with a fillip. He was of fair complexion and wore his hair rather long at the back, so much so as even to cover the nape of his neck, which was apparently a style affected by his family. His face was handsome, but would break out on a sudden with many pimples. His eyes were unusually large and, strange to say, had the power of seeing even at night and in the dark. But that was only for a short time when first opened after sleep, for they soon grew dim-sighted again. He strode along with his neck stiff and bent forward, usually with a stern countenance and for the most part in silence, never or very rarely conversing with his companions, and then speaking with great deliberation and with a kind of supple movement of his fingers. All of these mannerisms of his, which were disagreeable and signs of arrogance, were remarked by Augustus, who often tried to excuse them to the Senate and people by declaring that they were natural failings, and not intentional. He enjoyed excellent health, which was all but perfect during nearly the whole of his reign,[2] although from the thirtieth year of his age he took care of it according to his own ideas, without the aid or advice of physicians.

Although somewhat neglectful of the Gods and of religious matters, being addicted to astrology and firmly convinced that

---

[1] The average height of the Roman male was 5 feet 2 inches.

[2] Which has been used to support the contention that he could not have been as debauched as alleged. Nero's health was also good! (See *Nero*.)

everything was in the hands of fate, he was nevertheless im-moderately afraid of thunder. Whenever the sky was lower-ing, he always wore a laurel wreath, because it is said that kind of leaf is never touched by lightning.

He was greatly devoted to liberal studies in both languages. In his Latin oratory he followed Messala Corvinus, to whom he had given attention in his youth, when Messala was an old man. But he so obscured his style by excessive mannerisms and pedantry, that he was thought to speak much better off-hand than in a prepared address. He also composed a lyric poem, entitled "A Lament for the Death of Lucius Caesar," and made Greek verses in imitation of Euphorion, Rhianus, and Parthenius,[1] poets of whom he was very fond, placing their busts in the public libraries among those of the eminent writers of old. On this account many learned men vied with one another in issuing commentaries on their works and dedi-cating them to the Emperor. Yet his special aim was a knowl-edge of mythology, which he carried to a silly and laughable extreme; for he used to test even the grammarians,[2] a class of men in whom, as I have said, he was especially interested, by questions something like this: "Who was Hecuba's mother?" "What was the name of Achilles among the maid-ens?"[3] "What were the Sirens in the habit of singing?" More-over, on the first day that he entered the Senate after the death of Augustus, to satisfy at once the demands of filial piety and of religion, he offered sacrifice after the example of Minos with incense and wine, but without a fluteplayer, as Minos had done in ancient times on the death of his son.

Though he spoke Greek readily and fluently, yet he would not use it on all occasions and especially avoided it in the Senate. So much so that before using the word "monopo-lium,"[4] he begged pardon for the necessity of employing a foreign term. Again, when the word ἔμβλημα[5] was read in a

---

[1] Obscure Greek poets whose writings were full of either fabulous or love stories.

[2] Who were also teachers of literature.

[3] The daughters of King Lycomedes, in the Isle of Seyros, where he feigned himself a maiden.

[4] "Monopoly," a Greek word transliterated into Latin.

[5] The Greek word for inlaid ornaments of metal attached to cups and other vessels. There is no exact equivalent in Latin.

decree of the Senate, he recommended that it to be changed and a native word substituted for the foreign one; and if one could not be found, that the idea be expressed by several words, if necessary, and by periphrasis. On another occasion, when a soldier was asked in Greek to give testimony, he forbade him to answer except in Latin.

Twice only during the whole period of his retirement did he try to return to Rome. Once he sailed in a trireme as far as the gardens near the Naumachia,[1] after first posting a guard along the banks of the Tiber to keep off those who came out to meet him. The second time he came up the Appian Way as far as the seventh milestone. But he returned after merely having a distant view of the city walls, without approaching them, the first time for some unknown reason, the second through alarm at a portent. He had among his pets a serpent, and when he was going to feed it from his own hand, as his custom was, and discovered that it had been devoured by ants, he was warned to beware of the power of the multitude. So he went back in haste to Campania, fell ill at Astura, but recovering somewhat kept on to Circeii. To avoid giving any suspicion of his weak condition, he not only attended the games of the soldiers, but even threw down darts from his high seat at a board which was let into the arena. Immediately he was taken with a pain in the side, and then being exposed to a draught when he was overheated, his illness increased. For all that, he kept up for some time. While continuing his journey as far as Misenum he made no change in his usual habits, not even giving up his banquets and other pleasures, partly from lack of self-denial and partly to conceal his condition. Indeed, when the physician Charicles, having obtained leave of absence, on rising to leave the dining-room took his hand to kiss it, Tiberius, thinking that he was trying to feel his pulse, urged him to remain and take his place again, and prolonged the dinner to a late hour. Even then he did not give up his custom of standing in the middle of the dining-room with a Lictor by his side and addressing all the guests by name as they said farewell.

---

[1] The artificial lake near the Tiber where Julius Caesar exhibited a naval fight. (See *Julius.*)

Meanwhile, having read in the proceedings of the Senate that some of those under accusation, about whom he had written briefly, merely stating that they had been named by an informer, had been discharged without a hearing, he cried out in anger that he was held in contempt, and resolved to return to Capri at any cost, since he would not risk any step except from his place of refuge. Detained, however, by bad weather and the increasing violence of his illness, he died a little later in the villa of Lucullus, in the seventy-eighth year of his age and the twenty-third of his reign, on the seventeenth day before the Kalends of April, in the consulship of Gnaeus Acerronius Proculus and Gaius Pontius Nigrinus.

Some think that Gaius [1] gave him a slow and wasting poison, others that during convalescence from an attack of fever food was refused him when he asked for it. Some say that a pillow was thrown upon his face, when he came to and asked for a ring which had been taken from him during a fainting fit. Seneca writes that conscious of his approaching end, he took off the ring, held it a while, as if to give it to some one, but, putting it back, he clenched his left hand and lay for a long time motionless; and that he then suddenly called for his attendants, and on receiving no response, got up; but his strength failed him and he fell dead near the couch.

On his last birthday he dreamt that the Apollo of Temenos, a statue of remarkable size and beauty, which he had brought from Syracuse to be set up in the library of the new temple, appeared to him in a dream, declaring that it could not be dedicated by Tiberius. A few days before his death the lighthouse at Capri was wrecked by an earthquake. At Misenum the ashes from the glowing coals and embers which had been brought in to warm his dining-room, after they had died out and been for a long time cold, suddenly blazed up in the early evening and glowed without cessation until late at night.

The people were so glad of his death, that at the first news of it some ran about shouting, "Tiberius to the Tiber," while others prayed to Mother Earth and the Manes to allow

---

[1] Gaius Caligula (son of Germanicus), the next Emperor.

the dead man no abode except among the damned. Still others threatened his body with the hook and the Stairs of Mourning, especially embittered by a recent outrage, added to the memory of his former cruelty. It had been provided by decree of the Senate that the execution of the condemned should in all cases be put off for ten days, and it chanced that the punishment of some fell due on the day when the news came about Tiberius. The poor wretches begged the public for protection. But since in the continued absence of Gaius there was no one who could be approached and appealed to, the jailers, fearing to act contrary to the law, strangled them and cast out their bodies on the Stairs of Mourning. Therefore hatred of the tyrant waxed greater, since his cruelty endured even after his death. When the funeral procession left Misenum, many cried out that the body ought rather to be carried to Atella, and half-burned in the amphitheater. But it was taken to Rome by the soldiers and reduced to ashes with public ceremonies.

Two years before his death he had made two copies of a will, one in his own hand and the other in that of a freedman, but of the same content, and had caused them to be signed and sealed by persons of the very lowest condition. In this will he named his grandsons, Gaius, son of Germanicus, and Tiberius, son of Drusus, heirs to equal shares of his estate, each to be sole heir in case of the other's death. Besides, he gave legacies to several, including the Vestal Virgins, as well as to each and every man of the soldiers and the Commons of Rome, with separate ones to the masters of the city wards.

BOOK IV
GAIUS CALIGULA

GAIUS CALIGULA

GERMANICUS, father of Gaius Caesar, son of Drusus and the younger Antonia, after being adopted by his paternal uncle Tiberius, held the quaestorship five years before the legal age and passed directly to the consulship. When the death of Augustus was announced, he was sent to the army in Germany, where it is hard to say whether his filial piety or his courage was more conspicuous. For, although all the legions obstinately refused to accept Tiberius as Emperor, and offered him the rule of the State,[1] he held them to their allegiance. And later he won a victory over the enemy and celebrated a triumph. Then chosen Consul for a second time, before he entered on his term he was hurried off to restore order in the Orient, and after vanquishing the King of Armenia and reducing Cappadocia to the form of a province, died of a lingering illness at Antioch, in the thirty-fourth year of his age. There was some suspicion that he was poisoned. For besides the dark spots which appeared all over his body and the froth which flowed from his mouth, after he had been reduced to ashes his heart was found entire among his bones; and it is supposed to be a characteristic of that organ that when steeped in poison it cannot be destroyed by fire.

Now the belief was that he met his death through the wiles of Tiberius, aided and abetted by Gnaeus Piso.[2] This man had been made Governor of Syria at about that time, and realizing that he must give offense either to the father or the son, as if there were no alternative, he never ceased to show the bitterest enmity towards Germanicus in word and deed, even after the latter fell ill. In consequence Piso narrowly escaped being torn to pieces by the people on his return to Rome, and was condemned to death by the Senate.

---

[1] As told in *Tiberius*.
[2] Also discussed in *Tiberius*.

It is the general opinion that Germanicus possessed all the highest qualities of body and mind, to a degree never equalled by any one. He was a handsome man of extraordinary courage and surpassing ability in the oratory and learning of Greece and Rome. He was, besides, a man of unexampled kindliness endowed with a remarkable desire and capacity for winning men's regard and inspiring their affection. His legs were too slender for the rest of his figure, but he gradually brought them to proper proportions by constant horseback riding after meals. He often slew a foeman in hand-to-hand combat. He pleaded causes even after receiving the triumphal regalia. And among other fruits of his studies he left some Greek comedies. Unassuming at home and abroad, he always entered the free and federate towns without Lictors. Wherever he came upon the tombs of distinguished men, he always offered sacrifice to their shades. Planning to bury in one mound the old and scattered relics of those who fell in the overthrow of Varus, he was the first to attempt to collect and assemble them with his own hand. Even towards his detractors, whosoever they were and whatever their motives, he was so mild and lenient, that when Piso was annulling his decrees and maltreating his dependents, he could not make up his mind to break with him, until he found himself assailed also by potions and spells.[1] Even then he went no farther than formally to renounce Piso's friendship in the old-time fashion, and to bid his household avenge him, in case anything should befall him.

He reaped plentiful fruit from these virtues, for he was so respected and beloved by his kindred that Augustus (to say nothing of the rest of his relatives) after hesitating for a long time whether to appoint him his successor, had him adopted by Tiberius. He was so popular with the masses, that, according to many writers, whenever he came to any place or left one, he was sometimes in danger of his life from the crowds that met him or saw him off. In fact, when he returned from Germany after quelling the outbreak, all the cohorts of the praetorian guard went forth to meet him, although orders had been given that only two should go, and

---

[1] Fuller details are given by Tacitus, *Annals* II, 69.

the whole populace, regardless of age, sex, or rank, poured out of Rome as far as the twentieth milestone.

Yet far greater and stronger tokens of regard were shown at the time of his death and immediately afterwards. On the day when he passed away the temples were stoned and the altars of the Gods thrown down,[1] while some flung their household Gods into the street and cast out their newly born children.[2] Even barbarian peoples, so they say, who were engaged in war with us or with one another, unanimously consented to a truce, as if all in common had suffered a domestic tragedy. It is said that some princes put off their beards and had their wives' heads shaved, as a token of the deepest mourning and that even the King of Kings [3] suspended his exercise at hunting and the banquets with his grandees, which among the Parthians is a sign of public mourning.

At Rome when the community, in grief and consternation at the first report of his illness, was awaiting further news, and suddenly after nightfall a report at last spread abroad, on doubtful authority, that he had recovered, a general rush was made from every side to the Capitol with torches and victims, and the temple gates were all but torn off, that nothing might hinder them in their eagerness to pay their vows. Tiberius was roused from sleep by the cries of the rejoicing throng, who all united in singing:—

"Rome is safe, our country is safe, for our Germanicus is safe."

But when it was at last made known that he was no more, no solace could assuage the public grief nor any edict check it. It continued even during the festal days of the month of December.

The fame of the deceased and regret for his loss were increased by the horror of the times which followed, since all believed, and with good reason, that the cruelty of Tiberius, which soon burst forth, had been held in check through his respect and awe for Germanicus.

---

[1] For permitting such a man to die.
[2] Why raise children any more?
[3] A title assumed by various eastern potentates.

He had to wife Agrippina, daughter of Marcus Agrippa and Julia, who bore him nine children. Two of these were taken off when they were still in infancy, and one just as he was reaching the age of boyhood, a charming child, whose statue, in the guise of Cupid, Livia dedicated in the temple of the Capitoline Venus, while Augustus had another placed in his bedchamber and used to kiss it fondly whenever he entered the room. The other children survived their father, three girls, Agrippina, Drusilla, and Livilla, born in successive years, and three boys, Nero, Drusus, and Gaius Caesar. Nero and Drusus were adjudged public enemies by the Senate on the accusation of Tiberius.[1]

Gaius Caesar was born the day before the Kalends of September in the consulship of his father and Gaius Fonteius Capito. Conflicting testimony makes his birthplace uncertain. Gnaeus Lentulus Gaetulicus writes that he was born at Tibur, Plinius Secundus among the Treveri, in a village called Ambitarvium above the Confluence. Pliny adds as proof that altars are shown there, inscribed "For the Delivery of Agrippina." Verses which were in circulation soon after he became Emperor indicate that he was begotten in the winter-quarters of the legions:

"Born in a camp, reared with soldiers, he;
    A sign assured he would a ruler be."

I myself find in the public records that he first saw the light at Antium. Pliny charges Gaetulicus as guilty of a flattering lie, merely to soothe the vanity of a young, conceited prince, by giving him the added luster of being born in a city sacred to Hercules, adding that he advanced this false assertion with the more assurance, because, the year before the birth of Gaius, Germanicus really did have a son born to him at Tibur, also called Gaius Caesar, of whose lovable disposition and untimely death I have already spoken. Pliny has erred in his chronology. For the historians of Augustus agree that Germanicus was not sent to Germany until the close of his consulship, when Gaius was already born. Moreover, the inscription on the altar adds no strength to Pliny's view, for Agrip-

---

[1] See *Tiberius* for further details.

pina twice gave birth to daughters in that region, and any childbirth, regardless of sex, is called *puerperium*, since the men of old called girls *puerae*, just as they called boys *puelli*. Furthermore, we have a letter written by Augustus to his granddaughter Agrippina, a few months before he died, about the Gaius in question (for no other child of the name was still alive at that time), reading as follows: "Yesterday I arranged with Talarius and Asillius to bring you your boy Gaius on the fifteenth day before the Kalends of June, if it be the will of the Gods. I send with him besides one of my slaves who is a physician, and I have written Germanicus to keep him if he wishes. Farewell, my own Agrippina, and take care to come in good health to your Germanicus."

I think it is clear enough that Gaius could not have been born in a place to which he was first taken from Rome when he was nearly two years old. This letter also weakens our confidence in the verses, the more so because they are anony-mous. We must then accept the only remaining testimony, that of the public record, particularly since Gaius loved Antium as if it were his native soil, always preferring it to all other places of retreat, and even thinking, it is said, of transferring thither the seat and abode of the empire through weariness of Rome.

His surname Caligula [1] he derived from a joke of the troops, because he was brought up in their midst in the dress of a common soldier. To what extent besides he won their love and devotion by being reared in fellowship with them is especially evident from the fact that when they threatened mutiny after the death of Augustus and were ready for any act of madness, the mere sight of Gaius unquestionably calmed them. For they did not become quiet until they saw that he was being spirited away because of the danger from their outbreak and taken for protection to the nearest town. Then at last they became contrite, and laying hold of the carriage and stopping it, begged to be spared the disgrace which was being put upon them.

He attended his father also on his expedition to Syria. On his return from there he first lived with his mother and after

---

[1] "Little Boot." The *caliga*, or half-boot, studded with nails, was the usual shoe of the Roman soldier.

her banishment, with his great-grandmother Livia. When Livia died, though he was not yet of age, he spoke her eulogy from the rostra. Then he fell to the care of his grandmother Antonia, and in the nineteenth year of his age he was called to Capri by Tiberius, on the same day assuming the gown of manhood and shaving his first beard, but without any such ceremony as had attended the coming of age of his brothers. Although at Capri every kind of wile was resorted to by those who tried to lure him or force him to utter complaints, he never gave them any satisfaction, ignoring the ruin of his kindred as if nothing at all had happened, passing over his own ill-treatment with an incredible pretense of indifference, and so obsequious towards his grandfather and his household, that it was well said of him that no one had ever been a better slave or a worse master.

Yet even at that time he could not control his natural cruelty and viciousness, but he was a most eager witness of the tortures and executions of those who suffered punishment, revelling at night in gluttony and adultery, disguised in a wig and a long robe. He was also passionately devoted to the theatrical arts of dancing and singing, in which Tiberius very willingly indulged him, in the hope that through these his savage nature might be softened. This last was so clearly evident to the shrewd old man, that he used to say now and then that to allow Gaius to live would prove the ruin of himself and of all men, and that he was rearing a viper for the Roman people and a Phaethon for the world.

Not so very long afterward Gaius took to wife Junia Claudilla,[1] daughter of Marcus Silanus, a man of noble rank. He was then appointed Augur to succeed his brother Drusus. But before he was invested with the office he was advanced to that of Pontiff, with strong commendation of his dutiful conduct and general character. For, since the court was deserted and deprived of its other supports, after Sejanus had been suspected of hostile designs and presently put out of the way, he was little by little encouraged to look forward to the succession. To have a better chance of realizing this, after losing Junia in childbirth, he seduced

---

[1] Diminutive of Claudia. Suetonius often uses this more familiar form when speaking of women.

Ennia Naevia, wife of Macro, who at that time commanded the praetorian guard, even promising to marry her if he became Emperor, and guaranteeing this promise by an oath and a written contract. Having through her wormed himself into Macro's favor,[1] he poisoned Tiberius, as some think, and ordered that his ring be taken from him while he still breathed, and then suspecting that he was trying to hold fast to it, that a pillow be put over his face; or even strangled the old man with his own hand, immediately ordering the crucifixion of a freedman who cried out at the awful deed. And this is likely enough. For some writers say that Caligula himself later admitted, not it is true that he had committed parricide, but that he had at least meditated it at one time. For they say that he constantly boasted, in speaking of his filial piety, that he had entered the bedchamber of the sleeping Tiberius dagger in hand, to avenge the death of his mother and brothers, but that, seized with pity, he threw down the dagger and went out again; and that though Tiberius knew of this, he had never dared to make any inquiry or take any action.

By thus gaining the throne he fulfilled the highest hopes of the Roman people, or I may say of all mankind, since he was the prince most earnestly desired by the great part of the provincials and soldiers, many of whom had known him in his infancy, as well as by the whole body of the city populace, because of the memory of his father Germanicus and pity for a family that had been almost destroyed. Accordingly, when he set out from Misenum, though he was in mourning garb and escorting the body of Tiberius, yet his progress was marked by altars, victims, and blazing torches, and he was met by a dense and joyful throng, who called him besides other propitious names their "star," their "chick," their "babe," and their "nursling."

When he entered the city, full and absolute power was at once put into his hands by the unanimous consent of the Senate and of the mob, which forced its way into the House, and no attention was paid to the wish of Tiberius, who in his will had named his other grandson, still a boy, joint heir

---

[1] Macro was instrumental in the fall of Sejanus.

with Caligula. So great was the public rejoicing, that within the next three months, or less than that, more than a hundred and sixty thousand victims are said to have been slain in sacrifice.

A few days after this, when he crossed to the islands near Campania, vows were put up for his safe return, while no one let slip even the slightest chance of giving testimony to his anxiety and regard for his safety. But when he fell ill, they all spent the whole night about the Palace, some even vowing to fight as gladiators, while others posted placards offering their lives if the ailing prince were spared.[1] To this unbounded love of his citizens was added marked devotion from foreigners. Artabanus, for example, King of the Parthians, who was always outspoken in his hatred and contempt for Tiberius, voluntarily sought Caligula's friendship. He came to a conference with the consular Governor, and, crossing the Euphrates, paid homage to the Roman eagles and standards and to the statues of the Caesars.

Gaius himself tried to rouse men's devotion by courting popularity in every way. After eulogizing Tiberius with many tears before the assembled people and giving him a magnificent funeral, he at once posted off to Pandateria and the Pontian islands, to remove the ashes of his mother and brother to Rome; and in stormy weather, too, to make his filial piety the more conspicuous. He approached their remains with reverence and placed them in the urns with his own hands. With no less theatrical effect he brought them to Ostia in a bireme with a banner set in the stern, and from there up the Tiber to Rome, where he had them carried to the Mausoleum [2] on two biers by the most distinguished men of the order of Knights, in the middle of the day, when the streets were crowded. He appointed funeral sacrifices, too, to be offered each year with due ceremony, as well as games in the Circus in honor of his mother, providing a carriage to carry her image in the procession. But in memory of his father he gave to the month of September the name of Germanicus. After this,

---

[1] According to the widespread belief the death of one man might be redeemed with that of another. They were compelled to fulfill their vows.

[2] That built by Augustus.

by a single decree of the Senate, he heaped upon his grand-mother Antonia whatever honors Livia Augusta had ever enjoyed; took his uncle Claudius, who up to that time had been a Roman Knight, as his colleague in the consulship; adopted his brother [1] Tiberius on the day that he assumed the gown of manhood, and gave him the title of Chief of the Youth.[2] He caused the names of his sisters to be included in all oaths: "And I will not hold myself and my children dearer than I do Gaius and his sisters"; as well as in the propositions of the Consuls: "Favor and good fortune attend Gaius Caesar and his sisters."

With the same desire for popularity he recalled those who had been condemned to banishment; took no cognizance of any charges that remained untried from an earlier time; had all documents relating to the cases of his mother and brothers carried to the Forum and burned, to give no informer or witness occasion for further fear, having first loudly called the Gods to witness that he had neither read nor touched any of them. He refused a note which was offered him regarding his own safety, maintaining that he had done nothing to make any one hate him, and that he had no ears for informers.

He banished from the city the sexual perverts called spintriae,[3] barely persuaded not to drown them in the sea. The wrtings of Titus Labienus, Cremutius Cordus, and Cassius Severus, which had been suppressed by decrees of the Senate,[4] he allowed to be hunted up, circulated, and read, saying that it was wholly to his interest that everything which happened be handed down to posterity. He published the accounts of the empire, which had regularly been made public by Augustus, a practice discontinued by Tiberius. He allowed the magistrates unrestricted jurisdiction, without appeal to himself. He revised the lists of the Roman Knights strictly and scrupulously, yet with due moderation, publicly taking their horses from those guilty of any wicked or scandalous

---

[1] Son of his brother Drusus. He later put him to death. For which see Chapter XXIII.

[2] Originally the title of the Knights under forty-five who were in active service. Conferred on C. and L. Caesar by Augustus, it became the designation of the heir-apparent.

[3] About which see *Tiberius*.

[4] Because they were too frank, of course

act, but merely omitting to read the names of men convicted of lesser offenses. To lighten the labor of the jurors, he added a fifth division to the previous four. He tried also to restore the suffrage to the people by reviving the custom of elections.[1] He at once paid faithfully and without dispute the legacies named in the will of Tiberius, though this had been set aside, as well as in that of Julia Augusta, which Tiberius had suppressed. He remitted the tax of one half of one per cent on auction sales in Italy. He made good to many their losses from fires. And whenever he restored Kings to their thrones, he allowed them all the arrears of their taxes and their revenues which had accrued in the interval, as in the case of Antiochus of Commagene, where the confiscation would have amounted to a hundred million sesterces.[2] To make it known that he encouraged every kind of noble action, he gave eight hundred thousand sesterces [3] to a freedwoman, because she had kept silence about the guilt of her patron, though subjected to the utmost torture. Because of these acts, besides other honors, a golden shield was voted him, which was to be borne every year to the Capitol on an appointed day by the Colleges of Priests, escorted by the Senate, while boys and girls of noble birth sang the praises of his virtues in a choral ode. It was further decreed that the day on which he began to reign should be called the Parilia, as a token that the city had been founded a second time.

He held four consulships, one from the Kalends of July for two months, a second from the Kalends of January for thirty days, a third up to the Ides of January, and the fourth until the seventh day before the Ides of the same month. Of all these only the last two were continuous. The third he assumed at Lugdunum without a colleague, not, as some think, through arrogance or disregard of precedent, but because at that distance from Rome he had been unable to get news of the death of the other Consul just before the day of the Kalends. He twice gave the people a largess of

---

[1] Julius Caesar had shared it with them. Augustus had only kept the form. Tiberius had deprived the Roman people of the last remnant of their part in the government.

[2] $4,100,000.00.

[3] $32,800.00.

three hundred sesterces [1] each, and twice a lavish banquet to the Senate and the equestrian order, together with their wives and children. At the former of these he also distributed togas to the men, and to the women and children scarves of red and scarlet. Furthermore, to make a permanent addition to the public gayety, he added a day to the Saturnalia, and called it *Juvenalis*.

He gave several gladiatorial shows, some in the amphitheater of Taurus and some in the Saepta, in which he introduced pairs of African and Campanian boxers, the pick of both regions. He did not always preside at the games in person, but sometimes assigned the honor to the magistrates or to friends. He exhibited stage-plays continually, of various kinds and in many different places, sometimes even by night, lighting up the whole city. He also threw various sorts of gifts among the people to be scrambled for, and gave each man a basket of victuals. During the feasting he sent his share to a Roman Knight opposite him, who was eating with evident relish and appetite, while to a Senator for the same reason he gave a commission naming him Praetor out of the regular order. He also gave many games in the Circus, lasting from early morning until evening, introducing between the races now a baiting of panthers and now the maneuvers of the game called Troy; some, too, of special splendor, in which the Circus was strewn with red and green, while the charioteers were all men of senatorial rank. He also started some games off-hand, when a few people called for them from the neighboring balconies, as he was inspecting the outfit of the Circus from the Gelotian house.

Besides this, he devised a novel and unheard-of kind of show. He bridged the gap between Baiae and the mole at Puteoli, a distance of about thirty-six hundred paces, by bringing together merchant ships from all sides and anchoring them in a double line, after which a mound of earth was heaped upon them and fashioned in the manner of the Appian Way. Over this bridge he rode back and forth for two successive days, the first day on a caparisoned horse, himself resplendent in a crown of oak leaves, a buckler, a

---

[1] $15.00.

sword, and a cloak of cloth of gold; on the second, in the dress of a charioteer in a car drawn by a pair of famous horses, carrying before him a boy named Dareus, one of the hostages from Parthia, and attended by the entire praetorian guard and a company of his friends in Gallic chariots. I know that many have supposed that Gaius devised this kind of bridge in rivalry of Xerxes, who excited no little admiration by bridging the much narrower Hellespont; others, that it was to inspire fear in Germany and Britain, on which he had designs, by the fame of some stupendous work. But when I was a boy, I used to hear my grandfather say that the reason for the work, as revealed by the Emperor's confidential courtiers, was that Thrasyllus the astrologer had declared to Tiberius, when he was worried about his successor and inclined towards his natural grandson, that Gaius had no more chance of becoming Emperor than of riding about over the gulf of Baiae with horses.

He also gave shows in foreign lands, Athenian games at Syracuse in Sicily, and miscellaneous games at Lugdunum [Lyons] in Gaul. At the latter place he also gave a contest in Greek and Latin oratory, in which, they say, the losers gave prizes to the victors and were forced to compose eulogies upon them, while those who were least successful were ordered to erase their writings with a sponge or with their tongue, unless they elected rather to be beaten with rods or thrown into the neighboring river.

He completed the public works which had been half finished under Tiberius, namely the temple of Augustus and the theater of Pompey. He likewise began an aqueduct in the region near Tibur and an amphitheater beside the Saepta, the former finished by his successor Claudius, while the latter was abandoned. At Syracuse he repaired the city walls, which had fallen into ruin through lapse of time, and the temples of the Gods. He had planned, besides, to rebuild the palace of Polycrates at Samos, to finish the temple of the Didymaean Apollo at Ephesus, to found a city high up in the Alps, but, above all, to dig a canal through the Isthmus in Greece, and he had already sent a Chief Centurion to survey the work.

So much for Caligula as emperor. We must now tell of his career as a monster.

After he had assumed various surnames (for he was called "Pious," "Child of the Camp," "Father of the Armies," and "Greatest and Best of Caesars"), chancing to overhear some Kings, who had come to Rome to pay their respects to him, disputing at dinner about the nobility of their descent, he cried:

"Let there be one Lord, one King." [1]

And he came near assuming a crown at once and changing the semblance of a principate into the form of a monarchy. But on being reminded that he had risen above the elevation both of princes and Kings, he began from that time on to lay claim to divine majesty. He ordered that such statues of the Gods as were especially famous for their sanctity or their artistic merit, including that of Jupiter of Olympia,[2] should be brought from Greece, in order to remove their heads and put his own in their place. He built out a part of the Palace as far as the Forum, and making the temple of Castor and Pollux its vestibule, he often took his place between the divine brethren, and exhibited himself there to be worshiped by all comers, some of whom hailed him as Jupiter Latiaris. He also set up a special temple to his own godhead, with priests and with victims of the choicest kind. In this temple was a life-sized statue of the Emperor in gold, which was dressed each day in clothing such as he wore himself. The richest citizens used all their influence to become priests of his cult and bid high for the honor. The victims were flamingoes, peacocks, woodcock, guinea-hens and pheasants, offered day by day each after its own kind. At night he used constantly to invite the full and radiant moon to his embraces and his bed, while in the daytime he would talk confidentially with Jupiter Capitolinus, now whispering and then in turn putting his ear to the mouth of the God, now in louder and even angry language; for he was heard to make the threat: "Lift me up, or I'll lift thee." [3] Until, at last prevailed upon by the

---

[1] *Iliad* II, 204.
[2] By Pheidias.
[3] *Iliad* XXIII, 724, where after a long and indecisive wrestling bout Ajax thus challenges Ulysses to settle the contest.

entreaties of the God, as he said, to come and live with him, he built a bridge over the temple of the Deified Augustus, and thus joined his Palace to the Capitol. Presently, to be nearer yet, he laid the foundations of a new house in the court of the Capitol.

He did not wish to be thought the grandson of Agrippa, or called so, because of the latter's humble origin, and he grew very angry if any one in a speech or a song included Agrippa among the ancestors of the Caesars. He even boasted that his own mother was born in incest, which Augustus had committed with his daughter Julia. And, not content with this slur on the memory of Augustus, he forbade the celebration of his victories at Actium and off Sicily by annual festivals, on the ground that they were disastrous and ruinous to the Roman people. He often called his great-grandmother Livia Augusta "a Ulysses in woman's dress," and he had the audacity to accuse her of low birth in a letter to the Senate, alleging that her maternal grandfather, Aufidius Lurco, had been nothing but a Decurion of Fundi, whereas that he held high offices at Rome is proved by public records. When his grandmother Antonia asked for a private interview, he refused it except in the presence of the Praefect Macro. By indignities of this kind, and annoyances he caused her death, although some think that he also gave her poison. After she was dead, he paid her no honor, but viewed her burning pyre from his dining-room. He had his brother [1] Tiberius put to death without warning, suddenly sending a Tribune of the soldiers to do the deed; besides driving his father-in-law Silanus to end his life by cutting his throat with a razor. His charge against the latter was that Silanus had not followed him when he put to sea in stormy weather, but had remained behind in the hope of taking possession of the city in case he should be lost in the storm. His charge against Tiberius was that his breath smelled of an antidote taken to guard against being poisoned at his hand. Now as a matter of fact, Silanus was subject to sea-sickness and wished to avoid the discomforts of the voyage, while Tiberius had taken medicine for a chronic cough, which was growing worse. As for

---

[1] Son of his brother Drusus.

his uncle Claudius, he spared him merely as a laughing-stock.

He lived in habitual incest with all his sisters, and at a large banquet he placed each of them in turn below him, while his wife reclined above. Of these he is believed to have violated Drusilla when he was still a minor, and even to have been caught lying with her by his grandmother Antonia, at whose house they were brought up in company. Afterwards, when she was the wife of Lucius Cassius Longinus, an ex-consul, he took her from him and openly treated her as his lawful wife. Also when he was sick he made her heir to his property and the throne. When she died, he appointed a season of public mourning, during which it was a capital offense to laugh, bathe, or dine in company with one's parents, wife, or children. He was so beside himself with grief that suddenly fleeing the city by night and traversing Campania he went to Syracuse and hurriedly returned from there without cutting his hair or shaving his beard. And he never afterwards took oath about matters of the highest moment, even before the assembly of the people or in the presence of the soldiers, except by the godhead of Drusilla. The rest of his sisters he did not love with so great affection, nor honor so highly, but often prostituted them to his favorites. He therefore the more readily condemned them in the case of Aemilius Lepidus as adulteresses and privy to that conspiracy against him. And he not only made public letters in the handwriting of all of them, procured by fraud and seduction. He also consecrated to Mars the Avenger three swords with which his life was to have been taken, with an accompanying inscription containing the cause of his so doing.

It is not easy to decide whether in his marriages he acted more basely in contracting them, in repudiating them, or in continuing them. At the marriage of Livia Orestilla to Gaius Piso, he attended the ceremony himself, gave orders that the bride be taken to his own house, and within a few days divorced her. Two years later he banished her, because of a suspicion that in the meantime she had gone back to her former husband. Others write that being an invited guest at their wedding banquet, he sent word to Piso, who reclined opposite to him: "Don't take liberties with my wife," and at once carried

her off with him from the table, the next day issuing a proclamation that he had got himself a wife in the manner of Romulus and Augustus. When the statement was made that the
grandmother of Lollia Paulina, who was married to Gaius
Memmius, an ex-consul commanding armies, had once been a
remarkably beautiful woman, he suddenly called Lollia from
the province, separated her from her husband, and married
her. Then in a short time he put her away, with the command
never to have intercourse with any one. Though Caesonia was
neither beautiful nor young, and was already mother of three
daughters by another, besides being a woman of reckless extravagance and wantonness, he loved her not only more passionately but more faithfully, often exhibiting her to the
soldiers riding by his side, decked with cloak, helmet and
shield, and to his friends even in a state of nudity. He did not
honor her with the title of wife until she had borne him a
child, announcing on the selfsame day that he had married
her and that he was the father of her babe. This babe, whom
he named Julia Drusilla, he carried to the temples of all the
goddesses, finally placing her in the lap of Minerva and commending to her the child's nurture and training. And no evidence convinced him so positively that she was sprung from
his own loins as her savage temper, which was even then so
violent that she would try to scratch the faces and eyes of
the little children who played with her.

It would be trivial and pointless to add to this an account
of his treatment of his relatives and friends, Ptolemy, son of
King Juba, his cousin (for he was the grandson of Mark
Antony by Antony's daughter Selene), and in particular
Macro himself and even Ennia, who helped him to the throne.
All these were rewarded for their kinship and their faithful
services by violent deaths.

He was no whit more respectful or mild towards the Senate,
allowing some who had held the highest offices to run in their
togas for several miles beside his chariot and to wait on him at
table, standing napkin in hand either at the head of his couch,
or at his feet. Others he secretly put to death, yet continued
to send for them as if they were alive, after a few days falsely
asserting that they had committed suicide. When the Consuls
forgot to make proclamation of his birthday, he deposed them,

and left the state for three days without its highest magistrates. He flogged his Quaestor, who was charged with conspiracy, stripping off the man's clothes and spreading them under the soldiers' feet, to give them a firm footing as they beat him.

He treated the other orders with like insolence and cruelty. Being disturbed by the noise made by those who came in the middle of the night to secure the free seats in the Circus, he drove them all out with cudgels. In the confusion more than twenty Roman Knights were crushed to death, with as many matrons and a countless number of others. At the plays in the theater, sowing discord between the Commons and the Knights, he scattered the gift tickets ahead of time, to induce the rabble to take the seats reserved for the equestrian order. At a gladiatorial show he would sometimes draw back the awnings when the sun was hottest and give orders that no one be allowed to leave; then removing the usual equipment, he would match worthless and decrepit gladiators against mangy wild beasts, and have sham fights between householders who were of good repute, but conspicuous for some bodily infirmity. Sometimes too he would shut up the granaries and condemn the people to hunger.

The following are special instances of his innate brutality. When cattle to feed the wild beasts which he had provided for a gladiatorial show were rather costly, he selected criminals to be devoured, and, merely taking a place in the middle of a colonnade, he reviewed the line of prisoners without examining the charges and bade them be led away "from baldhead to baldhead." A man who had made a vow to fight in the arena, if the Emperor recovered, he compelled to keep his word, watched him as he fought sword in hand, and would not let him go until he was victorious, and then only after many entreaties. Another who had offered his life for the same reason, but delayed to kill himself, he turned over to his slaves, with orders to drive him through the streets decked with sacred boughs and fillets, calling for the fulfillment of his vow, and finally hurl him from the embankment. Many men of honorable rank were first disfigured with the marks of branding-irons and then condemned to the mines, to work at building roads, or to be thrown to the wild beasts; or else he shut them up in cages on all fours, like animals, or had them sawn asunder. Not all these punishments were for serious offenses, but merely for criticizing one of his shows, or for never having sworn by his Genius. He forced parents to attend the executions of their sons,[1] sending a litter for one man who pleaded ill health, and inviting another to dinner immediately after witnessing the death, and trying to rouse him to gayety and jesting by a great show of affability. He had the manager of his gladiatorial shows and beast-baitings beaten with chains in his presence for several successive days, and would not kill him until he was disgusted at the stench of his putrefied brain. He burned a writer of Atellan farces alive in the middle of the arena of the amphitheater, because of a humorous line of double meaning. When a Roman Knight on being thrown to the wild beasts loudly protested his innocence, he took him out, cut off his tongue, and put him back again.

Having asked a man who had been recalled from an exile of long standing, how in the world he spent his time there, the man replied by way of flattery: "I constantly prayed the Gods for what has come to pass, that Tiberius might die and you become Emperor." Thereupon Caligula, thinking that his exiles were likewise praying for his death, sent emissaries from island to island to butcher them all. Wishing to have one of the Senators torn to pieces, he induced some of the members to assail him suddenly, on his entrance into the House, with the charge of being a public enemy, to stab him with their writing-irons, and turn him over to the rest to be mangled. His cruelty was not sated until he saw the man's limbs, members, and bowels dragged through the streets and heaped up before him.

He added to the enormity of his crimes by the brutality of his language. He used to say that there was nothing in his own character which he admired and approved more highly than what he called his ἀδιατρεψία,[2] that is to say, his shameless impudence. When his grandmother Antonia gave him some advice, he was not satisfied merely not to listen but replied:

---

[1] Corroborated by Seneca, in *De Ira* II, 33.

[2] A stoic term for a stoic virtue, meaning "immovable rigor." This in Caligula was callous indifference. Therefore Suetonius explains it as "his shameless impudence."

"Remember that I have the right to do anything to any-body." When he was on the point of killing his brother, and suspected that he had taken drugs as a precaution against poison, he cried: "What! an antidote against Caesar?" After banishing his sisters, he made the threat that he not only had islands, but swords as well. An ex-praetor who had re-tired to Anticyra for his health, sent frequent requests for an extension of his leave. But Caligula ordered him put to death, adding that a man who had not been helped by so long a course of hellebore [1] needed to be bled. On signing the list of prisoners who were to be put to death every ten days, he said that he was clearing his accounts. Having condemned several Gauls and Greeks to death in a body, he boasted that he had subdued Gallograecia.

He seldom had any one put to death except by numerous slight wounds. "Strike so that he may feel he is dying," was his constant order, and soon became well known. When a different man than he had intended had been killed, through a mistake in the names, he said that the victim too had de-served the same fate. He often uttered the familiar line of the tragic poet [2]:

"Let them hate me, so they but fear me."

He often inveighed against all the Senators alike, as adherents of Sejanus and informers against his mother and brothers, producing the documents which he pretended to have burned, and upholding the cruelty of Tiberius as forced upon him, since he could not but believe so many accusers. He con-stantly railed at the equestrian order as devotees of the stage and arena. Angered at the rabble for applauding a faction which he opposed, he cried: "I wish the Roman people had but a single neck." When Tetrinius, the highwayman,

---

[1] Used in antiquity in treating madness, gout, and epilepsy. Anticyra, the refuge mentioned, was in Greece, and was celebrated for its growth of this herb.

[2] From *Atreus*, a tragedy by Accius (cir. 125 B.C.). Only fragments of his work remain.

was demanded,[1] he said all those who cried for him were Tetriniuses also. Once a band of five *retiarii*[2] in tunics, matched against the same number of *secutores*,[3] yielded without a struggle. But when their death was ordered, one of them caught up his trident and slew all the victors. Caligula bewailed this in a public proclamation as a most cruel murder, and expressed his horror of those who had had the heart to witness it.

He even used openly to deplore the state of his times, because they had been marked by no public disasters, saying that the rule of Augustus had been made famous by the Varus massacre, and that of Tiberius by the collapse of the amphitheater at Fidenae, while his own was threatened with oblivion because of its prosperity. And every now and then he wished for some slaughter of his armies, for famine, pestilence, fires, or a great earthquake.

His acts and words were equally cruel, even when he was indulging in relaxation and given up to amusement and feasting. While he was lunching or reveling capital examinations by torture were often made in his presence, and a soldier who was an adept at decapitation cut off the heads of those who were brought from prison. At Puteoli, at the dedication of the bridge that he contrived, as has been said, after inviting a number to come to him from the shore, on a sudden he had them all thrown overboard; and when some caught hold of the rudders of the ships, he pushed them off into the sea with boathooks and oars. At a public banquet in Rome he immediately handed a slave over to the executioners for stealing a strip of silver from the couches, with orders that his hands be cut off and hung from his neck upon his breast, and that he then be led about among the guests, preceded by a placard giving the reason for his punishment. When a gladiator who was practicing with him with wooden swords and fell on purpose, he stabbed him with a real dagger and then ran about with a palm-branch, as victors do Once when

---

[1] Either for punishment or to fight in the arena.
[2] Gladiators who wore no armor and fought with only a lance and a net.
[3] Gladiators who wore helmet and shield and fought with sword or leaden ball.

he stood by the altar dressed as a *popa*,[1] and a victim was brought up, he raised his mallet on high and slew the *cultrarius*.[1] At one of his more sumptuous banquets he suddenly burst into a fit of laughter, and when the Consuls, who were reclining next him, politely inquired at what he was laughing, he replied: "What do you suppose, except that at a single nod of mine both of you could have your throats cut on the spot?"

As a sample of his humor, he took his place beside a statue of Jupiter, and asked the tragic actor Apelles which of the two seemed to him the greater, and when he hesitated, Caligula had him flayed with whips, extolling his voice from time to time, when the wretch begged for mercy, as passing sweet even in his groans. Whenever he kissed the neck of his wife or sweetheart, he would say: "Off comes this beautiful head whenever I give the word." He even used to threaten now and then that he would resort to torture if necessary, to find out from his dear Caesonia why he loved her so passionately.

He assailed mankind of almost every epoch with no less envy and malice than insolence and cruelty. He threw down the statues of famous men, which for lack of room Augustus had moved from the court of the Capitol to the Campus Marius, and so utterly demolished them that they could not be set up again with their inscriptions entire. He then forbade for all time the erection of the statue of any living man anywhere, without his knowledge and consent. He even thought of destroying the poems of Homer, asking why he should not have the same privilege as Plato, who excluded Homer from his ideal commonwealth. More than that, he all but removed the writings and the busts of Vergil and of Titus Livius from all the libraries, railing at the former as a man of no talent and very little learning, and the latter as a verbose and careless historian. With regard to lawyers too, as if intending to do away with any practice of their profession, he often threatened that he would see to it, by Heaven, that they could give no advice contrary to his wish.

---

[1] The function of the *popa* was to stun the animal with a sledge-blow; that of the *cultrarius* to cut the victim's throat.

He took from all the noblest of the city the ancient devices of their families, from Torquatus his collar,[1] from Cincinnatus his lock of hair, from Gnaeus Pompeius the surname Great belonging to his ancient race. After inviting Ptolemy, whom I have mentioned before, to come from his kingdom he received him with honor, then suddenly had him executed for no other reason than that when giving a gladiatorial show, he noticed that Ptolemy on entering the theater attracted general attention by the splendor of his purple cloak. Whenever he ran across handsome men with fine heads of hair, he disfigured them by having the backs of their heads shaved.[2] There was a certain Aesius Proculus, son of a Chief Centurion, called Colosseros because of his remarkable size and handsome appearance. This man Caligula ordered to be suddenly dragged from his seat in the amphitheater and led into the arena, where he matched him first against a Thracian and then against a heavy-armed gladiator. When Proculus was victor in both contests, Caligula gave orders that he be bound at once, clad in rags, and then put to death, after first being led about the streets and exhibited to the women. In short, there was no one of such low condition or such abject fortune that he did not envy him such advantages as he possessed. Since the King of Nemi [3] had now held his priesthood for many years, he hired a stronger adversary to attack him. When one Porius, a gladiator who fought from a light chariot, was vigorously applauded on the day of one of the games for setting his slave free after a victory, Caligula rushed from the amphitheater in such haste that he trod on the fringe of his toga and went headlong down the steps, fuming and shouting that a people who are masters of the world give more honor to a gladiator for a trifling act than to their deified Emperors or to the one still present with them.

He respected neither his own chastity nor that of any one

---

[1] This collar of gold, taken from the neck of a gigantic Gaul killed in single combat by Titus Manlius, afterwards called Torquatus, was worn by his lineal male descendants. The family had become extinct but had been revived by Augustus in C. Nonius Asprenas.

[2] Because he himself was bald.

[3] The priest of Diana at Nemi, who must be a fugitive slave and obtain his office by slaying his predecessor.

cfse. He is said to have had unnatural relations with Marcus Lepidus, with Mnester, an actor in pantomimes, and with certain hostages. Valerius Catullus, a young man of a consular family, publicly proclaimed that he had violated the Emperor and worn himself out in commerce with him. To say nothing of his incest with his sisters and his notorious passion for Pyrallis, the prostitute, there was scarcely any woman of rank whom he did not approach. These as a rule he invited to dinner with their husbands, and as they passed by the foot of his couch, he would inspect them critically and deliberately, as if buying slaves, even putting out his hand and lifting up the face of any one who looked down in modesty. Then, as often as the fancy took him, he would leave the room and send for the one who pleased him best. Returning soon afterward with evident signs of what had occurred, he would openly commend or criticize his partner, recounting her charms or defects and commenting on her conduct. To some he personally sent a bill of divorce in the name of their absent husbands, and had it entered in the public records.

In reckless extravagance he outdid the prodigals of all times in ingenuity, inventing a new sort of baths and unnatural varieties of food and feasts. He would bathe in hot or cold perfumed oils, drink pearls of great price dissolved in vinegar, and set before his guests loaves and meats of gold, declaring that a man ought either to be frugal or Caesar. He even scattered large sums of money among the Commons from the top of the Julian Basilica for several days in succession. He also built Liburnian galleys [1] with ten banks of oars, with sterns set with gems, particolored sails, huge spacious baths, colonnades, and banquet-halls, and even a great variety of vines and fruit trees. In these he would feast even in the daytime amongst singers and dancers as he coasted along the shores of Campania. He built villas and country houses with utter disregard of expense, caring for nothing so much as to do what men said was impossible. So he built moles out into the deep and stormy sea, tunneled rocks of hardest flint, built up plains to the height of mountains and razed mountains to the level of the plain, all with incredible

---

[1] Such galleys, famous for their speed, commonly had but one or two banks of oars.

dispatch, since the penalty for delay was death. To make a long story short, vast sums of money, including the 2,700,-000,000 sesterces [1] which Tiberius Caesar had amassed, were squandered by him in less than the revolution of a year.

Having thus impoverished himself, from very need he turned his attention to pillage through a complicated and cunningly devised system of false accusations, auction sales, and imposts. He ruled that Roman citizenship could not lawfully be enjoyed by those whose forefathers had obtained it for themselves and their descendants, except in the case of sons, since "descendants" ought not to be understood as going beyond that degree. When grants of the deified Julius and Augustus were presented to him, he waved them aside as old and out of date. He also charged all those with making false returns, who, by any means whatsoever, had increased their property since the last census. [2] If any Chief Centurions since the beginning of Tiberius' reign had not named that Emperor or himself among their heirs, he set aside their wills on the ground of ingratitude. He also declared null and void the wills of all others who had said that they intended to make Caesar their heir when they died. When in this way he had aroused such fear among men that even persons unknown to him came to appoint him joint-heir with their friends, and in the case of parents with their children, he accused them of making game of him by continuing to live after such a declaration, and to many of them he sent poisoned cakes. He used further to conduct the trial of such cases in person, naming in advance the sum which he proposed to raise at each sitting, and not rising until it was made up. Impatient of the slightest delay, he once condemned in a single sentence more than forty who were accused on different counts, boasting to Caesonia, when she woke after a nap, of the great amount of business he had done while she was taking her siesta.

Appointing an auction, he put up and sold what was left from all the shows, personally soliciting bids and running them up so high, that some who were forced to buy articles at an enormous price and were thus stripped of their pos-

---

[1] $110,700,000.00.
[2] As an excuse to confiscate their estates.

sessions, opened their veins. A well-known incident is that
of Aponius Saturninus. He fell asleep on one of the benches,
and as the auctioneer was warned by Gaius not to overlook
the praetorian gentleman who kept nodding to him, the bidding was not stopped until thirteen gladiators were knocked
down to the unconscious sleeper at nine million sesterces.[1]

When he was in Gaul and had sold at immense figures the
jewels, furniture, slaves, and even the freedmen of his sisters
who had been condemned to death, finding the business so
profitable, he sent to the city for all the paraphernalia of the
old palace, seizing for its transportation even public carriages and animals from the bakeries, so that bread was often
scarce at Rome and many who had cases in court lost them
from inability to appear and meet their bail. To get rid of
this furniture, he resorted to every artifice of fraud and
imposition. Sometimes he would rail at the bidders for being
avaricious or not ashamed that they were richer than he.
At another time he would feign regret for allowing common
men to acquire the property of princes. Having learned that
a rich provincial had paid two hundred thousand sesterces [2]
to those who issued the Emperor's invitations to be smug-
gled in among the guests at one of his dinner-parties, he was
not in the least displeased that the honor of dining with him
was rated so high. But when next day the man appeared at
his auction, he sent a messenger to hand him some trifle or
other at the price of two hundred thousand sesterces and
say that he should dine with Caesar on his personal invitation.

He levied new and unheard-of taxes, at first through the
Publicans and then, because their profit was so great, through
the Centurions and Tribunes of the praetorian guard, no
class of commodities or persons being exempt from some
kind of tax or other. On all eatables sold in any part of the
city he levied a fixed and definite charge; on lawsuits and
legal processes begun anywhere, a fortieth part of the sum
involved, providing a penalty in case any one was found
guilty of compromising or abandoning a suit; on the daily
wages of porters, an eighth; on the earnings of prostitutes,

[1] $369,000.00.
[2] $8,200.00.

as much as each received for one embrace; and a clause was added to this chapter of the law, providing that those who had ever been prostitutes or acted as panders should be liable to this public tax, and that even matrimony should not be exempt.

When taxes of this kind had been proclaimed, but not published in writing, inasmuch as many offenses were committed through ignorance of the letter of the law, he at last, on the urgent demand of the people, had the law posted up, but in a very narrow place and in excessively small letters, to prevent the making of a copy. To leave no kind of plunder untried, he opened a brothel in his palace, setting apart a number of rooms and furnishing them to suit the grandeur of the place, where matrons and freeborn youths should stand exposed. Then he sent his pages about the Forums and courts to invite young men and old to enjoy themselves, lending money on interest to those who came and having clerks openly take down their names, as contributors to Caesar's revenues. He did not even disdain to make money from gaming, and to increase his gains by falsehood and even by perjury. Having on one occasion given up his place to the player next him and gone into the courtyard, he spied two wealthy Roman Knights passing by, ordered them to be seized at once and their property confiscated, and came back exultant, boasting that he had never played in better luck.

But when his daughter was born, complaining of his narrow means, and no longer merely of the burdens of a ruler but of those of a father as well, he took up contributions for the girl's maintenance and dowry. He also made proclamation that he would receive New Year's gifts, and on the Kalends of January took his place in the entrance to the Palace, to clutch the coins which a throng of people of all classes showered on him by handfuls and pocketfuls. Finally, seized with a mania for feeling the touch of money, he would often pour out huge piles of goldpieces in some open place, walk over them barefooted, and wallow in them for a long time with his whole body.

He had but one experience with military affairs or war, and that was not from any set purpose. For, having gone to

Mevania [1] to visit the river Clitumnus and its grove, he was reminded of the necessity of recruiting his bodyguard of Batavians and was seized with the idea of an expedition to Germany. So without delay he assembled legions and auxiliaries from all quarters, holding levies everywhere with the utmost strictness, and collecting provisions of every kind on an unheard-of scale. Then he began his march and made it at times so hurriedly and rapidly, that the praetorian cohorts were forced, contrary to all precedent, to lay their standards on the pack-animals and thus to follow him, and at other times so lazily and daintily that he was carried in a litter by eight bearers, requiring the inhabitants of the towns through which he passed to sweep the roads for him and sprinkle them to lay the dust.

On reaching his camp, to show his vigilance and strictness as a commander, he dismissed in disgrace the generals who were late in bringing in the auxiliaries from various places. In reviewing his troops he deprived many of the Chief Centurions who were well on in years of their rank, in some cases only a few days before they would have served their time, giving as a reason their age and infirmity. Then, railing at the rest for their avarice, he reduced the rewards given on completion of full military service to six thousand sesterces. [2]

All that he accomplished was to receive the surrender of Adminius, son of Cynobellinus, King of the Britons, who had been banished by his father and had deserted to the Romans with a small force. Yet as if the entire island had submitted to him, he sent a grandiloquent letter to Rome, commanding the couriers who carried it to ride in their post-chaise all the way to the Forum and the House, and not to deliver it to any one except the Consuls, in the temple of Mars the Avenger, before a full meeting of the Senate.

Presently, finding no one to fight with, he had a few Germans of his bodyguard taken across the river and concealed there, and word brought him after luncheon with great bustle and confusion that the enemy were close at hand. Upon this he rushed out with his friends and a part of the praetorian

---

[1] Birthplace of the poet Propertius.
[2] $246.00, half the amount established by Augustus.

cavalry to the woods close by, and after cutting the branches from some trees and adorning them like trophies, he returned by torchlight, taunting those who had not followed him as timorous and cowardly, and presenting his companions and the partners in his victory with crowns of a new kind and of a new name, ornamented with figures of the sun, moon and stars, and called *exploratoriae*. Another time some hostages were taken from a common school and secretly sent on ahead of him, when he suddenly left a banquet and pursued them with the cavalry as if they were runaways, caught them, and brought them back in fetters, in this farce too showing immoderate extravagance. On coming back to the table, when some announced that the army was assembled, he urged them to take their places just as they were, in their coats of mail. He also admonished them in the familiar line of Vergil to "bear up and save themselves for better days." [1]

While he was about these things he rebuked the distant Senate and people of Rome in a stern edict for indulging in revels and frequenting the theaters and their pleasant villas when Caesar was fighting battles and exposing himself to so many dangers.

Finally, as if resolved to make war in earnest, he drew up a line of battle on the shore of the ocean, placed his ballistas [2] and other artillery, and, no one knowing or able to imagine what he was going to do, he all of a sudden commanded they gather sea shells and fill their helmets and pockets with them, calling them "the spoils of ocean, due to the Capitol and the Palatine." As a monument of this victory he erected a lofty tower, from which lights were to shine at night to guide the course of ships, as from the Pharos. [3] Then promising the soldiers a gratuity of a hundred denarii [4] each, as if he had shown precedented liberality, he said, "Go your ways and be happy. Go your ways, you are rich."

Then turning his attention to his triumph, in addition to a few captives and deserters from the barbarians he chose all the tallest of the Gauls, and as he expressed it, those who

---

[1] *Aeneid* I, 207.
[2] Machines which cast stones.
[3] The lighthouse at Alexandria.
[4] About $15.00.

were "worthy of a triumph," as well as some of the chiefs. These he reserved for his parade, compelling them not only to dye their hair red and to let it grow long, but also to learn the language of the Germans and assume barbarian names. He also had the triremes in which he had entered the ocean carried overland to Rome for the greater part of the way. He wrote besides to his financial agents to prepare for a triumph at the smallest possible cost,[1] but on a grander scale than had ever before been known, since they had full power over the property of all men.

Before leaving the province he formed a design of unspeakable cruelty, that of butchering the legions that had begun the mutiny years before just after the death of Augustus,[1] because they had threatened his father Germanicus, their leader, and himself, at the time an infant. And though he was with difficulty turned from this mad purpose, he could by no means be prevented from persisting in his desire to decimate them. Accordingly he summoned them to an assembly unarmed, without even their swords, and surrounded them with armed horsemen. But seeing that some of the legionaries, suspecting his purpose, were stealing off to resume their weapons in case any violence should be offered them, he fled from the assembly and set out for the city in a hurry, turning all his ferocity upon the Senate, against which he uttered open threats, in order to divert the gossip about his own dishonor. He complained among other things that he had been cheated out of his fairly earned triumph, whereas a short time before he had himself given orders that on pain of death no action should be taken about his honors.

Therefore when he was met on the road by envoys from that distinguished body, begging him to hasten his return, he roared, "I will come, and this will be with me," frequently smiting the hilt of the sword which he wore at his side. He also made proclamation that he was returning, but only to those who desired his presence, the equestrian order and the people, for to the Senate he would never more be fellow-citizen nor prince. He even forbade any one of the Senators

---

[1] To himself personally.

to meet him. Then giving up or postponing his triumph, he entered the city on his birthday in an ovation.

Within four months he perished, having dared great crimes and meditating still greater ones. For he had made up his mind to move to Antium, and later to Alexandria, after first slaying the noblest members of the two orders. That no one may doubt this, let me say that among his private papers two notebooks were found with different titles, one called "The Sword" and the other "The Dagger," and both containing the names and marks of identification of those whom he had doomed to death. There was found besides a great chest full of divers kinds of poisons, which they say were later thrown into the sea by Claudius and so infected it as to kill the fish, which were thrown up by the tide upon the neighboring shores.

He was very tall and extremely pale, with a huge body, but very thin neck and legs. His eyes and temples were hollow, his forehead broad and grim, his hair thin and entirely gone on the top of his head, though his body was hairy. Because of this to look upon him from a higher place as he passed by, or for any reason whatever to mention a goat, was treated as a capital offense. While his face was naturally forbidding and ugly, he purposely made it even more savage, practicing all kinds of terrible and fearsome expressions before a mirror.

He was sound neither of body nor mind. As a boy he was troubled with the epilepsy, and while in his youth he had some endurance, yet at times because of sudden faintness he was hardly able to walk, to stand up, to collect his thoughts, or to hold up his head. He himself realized his mental infirmity, and thought at times of going into retirement to clear his brain. It is thought that his wife Caesonia gave him a drug intended for a love potion, which however had the effect of driving him mad. He was especially tormented with sleeplessness. For he never rested more than three hours at night, and even for that length of time he did not sleep quietly, but was terrified by strange apparitions, once for example dreaming that the spirit of the ocean talked with him. Therefore weary of lying in bed wide awake during the greater part of the night, he would now sit upon his couch, and now wander through the long colonnades, crying out from time to time for daylight and longing for its coming.

I think I may fairly attribute to mental weakness the existence of two exactly opposite faults in the same person, extreme assurance and, on the other hand, excessive timorousness. For this man, who so utterly despised the Gods, was wont at the slightest thunder and lightning to shut his eyes, to muffle up his head, and if they increased, to leap from his bed and hide under it. In his journey through Sicily, though he made all manner of fun of the miracles in various places, he suddenly fled from Messana by night, panic-stricken by the smoke and roaring from Aetna's crater. Full of threats as he was also against the barbarians, when he was riding in a chariot through a narrow defile on the far side of the Rhine, and some one said that there would be no slight panic if the enemy should appear anywhere, he immediately mounted a horse and hastily returned to the bridges. Finding them crowded with camp servants and baggage, in his impatience of any delay he was passed along from hand to hand over the men's heads. Soon after, hearing of an uprising in Germany, he made preparations to flee from Rome and equipped fleets for the purpose, finding comfort only in the thought that the provinces across the sea would at any rate be left him, in case the enemy should be victorious and take possession of the summits of the Alps, as the Cimbri, or even of the city, as the Senones had once done. And it was this, I think, that later inspired his assassins with the idea of pretending to the rioting soldiers that he had laid hands on himself in terror at the report of a defeat.

In his clothing, his shoes, and the rest of his attire he did not follow the usage of his country and his fellow-citizens; not always even that of his sex; or in fact, that of an ordinary mortal. He often appeared in public in embroidered cloaks covered with precious stones, with a long-sleeved tunic and bracelets; sometimes all in silks [1] and habited like a woman; at times in sandals or buskins, at times in the sort of shoes worn by light-armed soldiers, and sometimes in the low shoes which are used by females. Most often he exhibited himself

---

[1] Men were forbidden to wear silk.

with a golden beard, holding in his hand a thunderbolt, a trident, or a caduceus, emblems of the Gods. But sometimes he even appeared in the garb of Venus. He frequently wore the dress of a triumphing general, even before his campaign, and sometimes the breastplate of Alexander the Great, which he had taken from his sarcophagus.

As regards liberal studies, he gave little attention to literature but a great deal to oratory, and he was as ready of speech and eloquent as you please, especially if he had occasion to make a charge against any one. For when he was angry, he had an abundant flow of words and thoughts, and his voice and delivery were such that for very excitement he could not stand still and was clearly heard by those at a distance. When about to begin an harangue he threatened in such terms as "that he was about to draw the sword of his lucubrations," holding a polished and elegant style in such contempt that he used to say that Seneca, who was very popular just then, composed "mere school exercises," and that he was "sand without lime." He had the habit too of writing replies to the successful pleas of orators and composing accusations or vindications of important personages who were brought to trial before the Senate. And according as his pen had been more fluent in accusing or in defending he brought ruin or relief by his speech, while he would also invite the equestrian order by proclamation to come in and hear him.

Moreover he devoted himself with much enthusiasm to arts of other kinds and of great variety, appearing as a Thracian gladiator, as a charioteer, and even as a singer and dancer, fighting with the weapons of actual warfare, and driving in circuses built in various places. He was so carried away by his interest in singing and dancing that even at the public performances he could not refrain from singing with the tragic actor as he delivered his lines, or from openly imitating his gestures by way of praise or correction. Indeed, on the day when he was slain he seems to have ordered an all-night vigil for the sole purpose of taking advantage of the license granted by the time of year to make his first appearance on the stage. Sometimes he danced even at night, and once he summoned three Consulars to the Palace at the close of the second watch,[1] and when they arrived in great and deathly fear, he seated them on a stage and then on a sudden burst out with a great din of flutes and clogs,[2] dressed in a cloak and a tunic reaching to his heels, and after dancing a number went off again. And yet, varied as were his accomplishments, the man could not swim.

Toward those to whom he was devoted his partiality became madness. He used to kiss Mnester, the actor of pantomimes, even in the theater, and if any one made even the slightest sound while his favorite was dancing, he had him dragged from his seat and scourged him with his own hand. When a Roman Knight created a disturbance, he sent a Centurion to bid him go without delay to Ostia and carry to King Ptolemy in Mauretania a message the purport of which was: "Do neither good nor ill to the man whom I have sent you." He gave some Thracian gladiators command of his German bodyguard. He reduced the amount of armor of the *murmillones*.[3] When one Columbus had won a victory, but had suffered a slight wound, he had the place rubbed with a poison which he henceforth called "Columbinum." At least it was found mentioned under that name in his list of poisons. He was so passionately devoted to the green faction [4] that he constantly dined and spent the night in their stable, and in one of his revels with them he gave the driver Eutychus two million sesterces in gifts.[5] On the day before the games he used to send his soldiers to enjoin silence in the neighborhood, that the repose of his favorite horse *Incitatus*,[6] might not be disturbed. Besides a stall of marble, a manger of ivory, purple blankets and a collar of precious stones, he even gave this horse a house, with a retinue of slaves and fine furniture, for the more elegant entertainment of the

---

[1] About midnight, since the night was divided into four watches.

[2] The *scabellum* was attached to the feet of dancers and sounded an accompaniment to their movements.

[3] He disliked the gladiators known as *murmillones* because they were the usual opponents of his favorites, the Thracians.

[4] The charioteers in the Circus were divided into four parties, distinguished by their colors, which were red, white, blue, and green.

[5] $82,000.00. The host at a dinner party often gave guests gifts.

[6] "Flyer," "Go-ahead."

guests invited in the horse's name. It is also said that he intended to make him Consul.

During this frantic and riotous career several thought of attempting his life. But when one or two conspiracies had been detected and the rest were waiting for a favorable opportunity, two men made common cause and accomplished their purpose, with the connivance of his most influential freedmen and the officers of the praetorian guard. For these last, having been named, though falsely, as concerned in one of the former conspiracies against him, realized that Caligula hated and feared them. In fact, he exposed them to great odium by at once taking them aside and declaring, drawn sword in hand, that he would kill himself, if they too thought he deserved death. And from that time on he never ceased accusing them one to the other and setting them all at odds.

When they had decided to attempt his life at the exhibition of the Palatine games, as he went out at noon, Cassius Chaerea, Tribune of a cohort of the praetorian guard, claimed for himself the part of striking the first blow. For this man, already well along in years, Gaius had the habit of taunting in most scurrilous manner with wantonness and effeminacy. When he asked for the watchword Gaius would give him "Priapus" or "Venus," and when Chaerea had occasion to thank him for anything, he would hold out his hand to kiss, forming and moving it in an obscene fashion.

His approaching murder was foretold by many prodigies. The statue of Jupiter at Olympia, which he had ordered to be taken to pieces and moved to Rome, suddenly uttered such a peal of laughter that the scaffoldings collapsed and the workmen took to their heels. Immediately following this a man named Cassius came up who declared that he had been bidden in a dream to sacrifice a bull to Jupiter. The Capitol at Capua was struck by lightning on the Ides of March, and also the room of the doorkeeper of the Palace at Rome. Some inferred from the latter omen that danger was threatened to the owner at the hands of his guards; and from the former, the murder of a second distinguished personage, such as had taken place long before on that same day.[1] The soothsayer

---

[1] Referring, of course, to the murder of Julius Caesar.

Sulla too, when Gaius consulted him about his horoscope, declared that inevitable death was close at hand. The lots of Fortune at Antium warned him to beware of Cassius, and he accordingly ordered the death of Cassius Longinus, who was at the time proconsul of Asia, forgetting that the family name of Chaerea was Cassius. The day before he was killed he dreamt that he stood in heaven beside the throne of Jupiter and that the God struck him with the toe of his right foot and hurled him to earth. Some things which had happened on that very day shortly before he was killed were also regarded as portents. As he was sacrificing, he was sprinkled with the blood of a flamingo, and the pantomimic actor Mnester danced a tragedy [1] which the tragedian Neoptolemus had acted years before during the games at which Philip King of the Macedonians was assassinated. In a farce called "Laureolus," in which the chief actor falls as he is making his escape and vomits blood, several understudies [2] so vied with one another in giving evidence of their proficiency that the stage swam in blood. A nocturnal performance besides was rehearsing, in which scenes from the lower world were represented by Egyptians and Aethiopians.

On the ninth day before the Kalends of February at about the seventh hour he hesitated whether or not to get up for luncheon, since his stomach was still disordered from excess of food on the day before, but at length he came out at the persuasion of his friends. In the covered passage through which he had to pass, some boys of good birth, who had been summoned from Asia to appear on the stage, were rehearsing their parts, and he stopped to watch and encourage them. Had not the leader of the troop complained that he had a chill, he would have returned and had the performance given at once. From this point there are two versions of the story: Some say that as he was talking with the boys, Chaerea came up behind and gave him a deep cut in the neck, having first cried, "Do your duty," [3] and that then the Tribune

---

[1] Called *Cinyras,* the story of which is told by Ovid in *Metamorphoses* X.

[2] Understudies in Rome entertained the spectators after a play by imitating the actions of the star.

[3] Formula of the ritual at a sacrifice. The slayer raised his ax with the question, "Shall I not do it?" To which the priest replied, "Do it."

Cornelius Sabinus, who was the other conspirator and faced Gaius, stabbed him in the breast. Others say that Sabinus, after getting rid of the crowd through Centurions who were in the plot, asked for the watchword, as soldiers do, and that when Gaius gave him "Jupiter," he cried "So be it," [1] and as Gaius looked around, he split his jawbone with a blow of his sword. As he lay upon the ground and with writhing limbs called out that he still lived the others dispatched him with thirty wounds, for the general signal was "Strike again." Some even thrust their swords through his privates. At the beginning of the disturbance his litter bearers ran to his aid with their poles, and presently the Germans of his bodyguard, and they slew several of his assassins, as well as some inoffensive Senators.

He lived twenty-nine years and ruled three years, ten months and eight days. His body was conveyed secretly to the gardens of the Lamian family, where it was partly consumed on a hastily erected pyre and buried beneath a light covering of turf. Later his sisters on their return from exile dug it up, cremated it, and consigned it to the tomb. Before this was done, it is well known that the caretakers of the gardens were disturbed by ghosts, and that in the house where he was slain not a night passed without some fearsome apparition, until at last the house itself was destroyed by fire. With him died his wife Caesonia, stabbed with a sword by a Centurion, while his daughter's brains were dashed out against a wall.

One may form an idea of the state of those times by what followed. Not even after the murder was made known was it at once believed that he was dead, but it was suspected that Gaius himself had made up and circulated the report, to find out by that means how men felt towards him. The conspirators too had not agreed on a successor, and the Senate was so unanimously in favor of reëstablishing the republic that the Consuls called the first meeting, not in the Senate House, because it was named after Julius Caesar, but in the

---

[1] Another formula, which may also be translated "Take the fulfillment of your omen." As though Caligula having named Jupiter, God of the thunderbolt and instant death, should take indeed what that God dealt.

Capitol. Some in expressing their views proposed that the memory of the Caesars be done away with and their temples destroyed. Men further observed and commented on the fact that all the Caesars whose forename was Gaius perished by the sword, beginning with the one who was slain in the time of Cinna.[1]

---

[1] This was Gaius Julius Caesar Strabo, slain in 87 B.C. But the Dictator's father died a natural death, as did also Gaius Caesar, grandson of Augustus.

BOOK V

THE DEIFIED CLAUDIUS

THE DEIFIED CLAUDIUS

THE father of Claudius Caesar, Drusus, who at first had
the forename Decimus and later that of Nero, was born of
Livia within three months after her marriage to Augustus
(for she was with child at the time) and there was a suspicion
that he was begotten by his stepfather in adulterous intercourse. Certain it is that this verse at once became current:

"On certain persons fortune's smiles attend
   That they may children have at three months' end."

This Drusus, while holding the offices of Quaestor and
Praetor, was in charge of the war in Raetia and later of that in
Germany. He was the first Roman general to sail the northern
ocean, and beyond the Rhine with prodigious labor he constructed the huge canals which to this very day are called
by his name. Even after he had defeated the enemy in many
battles and driven them far into the wilds of the interior, he
did not cease his pursuit until the apparition of a barbarian
woman of more than human size, speaking in the Latin
tongue, forbade him to push his victory further. For these
exploits he received the honor of an ovation with the triumphal regalia. After his praetorship he immediately became
Consul and resumed his campaign, but died in his summer
camp, which for that reason was given the name of "Ac-
cursed." The body was carried by the leading men of the
free towns and colonies to Rome, where it was met and received by the Decuries of the Scribes, and buried in the
Campus Martius. But the army reared a monument in his
honor, about which the soldiers on a stated day each year
thereafter were to perform certain ceremonies[1] while the

[1] A *decursus*. The one about the funeral pyre of Augustus is described
by Dio, LVI, 42. After running around it in full armor, the soldiers
cast into the fire the military prizes which they had received from the
Emperor.

cities of Gaul were to offer prayers and sacrifices. The Senate, in adition to many other honors, voted him a marble arch adorned with trophies on the Appian Way, and the surname Germanicus for himself and his descendants. It is the general belief that he was as eager for glory as he was democratic by nature. For in addition to victories over the enemy he greatly desired to win the "noble trophies," [1] often pursuing the leaders of the Germans all over the field at great personal risk. And he made no secret of his intention of restoring the old-time form of government, whenever he should have the power. It is because of this, I think, that some have made bold to write that Augustus suspected him, recalled him from his province, and because he did not obey at once took him off by poison. This I have mentioned, rather not to pass it by, than that I think it true or even probable. For, as a matter of fact, Augustus loved him so dearly while he lived that he always named him joint-heir along with his sons, as he once declared in the Senate; and when he was dead, he eulogized him warmly before the people, praying the Gods to make his Caesars [2] like Drusus, and to grant him, when his time came, as glorious a death as they had given that hero. And not content with carving a laudatory inscription on his tomb in verses of his own composition, Augustus also wrote a memoir of his life in prose.

Drusus had several children by the younger Antonia, but was survived by only three, Germanicus, Livilla, and Claudius.

Claudius was born at Lugdunum on the Kalends of August in the consulship of Iullus Antonius and Fabius Africanus, the very day when an altar was first dedicated to Augustus in that town, and he received the name of Tiberius Claudius Drusus. Later, on the adoption of his elder brother into the Julian family, he took the surname Germanicus. He lost his father when he was still an infant, and throughout almost the whole course of his childhood and youth he suffered so severely from various obstinate disorders that the vigor of both his mind and his body was dulled, and even when he

---

[1] Spoils taken from an enemy's chief when slain in single combat by a Roman general.

[2] Gaius and Lucius, his grandsons through his daughter Julia.

reached the proper age he was not thought capable of any
public or private business. For a long time, even after he
reached the age of independence, he was subject to the supervision of others and under the direction of a teacher, of whom
he himself complains in a book of his, saying that he was a
barbarian and a former chief of muleteers, put in charge of
him for the express purpose of punishing him with all possible severity on every trifling occasion. It was also because
of his weak health that contrary to all precedent he wore a
cloak when he presided at the gladiatorial games which he
and his brother gave in honor of their father. On the day
when he assumed the gown of manhood he was taken in
a litter to the Capitol about midnight without the usual
ceremony.

Yet he gave no slight attention to liberal studies from his
earliest youth, and even published frequent specimens of his
attainments in each line. But even so he could not attain any
public position or inspire more favorable hopes of his future.

His mother Antonia often spoke of him as a monster of a
man, not finished but merely begun by Dame Nature, and if
she accused any one of dullness, she would say that he was a
bigger fool than her son Claudius. His grandmother Augusta
always treated him with the utmost contempt, very rarely
spoke to him, and when she admonished him it was in writing, briefly but severely, or through messengers. When his
sister Livilla heard that he would one day be Emperor, she
openly and loudly prayed that the Roman people might be
spared so cruel and undeserved a fortune. Finally to make it
clearer what opinions, favorable and otherwise, his great
uncle Augustus had of him, I have appended extracts from
his own letters:

"I have talked with Tiberius,[1] my dear Livia, as you requested, with regard to what is to be done with your grandson Tiberius [2] at the games of Mars. Now we are both agreed
that we must decide once for all what plan we are to adopt
in his case. For if he be sound [3] and, to say, complete,

---

[1] That is, Claudius.

[2] The future Emperor.

[3] That is, if he have his five senses. Augustus, in this letter, as in the
two following, employs a number of Greek words and phrases.

what reason have we for doubting that he ought to be advanced through the same grades and steps through which his brother has been advanced? But if we realize that he is wanting and defective in soundness of body and mind, we must not furnish the means of ridiculing both him and us to a public which is wont to scoff at and deride such things. Surely we shall always be in a stew, if we deliberate about each separate occasion and do not make up our minds in advance whether we think he can hold public offices or not. However, as to the matters about which you ask my present advice, I do not object to his having charge of the banquet of the priests at the games of Mars, if he will allow himself to be advised by his kinsman the son of Silvanus, so as not to do anything to make himself conspicuous or ridiculous. That he should view the games in the Circus from the Imperial box does not meet with my approval, for he will be conspicuous if exposed to full view in the front of the auditorium. I am opposed to his going to the Alban Mount or being in Rome on the days of the Latin festival. For, why should he not be made Prefect of the city if he is able to attend his brother to the Mount? You have my views, my dear Livia, to wit that I desire that something be decided once for all about the whole matter, to save us from constantly wavering between hope and fear. Moreover, you may, if you wish, give this part of my letter to our kinswoman Antonia also to read." Again in another letter:

"I certainly shall invite the young Tiberius to dinner every day during your absence, to keep him from dining alone with his friends Sulpicius and Athenodorus. I do wish that he would choose more carefully and in a less scatter-brained fashion some one to imitate in his movements, bearing, and gait. The poor fellow is unlucky. For in important matters, where his mind does not wander, the nobility of his character is apparent enough." Also in a third letter:

"Confound me, dear Livia, if I am not surprised that your grandson Tiberius could please me with his declaiming. How in the world any one who is so lacking in clarity in his conversation can speak with clarity and propriety when he declaims, is more than I can see."

There is no doubt at all what Augustus later decided, and

that he left him invested with no office other than the sacerdotal dignity of Augur, not even naming him as one of his
heirs, save in the third degree [1] and to a sixth part of his
estate, among those who were all but strangers. While the
legacy that he left him was not more than eight hundred
thousand sesterces.[2]

His paternal uncle Tiberius gave him the consular regalia,
when he asked for office. But when he urgently requested the
actual position, Tiberius merely replied by a note in these
words: "I have sent you forty gold-pieces for the Saturnalia
and the Sigillaria." [3] Then at last Claudius abandoned all
hope of advancement and gave himself up to idleness, living
in obscurity now in his house and gardens in the suburbs,
and sometimes at a villa in Campania. Moreover from his
intimacy with the lowest of men he incurred the reproach of
drunkenness and gambling, in addition to his former reputation for dullness. Yet all this time, despite his conduct, he
never lacked attention from individuals or respect from the
public.

The equestrian order twice chose him as their patron, to
head a deputation on their behalf: once when they asked
from the Consuls the privilege of carrying the body of Augustus to Rome on their shoulders, and again when they offered
them their congratulations on the downfall of Sejanus. They
even used to rise and put off their cloaks when he appeared
at the public shows. The Senate too voted that he be made
a special member of the Priests of Augustus,[4] who were
usually chosen by lot, and later, when he lost his house by
fire, that it should be rebuilt at the public expense, and that
he should have the honor of giving his opinion among the
Consulars. This second decree was however repealed, since
Tiberius urged Claudius's infirmity as a reason, and promised
that he would make the loss good through his own generosity.

---

[1] And such had little or no prospect of receiving their inheritance.

[2] $32,800.00.

[3] December 21 and 22, an extension of the joyous Saturnalia. It was
customary on these days to make presents of little images of various
sorts called *sigilla*.

[4] The order founded by Tiberius for the worship of the Deified Augustus.

Yet when Tiberius died, he named Claudius only among his heirs in the third degree, to a third part of his estate, although he gave him in addition a legacy of about two million sesterces,[1] and expressly commended him besides to the armies and to the Senate and people of Rome with the rest of his kinsfolk.

It was only under his brother's son Gaius Caligula, who in the early part of his reign tried to gain popularity by every device, that he at last began his official career, holding the consulship as his colleague for two months. And it chanced that as he entered the Forum for the first time with the fasces, an eagle that was flying by lit upon his shoulder. He was also allotted a second consulship, to be held four years later,[2] and several times he presided at the shows in place of Caligula, and was greeted by the people now with "Success to the Emperor's uncle!" and now with "All hail to the brother of Germanicus!"

But all this did not save him from constant insults. For, if he came to dinner a little after the appointed time, he took his place with difficulty, and only after making the round of the dining-room. Whenever he went to sleep after dinner, which was a habit of his, he was pelted with the stones of olives and dates, and sometimes he was awakened by the jesters with a whip or cane, in pretended sport. They used also to put slippers on his hands as he lay snoring, so that when he was suddenly aroused he might rub his face with them.

But he was exposed also to actual dangers. First, in his own consulship, when, having been too remiss in contracting for and erecting the statues of the Emperor's brothers, Nero and Drusus, he was very near being deprived of his office. Afterwards he was continually harassed by all kinds of accusations, brought against him by strangers or even by his own domestics. Finally, when the conspiracy of Lepidus and Gaetulicus was detected and he was sent to Germany as one of the envoys to congratulate the Emperor, he was really in peril of his life, since Caligula raged and fumed because his

---

[1] $82,000.00.

[2] Caligula appointed a number of Consuls at once and they drew lots for the year they should serve.

uncle of all men had been sent to him, as if to a child in need of a guardian. So great, indeed, was his wrath that some have written that Claudius was even thrown into the river clothes and all, just as he had come. Moreover, from that time on he always gave his opinion in the Senate last among the Consulars, having the question put to him after all the rest by way of humiliation. A case involving the forgery of a will was even admitted, in which Claudius himself was one of the signers. At last he was forced to pay eight million sesterces [1] to enter a new priesthood, which reduced him to such straitened circumstances that he was unable to meet the obligation incurred to the treasury. Whereupon, by edict of the Prefects, his property was advertised for sale to meet the deficiency, in accordance with the law regulating confiscations.

Having spent the greater part of his life under these and like circumstances, he became Emperor in his fiftieth year by a remarkable freak of fortune.

When the assassins of Caligula shut out the crowd under pretense that the Emperor wished to be alone, Claudius was ousted with the rest and withdrew to an apartment called the Hermaeum. A little later, in great terror at the news of the murder, he stole away to a balcony hard by and hid among the curtains which hung before the door. As he cowered there, a common soldier, who was prowling about at random, saw his feet, and intending to ask who he was, pulled him out and he recognized him. When Claudius fell at his feet in terror, he hailed him as Emperor. Then he took him to the rest of his comrades, who were as yet in a condition of uncertainty and purposeless rage. These placed him in a litter, took turns in carrying it, since his own bearers had made off, and bore him in a state of despair and terror to the Camp, while the throng that met him pitied him, as an innocent man who was being hurried off to execution. Received within the rampart, he spent the night among the sentries, somewhat recovered from his fright, but in no great hopes of the succession. For the Consuls with the Senate and the city cohorts, resolved on maintaining the public liberty, had taken possession of the Forum and the Capitol. When

---

[1] $328,000.00.

he too was summoned to the House by the Tribunes of the Commons, to give his advice on the situation, he sent word that "he was detained by force and compulsion." But the next day, since the Senate was dilatory in putting through its plans because of the tiresome bickering of those who held divergent views, while the populace, who stood about the hall, called for one ruler and expressly named Claudius, he allowed the alarmed assembly of the soldiers to swear allegiance to him, and promised each man fifteen thousand sesterces.[1] Thus was he the first of the Caesars who resorted to bribery to secure the fidelity of the troops.

As soon as his power was firmly established, he considered it of foremost importance to obliterate the memory of the two days when men had thought of changing the form of government. Accordingly he made a decree that all that had been done and said during that period should be pardoned and forever forgotten. He kept his word, too, save only that a few of the Tribunes and Centurions who had conspired against Caligula were put to death, both to make an example of them and because he knew that they had also demanded his own death.

Then turning to the duties of family loyalty, he adopted as his most sacred and frequent oath "By Augustus." He had the Senate vote divine honors to his grandmother Livia, with a chariot to be drawn by elephants [2] in the procession at the Circus, as had been appointed for Augustus, and public offerings to the shades of his parents; also annual games in the Circus on his father's birthday, and for his mother a carriage to bear her image through the Circus and the surname of Augusta, which she had declined during her lifetime. In memory of his brother,[3] whom he took every opportunity of honoring, he brought out a Greek comedy in the contest at Naples and awarded it the crown in accordance with the decision of the judges. He did not leave even Mark Antony unhonored or without grateful mention, declaring once in a proclamation that he requested the more earnestly that the birthday of his father Drusus be celebrated because

---

[1] $615.00.
[2] For carrying her image.
[3] Germanicus.

it was the same as that of his grandfather Antony. He completed the marble arch to Tiberius near Pompey's theater, which had been voted some time before by the Senate, but left unfinished. Even in the case of Caligula, while he annulled all his acts, yet he would not allow the day of his death to be added to the festivals, although it was also the beginning of his own reign.

But in adding to his own dignity he was modest and unassuming, refraining from taking the forename Imperator, refusing excessive honors, and passing over the betrothal of his daughter and the birthday of a grandson in silence and with merely private ceremonies. He recalled no one from exile except with the approval of the Senate. He obtained from the members as a favor the privilege of bringing into the House with him the Prefect of the praetorian guard and the Tribunes of the Soldiers, and the ratification of the judicial acts of his agents in the provinces. He likewise obtained from the Consuls permission to hold fairs on his private estates. He often appeared as one of the advisers at cases tried before the magistrates. And when they gave games, he also arose with the rest of the audience and showed his respect by acclamations and applause. When the Tribunes of the Commons appeared before him as he sat upon the tribunal, he apologized to them because for lack of room he could not hear them unless they stood up.

By such conduct he won so much love and devotion in a short time, that when it was reported that he had been waylaid and killed on a journey to Ostia the people were horror-stricken, and with dreadful execrations continued to assail the soldiers as traitors, and the Senate as murderers, until finally one or two men, and later several, were brought forward upon the rostra by the magistrates and assured the people that Claudius was safe and on his way to the city.

Yet he did not remain throughout without experience of treachery, but he was attacked by individuals, by a conspiracy, and finally by a civil war. A man of the Commons was caught near his bed-chamber in the middle of the night, dagger in hand. And two members of the equestrian order were found lying in wait for him in public places, one ready to attack him with a sword-cane as he came out of the theater, the other with a hunting knife as he was sacrificing in the temple of Mars. Asinius Gallus and Statilius Corvinus, grandsons of the orators, Pollio and Messala, conspired to overthrow him, aided by a number of his own freedmen and slaves. The civil war was set on foot by Furius Camillus Scribonianus, Governor of Dalmatia, but his rebellion was put down within five days, since the legions which had changed their allegiance were turned from their purpose by superstitious fear for, when the order was given to march to their new commander, by some providential chance the eagles could not be adorned nor the standards pulled up and moved.[1]

He held four consulships in addition to his original one. Of these the first two were in successive years, while the other two followed at intervals of four years each, the last for six months, the others for two. In his third he was substituted for one of the Consuls who had died, a thing which was without precedent in the case of an Emperor. He administered justice most conscientiously both as Consul and when out of office, even on his own anniversaries and those of his family, and sometimes even on festivals of ancient date and days of ill-omen. He did not always follow the letter of the laws, but modified their severity or lenity in many cases according to his own notions of equity and justice. For to those who lost their suits before private judges by insisting upon more than appeared to be their due he allowed a new trial, while he even exceeded the punishment appointed by law and condemned to the wild beasts those who were convicted of especially heinous crimes.

But in hearing and deciding cases he showed strange inconsistency of temper, for he was now careful and shrewd, sometimes hasty and inconsiderate, occasionally silly and like a crazy man. In revising the lists of the Decuries for court duty, he disqualified a man who had presented himself without mentioning that he was immune because of the number of his children, on the ground that he had a passion for jury-duty. Another one of them, who was challenged by his op-

---

[1] Bad signs. On breaking camp the eagles were decorated with garlands and anointed with perfumes.

ponents about a suit of his own, said that it did not properly come before Caesar's tribunal, but the ordinary courts; whereupon Claudius compelled him at once to bring the case before him, saying that the man would show in a case affecting his own interests how just a juror he would be in the affairs of others. When a woman refused to recognize her son, and the evidence on both sides was conflicting, he forced her to admit the truth by ordering her to marry the young man. Whenever one party to a suit was absent, he was prone to decide in favor of the one who was present, without considering whether his opponent had failed to appear through his own fault or from a necessary cause. On a man's being convicted of forgery, some one cried out that his hands ought to be cut off; whereupon Claudius insisted that an executioner be summoned at once with knife and block. In a case involving citizenship a fruitless dispute arose among the advocates as to whether the defendant ought to make his appearance in the toga or in a Greek mantle, and the Emperor, with the idea of showing absolute impartiality, made him change his garb several times, according as he was accused or defended.[1] In one case he is credited with having rendered the following decision, which he had actually written out beforehand: "I decide in favor of those who have told the truth."

By such acts as these he so discredited himself that he was held in general and open contempt. One man in making excuses for a witness that the Emperor had summoned from one of the provinces, said that he could not appear, but for a long time would give no reason. At last, after a long series of questions, he said: "He's dead; I think the excuse is a lawful one." Another in thanking the Emperor for allowing him to defend his client added "After all, it is usual." I myself used to hear older men say that the pleaders took such advantage of his good-nature, that they would not only call him back when he left the tribunal, but would catch hold of the fringe of his robe, and sometimes of his foot, and thus detain him. To prevent any surprise at this, I may add that a common Greek pettifogger let slip this remark in a hot de-

[1] Only a Roman citizen had the right to wear the toga.

bate: "You are both an old man and a fool." All the world knows that a Roman Knight, who was tried for improper conduct towards women on a false charge trumped up by unscrupulous enemies, seeing common strumpets called as witnesses against him and their testimony admitted, hurled the stylus and tablets which he held in his hand into the Emperor's face with such force as to cut his cheek badly, at the same time loudly reviling his cruelty and stupidity.

He also assumed the office of Censor, which had long been discontinued, ever since the term of Plancus and Paulus. But in this office too he was variable, and both his theory and his practice were inconsistent. In his review of the Knights he let off a young man of evil character, whose father said that he was perfectly satisfied with him, without any public censure, saying "He has a censor of his own." Another who was notorious for corruption and adultery he merely admonished to be more restrained in his indulgence, or at any rate more circumspect, adding, "For why should I know what mistress you keep?" When he had removed the mark of censure affixed to one man's name, yielding to the entreaties of the latter's friends, he said: "But let the erasure be seen." He not only struck from the list of jurors a man of high birth, a leading citizen of the province of Greece, because he did not know Latin, but even deprived him of the rights of citizenship. Nor in this review would he permit any one to render the account of his life by an advocate, but obliged each man to speak for himself in the best way he could. And he degraded many, some contrary to their expectation and on the novel charge that they had left Italy without consulting him and obtaining leave of absence. One man he so treated merely because he had been companion to a King in his province, citing the case of Rabirius Postumus, who in bygone days had been tried for treason because he had followed Ptolemy to Alexandria, to recover a loan. When he attempted to degrade still more, he found them in most cases blameless. For, owing to the great carelessness of his agents, but to his own greater shame, those whom he accused of celibacy, childlessness, or lack of means proved that they were married, or fathers, or well-to-do. In fact, one man, who was charged with having stabbed himself stripped off his clothing and showed a body without a scar.

Other noteworthy acts of his censorship were the following. He had a silver chariot of costly workmanship, which was offered for sale in the Sigillaria,[1] bought and cut to pieces in his presence. In one single day he made twenty proclamations, among them two: in one of which he advised everybody that when the yield of the vineyards is bountiful the wine casks should be well smeared with pitch; and in the other that nothing was so effective a cure for snake-bite as the juice of the yew tree.

He made but one campaign and that of little importance. When the Senate voted him the triumphal regalia, thinking the honor beneath the imperial dignity and desiring the glory of a legitimate triumph, he chose Britain as the best place for gaining it, a land that had been attempted by no one since the Deified Julius and was just at that time in a state of rebellion because of the refusal to return certain deserters. On the voyage thither from Ostia he was nearly cast away twice in furious north-westers, off Liguria and near the Stoechades[2] islands. Therefore he made the journey from Massilia[3] all the way to Gesoriacum[4] by land, crossed from there, and without any battle or bloodshed received the submission of a part of the island, returned to Rome within six months after leaving the city, and celebrated a triumph of great splendor. To witness the sight he allowed not only the Governors of the provinces to come to Rome, but even some of the exiles. And among the tokens of his victory he set a naval crown on the gable of the Palace beside the civic crown, as a sign that he had crossed and, as it were, subdued the Ocean. His wife Messalina followed his chariot in a carriage, as did also those who had won the triumphal regalia in the same war. The rest marched on foot in purple-bordered togas, except Marcus Crassus Frugi, who rode a caparisoned horse and wore a tunic embroidered with palms, because he was receiving the honor for the second time.

---

[1] There was both a quarter and a street in Rome by this name.
[2] Iles d'Hyères, off Toulon.
[3] Marseilles.
[4] Boulogne.

He always gave scrupulous attention to the care of the city and the supply of grain. On the occasion of a stubborn fire in the Aemiliana [1] he remained in the Diribitorium [2] for two nights, and when a body of soldiers and of his own slaves could not give sufficient help, he summoned the Commons from all parts of the city through the magistrates, and placing bags full of money before them, urged them to the rescue, paying each man on the spot a suitable reward for his services.

When there was a scarcity of grain because of long-continued droughts, he was once stopped in the middle of the Forum by a mob and so pelted with abuse and at the same time with pieces of bread, that he was barely able to make his escape to the Palace by a back door. After this experience he resorted to every possible means to bring grain to Rome, even in the winter season. To the merchants he held out the certainty of profit by assuming the expense of any loss that they might suffer from storms. To those who would build merchant ships he offered large bounties adapted to the condition of each, namely: to a citizen, exemption from the *lex Papia Poppaea;* [3] to those who had limited citizenship, the rights of full citizenship; to women, the privileges allowed the mothers of four children. And all these provisions are in force to-day.

The public works which he completed were great and essential rather than numerous. They were in particular the following.

An aqueduct begun by Caligula. Also the outlet of Lake Fucinus and the harbor at Ostia, although in the case of these two he knew that Augustus had refused the former to the Marsians in spite of their frequent requests, and that the latter had often been thought of by the Deified Julius, but given up because of its difficulty. He brought to the city on stone arches the cool and abundant founts of the Claudian

---

[1] A suburb of Rome, north of the city and outside the Servian wall.

[2] Dio (LV, 8) calls this the largest building ever covered by a single roof. It was in the Campus Martius. In it the votes were sorted and counted.

[3] After the failure of Augustus' marriage law (See *Augustus*) this less rigorous one was passed, 9 A.D.

aqueduct, one of which is called Caeruleus and the other Curtius and Albudignus, and at the same time the spring of the new Anio, distributing them into many beautifully ornamented pools. He made the attempt on the Fucine Lake as much in the hope of gain as of glory, inasmuch as there were some who agreed to drain it at their own cost, provided the land that was uncovered be given to them. He finished the outlet, which was three miles in length, partly by leveling and partly by tunneling a mountain, a work of great difficulty and requiring eleven years, although he had thirty thousand men at work all the time without interruption. He constructed the harbor at Ostia by building curving breakwaters on the right and left, while before the entrance he placed a mole of deep water. To give this mole a firmer foundation, he first sank the ship in which the great obelisk [1] had been brought from Egypt, and then securing it by piles, built upon it a very lofty tower after the model of the Pharos at Alexandria, to be lighted at night to guide the course of ships.

He very often distributed largesses to the people. He also gave several splendid shows, not merely the usual ones in the customary places, but some of a new kind and some revived from ancient times, and in places where no one had ever given them before. He opened the games at the dedication of Pompey's theater, which he had restored when it was damaged by a fire, from a raised seat in the orchestra, after first offering sacrifice at the temples in the upper part of the auditorium and coming down through the tiers of seats while all sat in silence. He also celebrated secular games, alleging that they had been given too early by Augustus and not reserved for the regular time, although he himself writes in his own History that when they had been discontinued for a long time, Augustus restored them to their proper place after a very careful calculation of the intervals. Therefore the herald's proclamation was greeted with laughter, when he invited the people in the usual formula to games "which no one had ever seen or would ever see again." For some were still living who had seen them before, and some actors who had

---

[1] Brought by Caligula from Heliopolis. Now standing before St. Peter's.

appeared at the former performance appeared at that time as well. He often gave games in the Vatican Circus [1] also, at times with a beast-baiting between every five races. But the Great Circus he adorned with barriers of marble and gilded goals, whereas before they had been of common seats to the Senators, who had been in the habit of viewing the games with the rest of the people. In addition to the chariot races he exhibited the game called Troy and also panthers, which were hunted down by a squadron of the praetorian cavalry under the lead of the Tribunes and the Prefect himself. He also exhibited Thessalian horsemen, who drive wild bulls all over the arena, leaping upon them when they are tired out and throwing them to the ground by the horns.

He gave many gladiatorial shows and in many places: one in yearly celebration of his accession, in the Praetorian Camp without wild beasts and fine equipment, and one of the regular and usual kind in the Saepta; another in the same place not in the regular list, short and lasting but a few days, to which he was the first to apply the name of *sportula*, because before giving it for the first time he made proclamation that he invited the people "as it were to an extempore meal, hastily prepared." Now there was no form of entertainment at which he was more familiar and free, even thrusting out his left hand,[2] as the Commons did, and counting aloud on his fingers the gold pieces which were paid to the victors; and ever and anon he would address the audience, and invite and urge them to merriment, calling them "masters" from time to time, and interspersing feeble and far-fetched jokes. For example, when they called for Palumbus [3] he promised that they should have him, "if he could be caught." The following, however, was both exceedingly timely and salutary: when he had granted the wooden sword [4] to one of those gladiators who fight from a light chariot, for whose discharge four sons begged, and the act was received with loud and general applause, he at once circulated a note, pointing out

---

[1] Built by Caligula where St. Peter's now stands.

[2] Undignified in an Emperor. The left arm was kept close to the body and covered decently in the folds of the toga.

[3] "The Dove," nickname of a gladiator.

[4] The symbol of discharge.

to the people how greatly they ought to desire children, since
they saw that they brought favor and protection even to a
gladiator. He gave representations in the Campus Martius
of the storming and sacking of a town in the manner of real
warfare, as well as of the surrender of the Kings of the
Britons, and presided clad in a general's cloak. Even when
he was on the point of letting out the water from Lake
Fucinus he gave a sham sea-fight first. But when the combatants cried out, "Hail, Emperor, they who are about to
die salute thee," he replied, "Or not." [1] Taking this to mean
he wished to excuse them from this encounter, they all refused to fight. Upon this he hesitated for some time about
destroying them all with fire and sword, but at last leaping
from his throne and running along the edge of the lake with
his ridiculous tottering gait, he induced them to fight, partly
by threats and partly by promises. At this performance a
Sicilian and a Rhodian fleet engaged, each numbering twelve
triremes, and the signal was sounded on a horn by a silver
Triton, which was raised from the middle of the lake by a
mechanical device.

Touching religious ceremonies and civil and military customs, as well as the condition of all classes at home and
abroad, he corrected various abuses, revived some old customs or even established new ones. In admitting priests into
the various colleges he never named any one until he had
first taken oath. He scrupulously observed the custom of
having the Praetor call an assembly and proclaim a holiday,
whenever there was an earthquake within the city, as well
as that of offering up a supplication whenever a bird of ill-
omen was seen on the Capitol. This last he himself conducted
in his capacity of Chief Priest, first reciting the form of words
to the people from the rostra, after all mechanics and slaves
had been ordered to withdraw.

The season for holding court, formerly divided into a winter and a summer term, he made continuous. Jurisdiction in
cases of trust, which it had been usual to assign each year
and only to magistrates in the city, he delegated for all time
and extended to the Governors of the provinces. He an-

---

[1] About to die. One of Claudius' feeble jokes.

nulled a clause added to the *lex Papia Poppaea* by Tiberius, implying that men of sixty could not beget children. He made a law that guardians might be appointed for orphans by the Consuls, contrary to the usual procedure, and that those who were banished from a province by its magistrates should also be debarred from the city and from Italy. He himself imposed upon some a new kind of punishment, by forbidding them to go more than three miles outside of the city.

When about to conduct business of special importance in the House, he took his seat between the two Consuls or on the Tribunes' bench. He reserved to himself the granting of permission to travel, which had formerly been requested of the Senate.

He gave the consular regalia even to the second grade of stewards. If any refused senatorial rank,[1] he took from them that of Knight also. Though he had declared at the beginning of his reign that he would choose no one as a Senator who did not have a Roman citizen for a great-great-grandfather, he gave the broad stripe even to a freedman's son, but only on condition that he should first be adopted by a Roman Knight. Even then, fearful of criticism, he declared that the Censor, Appius Caecus, the ancient founder of his family, had admitted the sons of freedmen into the Senate. But he did not know that in the days of Appius and for some time afterwards the term "freedmen" designated, not those who were themselves manumitted, but their freeborn sons. He obliged the College of Quaestors to give a gladiatorial show in place of paving the roads; then depriving them of their official duties at Ostia and in Gaul, he restored to them the charge of the treasury of Saturn,[2] which had in the meantime been administered by Praetors, or by ex-praetors, as in our time.

He gave the triumphal regalia to Silanus, his daughter's affianced husband, who was still a boy, and conferred them on older men so often and so readily, that a joint petition was circulated in the name of the legions, praying that those emblems be given the Consular-Governors at the same time

---

[1] A common reason for this was the desire to engage in business, which Senators were not allowed to do.

[2] The state treasury in the temple of Saturn in the Forum.

with their armies, to prevent their seeking all sorts of pre-
texts for war. To Aulus Plautius he also granted an ovation,[1]
going out to meet him when he entered the city, and honoring
him by walking on his left as they went to the Capitol and
back. He allowed Gabinius Secundus to assume the surname
of Cauchius because of his conquest of the Cauchi, a German nation.

His military organization of the Knights was this: after
the command of a cohort they were promoted to head a
division of cavalry, and after that to Tribune of a legion.
He also instituted a series of military positions and a kind
of fictitious service, which is called "supernumerary" and
could be performed *in absentia* and in name only. He even
had the Senate pass a decree forbidding soldiers to enter the
houses of Senators to pay their respects. He confiscated the
property of those freedmen who passed as Roman Knights,
and reduced to slavery again such as were ungrateful and a
cause of complaint to their patrons, declaring to their advocates that he would not entertain any suit they might bring
against their own freedmen. When certain men were exposing their sick and worn out slaves on the Island of Aesculapius [2] because of the trouble of treating them, Claudius
decreed that all such slaves were free, and that if they recovered, they should not return to the control of their
master. But if any one preferred to kill such a slave rather
than to abandon him, he was liable to the charge of murder.
He provided by an edict that travelers should not pass
through the towns of Italy except on foot, or in a chair
or litter. He stationed a cohort at Puteoli and one at Ostia,
to guard against the danger of fires.

He forbade men of foreign birth to use the Roman names
so far as those of the clans were concerned. Those who usurped
the privileges of Roman citizenship he executed in the Esquiline field. He restored to the Senate the provinces of Achaia
and Macedonia, which Tiberius had taken into his own charge.
He deprived the Lycians of their independence because of
deadly intestine feuds, and restored theirs to the Rhodians,
since they had given up their former faults. He allowed the

---

[1] To reward his able services as commander of the army in Britain.
[2] In the Tiber at Rome, opposite the Campus Martius.

people of Ilium perpetual exemption from tribute, on the ground that they were the founders of the Roman race, reading upon the occasion an ancient letter of the Senate and people of Rome written in Greek to King Seleucus, in which they promised him their friendship and alliance only on condition that he should keep their kinsfolk of Ilium free from every burden. Since the Jews constantly made disturbances at the instigation of Chrestus,[1] he expelled them from Rome. He allowed the envoys of the Germans to sit in the orchestra, being moved to do so by their naïve self-confidence. For, when they had been taken to the seats occupied by the common people and saw the Parthian and Armenian envoys sitting with the Senate, they moved of their own accord to the same part of the theater, protesting that their merits and rank were no whit inferior. He utterly abolished the cruel and inhuman religion of the Druids among the Gauls, which under Augustus had merely been prohibited to Roman citizens. On the other hand, he even attempted to transfer the Eleusinian rites from Attica to Rome, and had the temple of Venus Erycina in Sicily, which had fallen to ruin through age, restored at the expense of the treasury of the Roman people. He struck his treaties with foreign princes in the Forum, sacrificing a pig and reciting the ancient formula of the Fetial Priests.[2] But these and other acts, and in fact almost the whole conduct of his reign, were dictated not so much by his own judgment as that of his wives and freedmen, since he nearly always acted in accordance with their interests and desires.

He was betrothed twice at an early age: to Aemilia Lepida, great-granddaughter of Augustus, and to Livia Medullina, who also had the surname of Camilla and was descended from the ancient family of Camillus the Dictator. He put away the former before their marriage, because her parents had offended Augustus. The latter was taken ill and died on

---

[1] Roman and Greek form of Christus. But Jesus Christ was supposed to have been crucified in Tiberius' reign. A good example of how hazy the early Jewish-Christian question was in the minds of contemporary enlightened Romans.

[2] They ratified treaties and formally declared war after satisfaction had been refused.

the very day which had been set for the wedding. He then married Plautia Urgulanilla, whose father had been honored with a triumph, and later Aelia Paetina, daughter of an ex-consul. He divorced both these, Paetina for trivial offenses, but Urgulanilla because of scandalous lewdness and the suspicion of murder. Then he married Valeria Messalina, daughter of his cousin Messala Barbatus. But when he learned that besides other shameful and wicked deeds she had actually married Gaius Silius, and that a formal contract had been signed in the presence of witnesses,[1] he put her to death and declared before the assembled praetorian guard that inasmuch as his marriages did not turn out well, he would remain a widower, and if he did not keep his word, he would not refuse death at their hands. Yet he could not refrain from at once planning another match, even with Paetina, whom he had formerly discarded, and with Lollia Paulina, who had been the wife of Gaius Caesar. But his affections were ensnared by the wiles of Agrippina, daughter of his brother Germanicus, aided by the right of exchanging kisses and the opportunities for endearments offered by their relationship. And at the next meeting of the Senate he induced some of the members to propose that he be compelled to marry Agrippina, on the ground that it was for the interest of the State, and that others be allowed to contract similar marriages, which up to that time had been regarded as incestuous. And he married her with hardly a single day's delay. But none were found to follow his example save a freedman and a Chief Centurion, at the solemnization of whose nuptials both he and Agrippina attended.

He had children by three of his wives: by Urgulanilla, Drusus and Claudia; by Paetina, Antonia; by Messalina, Octavia and a son, at first called Germanicus and later Britannicus. He lost Drusus just before he came to manhood, for he was strangled by a pear which he had thrown in the air in play and caught in his open mouth. A few days before this

---

[1] Suetonius does not tell all. The occasion was celebrated with a magnificent supper, to which Messalina invited a large company. Lest they think the affair mere frolic, not meant to be consummated, the adulterous pair ascended the nuptial couch in the presence of the astonished guests.

he had betrothed him to the daughter of Sejanus, which makes me wonder all the more that some say that Drusus was treacherously slain by Sejanus. Claudia was the offspring of his freedman Boter, and although she was born within five months after the divorce [1] and Claudius had begun to rear her, yet he ordered her to be cast out naked at her mother's door and disowned. He gave Antonia in marriage to Gnaeus Pompeius Magnus, and later to Faustus Sulla, both young men of high birth, and Octavia to his stepson Nero, after she had previously been betrothed to Silanus. Britannicus was born on the twenty-second day of his reign and in his second consulship. When he was still very small, Claudius would often take him in his arms and commend him to the assembled soldiers, and to the people at the games, holding him in his lap or in his outstretched hands, and he would wish him happy auspices, joined by the applauding throng. Of his sons-in-law he adopted Nero, while Pompeius and Silanus he not only declined to adopt, but even put to death.

Of his freedmen he had special regard for the eunuch Posides, whom he even presented with the headless spear [2] at his British triumph, along with those who had served as soldiers. He was equally fond of Felix, giving him the command of cohorts and of troops of horse, as well as of the province of Judaea; and he became the husband of three Queens. Also of Harpocras, to whom he granted the privilege of riding through the city in a litter and of giving public entertainments. [3] Still higher was his regard for Polybius, his literary adviser, who often walked between the two Consuls. But most of all he was devoted to his secretary Narcissus and his treasurer Pallas, and he gladly allowed them to be honored in addition by a decree of the Senate, not only with immense gifts, but even with the insignia of Quaestors and Praetors. Besides this he permitted them to amass such wealth by plunder, that when he once complained of the low state of his funds, the witty answer was made that he would have enough and to spare, if he were taken into partnership by his two freedmen.

---

[1] Of Claudius from Urgulanilla.
[2] A common military prize.
[3] Otherwise restricted to Knights.

Wholly under the control of these and of his wives, as I have said, he played the part, not of a prince, but of a servant, lavishing honors, the command of armies, pardons or punishments, according to the interests of each of them, or even their wish or whim; and that too for the most part in ignorance and blindly. Not to go into details about less important matters (such as revoking his grants, rescinding his decisions, substituting false letters patent, or even openly changing those which he had issued), he put to death his father-in-law Appius Silanus and the two Julias, daughters of Drusus and Germanicus, on an unsupported charge and giving them no opportunity for defense; also Gnaeus Pompeius, the husband of his elder daughter, and Lucius Silanus who was betrothed to his younger one. Of these Pompey was stabbed in the embraces of a favorite youth, while Silanus was compelled to abdicate his praetorship four days before the Kalends of January and to take his own life at the beginning of the year, the very day of the marriage of Claudius and Agrippina. He inflicted the death penalty on thirty-five Senators and more than three hundred Roman Knights with such easy indifference, that when a Centurion in reporting the death of an ex-consul said that his order had been carried out, he replied that he had given no order. But he nevertheless approved the act, since his freedmen declared that the soldiers had done their duty in hastening to avenge their Emperor without instructions. It is, however, beyond all belief, that at the marriage which Messalina had contracted with her paramour Silius he signed the contract for the dowry with his own hand, being induced to do so on the ground that the marriage was a feigned one, designed to avert and turn upon another a danger which was inferred from certain portents to threaten the Emperor himself.

He possessed majesty and dignity of appearance, but only when he was standing still or sitting, and especially when he was lying down. For he was tall but not slender, with an attractive face, becoming white hair, and a full neck. But when he walked, his weak knees gave way under him and he had many disagreeable traits both in his lighter moments and when he was engaged in business. His laughter was unseemly and his anger still more disgusting, for he would foam at the mouth and trickle at the nose. He stammered besides and his head was very shaky at all times, but especially when he made the least exertion.

Though previously his health was bad, it was excellent while he was Emperor except for attacks of pain in the stomach, which he said all but drove him to suicide.

He gave frequent and grand dinner parties, as a rule in spacious places, where six hundred guests were often entertained at one time. He even gave a banquet close to the outlet of the Fucine Lake and was well-nigh drowned, when the water was let out with a rush and deluged the place. He always invited his own children to dinner along with the sons and daughters of distinguished men, having them sit at the feet of the couches as they ate, after the old time custom. When a guest was suspected of having stolen a golden bowl the day before, he invited him again the next day, but set before him an earthenware cup. He is even said to have thought of an edict allowing the privilege of breaking wind quietly or noisily at table, having learned of a man who endangered his own life by restraining himself through modesty.

He was eager for food and drink at all times and in all places. Once when he was holding court in the forum of Augustus and had caught the savor of a meal which was preparing for the priests of Mars in the temple of that God hard by, he left the tribunal, went up where the priests were, and took his place at their table. He hardly ever left the dining-room until he was stuffed and soaked. He then went to sleep at once, lying on his back with his mouth open, and a feather was put down his throat to relieve his stomach. He slept but little at a time, for he was usually awake before midnight. But he would sometimes drop off in the daytime while holding court and could hardly be roused when the advocates raised their voices for the purpose. He was immoderate in his passion for women, but wholly free from unnatural vice. He was greatly devoted to gaming, even publishing a book on the art, and he actually used to play while driving, having the board so fitted to his carriage as to prevent his game from being disturbed.

That he was of a cruel and bloodthisty disposition was shown in matters great and small. He always exacted examination by torture and the punishment of parricides [1] at once and in his presence. When he was at Tibur and wished to see an execution in the ancient fashion,[2] no executioner could be found after the criminals were bound to the stake. Whereupon he sent to fetch one from the city and continued to wait for him until nightfall. At any gladiatorial show, either his own or another's, he gave orders that even those who fell accidentally should be slain, in particular the net-fighters, so that he could watch their faces as they died. When a pair of gladiators had fallen by mutually inflicted wounds, he at once had some little knives made from both their swords for his use. He took such pleasure in the combats with wild beasts and of those that fought at noonday, that, anticipating the first, he would go down to the arena at daybreak, and, not to miss the second, he would keep his seat after dismissing the people for luncheon at midday. In addition to the appointed combatants, he would for trivial and hasty reasons match others, even the carpenters, the assistants, and men of that class, if any automatic device, pageant piece, or anything else of the kind had not worked well. He even forced one of his pages to enter the arena just as he was, in his toga.

But there was nothing for which he was so notorious as timidity and suspicion. Although in the early days of his reign, as we have said, he made a display of simplicity, he never ventured to go to a banquet without being surrounded by guards with lances and having his soldiers wait upon him in place of the servants. And he never visited a man who was ill without having the patient's room examined beforehand and his pillows and bed-clothing felt over and shaken out. Afterwards he even subjected those who came to pay their morning calls to search, sparing none the strictest examination. Indeed, it was not until late, and then reluctantly, that he gave up having women and young boys and girls grossly mishandled, and the cases for pens and stylii taken from every man's attendant or scribe. When Camillus began his

---

[1] Seneca, *de Clementia* (I, 23), says Claudius had more parricides sewn in leather bags and drowned in five years' time than in all former time.

[2] For a description of which see *Nero*.

revolution, he felt sure that Claudius could be intimidated without resorting to war. And in fact when he ordered the Emperor in an insulting, threatening, and impudent letter to give up his throne and betake himself to a life of privacy and retirement, Claudius called together the leading men and asked their advice about complying.

He was so terror-stricken by unfounded reports of conspiracies that he tried to abdicate. When, as I have mentioned before, a man with a dagger was caught near him as he was sacrificing, he summoned the Senate in haste by criers and loudly and tearfully bewailed his lot, saying that there was no safety for him anywhere, and for a long time would not appear in public. His ardent love for Messalina too was cooled, not so much by her unseemly and insulting conduct, as through fear of danger, since he believed that her paramour Silius aspired to the throne. On that occasion he made a shameful and cowardly flight to the praetorian camp, doing nothing all the way but ask whether his throne was secure.

No suspicion was too trivial, nor the inspirer of it too insignificant, to drive him on to precaution and vengeance, once a slight uneasiness entered his mind. One of two parties to a suit, when he made his morning call, took Claudius aside, and said that he had dreamed that he was murdered by some one; then a little later pretending to recognize the assassin, he pointed out his opponent, as he was handing in his petition. The latter was immediately seized, as if caught red-handed, and hurried off to execution. It was in a similar way, they say, that Appius Silanus met his downfall. When Messalina and Narcissus had put their heads together to destroy him, they agreed on their parts and the latter rushed into his patron's bed-chamber before daybreak in pretended consternation, declaring that he had dreamed that Appius had made an attack on the Emperor. Then Messalina, with assumed surprise, declared that she had had the same dream for several successive nights. A little later, as had been arranged, Appius, who had received orders the day before to come at that time, was reported to be forcing his way in, and as if this were proof positive of the truth of the dream, his immediate accusation and death were ordered. And Claudius did not hesitate to recount the whole affair to the Senate next day and to thank the freedman, Narcissus, for watching over his Emperor's safety even in his sleep.

He was conscious of his tendency to wrath and resentment and excused both in an edict, drawing a distinction between them and promising that the former would be short and harmless and the latter not without cause. After sharply rebuking the people of Ostia, because they had sent no boats to meet him when he entered the Tiber, and in such bitter terms that he wrote that they had reduced him to the rank of a commoner, he suddenly forgave them and all but apologized. He repulsed with his own hand men who approached him in public at unseasonable times. He also banished a Quaestor's clerk without a hearing, as well as a Senator of praetorian rank, although they were blameless: the former for going too far in pleading a suit against him before he became Emperor; the latter, because, when Aedile, he had fined the tenants of Claudius's estates for violating the law forbidding the selling of cooked victuals, and had whipped his bailiff when he remonstrated. And with the same motive he took from the Aediles the regulation of the cook-shops.

He did not even keep quiet about his own stupidity, but in certain brief speeches he declared that he had purposely feigned it under Caligula, because otherwise he could not have escaped alive and attained his present station. But he convinced no one, and within a short time a book was published, the title of which was "The Elevation of Fools" and its thesis that no one feigned folly.

Among other things men have marveled at his absent-mindedness and blindness, or to use the Greek terms, his μετεωρία and ἀβλεψία. When he had put Messalina to death, he asked shortly after taking his place at the table why the Empress did not come. He caused many of those whom he had condemned to death to be summoned the very next day to consult with him or game with him, and sent a messenger to upbraid them for sleepy-heads when they delayed to appear. When he was planning his unlawful marriage with Agrippina, in every speech that he made he constantly called her his daughter and nursling, born and brought up in his arms. Just before his adoption of Nero, as if it were not bad enough to adopt a stepson when he had a grown-up son of his own, he publicly declared more than once that no one had ever been taken into the Claudian family by adoption.

In short, he often showed such heedlessness in word and act that one would suppose that he did not know or care to whom, with whom, when, or where he was speaking. When a debate was going on about the butchers and vintners, he cried out in the House: "Now, pray, who can live without a snack," and then went on to describe the abundance of the old taverns to which he himself used to go for wine in earlier days. He gave as one of his reasons for supporting a candidate for the quaestorship, that the man's father had once given him cold water when he was ill and needed it. Once when a witness had been brought before the Senate, he said: "This woman was my mother's freedwoman and tire-woman, but she always regarded me as her patron. I mention this because there are still some in my household now who do not look on me as patron." When the people of Ostia made a public petition to him, he flew into a rage on the very tribunal and bawled out that he had no reason for obliging them; that he was surely free if any one was. In fact every day, and almost every hour and minute, he would make such remarks as these; "What! do you take me for a Telegenius?" [1] "Scold me, but hands off!" and many others of the same kind which would be unbecoming even in private citizens, not to mention a prince who lacked neither eloquence nor culture, but on the contrary constantly devoted himself to liberal pursuits.

He began to write a history in his youth with the encouragement of Titus Livius [2] and the direct help of Sulpicius Flavus. But when he gave his first reading to a large audience, he had difficulty in finishing, since he more than once threw cold water on his own performance. For at the beginning of the reading the breaking down of several benches by a fat man raised a laugh, and even after the disturbance was quieted, Claudius could not keep from recalling the incident and renewing his guffaws. Even while he was Emperor

---

[1] Obviously some man proverbial for his folly. Nothing is known about him.

[2] This famous historian died in A.D. 17 during the reign of Tiberius at which time Claudius was about 27.

he wrote a good deal and gave constant recitals through a professional reader. He began his history with the death of the Dictator Caesar, but passed to a later period and took a fresh start at the end of the civil war, realizing that he was not allowed to give a frank or true account of the earlier times, since he was often taken to task both by his mother and his grandmother.[1] He left two books of the earlier history, but forty-one of the later. He also composed an autobiography in eight books, lacking rather in good taste than in style, as well as a "Defense of Cicero against the writings of Asinius Gallus," a work of no little learning. Besides this he invented three new letters and added them to the alphabet, maintaining that they were greatly needed.[2] He published a book on their theory when he was still in private life, and when he became Emperor had no difficulty in bringing about their general use. These characters may still be seen in numerous books, in the record of daily events, and in inscriptions on public buildings.

He gave no less attention to Greek studies, taking every occasion to declare his regard for that language and its superiority. To a foreigner who held forth both in Greek and in Latin he said: "Since you are ready with both our tongues"; and in commending Achaia to Senators he declared that it was a province dear to him through the association of kindred studies; while in the Senate he often replied in that language to Greek envoys. Indeed he quoted many Homeric lines from the tribunal, and whenever he had punished an enemy or a conspirator, he commonly gave the Tribune of the guard this verse when he asked for the usual watchword:

"Ward off stoutly the man who first assails you." [3]

At last he even wrote historical works in Greek: twenty books of Etruscan History and eight of Carthaginian. Because of these works there was added to the old Museum at Alexandria a new one called after his name, and it was provided that in the one his Etruscan History should be read each year

[1] Daughter and widow respectively of Mark Antony.

[2] Ⱶ, to represent a sound between i and u; Ↄ for bs or ps; Ⱶ for consonantal u.

[3] Iliad XXIV, 369.

from beginning to end, and in the other his Carthaginian, by various readers in turn, in the manner of public recitations.

Towards the end of his life he had shown some plain signs of repentance for his marriage with Agrippina and his adoption of Nero. For, when his freedmen expressed their approval of a trial in which he had the day before condemned a woman for adultery, he declared that it had been his destiny also to have wives who were all unchaste, but not unchastened. And shortly afterwards meeting Britannicus,[1] he hugged him close and urged him to grow up and receive from his father an account of all that he had done, adding in Greek, "He who dealt the wound will heal it." When he expressed his intention of giving Britannicus the gown of manhood, since his stature justified it though he was still young and immature, he added: "That the Roman people may at last have a genuine Caesar."

Not long afterwards he also made his will and sealed it with the seals of all the magistrates. But before he could go any further, he was cut short by Agrippina, who was being accused besides of many other crimes both by her own conscience and by informers.

That Claudius was poisoned is the general belief, but when it was done and by whom is disputed. Some say that it was his taster, the eunuch Halotus, as he was banqueting on the Citadel with the priests. Others say that at a family dinner Agrippina served the drug to him with her own hand in mushrooms, a dish of which he was extravagantly fond. Reports also differ as to what followed. Many say that as soon as he swallowed the poison he became speechless, and after suffering excruciating pain all night, died just before dawn. Some say that he first fell into a stupor, then vomited up the whole contents of his overloaded stomach, and was given a second dose, perhaps in a gruel, under pretense that he must be refreshed with food after his exhaustion, or administered in an enema, as if he were suffering from a surfeit and required relief by that form of evacuation as well.

His death was kept quiet until all the arrangements were made about the succession. Accordingly vows were offered

---

[1] His own son, by Messalina; later poisoned by Nero, his adopted son.

for his safety, as if he were still ill, and the farce was kept up by bringing in comic actors, under pretense that he had asked to be entertained in that way. He died on the third day before the Ides of October in the consulship of Asinius Marcellus and Acilius Aviola, in the sixty-fourth year of his age and the fourteenth of his reign. He was buried with regal pomp and enrolled among the Gods, an honor neglected and finally annulled by Nero, but later restored to him by Vespasian.

The principal omens of his death were the following: the rise of a long-haired star, commonly called a comet; the striking of his father Drusus' tomb by lightning; and the fact that many magistrates of all ranks had died that same year. There are besides some indications that he himself was not unaware of his approaching end, and that he made no secret of it. For, when he was appointing the Consuls, he made no appointment beyond the month when he died. On his last appearance in the Senate, after earnestly exhorting his children to harmony, he begged the members to watch over the tender years of both. And in the last cause he heard from the tribunal he declared more than once that he had reached the end of a mortal career, although all who heard him shrank at the ominous words and prayed "may God forbid."

BOOK VI

NERO

NERO

OF the Domitian family two branches have acquired distinction, the Calvini and the Ahenobarbi. The latter have as
the founder of their race and the origin of their surname
Lucius Domitius, to whom, as he was returning from the
country, there once appeared twin youths of more than mortal majesty, so it is said, and bade him carry to the Senate
and people the news of a victory, which was as yet unknown.[1]
And as a token of their divinity it is said that they stroked
his cheeks and turned his black beard to a ruddy hue, like
that of bronze. This sign was perpetuated in his descendants,
a great part of whom had red beards. After they had attained
seven Consulships, a Triumph, and two Censorships, and
were enrolled among the patricians, they all continued to use
the same surname. They confined their forenames to Gnaeus
and Lucius, and used even these with a noteworthy variation,
now conferring each one on three members of the family in
succession, and now giving them to individual members in
turn. Thus the first, second, and third of the Ahenobarbi, we
are told, were called Lucius, the next three in order Gnaeus,
while all those that followed were called in turn first Lucius
and then Gnaeus. It seems to me worth while to give an account of several members of this family, to show more clearly
that Nero so far degenerated from the noble qualities of his
ancestors that he retained only their vices, as if those alone
had been transmitted to him by natural inheritance.

To begin then somewhat far back, his great-grandfather's
grandfather, Gnaeus Domitius, when Tribune of the Commons, was enraged at the Pontiffs for choosing another than
himself in his father's place among them, and transferred the
right of filling vacancies in the priesthoods from the colleges

---

[1] Castor and Pollux were the youths, the victory that at Lake Regillus,
498 B.C.

themselves to the people. Then having vanquished the Allobroges and the Arverni [1] in his consulship, he rode through the province on an elephant, attended by a throng of soldiers, in a kind of triumphal procession.[2] He it was of whom the orator Licinius Crassus said that it was not surprising that he had a brazen beard, since he had a face of iron and a heart of lead. His son, who was Praetor at the time, summoned Gaius Ceasar to an investigation before the Senate at the close of his consulship, because it was thought that his administration had been in violation of the auspices and the laws. Afterwards in his own consulship he tried to deprive Caesar of the command of the armies in Gaul, and being named Caesar's successor by his party, was taken prisoner at Corfinium at the beginning of the civil war. Granted his freedom, he at first gave courage by his presence to the people of Massilia, who were hard pressed by their besiegers, but suddenly abandoned them and at last fell in the battle at Pharsalus. He was a man of no great resolution, though he had a violent temper, and when he once attempted to kill himself in a fit of despair and terror, he so shrank from the thought of death that he changed his mind and vomited up the poison, conferring freedom on his physician, since, knowing his master, he had purposely given him what was not a fatal dose. When Gnaeus Pompeius brought forward the question of the treatment of those who were neutral and sided with neither party, he alone was for regarding them as hostile.

He left a son, who was beyond all question better than the rest of the family. He was condemned to death by the Pedian law among those implicated in Caesar's death, though he was guiltless, and accordingly joined Brutus and Cassius, who were his near relatives. After the death of both leaders he retained the fleet of which he had previously been made commander, and even added to it, and it was not until his party had been everywhere routed that he surrendered it to Mark Antony, of his own free will and as though he were conferring a great favor. He too was the only one of those condemned

---

[1] The Allobroges were a tribe of Gauls inhabiting modern Dauphiny and Savoy, the Arverni the environs of modern Auvergne.

[2] Suetonius' error. It was the father of the Tribune who defeated the Allobroges.

by that same law who was allowed to return to his native land, where he successively held all the highest offices. When the civil strife was subsequently renewed, he was appointed one of Antony's lieutenants and offered the chief command by those who were ashamed of Cleopatra. But not daring, on account of a sudden illness with which he was seized, either to accept it or yet positively to refuse it, he went over to the side of Augustus, and a few days later died. Even he did not escape with an unblemished reputation, for Antony openly declared that he had changed sides from desire for the com·pany of his mistress, Servilia Nais.

He was the father of the Domitius who was later well known from being named in Augustus' will as the purchaser of his goods and chattels.[1] He was a man less famous in his youth for his skill in driving than he was later for winning the insignia of a triumph in the war in Germany. But he was haughty, extravagant, and cruel, and when he was only an Aedile, he forced the Censor Lucius Plancus to make way for him on the street. While holding the offices of Praetor and Consul, he brought Roman Knights and matrons on the stage to act a farce. He gave beast-baitings both in the Circus and in all the regions of the city, and also a gladiatorial show, but with such inhuman cruelty that Augustus, after his private warning was disregarded, was forced to restrain him by an edict.

He had by the elder Antonia a son Domitius who became the father of Nero, a man hateful in every walk of life. For, when he had gone to the East on the staff of the young Gaius Caesar, he slew one of his own freedmen for refusing to drink as much as he was ordered, and when he was in consequence dismissed from the number of Gaius' friends, he lived not a whit less lawlessly. On the contrary, in a village on the Appian Way, suddenly whipping up his team, he purposely ran over and killed a boy. And at Rome, right in the Forum, he gouged out the eye [2] of a Roman Knight for being too outspoken in chiding him. He was moreover so dishonest that he not only cheated some bankers of the prices of wares which he had

---

[1] Thabis, his executor, who symbolically purchased all property named in the will before he made the designated payments to the heirs
[2] A favorite mode of attack among the Italians.

bought, but in his praetorship he even defrauded the victors in the chariot races of the amount of their prizes. When for this reason he was held up to scorn by the jests of his own sister, and the managers of the troupes made complaint, he issued an edict [1] that the prizes should thereafter be paid on the spot. Just before the death of Tiberius he was also charged with treason, as well as with acts of adultery and with incest with his sister Lepida, but escaped owing to the change of rulers and died of dropsy at Pyrgi, after acknowledging Nero son of Agrippina, the daughter of Germanicus.

Nero was born at Antium nine months after the death of Tiberius, on the eighteenth day before the Kalends of January, just as the sun rose, so that he was touched by its rays almost before he could be laid upon the ground. Many people at once made many direful predictions from his horoscope, and a remark of his father Domitius was also regarded as an omen. For, while receiving the congratulations of his friends, he said that nothing that was not abominable and a public bane could be born of Agrippina and himself. Another manifest indication of Nero's future unhappiness occurred on his naming day.[2] For, when Gaius Caesar was asked by his sister to give the child whatever name he liked, he looked at his uncle Claudius, who later became Emperor and adopted Nero, and said that he gave him his name. This he did, not seriously, but in jest, and Agrippina scorned the proposal, because at that time Claudius was one of the laughing-stocks of the court.

At the age of three he lost his father, being left heir to a third of his estate. But even this he did not receive in full, since his fellow heir Gaius [3] seized all the property. Then his mother was banished too, and he was brought up at the house of his aunt Lepida almost in actual want, under two tutors, a dancer and a barber. But when Claudius became emperor, Nero not only recovered his father's property, but was also enriched by an inheritance from his stepfather, Passienus Crispus. When his mother was recalled from banishment and reinstated, he became so prominent through her influence

[1] In his capacity of Praetor.
[2] For boys the 9th day after birth.
[3] Caligula.

that it leaked out that Messalina, wife of Claudius, had sent emissaries to strangle him as he was taking his noonday nap, regarding him as a rival of Britannicus. An addition to this bit of gossip is, that the would-be assassins were frightened away by a snake which darted out from under his pillow. The only foundation for this tale was, that there was found in his bed near the pillow the slough of a serpent. All the same, at his mother's desire he had the skin enclosed in a golden bracelet, and wore it for a long time on his right arm. But when at last the memory of his mother grew hateful to him, he threw it away, and afterwards in the time of his extremity sought it again in vain.

While he was still a young, half-grown boy he took part in the game of Troy at a performance in the Circus with great self-possession and success. In the eleventh year of his age he was adopted by Claudius and consigned to the training of Annaeus Seneca,[1] who was then already a Senator. They say that on the following night Seneca dreamed that he was teaching Gaius Caligula, and Nero soon proved the dream prophetic by revealing the cruelty of his disposition at the earliest possible opportunity. For merely because his brother Britannicus had, after his adoption, greeted him as usual as Ahenobarbus, he tried to convince his father[2] that Britannicus was a changeling. Also when his aunt Lepida was accused, he publicly gave testimony against her, to gratify his mother, who was using every effort to ruin Lepida.

At his formal introduction into public life he announced a largess to the people and a gift of money to the soldiers, ordered a parade of the praetorian guard and headed them shield in hand. After this he returned thanks to his father in the Senate. In the latter's consulship he pleaded before him the cause of the people of Bononia in Latin, and of those of Rhodes and Ilium in Greek. His first appearance as judge was when he was Prefect of the City during the Latin Festival, when the most celebrated pleaders vied with one another in bringing before him, not trifling and brief cases according

---

[1] This famous stoic and philosophical writer had, shortly before the death of Tiberius, been released from an eight-year exile in Corsica. He afterwards fell a victim to the jealousy and cruelty of Nero.

[2] His adoptive father, Claudius.

to the usual custom, but many of the highest importance, though this had been forbidden by Claudius. Shortly afterwards he took Octavia to wife and gave games and a beast-baiting in the Circus, that health might be vouchsafed Claudius.

When the death of Claudius was made public, Nero, who was seventeen years old, went forth to the watch between the sixth and seventh hour, since no earlier time for the formal beginning of his reign seemed suitable because of bad omens throughout the day. Hailed Emperor on the steps of the Palace, he was carried in a litter to the praetorian camp, and after a brief address to the soldiers was taken from there to the House. He did not leave there until evening, and, of the unbounded honors that were heaped upon him, he refused but one, the title of Father of his Country, and that because of his youth.

Then beginning with a display of filial piety, he gave Claudius a magnificent funeral, spoke his eulogy, and deified him. He paid the highest honors to the memory of his father Domitius. He left to his mother the management of all public and private business. Indeed, on the first day of his rule he gave to the Tribune on guard the watchword "The Best of Mothers," and afterwards he often rode with her through the streets in her litter. He established a colony at Antium, where he settled the veterans of the praetorian guard together with the richest Chief Centurions, whom he compelled to change their residence. And he also made a harbor there at great expense.

To make his good intentions still more evident, he declared that he would rule according to the principles of Augustus, and he let slip no opportunity for acts of generosity and mercy, or even for displaying his affability. The more oppressive sources of revenue he either abolished or moderated. He reduced the rewards paid to informers against violators of the Papia-Poppaean law to one-fourth of the former amount. He distributed four hundred sesterces [1] to each man of the people, and granted to the most distinguished of the Senators who were without means an annual salary, to some as much

----

[1] $16.40.

as five hundred thousand sesterces.[1] To the praetorian cohorts he gave a monthly allowance of grain free of cost. When he was asked according to custom to sign the warrant for the execution of a man who had been condemned to death, he said: "How I wish I had never learned to write!" He greeted men of all orders off-hand and from memory. When the Senate returned thanks to him, he replied, "When I shall have deserved them." He admitted even the Commons to witness his exercises in the Campus, and often declaimed in public. He read his poems too, not only at home but in the theater as well, so greatly to the delight of all that a thanksgiving[2] was voted because of his recital, while those publicly read were inscribed in letters of gold and dedicated to Jupiter of the Capitol.

He gave many entertainments of different kinds: the *Juvenales*,[3] chariot races in the Circus, stage-plays, and a gladiatorial show. At the first mentioned he had even old men of consular rank and aged matrons take part. For the games in the Circus he assigned places to the Knights apart from the rest,[4] and even matched chariots drawn by four camels. At the plays which he gave for the "Eternity of the Empire," which by his order were called the *Ludi Maximi,* parts were taken by several men and women of both the senatorial order and that of the Knights. A well-known Knight mounted an elephant and slid down a rope. A Roman play of Afranius, too, was staged, entitled "The Fire," and the actors were allowed to carry off the furniture of the burning house and keep it. Every day all kinds of presents were thrown to the people. These included a thousand birds of every kind each day, various kinds of food, tickets for grain, clothing, gold, silver, precious stones, pearls, paintings, slaves, beasts of burden, even trained wild animals, and finally, ships, blocks of houses, and farms.

These plays he viewed from the top of the proscenium. At the gladiatorial show, which he gave in a wooden amphi-

---

[1] $20,500.00

[2] An honor previously conferred only on generals after a great victory.

[3] In commemoration of the first shaving of his beard.

[4] Formerly done only at the theater, though Augustus had given the Senators special seats at other public spectacles.

theater, erected in the district of the Campus Martius within the space of a single year, he had no one put to death, not even criminals. But he compelled four hundred Senators and six hundred Roman Knights, some of whom were well to do and of unblemished reputation, to fight in the arena. Even those who fought with the wild beasts and performed the various services in the arena were of the same orders. He also exhibited a naval battle in salt water with sea monsters swimming about in it. He also presented pyrrhic dances by some Greek youths, handing each of them certificates of Roman citizenship at the close of his performance. The pyrrhic dances represented various scenes. In one a bull mounted Pasiphae, who was concealed in a wooden statue of a cow, or at least many of the spectators thought so. Icarus at his very first attempt to fly fell close by the imperial couch and bespattered the Emperor with his blood. For Nero very seldom presided at the games, but used to view them while reclining on a couch, at first through small openings, though later with his entire box uncovered.

He was likewise the first to establish at Rome a quinquennial contest in three parts, in the Greek manner, that is in music, gymnastics, and horse-racing, which he called the *Neronia,* dedicating at the same time his baths and gymnasium [1] where he supplied every member of the senatorial and equestrian orders with rubbing oil. To preside as judges over the whole contest he appointed ex-consuls, chosen by lot, who occupied the seats of the Praetors. Then he went down into the orchestra among the Senators and accepted the prize for Latin oratory and verse, for which all the most eminent men had contended but which was given to him with their unanimous consent. But when that for lyre-playing was also offered him by the judges, he knelt before it and ordered that it be laid at the feet of Augustus' statue. At the gymnastic contest, which he gave in the Saepta, he shaved his first beard to the accompaniment of a splendid sacrifice of bullocks, put it in a golden box adorned with pearls of great price, and dedicated it in the Capitol. He invited the Vestal

---

[1] Adjoining buildings in the Campus Martius, near the Pantheon. No trace of them remains.

Virgins also to witness the contests of the athletes,[1] because at Olympia the priestesses of Ceres were allowed the same privilege.

I may fairly include among his shows the entrance of Tiridates into the city. He was a King of Armenia, whom Nero induced by great promises to come to Rome. Since he was prevented by bad weather from exhibiting him to the people on the day appointed by proclamation, he produced him at the first favorable opportunity, with the praetorian cohorts drawn up in full armor about the temples in the Forum, while he himself sat in a curule chair on the rostra in the attire of a triumphing general, surrounded by military ensigns and standards. As the King approached along a sloping platform, the Emperor at first let him fall at his feet, but raised him with his right hand and kissed him. Then, while the King made supplication, Nero took the turban from his head and replaced it with a diadem, while a man of praetorian rank translated the words of the suppliant and proclaimed them to the throng. From there the King was taken to the theater, and when he had again done obeisance, Nero gave him a seat at his right hand. Because of all this Nero was hailed as Imperator, and after depositing a laurel wreath in the Capitol,[2] he closed the two doors of the temple of Janus, as a sign that no war was left anywhere.

He held four consulships, the first for two months, the second and the last for six months each, the third for four months. The second and third were in successive years, while a year intervened between these and each of the others.

In the administration of justice he was reluctant to render a decision to those who presented cases, except on the following day and in writing. His procedure was, instead of continuous pleadings, to have each point presented separately by the parties in turn. Furthermore, whenever he withdrew for consultation, he did not discuss any matter with all his advisers in a body, but had each of them give his opinion in written form. These he read silently and in private and then

---

[1] Augustus had prohibited all women from the gladiatorial fights and the athletic contests.

[2] Which was usual only after a triumph.

gave a verdict according to his own inclination, as if it were the view of the majority.

For a long time he would not admit the sons of freedmen to the Senate and he refused office to those who had been admitted by his predecessors. Candidates who were in excess of the number of vacancies received the command of a legion as compensation for the postponement and delay. He commonly appointed Consuls for a period of six months. When one of them died just before the Kalends of January, he appointed no one in his place, expressing his disapproval of the old precedent of Caninus Rebilus, who was Consul but one day. He conferred the triumphal regalia even on men of the rank of Quaestor, as well as on some of the Knights, and sometimes for other than military services. As regards the speeches which he sent to the Senate on various matters, he passed over the Quaestors, whose duty it was to read them, and usually had them presented by one of the Consuls.

He devised a new form for the buildings of the city and in front of the houses and apartments he erected porches, from the flat roofs of which fires could be fought.[1] These he put up at his own cost. He had also planned to extend the walls as far as Ostia and to bring the sea from there to Rome by a canal.

During his reign many abuses were severely punished and put down, and not a few new laws were made: a limit was set to expenditures; the public banquets were confined to a distribution of food; the sale of any kind of cooked viands in the taverns was forbidden, with the exception of pulse and vegetables, whereas before every sort of dainty was exposed for sale. Punishment was inflicted on the Christians, a class of men given to a new and mischievous superstition.[2] He put an end to the diversions of the chariot drivers, who from immunity of long standing claimed the right of ranging at large and amusing themselves by cheating and robbing the

---

[1] This was undoubtedly after the great fire.

[2] Tacitus, in *Annals* XIII, 32, calls the Christian religion "a foreign and deadly superstition." Pliny in Letter 97 of Book X calls it "a depraved, wicked, and outrageous superstition."

people. The pantomimic actors and their partisans were banished from the city.[1]

It was in his reign that a protection against forgers was first devised, by having no tablets signed that were not bored with holes through which a cord was thrice passed.[2] In the case of wills it was provided that the first two leaves should be presented to the signatories with only the name of the testator written upon them, and that no one who wrote a will for another should put down a legacy for himself; further, that clients should pay a fixed and reasonable fee for the services of their lawyers, but nothing at all for the court, which was to be gratuitous, the charges for it to be paid by the public treasury. It was also ordained that the pleading of cases connected with the treasury should be transferred to the Forum and a board of arbiters, and that all appeals from the juries should be made to the Senate.

So far from being actuated by any wish or hope of increasing or extending the empire, he even thought of withdrawing the army from Britain and changed his purpose only because he was ashamed to seem to belittle the glory of his father.[3] He increased the provinces only by the realm of Pontus, when it was given up by Polemon, and that of Cottius in the Alps on the latter's death.

He planned but two foreign tours, to Alexandria and Achaia. The former he gave up on the very day when he was to have started, disturbed by a threatening portent. For as he was making the round of the temples and had sat down in the shrine of Vesta, first the fringe of his garment caught when he attempted to get up, and then such darkness overspread his eyes that he could see nothing. In Achaia he attempted to cut through the Isthmus [4] and called together the praetorians and urged them to begin the work. Then, at a signal given on a trumpet, he was first to break ground

---

[1] Because of their disorderly conduct. But his was worse.

[2] The tablets consisted of three leaves, two of which were bound together and sealed. The contract was written twice, on the open leaf and on the closed ones. In cases of dispute the seals were broken and the two versions compared.

[3] Claudius, his adoptive father.

[4] Of Corinth.

with a mattock and to carry off a basketful of earth upon his shoulders. He also prepared for an expedition to the Pass of the Caspian Mountains, after enrolling a new legion of raw recruits of Italian birth, each six feet tall,[1] which he called the "phalanx of Alexander the Great."

I have brought together these acts of his, some of which are beyond criticism, while others are even deserving of no slight praise, to separate them from his shameful and criminal deeds, of which I shall proceed now to give an account.

Having gained some knowledge of music in addition to the rest of his early education, as soon as he became Emperor he sent for Terpnus, the greatest master of the lyre in those days, and after listening to him sing after dinner for many successive days until late at night, he little by little began to practice himself, neglecting none of the exercises which artists of that kind are in the habit of following, to preserve or strengthen their voices. For he used to lie upon his back and hold a leaden plate on his chest, purge himself by the syringe and by vomiting, and deny himself fruits and all foods injurious to the voice. Finally encouraged by his progress, although his voice was weak and husky, he began to long to appear on the stage, and every now and then in the presence of his intimate friends he would quote a Greek proverb meaning "Hidden music counts for nothing." And he made his début at Naples, where he did not cease singing until he had finished the number which he had begun, even though the theater was shaken by a sudden earthquake shock.[2] In the same city he sang frequently and for several successive days. Even when he took a short time to rest his voice, he could not keep out of sight but went to the theater after bathing and dined in the orchestra with the people all about him, promising them in Greek, that when he had wetted his whistle a bit, he would ring out something good and loud. He was greatly taken too with the rhythmic applause of some Alexandrians, who had flocked to Naples from a fleet that had lately arrived, and summoned more men from

---

[1] Roman measure. A little under 5 ft. 10 in. English.

[2] It collapsed in consequence, but not till the audience had dispersed. Tacitus says nothing about the quake, but corroborates the fall of the building immediately after the performance.

Alexandria. Not content with that, he selected some young
men of the order of Knights and more than five thousand
sturdy young commoners, to be divided into groups and learn
the Alexandrian styles of applause, which they called "the
bees," "the roof-tiles," and "the bricks." [1] These men were
noticeable for their thick hair and fine apparel. Their left
hands were bare and without rings, and they played thin
"claques" vigorously whenever Nero sang. The leaders of
these bands were paid four hundred thousand sesterces each.[2]

Considering it of great importance to appear in Rome as
well, he repeated the contest of the *Neronia* before the appointed time, and when there was a general call for his "divine
voice," he replied that if any wished to hear him, he would
favor them in the gardens. But when the guard of the soldiers which was then on duty seconded the entreaties of the
people, he gladly agreed to appear at once. So without delay
he had his name added to the list of the lyre-players who entered the contest, and casting his own lot into the urn with
the rest, he came forward in his turn, attended by the Prefects of the Guard carrying his lyre, and followed by the
Tribunes of the soldiers and his intimate friends. Having
taken his place and finished his preliminary speech, he announced through the ex-consul Cluvius Rufus that "he would
sing Niobe." And he kept at it until late in the afternoon,
putting off the award of the prize for that event and postponing the rest of the contest to the next year, to have an
excuse for singing oftener. But since even that seemed too
long to wait, he did not cease to appear in public from time
to time. He even thought of taking part in private performances among the professional actors, and a Praetor offered
a million sesterces [3] for his services. He also put on the mask
and sang tragedies representing Gods and heroes and even
heroines and Goddesses, having the masks fashioned in the
likeness of his own features or those of the women of whom
he chanced to be enamored. Among other themes he sang

---

[1] The first seems to have derived its name from the sound, which was
like the humming of bees, the second and third from clapping the hands,
held rounded or hollowed like roof-tiles, or held flat like bricks.

[2] $16,400.00

[3] $41,000.00

"Canace in Labor," [1] "Orestes the Matricide," "The Blinding of Oedipus" and the "Frenzy of Hercules." At the last named performance they say that a young recruit, posted at the entrance of the stage, seeing him in rags and bound with chains, as the argument of the play required, rushed forward to lend him aid.

From his earliest years he had a special passion for horses and talked constantly about the games in the Circus, though he was forbidden to do so. Once when he was lamenting with his fellow pupils the fate of a charioteer of the "Greens," who was dragged by his horses, and his preceptor scolded him, he told a lie and pretended that he was talking of Hector. At the beginning of his reign he used to play every day with ivory chariots on a board, and he came from the country to all the games, even the most insignificant, at first secretly, and then so openly that no one doubted that he would be in Rome on that particular day. He made no secret of his wish to have the number of prizes increased, and in consequence more races were added and the performance was continued to a late hour, while the managers of the troupes no longer thought it worth while to produce their drivers at all except for a full day's racing. He soon longed to drive a chariot himself and even to show himself frequently in public. So after a trial exhibition in his gardens before his slaves and the dregs of the populace, he gave all an opportunity of seeing him in the Circus Maximus, one of his freedmen dropping the napkin [2] from the place usually occupied by the magistrates.

Not content with showing his proficiency in these arts at Rome, he went to Achaia, as I have said, influenced especially by the following consideration. The cities in which it was the custom to hold contests in music had adopted the rule of sending all the lyric prizes to him. These he received with the greatest delight, not only giving audience before all others

---

[1] Canace, daughter of an Etrurian King, whose incestuous intercourse with her brother was detected in consequence of the cries of an infant she had delivered. Whereupon she killed herself with a sword her father had sent her for the purpose. It was a joke in Rome that when Nero was performing this piece "he was laboring in child-birth."

[2] The signal for the start.

to the envoys who brought them, but even inviting them to his private table. When some of them begged him to sing during dinner and greeted his performance with extravagant applause, he declared that "the Greeks were the only ones who had an ear for music and that they alone were worthy of his efforts." So he took ship without delay and immediately on arriving at Cassiope [1] made a preliminary appearance as a singer at the altar of Jupiter Cassius, and then went the round of all the contests.

To make this possible, he gave orders that even those which came in different years should be brought in the compass of one, so that some had even to be given twice. At Olympia, likewise, he introduced a musical competition, contrary to custom. To avoid being distracted or hindered in any way while busy with these contests, he replied to his freedman Helius, who reminded him that the affairs of the city required his presence, in these words: "However much it may be your advice and your wish that I should return speedily, yet you ought rather to counsel me and to hope that I may return worthy of Nero."

While he was singing no one was allowed to leave the theater even for the most urgent reasons. And so it is said that some women gave birth to children there, while many who were worn out with listening and applauding, secretly leaped from the side of the theater, since the gates at the entrance were closed, or feigned death and were carried out as if for burial. The trepidation and anxiety with which he took part in the contests, his keen rivalry of his opponents and his awe of the judges, can hardly be credited. As if his rivals were of quite the same station as himself, he used to show respect to them and try to gain their favor, while he slandered them behind their backs, sometimes assailed them with abuse when he met them, and even bribed those who were especially proficient.

Before beginning, he would address the judges in the most deferential terms, saying that he had done all that could be done, but the issue was in the hands of Fortune, though they, being men of wisdom and experience, ought to exclude

---

[1] Now Corfu.

from their judgment what was merely accidental. When they bade him take heart, he withdrew with greater confidence, but not even then without anxiety, interpreting the silence and modesty of some as sullenness and ill-nature, and declaring that he had his suspicions of them.

In competition he observed the rules most scrupulously, never daring to clear his throat and even wiping the sweat from his brow with his arm.[1] Once indeed, during the performance of a tragedy, when he had dropped his scepter but quickly recovered it, he was terribly afraid that he might be excluded from the competition because of his slip, and his confidence was restored only when his accompanist swore that it had passed unnoticed amid the delight and applause of the people. When the victory was won, he made the announcement himself. It was for that reason he always took part in the contests of the heralds.[2] To obliterate the memory of all other victors in these sacred contests and leave no trace of them, their statues and busts were all thrown down by his order, dragged off with hooks, and cast into privies.

He also drove a chariot in many places, at Olympia even a ten-horse team, although in one of his own poems he had criticized Mithridates for just that thing. But after he had been thrown from the car and put back in it, he was unable to hold out and gave up before the end of the course. But he received the crown just the same. On his departure he presented the entire province with freedom and at the same time gave the judges Roman citizenship and a large sum of money. These favors he announced in person on the day of the Isthmian Games, standing in the middle of the stadium.

On his way back from Greece, he entered Naples through a breach made in the city wall, as is customary with victors in the sacred games, since it was at that city he had made his début as an artist. In like manner he entered Antium, then Albanum, and finally Rome. But at Rome he rode in the chariot which Augustus had used in his triumphs in days gone by, and wore a purple robe and a Greek cloak adorned with stars of gold, bearing on his head the Olympic crown

---

[1] The rules forbade the use of a handkerchief.
[2] Heralds for the great festivals were selected by competition.

and holding the Pythian crown in his right hand, while the rest were carried before him with inscriptions telling where he had won them and against what competitors, and giving the titles of the songs or the subject of the plays. His chariot was followed by his claque as by the escort of a triumphal procession, who shouted that they were the attendants of Augustus and the soldiers of his triumph. Having had the arch of the Circus Maximus taken down, he made his way through it across the Velabrum and the Forum to the Palatine and the temple of Apollo. All along the route victims were slain, the streets were sprinkled from time to time with perfume, while birds, ribbons, and sweetmeats were showered upon him. He placed the sacred crowns in his bed-chambers around his couches, as well as statues representing him in the guise of a lyre-player, which was the device he had stamped on a coin. So far from neglecting or relaxing his practice of the art after this, he never addressed the soldiers except by letter or in a speech delivered by another, to save his voice. He never did anything for amusement or in earnest without a teacher of voice at his side to warn him to spare his vocal organs and hold a handkerchief to his mouth. To many men he offered his friendship or announced his hostility, according as they had applauded him lavishly or grudgingly.

Although at first his acts of wantonness, lust, extravagance, avarice and cruelty were gradual and secret, and might be condoned as follies of youth, yet even then their nature was such that no one doubted that they were defects of his character and not due to his time of life. No sooner was twilight over than he would slip on the disguise of a cap or a wig and go to the taverns or range about the streets playing pranks, which however were very far from harmless. For he used to beat men as they came home from dinner, stabbing any who resisted him and throwing them into the sewers. He would even break into shops and rob them, setting up a market in the Palace, where he divided the booty which he took, sold it at auction, and then squandered the proceeds. In the scuffles which took place on such occasions he often ran the risk of losing his eyes or even his life, for he was beaten almost to death by a man of the senatorial order whose wife he had handled indecently. Warned by this, he never afterwards ventured to appear in public at that hour without having Tribunes follow him at a distance and unobserved. Even in the daytime he would be carried privately to the theater in a sedan, where he would take a place in the upper part of the proscenium from which he not only witnessed the brawls of the pantomimic actors but also egged them on. When they came to blows and stones and pieces of broken benches began to fly about he himself threw many missiles at the people and even broke a Praetor's head.

Little by little, however, as his vices grew stronger, he dropped jesting and secrecy and with no attempt at disguise openly broke out into worse crime.

He prolonged his revels from midday to midnight, often livening himself by a warm plunge, or, if it were summer, into water cooled with snow. Sometimes too he closed the inlets of the Naumachia [1] and banqueted there in public, or in the Campus Martius, or in the Circus Maximus, waited on by harlots and dancing girls from all over the city. Whenever he drifted down the Tiber to Ostia, or sailed about the Gulf of Baiae, booths were set up at intervals along the banks and shores, fitted out as brothels and eating-houses, before which were matrons who played the part of bawds and hostesses, soliciting him from every side to come ashore. He also coerced his friends to give him banquets, one of whom spent four million sesterces [2] on a dinner at which turbans were the favor, and another a considerably larger sum on one at which roses were distributed.

Besides abusing freeborn boys and seducing married women, he debauched the Vestal Virgin Rubria. The freedwoman Acte he all but made his lawful wife, after bribing some ex-consuls to perjure themselves by swearing that she was of royal birth. He castrated the boy Sporus and actually tried to make a woman of him. He married him with all the usual ceremonies, including a dowry and a bridal veil, took him to his house attended by a great throng, and treated him as his wife. And the witty jest that some one made is still current, that it would have been well for the world if Nero's

---

[1] The great basin made for sea-fights.
[2] $164,000.00.

father Domitius had had that kind of wife. This Sporus, decked out with the finery of the Empresses and riding in a litter, he took with him to the assizes and marts of Greece, and later at Rome through the Street of the Images, fondly kissing him from time to time. That he even desired illicit relations with his own mother,[1] and was kept from it by her enemies, who feared that such a relationship might give the reckless and insolent woman too great influence, was notorious, especially after he added to his concubines a courtesan who was said to look very like Agrippina. Even before that, so they say, whenever he rode in a litter with his mother, he had incestuous relations with her, which were betrayed by the stains on his clothing.

He so prostituted his own chastity that after defiling almost every part of his body, he at last devised a kind of game, in which, covered with the skin of some wild animal, he was let loose from a cage and attacked the private parts of men and women, who were bound to stakes, and when he had sated his mad lust, was dispatched by his freedman Doryphorus. For he was even married to this man in the same way that he himself had married Sporus, going so far as to imitate the cries and lamentations of a maiden being deflowered. I have heard from some men that it was his unshaken conviction that no man was chaste or pure in any part of his body, but that most of them concealed their vices and cleverly drew a veil over them; and that therefore he pardoned all other faults in those who confessed to him their lewdness.

He thought that there was no other way of enjoying riches and money than by riotous extravagance, declaring that only stingy and niggardly fellows kept a correct account of what they spent, while fine and genuinely magnificent gentlemen wasted and squandered. Nothing in his uncle Gaius so excited his envy and admiration as the fact that he had in so short a time run through the vast wealth which Tiberius had left him. Accordingly he made presents and wasted

---

[1] It is said the advances were made by Agrippina, with flagrant indecency, to secure her power over him. See Tacitus *Annals* XIV, 2.

money without stint. On Tiridates,[1] though it would seem hardly within belief, he spent eight hundred thousand sesterces[2] a day, and on his departure presented him with more than a hundred millions.[3] He gave the lyre-player Menecrates and the gladiator Spiculus properties and residences equal to those of men who had celebrated triumphs. He enriched the monkey-faced usurer Paneros with estates in the country and in the city and had him buried with almost regal splendor. He never wore the same garment twice. He played at dice for four hundred thousand sesterces a point.[4] He fished with a golden net drawn by cords woven of purple and scarlet threads. It is said that he never made a journey with less than a thousand carriages, his mules shod with silver and their drivers clad in wool of Canusium, attended by a train of Mazaces[5] and couriers with bracelets and trappings.

There was nothing however in which he was more ruinously prodigal than in building. He made a palace extending all the way from the Palatine to the Esquiline, which at first he called the House of Passage, but when it was burned shortly after its completion and rebuilt, the Golden House. Its size and splendor will be sufficiently indicated by the following details. Its vestibule was high enough to contain a colossal statue of the Emperor a hundred and twenty feet high. So large was this house that it had a triple colonnade a mile long. There was a lake in it too, like a sea, surrounded with buildings to represent cities, besides tracts of country, varied by tilled fields, vineyards, pastures and woods, with great numbers of wild and domestic animals. In the rest of the house all parts were overlaid with gold and adorned with jewels and mother-of-pearl. There were dining-rooms with fretted ceilings of ivory, whose panels could turn and shower down flowers and were fitted with pipes for sprinkling the guests with perfumes. The main banquet hall was circular and constantly revolved day and night, like the heavens. He had baths supplied with sea water and sulphur water.

---

[1] The same whom Nero exhibited to the people as told earlier.
[2] $32,800.00.
[3] $4,100,000.00.
[4] $16,400.00.
[5] Celebrated horsemen from Mauretania (North Africa).

When the edifice was finished in this style and he dedicated it, he deigned to say nothing more in the way of approval than that he was at last beginning to be housed like a human being.

He also began a pool, extending from Misenum to the lake of Avernus, roofed over and enclosed in colonnades, into which he planned to turn all the hot springs in every part of Baiae. He likewise projected a canal to extend from Avernus all the way to Ostia, to enable the journey to be made by ship yet not by sea: its length was to be a hundred and sixty miles and its breadth sufficient to allow ships with five banks of oars to pass each other. For the execution of these projects he had given orders that the prisoners all over the empire should be transported to Italy, and that those who were convicted even of capital crimes should be punished in no other way than by sentence to this work.

He was led to such mad extravagance, in addition to his confidence in the resources of the empire, by the hope of a vast hidden treasure, suddenly inspired by the assurance of a Roman Knight, who declared positively that the enormous wealth which Queen Dido had taken with her of old in her flight from Tyre was hidden away in huge caves in Africa and could be recovered with but trifling labor.

When this hope proved false, he resorted to false accusations and robbery, being at the end of his resources and so utterly impoverished that he was obliged to postpone and defer even the pay of the soldiers and the rewards due to the veterans.

First of all he made a law, that instead of one-half, five-sixths of the property of deceased freedmen should be made over to him, if without good and sufficient reason they bore the name of any family with which he himself was connected. Further, that the estates of those who were ungrateful to their Emperor [1] should belong to the privy purse, and that the lawyers who had written or dictated such wills should not go unpunished. Finally, that any word or deed on which an informer could base an action should come under the law

---

[1] Those, that is, who had left him nothing in their wills, or what he considered less than his due.

against treason. He demanded the return of the rewards which he had given in recognition of the prizes conferred on him by any city in any competition. Having forbidden the use of amethystine or Tyrian purple dyes, he secretly sent a man to sell a few ounces on a market day and then closed the shops of all the dealers.[1] It is even said that when he saw a matron in the audience at one of his recitals clad in the forbidden color he pointed her out to his agents, who dragged her out and stripped her on the spot, not only of her garment, but also of her property. He never appointed any one to an office without adding: "You know what my needs are," and "Let us see to it that no one possess anything." At last he stripped many temples of their gifts and melted down the images of gold and silver, including those of the guardian Gods of Rome [2] which, however, Galba soon afterwards restored.

He began his career of parricide and murder with Claudius, for even if he was not the instigator of the Emperor's death, he was at least privy to it, as he openly admitted. For he used afterwards to laud mushrooms, the vehicle in which the poison was administered to Claudius, as "the food of the Gods," as the Greek proverb has it. At any rate, after Claudius' death he vented on him every kind of insult, in act and word,[3] charging him now with folly and now with cruelty. For it was a favorite joke of his to say that Claudius had ceased "to play the fool" among mortals, lengthening the first syllable of the word *morari*.[4] And he disregarded many of his decrees and acts as the work of a madman and a dotard. Finally, he neglected to enclose the place where his body was burned except with a low and mean wall.

He attempted the life of Britannicus by poison, not less from jealousy of his voice (for it was more agreeable than his own) than from fear that he might sometime win a higher place than himself in the people's regard because of the

---

[1] As an excuse to confiscate their property.

[2] Called *Penates*. They were Jupiter, Juno, Apollo, Minerva, Neptune.

[3] Suetonius says that Nero began by honoring the memory of Claudius.

[4] By which pronunciation he changed the sense of the phrase from "linger among mortals" to "play the fool among mortals."

memory of his father. He procured the potion from an arch-poisoner, one Locusta, and when the effect was slower than he anticipated, merely physicking Britannicus, he called the woman to him and flogged her with his own hand, charging that she had administered a medicine instead of a poison. When she said in excuse that she had given a smaller dose to shield him from the odium of the crime, he replied: "It's likely that I am afraid of the Julian law." So he forced her to mix as swift and instant a potion as she knew how in his own room before his very eyes. Then he tried it on a kid, and as the animal lingered for five hours, had the mixture steeped again and again and threw some of it before a pig. The beast instantly fell dead, whereupon he ordered that the poison be taken to the dining-room and given to Britannicus. The boy dropped dead at the very first taste, but Nero lied to his guests and declared that he was seized with the falling sick-ness, to which he was subject, and the next day had him hastily and unceremoniously buried in a pouring rain. He rewarded Locusta for her eminent services with a full par-don and large estates in the country, and actually sent her pupils.

His mother offended him by too strict surveillance and criticism of his words and acts, but at first he confined his resentment to frequent endeavors to bring upon her a burden of unpopularity by pretending that he would abdicate the throne and go off to Rhodes. Then depriving her of all her honors and of her guard of Roman and German soldiers, he even forbade her to live with him and drove her from the Palace. After that he passed all bounds in harrying her, bribing men to annoy her with lawsuits while she remained in the city, and after she had retired to the country, to pass her house by land and sea and break her rest with abuse and mockery. At last terrified by her violence and threats, he de-termined to have her life, and after thrice attempting it by poison and finding that she had made herself immune by antidotes, he tampered with the ceiling of her bedroom, con-triving a mechanical device for loosening its panels and drop-ping them upon her while she slept. When this leaked out through some of those connected with the plot, he devised

a collapsible boat,[1] to destroy her by shipwreck or by the falling in of its cabin. Then he pretended a reconciliation and invited her in a most cordial letter to come to Baiae and celebrate the feast of Minerva with him. On her arrival, instructing his captains to wreck the galley in which she had come, by running into it as if by accident, he detained her at a banquet, and when she would return to Bauli, offered her his contrivance in place of the craft which had been damaged, escorting her to it in high spirits and even kissing her breasts as they parted. The rest of the night he passed sleepless in intense anxiety, awaiting the outcome of his design. On learning that everything had gone wrong and that she had escaped by swimming, driven to desperation he secretly had a dagger thrown down beside her freedman Lucius Agermus, when he joyfully brought word that she was safe and sound. He then ordered that the freedman be seized and bound, on the charge of having been hired by her to kill the Emperor, and that his mother be put to death, giving out that she had committed suicide to escape the consequences of her detected guilt. Trustworthy authorities add still more gruesome details: that he hurried off to view the corpse, handled her limbs, criticizing some and commending others,[2] and that becoming thirsty meanwhile, he took a drink. Yet he could not either then or ever afterwards endure the stings of conscience, though soldiers, Senate and people tried to hearten him with their congratulations. For he often owned that he was hounded by his mother's ghost and by the whips and blazing torches of the Furies. He even had rites performed by the Magi, in the effort to summon her shade and entreat it for forgiveness. Moreover, in his journey through Greece he did not venture to take part in the Eleusinian mysteries, since at the beginning the godless and wicked are warned by the herald's proclamation to go hence.

To matricide he added the murder of his aunt. When he once visited her as she was confined to her bed from costiveness, and she, as old ladies will, stroking his downy beard (for he was already well grown) happened to say fondly:

---

[1] Invented by his freedman Anicetus.
[2] Tacitus in *Annals* XIV, 9, says that some denied this.

"As soon as I receive this,[1] I shall gladly die," he turned to those with him and said as if in jest: "I'll take it off at once." Then he bade the doctors give the sick woman an over-dose of physic and seized her property before she was cold, suppressing her will, that nothing might escape him.

Besides Octavia [2] he later took two wives, Poppaea Sabina, daughter of an ex-quaestor and previously married to a Roman Knight, and then Statilia Messalina, daughter of the great-granddaughter of Taurus, who had been twice Consul and awarded a Triumph. To possess the latter he slew her husband Atticus Vestinus while he held the office of Consul. He soon grew tired of living with Octavia, and when his friends took him to task, replied that "she ought to be con-tent with the insignia of wifehood." Presently after several vain attempts to strangle her, he divorced her on the ground of barrenness, and when the people took it ill and openly re-proached him, he banished her besides. Finally he had her put to death on a charge of adultery that was so shameless and unfounded, that when all who were put to the torture maintained her innocence, he bribed his former preceptor Anicetus to make a pretended confession that he had tricked her out of her chastity. He dearly loved Poppaea, whom he married twelve days after his divorce from Octavia, yet he caused her death too by kicking her when she was pregnant and ill, because she had scolded him for coming home late from the races. By her he had a daughter, Claudia Augusta, but lost her when she was still an infant.

Indeed there is no kind of relationship that he did not vio-late in his career of crime. He put to death Antonia, daughter of Claudius, for refusing to marry him after Poppaea's death, charging her with an attempt at revolution. And he treated in the same way all others who were in any way con-nected with him by blood or by marriage. Among these was the young Aulus Plautius, whom he forcibly defiled before his death, saying "Let my mother come now and kiss my suc-cessor," openly charging that Agrippina had loved Plautius and that this had roused him to hopes of the throne. Rufrius

---

[1] That is, "as soon as I see you a man." What Nero did with the first hair from his chin Suetonius has already told.

[2] Daughter of Claudius by Messalina.

Crispinus, a mere boy, his stepson and the child of Poppaea, he ordered to be drowned by the child's own slaves while he was fishing, because it was said that he used to play at being a general and an emperor. He banished his nurse's son Tuscus, because when Procurator in Egypt, he had bathed in some baths which were built for a visit of Nero's. He drove his tutor Seneca to suicide, although when the old man often pleaded to be allowed to retire and offered to give up his estates, he had sworn most solemnly that he did wrong to suspect him and that he would rather die than harm him. He sent poison to Burrus, Prefect of the Guard, in place of a throat medicine which he had promised him. The old and wealthy freedmen who had helped him first to his adoption and later to the throne, and aided him by their advice, he killed by poison, administered partly in their food and partly in their drink.

Those outside his family he assailed with no less cruelty. It chanced that a comet had begun to appear on several successive nights, a thing which is commonly believed to portend the death of great rulers. Worried by this, and learning from the astrologer Balbillus that Kings usually averted such omens by the sacrifice of some illustrious person, thus bringing the danger foreboded to their own persons onto the heads of their chief men, he resolved on the death of all the eminent men of the State. Indeed, all the more firmly, and with some semblance of justice, after the discovery of two conspiracies. The earlier and more dangerous of these was that of Piso at Rome; the other was set on foot by Vinicius at Beneventum and detected there. The conspirators made their defense in triple sets of fetters, some voluntarily admitting their guilt, some even maintaining they were trying to do him a favor, saying that there was no way except by death that they could help a man disgraced by every kind of wickedness. The children of those who were condemned were banished or put to death by poison or starvation. A number are known to have been slain all together at a single meal along with their preceptors and attendants, while others were prevented from earning their daily bread.

After this he showed neither discrimination nor moderation in putting to death whomsoever he pleased on any pretext whatever. To mention but a few instances: Salvidienus Orfitus was charged with having rented three shops which formed part of his house near the Forum to certain states as their headquarters in Rome; Cassius Longinus, a blind jurist, with retaining in the old family tree of his house the mask of Gaius Cassius, the assassin of Julius Caesar; Paetus Thrasea with having a sullen mien, like that of a preceptor. To those who were bidden to die he never granted more than an hour's respite, and to avoid any delay, he brought physicians who were at once to "attend to" such as lingered, for that was the term he used for killing them by opening their veins. It is even believed that it was his wish to throw living men to be torn to pieces and devoured by a monster of Egyptian birth, who would gnaw raw flesh and anything else that was given him. Transported and puffed up with such successes, as he considered them, he boasted that no prince had ever known what power he really had, and he often threw out unmistakable hints that he would not spare even those of the Senate who survived, but would one day blot out the whole order from the State and hand over the rule of the provinces and the command of the armies to the Roman Knights and to his freedmen. Certain it is that neither on beginning a journey nor on returning did he ever kiss any member of it, or even return his greeting. And at the formal opening of the work at the Isthmus the prayer which he uttered in a loud voice before a great throng was, that the event might result favorably "for himself and the people of Rome," thus suppressing any mention of the Senate.

But he showed no greater mercy to the people or the walls of his capital. When some one in a general conversation said:

"When I am dead, be earth consumed by fire,"[1]

he rejoined "Nay, rather while I live," and his action was wholly in accord. For under cover of displeasure at the ugliness of the old buildings and the narrow, crooked streets, he set fire to the city[2] so openly that several ex-consuls did

---

[1] But see Tacitus (*Annals*, XV, 38), whose report of this event, as also Dio's (LXII, 18), differs from Suetonius'.

[2] A line believed to be from *Bellerophon*, a lost play of Euripides. Dio, LVIII, 23, reports Tiberius as quoting it.

not venture to lay hands on his household servants although they caught them on their estates with tow and firebrands, while some granaries near the Golden House, on a plot of ground he particularly desired, were demolished by engines of war and then set on fire, because their walls were of stone. For six days and seven nights destruction raged, while the people were driven for shelter to monuments and tombs. At that time, besides an immense number of apartment houses, the private houses of leaders of old were burned, still adorned with trophies of victory, and the temples of the Gods vowed and dedicated by the Kings and later in the Punic and Gallic wars, and whatever else interesting and noteworthy had survived from antiquity. Viewing the conflagration from the tower of Maecenas and exulting, as he said, in "the beauty of the flames," he sang the whole of the "Sack of Troy," [1] dressed up in his regular stage costume. Furthermore, to gain from this calamity too all the spoil and booty possible, while promising the removal of the débris and dead bodies free of cost he allowed no one to approach the ruins of his own property. And from the contributions which he not only received, but even demanded, he nearly bankrupted the provinces and exhausted the resources of individuals.

To all the disasters and abuses thus caused by the prince there were added certain accidents of fortune: a plague which in a single autumn entered thirty thousand deaths in the registers of Venus Libitina; a disaster in Britain, where two important towns were sacked and great numbers of citizens and allies were butchered; a shameful defeat in the Orient, in consequence of which the legions in Armenia were sent under the yoke and Syria was all but lost. It is surprising and of special note that all this time he bore nothing with more patience than the curses and abuse of the people, and was particularly lenient towards those who assailed him with gibes and lampoons. Of these many were posted or circulated both in Greek and Latin, for example the following:

"Orestes and Alcmeon, both, their mothers slew.
What Nero does is therefore nothing new."

---

[1] In whose temple funeral outfits and a register of deaths were kept.

"Sprung from Aeneas, pious, wise, and great,
Who says our Nero is degenerate?
Safe through the flames one bore his sire. The other,
To save himself, took off his loving mother."

"While Nero sweetly struck his lyre
Apollo strung his bow.
Our prince is now the God of fire
The other God, our foe."

"All Rome's become one house. To Veii fly,
Unless it stretch to Veii, bye and bye." [1]

But he made no effort to find the authors, and when some of them were reported to the Senate by an informer, he forbade their being very severely punished. As he was passing along a public street, the Cynic Isidorus loudly taunted him, "because he was a good singer of the ills of Nauplius, but made ill use of his own goods." Datus also, an actor of Atellan farces, in a song beginning:

"Good-by, papa, good-by, mamma,"

represented drinking and swimming in pantomime, referring of course to the death of Claudius and Agrippina; and in the final tag,

"Now Orcus guides your steps,"

he indicated the Senate by a gesture.[2] Nero contented himself with banishing the actor and the philosopher from the city, either because he was impervious to all insults, or to avoid sharpening men's wits by showing his vexation.

After the world had put up with such a ruler for nearly fourteen years, it at last cast him off, and the Gauls took the first step under the lead of Julius Vindex, who at that time governed their province as Propraetor.

---

[1] Pliny remarks that the "Golden House" of Nero was swallowing up all Rome. Veii was one of the most ancient Etruscan cities, long a powerful rival of Rome, and but twelve miles north. The Romans almost abandoned their own city after its sack by the Gauls in 390 B.C. and removed there. Hardly a vestige of it remains.

[2] Alluding to Nero's plan to send all the Senators to the Underworld where Orcus, or Pluto, would lead them.

Astrologers had predicted to Nero that he would one **day** be repudiated, which was the occasion of that well-known **saying** of his: "A humble art affords us daily bread,"[1] doubtless uttered to justify him in practicing the art of lyreplaying, as an amusement while Emperor, but a necessity for a private citizen. Some of them, however, had promised him the rule of the East, when he was cast off, a few expressly naming the sovereignty of Jerusalem, and several of the restitution of all his former fortunes. Inclining rather to this last hope, after losing Armenia and Britain and recovering both, he began to think that he had suffered the misfortunes which fate had in store. And after consulting the oracle at Delphi and being told that he must look out for the seventy-third year, assuming that he would die only at that period, and taking no account of Galba's years, he felt so confident not only of old age, but also of unbroken and unusual good fortune, that when he had lost some articles of great value by shipwreck, he did not hesitate to say among his intimate friends that the fish would bring them back to him.

He was at Naples when he learned of the uprising of the Gallic provinces, on the anniversary of his mother's murder, and received the news with such calmness and indifference that he incurred the suspicion of actually rejoicing in it, because it gave him an excuse for pillaging those wealthy provinces according to the laws of war. And he at once proceeded to the gymnasium, where he watched the contests of the athletes with rapt interest. At dinner too when interrupted by a more disturbing letter, he fired up only so far as to threaten vengeance on the rebels. In short for eight whole days he made no attempt to write a reply to any one and gave no commission or command, but blotted out the affair with silence.

At last he was driven by numerous insulting edicts of Vindex, to urge the Senate in a letter to avenge him and th' state, alleging a throat trouble as his excuse for not appearing in person. Yet there was nothing which he so much re-

---

[1] Dio (LXIII, 27) writes that Nero when planning to kill the Senators, burn Rome, and sail to Alexandria, said: "Even though we be driven from our empire, yet this little artistic gift of ours will support us there."

sented as the taunt that he was a wretched lyre-player and
that he was addressed as Ahenobarbus instead of Nero.[1]
With regard to his family name, which was cast in his teeth
as an insult, he declared that he would resume it and give up
that of his adoption. He used no other arguments to show the
falsity of the rest of the reproaches than that he was actually
taunted with being unskilled in an art to which he had devoted so much attention and in which he had so perfected
himself, and he asked various individuals from time to time
whether they knew of any artist who was his superior.

Finally, beset by message after message, he returned to
Rome in a panic. But on the way, when but slightly encouraged by an insignificant omen, for he noticed a monument on
which was sculptured the overthrow of a Gallic soldier by a
Roman horseman, who was dragging him along by the hair,
he leaped for joy at the sight and lifted up his hands to
heaven. But not even then did he personally address the
Senate or the people, but only called some of the leading men
to his house and after a hasty consultation spent the rest of
the day in exhibiting some water-organs [2] of a new and hith-
erto unknown form, explaining their several features and
lecturing on the theory and complexity of each of them and
he even declared that he would presently produce them all in
the theater "with the kind permission of Vindex."

Thereafter, having learned that Galba also and the Spanish provinces had revolted, he fainted and lay for a long
time insensible, without a word and all but dead. When he
came to himself, he rent his robe and beat his brow, declaring that it was all over with him. And when his old nurse tried
to comfort him by reminding him that similar evils had befallen other princes before him, he declared that unlike all
others he was suffering the unheard of and unparalleled fate
of losing the supreme power while he still lived. Nevertheless
he did not abandon or amend his slothful and luxurious

[1] Lucius Domitius Ahenobarbus was Nero's original name, being the
son of Cn. Domitius Ahenobarbus and Agrippina, one of Germanicus'
daughters. But after Agrippina married her uncle, the Emperor Claudius, the stepson's name was changed to Nero Claudius Caesar Drusus
Germanicus.

[2] The prototype of our pipe-organs. Water was the inflating power
Vitruvius (IV, IX) attributes its invention to Ctesibus of Alexandria.

habits. On the contrary, whenever any good news came from the provinces, he not only gave lavish feasts, but even ridiculed the leaders of the revolt in verses set to wanton music, which have since become public, and accompanied them with gestures. In the theater, where he had been secretly carried as usual, he sent word to an actor who was making a hit that he was taking advantage of the Emperor's busy days.

At the very beginning of the revolt it is believed that he formed many plans of monstrous wickedness, but in no way inconsistent with his character: to depose and assassinate the commanders of the armies and the governors of the provinces, on the ground that they were all united in a conspiracy against him; to massacre all the exiles everywhere and all men of Gallic birth in the city: the former, to prevent them from joining the rebels; the latter, as sharing and abetting the designs of their countrymen; to turn over the Gallic provinces to his armies to ravage; to poison the entire Senate at banquets; to set fire to the city, first letting the wild beasts loose, that it might be harder for the people to protect hemselves. But he was deterred from these designs, not so much by any compunction, as because he despaired of being able to carry them out, and feeling obliged to take the field, he deposed the Consuls before the end of their term and assumed the office alone in place of both of them, alleging that it was fated that the Gallic provinces could not be subdued except by a Consul. Having assumed the fasces,[1] he declared as he was leaving the dining-room after a banquet, leaning on the shoulders of his comrades, that immediately on setting foot in the province he would go before the soldiers unarmed and do nothing but weep; and having thus led the rebels to change their purpose, he would next day rejoice among his rejoicing subjects and sing paeans of victory, which he ought at that very moment to be composing.

In preparing for his campaign his first care was to select wagons to carry his theatrical instruments, to have the hair of his concubines, whom he planned to take with him, trimmed man-fashion, and to equip them with Amazonian axes and shields. Next he summoned the city tribes to enlist,

---

[1] The symbol of consular authority.

and when no eligible person responded, he ordered all masters
to send a certain number of slaves, accepting only the choicest from each household and not even exempting paymasters
and secretaries. He also required all classes to contribute a
part of their incomes, and all tenants of private houses and
apartments to pay a year's rent at once to the privy purse.
With great fastidiousness and strictness he demanded newly
minted coin, refined silver, and pure gold, so that many
openly refused to make any contribution at all, unanimously
demanding that he should rather compel the informers to
give up whatever rewards had been paid them.

The bitter feeling against him was increased because he
also turned the high cost of grain to his profit. For, as it
happened just at that time of famine, a ship was reported
arrived from Alexandria but freighted with sand for the
court wrestlers.

When he had thus aroused the hatred of all, there was no
form of insult to which he was not subjected. A lock of hair
was placed on the head of his statue with the inscription in
Greek: "Now there is a real contest and you must at last
surrender." To the neck of another statue a sack was tied
and with it the words: "I have done what I could, but you
have earned the sack.[1] People wrote on the columns that by
his singing he had stirred up even the Gauls.[2] When night
came on, many men pretended to be wrangling with their
slaves and kept calling out for a vindicator.[3]

In addition he was frightened by manifest portents from
dreams, auspices and omens, both old and new. He had never
been in the habit of dreaming before he killed his mother.
But after that he had such nightmares as: that he was steer-
ing a ship and the helm was wrenched from his hands; that he
was dragged by his wife Octavia into thickest darkness; that
now he was covered with a swarm of winged ants; or again,
that the statues of all the heroes dedicated in Pompey's
theater had surrounded him and blocked his way; that a

---

[1] The one in which parricides were sewn up.

[2] A double pun. *Galli* means both "cocks" and "Gauls"; *cantare* "to
crow" as well as "to sing."

[3] Another pun. *Vindex* signifying both the leader of the revolt in Gaul
and one who punishes unruly servants.

Spanish steed of which he was very fond was changed into the form of an ape in the hinder parts of its body, and its head, which alone remained unaltered, gave forth tuneful neighs. The doors of the Mausoleum flew open of their own accord, and a voice was heard from within summoning him by name. After his domestic Gods had been adorned on the Kalends of January, they fell to the ground in the midst of the preparations for the sacrifice. As he was taking the auspices, Sporus made him a present of a ring with a stone on which was engraved the rape of Proserpina. When the vows were to be taken [1] and a great throng of classes had assembled, the keys of the Capitol could not be found for a long time. When a speech of his in which he assailed Vindex was being read in the Senate, at the words "the wretches will suffer punishment and a fitting end will soon be made of them," all who were present cried out with one voice: "You will make it, Augustus." Men had also not failed to notice that the last piece which he sang in public was "Oedipus in Exile," and that he ended with the line:

"Wife, father, mother drive me to my death."

In the meanwhile, when word came that the other armies had revolted, he tore to pieces the dispatches which were handed to him as he was dining, tipped over the table, and dashed to the ground two favorite drinking cups, which he called "Homeric," because they were carved with scenes from Homer's poems. Then taking some poison from Locusta and putting in into a golden box, he crossed over into the Servilian gardens, where he tried to induce the Tribunes and Centurions of the Guard to accompany him in his flight, first sending his most trustworthy freedmen to Ostia, to get a fleet ready. But when some gave evasive answers and some openly refused, one even cried:

"Is it, then, such a dreadful thing, to die?" [2]

Whereupon he turned over various plans in his mind, whether

----

[1] On the 1st of January, for the prosperity of the Emperor and the State.

[2] Vergil, *Aeneid*, XII, 646.

to go as a suppliant to the Parthians or to Galba, or to appear to the people on the rostra, dressed in black, and beg as pathetically as he could for pardon for his past offenses; and if he could not soften their hearts, to entreat them at least to allow him the prefecture of Egypt. Afterwards a speech composed for this purpose was found in his writing desk. But it is thought that he did not dare to deliver it for fear of being torn to pieces before he could reach the Forum.

Having therefore put off further consideration to the following day, he awoke about midnight and finding that the guard of soldiers had left, he sprang from his bed and sent for all his friends. Since no reply came back from any one, he went himself to their rooms with a few followers. But finding that all the doors were closed and that no one replied to him he returned to his own chamber, from which now the very caretakers had fled, taking with them even the bed-clothing and the box of poison. Then he at once called for the gladiator Spiculus or any other skillful killer at whose hand he might find death, and when no one appeared, he cried "Have I then neither friend nor foe?" and ran out as if to throw himself into the Tiber.

Changing his purpose again, he sought for some retired place, where he could hide and collect his thoughts. And when his freedman Phaon offered his villa in the suburbs between the Via Nomentana and the Via Salaria near the fourth milestone, just as he was, barefooted and in his tunic, he put on a faded cloak, covered his head, and holding a handkerchief before his face, mounted a horse with only four attendants, one of whom was Sporus. At once he was startled by a shock of earthquake and a flash of lightning full in his face, and he heard the shouts of the soldiers from the camp hard by, as they prophesied destruction for him and success for Galba. He also heard one of the wayfarers whom he met say: "These men are after Nero," and another ask: "Is there anything new in the city about Nero?" Then his horse took fright at the smell of a corpse which had been thrown out into the road, his face was exposed, and a retired soldier of the Guard recognized him and saluted him. When they came to a by-path leading to the villa, they turned the horses loose and he made his way amid bushes and brambles and along a path through a thicket of reeds to the back wall of the house, with great difficulty and only when a robe was thrown down for him to walk on. Here the aforesaid Phaon urged him to hide for a time in a pit, from which sand had been dug, but he declared that he would not go under ground while still alive, and after waiting for a while until a secret entrance into the villa could be made, he scooped up in his hand some water to drink from a pool close by, saying: "This is Nero's distilled water." [1] Then, as his cloak had been torn by the thorns, he pulled out the twigs which had pierced it, and crawling on all fours through a narrow passage that had been dug, he entered the villa and lay down in the first room he came to, on a couch with a common mattress, over which an old cloak had been thrown. Though suffering from hunger and renewed thirst, he refused some coarse bread which was offered him, but drank a little lukewarm water.

At last, while his companions one and all urged him to save himself as soon as possible from the indignities that threatened him, he bade them dig a grave in his presence, proportioned to the size of his own person, collect any bits of marble that could be found, and at the same time bring water and wood for presently disposing of his body.[2] As each of these things was done, he wept and said again and again: "What an artist the world is losing!"

While he hesitated, a letter was brought to Phaon by one of his couriers. Nero snatching it from his hand read that he had been pronounced a public enemy by the Senate, and that they were seeking him to punish him in the ancient fashion. And he asked what manner of punishment that was. When he learned that the criminal was stripped naked, fastened by the neck in a forked stake and then beaten to death with rods, in mortal terror he seized two daggers which he had brought with him, and then, after trying the point of each, put them up again, pleading that the fated hour had not yet come. Now he would beg Sporus to begin to lament and wail, and now entreat some one to help him take his life by setting him the example. Anon he reproached himself for his cowardice in

---

[1] Pliny tells us in *Natural History* (XXXIII, 3) that Nero had his drinking water boiled, to clear it from impurities, then cooled with ice.

[2] Water for washing the corpse, fire for burning it.

such words as these: "To live despoiled, disgraced—this does
not become Nero, does not become him—one should be reso-
lute at such times—come, rouse thyself!" And now the horsemen were at hand who had orders to take him off alive. When
he heard them, he quavered:

"The trampling of swift-footed studs is in my ear," [1]

and drove a dagger into his throat, aided by Epaphroditus
his private secretary.[2] He was all but dead when a Centurion
rushed in, and as he placed a cloak to the wound, pretending
that he had come to aid him, Nero merely gasped: "Too late!"
and "This is fidelity!" With these words he was gone, his eyes
so set and starting from their sockets that all who saw him
shuddered with horror. First and beyond all else he had
forced from his companions a promise to let no one have his
head, but to contrive in some way that he be buried un-
mutilated. And this was granted by Icelus, Galba's freedman, who had shortly before been released from the bondage
to which he was consigned at the beginning of the revolt.

He was buried at a cost of two hundred thousand sesterces [3]
and laid out in white robes embroidered with gold, which he
had worn on the Kalends of January. His ashes were deposited
by his nurses, Egloge and Alexandria, accompanied by his
mistress Acte, in the family tomb of the Domitii on the summit of the Hill of Gardens,[4] which is visible from the Campus
Martius. In that monument his sarcophagus of porphyry, with
an altar of marble from Luna standing above it, is enclosed
by a balustrade of Thasian stone.

He was about the average height, his body marked with
spots and malodorous, his hair light blond, his features regular rather than attractive, his eyes blue and somewhat weak,
his neck overthick, his belly prominent, and his legs very
slender. His health was good, for though indulging in every
kind of riotous excess, he was ill but three times in all during
the fourteen years of his reign, and even then not enough to

---

[1] *Iliad*, X, 535.

[2] For his death see *Domitian*.

[3] $8,200.00.

[4] The Pincian Hill, where the statue, "The Dying Gladiator," was
discovered.

give up wine or any of his usual habits. He was utterly shameless in the care of his person and in his dress, always having his hair arranged in tiers of curls, and during the trip to Greece also letting it grow long and hang down behind. And he often appeared in public in a dinner-gown [1] with a handkerchief bound about his neck, ungirt and unshod.

When a boy he took up almost all the liberal arts. But his mother turned him from philosophy, warning him that it was a drawback to one who was going to rule, while Seneca kept him from reading the early orators, to make his admiration for his teacher endure the longer. Turning therefore to poetry, he wrote verses with eagerness and without labor, and did not, as some think, publish the work of others as his own. There have come into my hands note-books and papers with some well-known verses of his, written with his own hand and in such a manner that it was perfectly evident that they were not copied or taken down from dictation, but worked out exactly as one writes when thinking and creating; so many instances were there of words erased or struck through and written above the lines. He likewise had no slight interest in painting and sculpture.

But above all he was carried away by a craze for popularity and he was jealous of all who in any way stirred the feeling of the mob. It was the general belief that after his victories on the stage he would at the next lustrum have competed with the athletes at Olympia. For he practiced wrestling constantly, and all over Greece he had always viewed the gymnastic contests after the fashion of the judges, sitting on the ground in the stadium; and if any pairs of contestants withdrew too far from their positions, he would force them forward with his own hand. Since he was acclaimed as the equal of Apollo in music and of the Sun in driving a chariot, he had planned to emulate the exploits of Hercules as well. And they say that a lion had been specially trained for him to kill naked in the arena of the amphitheater before all the people, with a club or by the clasp of his arms.

Towards the end of his life, in fact, he had publicly vowed

---

[1] A loose gown of bright-colored silk, worn by men at dinner during the Saturnalia, but only by women at other times.

that if he retained his power, he would at the games in celebration of his victory give a performance on the water-organ,
the flute, and the bagpipes, and that on the last day he would
appear as an actor and dance "Vergil's Turnus." Some even
assert that he put the actor Paris to death as a dangerous
rival.

He had a longing for immortality and undying fame,
though it was ill-regulated. With this in view he took their
former appellations from many things and numerous places
and gave them new ones from his own name. He also called
the month of April Neroneus and was minded to name Rome
Neropolis.

He utterly despised all cults, with the sole exception of
that of the Syrian Goddess,[1] and even acquired such a contempt for her that he made water on her image, after he was
enamored of another superstition, which was the only one
to which he constantly clung. For he had received as a gift
from some unknown man of the Commons, as a protection
against plots, a little image of a girl. Since a conspiracy came
to light immediately after, he continued to venerate it as a
powerful divinity and to offer three sacrifices to it every day,
encouraging the belief that through its communication he
had knowledge of the future. A few months before his death
he did attend an inspection of victims, but could not get a
favorable omen.

He met his death in the thirty-second year of his age, on
the anniversary of the murder of Octavia, and such was the
public rejoicing that the people put on caps[2] and ran about
all over the city. Yet there were some who for a long time
decorated his tomb with spring and summer flowers, and now
produced his statues on the rostra in the fringed toga, and
now his edicts, as if he were still alive and would shortly return and deal destruction to his enemies. Nay more, Vologaesus, King of the Parthians, when he sent envoys to the
Senate to renew his alliance, earnestly begged this too, that

---

[1] Atargatis, the Syrian Venus.
[2] Freedmen wore caps.

honor be paid to the memory of Nero. In fact, twenty years later, when I was a young man, a person of obscure origin appeared, who gave out that he was Nero, and the name was still in such favor with the Parthians that they supported him vigorously and surrendered him with great reluctance.

BOOK VII

GALBA, OTHO, AND VITELLIUS

GALBA

THE race of the Caesars ended with Nero. That this would be so was shown by many portents and especially by two very significant ones. Years before, as Livia was returning to her estate near Veii, immediately after her marriage with Augustus, an eagle which flew by dropped into her lap a white hen, holding in its beak a sprig of laurel, just as the eagle had carried it off. Livia resolved to rear the fowl and plant the sprig, whereupon such a great brood of chickens was hatched that to this day the villa is called *The Hen Roost*, and such a grove of laurel sprang up, that the Caesars gathered their laurels from it when they were going to celebrate triumphs. Moreover it was the habit of those who triumphed to plant other branches at once in that same place, and it was observed that just before the death of each of them the tree which he had planted withered. Now in Nero's last year the whole grove died from the root up, as well as all the hens. Furthermore, when shortly afterwards the temple of the Caesars was struck by lightning, the heads fell from all the statues at the same time, and Augustus' scepter was dashed from his hand.

Nero was succeeded by Galba, who was related in no degree to the house of the Caesars, although unquestionably of noble origin and of an old and powerful family. For he always added to the inscriptions on his statues that he was the great-grandson of Quintus Catulus Capitolinus, and when he became Emperor he even displayed a family tree in his hall in which he carried back his ancestry on his father's side to Jupiter and on his mother's to Pasiphae, the wife of Minos.

It would be a long story to give in detail his illustrious ancestors and the honorary inscriptions of the entire race, but I shall give a brief account of his immediate family. It is uncertain why the first of the Sulpicii who bore the surname Galba assumed the name, and whence it was derived. Some think that it was because after having for a long time unsuccessfully besieged a town in Spain, he at last set fire to it by torches smeared with *galbanum;* [1] others because during a long illness he made constant use of *galbeum,* that is to say of remedies wrapped in wool; still others, because he was a very fat man, such as the Gauls term *galba,* or because he was, on the contrary, as slender as the insects called *galbae,* which breed in oak trees.

The family acquired distinction from Servius Galba, who became Consul and was decidedly the most eloquent speaker of his time. This man, they say, was the cause of the war with Viriathus, because while governing Spain as Propraetor, he treacherously massacred thirty thousand of the Lusitanians. His grandson had been one of Caesar's lieutenants in Gaul, but angered because his commander caused his defeat for the consulship, he joined the conspiracy with Brutus and Cassius, and was consequently condemned to death by the Pedian law. From him were descended the grandfather and the father of the Emperor Galba. The former, who was more eminent for his learning than for his rank—for he did not advance beyond the grade of Praetor—published a voluminous and painstaking history. The father attained the consulship, and although he was short of stature and even hunchbacked, besides being only an indifferent speaker, was an industrious pleader at the bar. He married Mummia Achaica, the granddaughter of Catulus and great-granddaughter of Lucius Mummius who destroyed Corinth; and later Livia Ocellina, a very rich and beautiful woman, who however is thought to have sought marriage with him because of his high rank, and the more eagerly when, in response to her frequent advances, he took off his robe in private and showed her his deformity, so as not to seem to deceive her by concealing it. By Achaica he had two sons, Gaius and Servius. Gaius, who was the elder, left Rome after squandering the greater part of his estate, and committed suicide because Tiberius would not allow him to take part in the allotment of the provinces in his year.

---

[1] The gum resin from a species of *Terula* growing on deserts in Persia.

The Emperor Servius Galba was born in the consulship of Marcus Valerius Messala and Gnaeus Lentulus, on the ninth day before the Kalends of January, in a country house situated on a hill near Tarracina, on the left as you go towards Fundi. Adopted by his stepmother Livia, he took her name and the surname Ocella, and also changed his forename; for he used Lucius, instead of Servius, from that time until he became Emperor. It is well known that when he was still a boy and called to pay his respects to Augustus with others of his age, the Emperor pinched his cheek and said in Greek: "Thou too, child, wilt have a nibble at this power of mine." Tiberius too, when he heard that Galba was destined to be Emperor, but in his old age, said: "Well, let him live then, since that does not concern me." Again, when Galba's grandfather was busy with a sacrifice to avert a stroke of lightning, and an eagle snatched the intestines from his hand and carried them to an oak full of acorns, the prediction was made that the highest dignity would come to the family, but late; whereupon he said with a laugh: "Very likely, when a mule has a foal!" Afterwards when Galba was beginning his revolt, nothing gave him so much encouragement as the foaling of a mule, and while the rest were horrified and looked on it as an unfavorable omen, he alone regarded it as most propitious, remembering the sacrifice and his grandfather's saying.

When he assumed the gown of manhood, he dreamt that Fortune said that she was tired of standing before his door, and that unless she were quickly admitted, she would fall a prey to the first comer. When he awoke, opening the door of the hall, he found close by the threshold a bronze statue of Fortune more than a cubit high. This he carried in his arms to Tusculum, where he usually spent the summer, and consecrated it in a room of his house. And from that time on he honored it with sacrifices every month and with an all-night vigil once a year.

Even before he reached middle life, he persisted in keeping up an old and forgotten custom of his country, which survived only in his own household, of having his freedmen and slaves appear before him twice a day in a body, greeting him in the morning and bidding him farewell at evening, one by one.

Among other liberal studies he applied himself to the law. He also assumed a husband's duties, but after losing his wife Lepida and two sons whom he had by her, he remained a widower. And he could not be tempted afterwards by any match, not even with Agrippina, who no sooner lost Domitius by death than she set her cap for Galba so obviously, even before the death of his wife, that Lepida's mother scolded her roundly before a company of matrons and went so far as to slap her.

He showed marked respect to Livia Augusta,[1] to whose favor he owed great influence during her lifetime and by whose last will he almost became a rich man, for he had the largest bequest among her legatees, one of fifty million sesterces.[2] But because the sum was designated in figures and not written out in words, Tiberius, who was her heir, reduced the bequest to five hundred thousand,[3] and Galba never received even that amount.

He began his career of office before the legal age, and in celebrating the games of the Floralia in his praetorship he gave a new kind of exhibition, namely of elephants walking the rope. Then he governed the province of Aquitania for nearly a year and soon afterwards held a regular consulship for six months. It chanced that in this office he succeeded Lucius [4] Domitius, the father of Nero, and was succeeded by Salvius Otho, the father of the Emperor Otho, a kind of omen of what happened later, when he became Emperor between the reigns of the sons of these two men.

Appointed by Gaius Caesar to supersede Gaetulicus as Governor of Upper Germany, the day after he appeared before the legions he put a stop to their applause at a festival which chanced to fall at that time, by issuing a written order to keep their hands under their cloaks; and immediately this verse was bandied about the camp:

> "Learn, soldier, how in arms to use your hands,
> Galba now, not Gaetulicus, commands."

[1] Widow of Augustus.

[2] $2,050,000.00.

[3] $20,500.00.

[4] Either Suetonius is in error or the manuscripts; the name should be Gnaeus.

With equal strictness he put a stop to the requests for furloughs. He got both the veterans and the new recruits into condition by plenty of hard work, speedily checked the barbarians, who had already made inroads even into Gaul, and when Gaius [1] arrived, Galba and his army made such a good impression, that out of the great body of troops assembled from all the provinces none received greater commendation or richer rewards. Galba particularly distinguished himself, while directing the military maneuvers shield in hand, by actually running for twenty miles close beside the Emperor's chariot.

When the murder of Gaius was announced, although many urged Galba to take advantage of the opportunity, he preferred quiet. Hence he was in high favor with Claudius, became one of his staff of intimate friends, and was treated with such consideration that the departure of the expedition to Britain was put off because Galba was taken with a sudden illness, of no great severity. He governed Africa for two years with the rank of Proconsul, being specially chosen [2] to restore order in the province, which was disturbed both by internal strife and by a revolt of the barbarians. And he was successful, owing to his insistence on strict discipline and his observance of justice even in trifling matters. When provisions were scarce during some expedition, a soldier was accused of having sold wheat left from his rations at a hundred denarii a peck. Galba gave orders that when the man began to lack food, he should receive aid from no one, and he starved to death. On another occasion when he was holding court and the question of the ownership of a beast of burden was laid before him, as the evidence on both sides was slight and the witnesses unreliable, so that it was difficult to get at the truth, he ruled that the beast should be led with its head muffled up to the pool where it was usually watered, that it should then be unmuffled, and should belong to the man to whom it returned to its own accord after drinking.

His services in Africa at that time, and previously in Germany, were recognized by the triumphal regalia and three

---

[1] For whose German exploits see *Caligula*.

[2] Except in special cases, like this, Governors were appointed by lot from among those eligible.

priesthoods, for he was chosen a member of the Fifteen,[1] made one of the Brotherhood of Titius [2] and priest of Augustus.[3] After that he lived for the most part in retirement until about the middle of Nero's reign, never going out even for recreation without taking a million sesterces in gold with him in a second carriage,[4] until at last, while he was staying in the town of Fundi, Hispania Tarraconensis was offered him. And it fell out that as he was offering sacrifice in a public temple after his arrival in the province, the hair of a young attendant who was carrying an incense-box suddenly turned white all over his head, and there were some who did not hesitate to interpret this as a sign of a change of rulers and of the succession of an old man to a young one; that is to say, of Galba to Nero. Not long after this lightning struck a lake of Cantabria and twelve axes were found there, an unmistakable token of supreme power.

For eight years he governed the province in a variable and inconsistent manner. At first he was vigorous and energetic and even over-severe in punishing offenses. For he cut off the hands of a money-lender who carried on his business dishonestly and nailed them to his counter and he crucified a man for poisoning his ward, whose property he was to inherit in case of his death. When the man invoked the law and declared that he was a Roman citizen, Galba, pretending to lighten his punishment by some consolation and honor, ordered that a cross much higher than the rest and painted white be set up, and the man transferred to it. But he gradually changed to sloth and inaction, so as to give Nero no cause for jealousy because, as he used to say himself, no one could be forced to render an account for doing nothing.

As he was holding the assizes at New Carthage, he learned of the rebellion of the Gallic provinces through an urgent appeal for help from the Governor of Aquitania. Then came letters from Vindex, calling upon him to make himself the liberator and leader of mankind. So without much hesitation he accepted the proposal, led by fear as well as by hope. For

---

[1] Supervisors of Sacrifices and the Sibylline Books.
[2] A priesthood which perpetuated certain ancient Sabine rites.
[3] Tiberius instituted the worship of Augustus.
[4] $41,000.00; so, if need be, he could leave the country at once.

he had intercepted dispatches ordering his own death, which had been secretly sent by Nero to his agents. He was encouraged too, in addition to most favorable auspices and omens, by the prediction of a young girl of high birth, and the more so because the priest of Jupiter at Clunia, directed by a dream, had found in the inner shrine of his temple the very same prediction, likewise spoken by an inspired girl two hundred years before. And the purport of the verses was that one day there would come forth from Spain the ruler and lord of the world.

Accordingly, pretending that he was going to attend to the manumitting of slaves, he mounted the tribunal. On the front of it he had set up as many images as he could find of those who had been condemned and put to death by Nero, having by his side a boy of noble family, whom he had summoned for that very purpose from his place of exile hard by in the Balearic Isles. But instead he began to deplore the state of the times. When he was forthwith hailed as Emperor, he declared that he was their Governor, representing the Senate and people of Rome. Then proclaiming a holiday, he enrolled from the people of the province legions and auxiliaries in addition to his former force of one legion, two divisions of cavalry, and three cohorts. But from the oldest and most experienced of the nobles he chose a kind of Senate, to whom he might refer matters of special importance whenever it was necessary. He also chose young men of the order of Knights, who were to have the title of Volunteers and keep guard before his bedchamber in place of the regular soldiers, without losing their right to wear the gold ring. He also sent proclamations broadcast throughout the province, urging all men individually and collectively to join the revolution and aid the common cause in every possible way.

At about this same time, during the fortification of a town which he had chosen as the seat of war, a ring of ancient workmanship was found, containing a precious stone engraved with a Victory and a trophy. Immediately afterwards a ship from Alexandria loaded with arms arrived at Dertosa [1] without a pilot, without a single sailor or passenger, removing

---

[1] Now Corunna.

all doubt in any one's mind that the war was just and holy and undertaken with the approval of the Gods. Then suddenly and unexpectedly the whole plan was almost brought to naught. One of the two divisions of cavalry, repenting of its change of allegiance, attempted to desert Galba as he was approaching his camp and was with difficulty prevented. Some slaves too, whom one of Nero's freedmen had given Galba with treachery in view, all but slew him as he was going to the bath through a narrow passage-way. In fact they would have succeeded, had they not conjured one another not to miss the opportunity and so been questioned as to what the opportunity was to which they referred. For when they were put to the torture, a confession was wrung from them.

To these great perils was added the death of Vindex, by which he was especially panic-stricken and came near taking his own life, in the belief that all was lost. But when some messengers came from the city, reporting that Nero was dead and that all the people had sworn allegiance to him, he laid aside the title of Governor and assumed that of Caesar. He then began his march to Rome in a general's cloak with a dagger hanging from his neck in front of his breast; and he did not resume the toga until he had overthrown those who were plotting against him, Nymphidius Sabinus, Prefect of the praetorian guard at Rome, and the Governors of Germany and Africa, Fonteius Capito and Clodius Macer.

His double reputation for cruelty and avarice had gone before him. Men said that he had punished the cities of the Spanish and Gallic provinces which had hesitated about taking sides with him by heavier taxes and some even by the razing of their walls, putting to death the Governors and imperial deputies along with their wives and children. Further, that he had melted down a golden crown of fifteen pounds' weight, which the people of Tarraco had taken from their ancient temple of Jupiter and presented to him, with orders that the three ounces which were found lacking be exacted from them. This reputation was confirmed and even augmented immediately on his arrival in the city. For having compelled some marines whom Nero had made regular soldiers to return to their former positions as rowers, upon their refusing and obstinately insisting they remain under the eagle and standards, he not only dispersed them by a cavalry charge, but even decimated them. He also disbanded a cohort of Germans, whom the previous Caesars had made their bodyguard and had found absolutely faithful in many emergencies, and sent them back to their native country without any rewards, alleging that they were more favorably inclined toward Gnaeus Dolabella, near whose gardens they had their camp. The following tales too were told in mockery of him, whether truly or falsely: that when an unusually elegant dinner was set before him, he groaned aloud; and when his duly appointed steward presented his expense account, he handed him a dish of beans in return for his industry and carefulness; and that when the flute player Canus greatly pleased him, he presented him with five denarii,[1] which he took from his own purse with his own hand.[2]

Accordingly his coming was not so welcome as it might have been, and this was apparent at the first performance in the theater. For when the actors of an Atellan farce began the familiar lines

"Here comes Reuben from his farm"

all the spectators at once finished the song in chorus and repeated it several times with appropriate gestures, beginning with that verse.

Thus his popularity and prestige were greater when he won, than while he ruled the empire, though he gave many proofs of being an excellent prince. But he was by no means so much loved for those qualities as he was hated for his acts of the opposite character.

He was wholly under the control of three men, who were commonly known as his tutors because they lived with him in the palace and never left his side. They were Titus Vinius, one of his generals in Spain, a man of unbounded covetousness; Cornelius Laco, advanced from the position of judge's

---

[1] $0.75.

[2] Plutarch (*Galba*, XVI) says the gift was of gold pieces and that Galba said it came from his own and not the public purse. Galba's frugality was regarded as stinginess by a people accustomed to Nero's extravagance.

assistant to that of Prefect of the Guard and intolerably naughty and indolent; and his own freedman Icelus, who had only just before received the honor of the gold ring and the surname of Marcianus, yet already aspired to the highest office open to the equestrian order.[1] To these brigands, each with his different vice, he so entrusted and handed himself over as their tool, that his conduct was far from consistent. For at one time he was more exacting and niggardly, and at another more extravagant and reckless than became a prince chosen by the people and of his time of life.

He condemned to death divers distinguished men of both orders on trivial suspicions without a trial. He rarely granted Roman citizenship, and the privileges due those who had three children to only one or two at most, and even to those only for a fixed and limited time. When the jurors petitioned that a sixth division be added to their number, he not only refused, but even deprived them of the privilege granted by Claudius, of not being summoned for court duty in winter and at the beginning of the year.

It was thought too that he intended to limit the offices open to Senators and Knights to a period of two years, and to give them only to such as did not wish them and declined them. He had all the grants of Nero revoked,[2] allowing only a tenth part to be retained. He exacted repayment of these with the help of fifty Roman Knights, stipulating that even if the actors and athletes had sold anything that had formerly been given them, it should be taken away from the purchasers, in case the recipient had spent the money and could not repay it. On the other hand, there was nothing that he did not allow his friends and freedmen to sell at a price or bestow as a favor, taxes and freedom from taxation, the punishment of the guiltless and impunity for the guilty. Nay more, when the Roman people called for the punishment of Halotus and Tigellinus, the most utterly abandoned of all Nero's creatures, not content with saving their lives, he honored Halotus with a very important stewardship and in

---

[1] Prefect of the praetorian guard.
[2] Which, according to Tacitus (*Histories*, I, 20) amounted to over $90,200,000.00.

the case of Tigellinus even issued an edict rebuking the people for their cruelty.

Having thus incurred the hatred of almost all men of every class, he was especially detested by the soldiers. For although their officers [1] had promised them a larger gift than common when they swore allegiance to Galba in his absence, so far from keeping the promise, he declared more than once that it was his habit to levy troops, not buy them. Because of this he embittered the soldiers all over the empire. The praetorians he filled besides with both fear and indignation by discharging many of them from time to time as under suspicion of being partisans of Nymphidius. But loudest of all was the grumbling of the army in Upper Germany, because it was defrauded of the reward for its services against the Gauls and Vindex. Hence they were the first to venture on mutiny, refusing on the Kalends of January to swear allegiance to any one save the Senate, and at once resolving to send a deputation to the praetorians with the following message: that the Emperor created in Spain did not suit them and the Guard must choose one who would be acceptable to all the armies.

When this was reported to Galba, thinking that it was not so much his age as his lack of children that was criticized, he picked out Piso Frugi Licianus from the midst of the throng at one of his morning receptions, a young man of noble birth and high character, who had long been one of his special favorites and always named in his will as heir to his property and his name. Calling him son, he led him to the praetorian camp and adopted him before the assembled soldiers. But even then he made no mention of largess, thus making it easier for Marcus Salvius Otho to accomplish his purpose within six days after the adoption.

Many prodigies in rapid succession from the very beginning of his reign had foretold Galba's end exactly as it happened. When victims were being slain to right and left in

---

[1] According to Plutarch (*Galba*, 2) it was Nymphidius Sabinus, Prefect of the praetorian guard, who made this promise. Other officers doubtless followed his example. This failure to give the soldiers the donative to which they had become accustomed contributed more to Galba's ruin than even the odium he incurred by the rapaciousness of his favorites.

every town along his way,[1] an ox, maddened by the stroke of an ax, broke its bonds and charged the Emperor's chariot, and as it raised its feet, deluged him with blood. And as Galba dismounted, one of his guards, pushed forward by the crowd, almost wounded him with his lance. Again, as he entered the city, and later the Palace, he was met by a shock of earthquake and a sound like the lowing of kine. There followed even clearer signs. He had set apart from all the treasure a necklace fashioned of pearls and precious stones, for the adornment of his statue of Fortune at Tusculum. This on a sudden impulse he consecrated to the Capitoline Venus, thinking it worthy of a more august position. The next night Fortune appeared to him in his dreams, complaining of being robbed of the gift intended for her and threatening in her turn to take away what she had bestowed. When Galba hastened in terror to Tusculum at daybreak, to offer expiatory sacrifices because of the dream, and sent on men to make preparations for the ceremony, he found on the altar nothing but warm ashes and beside it an old man dressed in black, holding the incense in a glass dish and the wine in an earthen cup.[2] It was also remarked that as he was sacrificing on the Kalends of January, the garland fell from his head, and that as he took the auspices, the sacred chickens flew away. As he was on the point of addressing the soldiers on the day of the adoption, his camp chair, through the forgetfulness of his attendants, was not placed on the tribunal, as is customary, and in the Senate his curule chair was set wrong side foremost.

As he was offering sacrifice on the morning before he was killed, a soothsayer warned him again and again to look out for danger, since assassins were not far off.

Not long after this he learned that Otho held possession of the camp of the praetorian guard. When several advised him to proceed thither as soon as possible, saying that he could win the day by his presence and prestige, he decided to do no more than hold his present position and strengthen it

---

[1] From Spain to Rome.

[2] The fire should have been blazing brightly and a youth clad in white should have carried the incense and wine in more costly receptacles.

by getting together a guard of the legionaries, who were en-
camped in many different quarters of the city. He did however put on a linen cuirass, though he openly declared that
it would afford little protection against so many swords. But
he was lured out by false reports, circulated by the conspirators to induce him to appear in public. For when a few
rashly assured him that the trouble was over, that the rebels
had been overthrown, and that the rest were coming in a
body to offer their congratulations, ready to submit to all his
orders, he went out to meet them with so much confidence,
that when one of the soldiers boasted that he had slain Otho,
he asked him, "On whose authority?" and then he went on
as far as the Forum. There the horsemen who had been bidden
to slay him, spurring their horses through the streets and
dispersing the crowd of civilians, caught sight of him from a
distance and halted for a moment. Then they rushed upon
him and butchered him, abandoned by his followers.

Some say that at the beginning of the disturbance he cried
out, "What mean you, fellow soldiers? I am yours and you
are mine," and that he even promised them the largess. But
the more general account is, that he offered them his neck
without resistance, urging them to do their duty and strike,
since it was their will. It might seem very surprising that
none of those present tried to lend aid to their Emperor, and
that all who were sent for treated the summons with contempt except a company of German troops. These, because
of his recent kindness in showing them great indulgence when
they were weakened by illness, flew to his help, but through
their unfamiliarity with the city took a roundabout way and
arrived too late.

He was killed beside the Lake of Curtius [1] and was left
lying just as he was, until a common soldier, returning from
a distribution of grain, threw down his load and cut off the
head. Then, since there was no hair by which to grasp it,
he put it under his robe, but later thrust his thumb into the
mouth and so carried it to Otho. He handed it over to his
servants and camp-followers, who set it on a lance and
paraded it about the camp with jeers, crying out from time

---

[1] In the Forum.

to time, "Galba, thou Cupid, take joy in thy vigor!" The special reason for this saucy jest was, that the report had gone abroad a few days before, that when some one had congratulated him on still looking young and vigorous, he replied:

"As yet my strength is unimpaired." [1]

From these it was brought by a freedman of Patrobius Neronianus for a hundred pieces of gold [2] and thrown aside in the place where his patron had been executed by Galba's order. At last, however, his steward Argivus consigned it to the tomb with the rest of the body in Galba's private gardens on the Aurelian Road.

He was of average height, very bald, with blue eyes and a hooked nose. His hands and feet were so distorted by gout that he could not endure a shoe for long, unroll a book, or even hold one. The flesh on his right side too had grown out and hung down to such an extent, that it could with difficulty be held in place by a bandage.

It is said that he was a heavy eater and in winter time was in the habit of taking food even before daylight, while at dinner he helped himself so lavishly that he would have the leavings which remained in a heap before him passed along and distributed among the attendants who waited on him.[3] He was much inclined to unnatural desire, and in gratifying it preferred full-grown, strong men. They say that when Icelus, one of his old-time favorites, brought him news in Spain of Nero's death, he not only received him openly with the fondest kisses, but begged him to prepare himself without delay and took him privately aside.

He met his end in the seventy-third year of his age and the seventh month of his reign. The Senate, as soon as it was allowed to do so, voted him a statue standing upon a column adorned with the beaks of ships, in the part of the Forum where he was slain. But Vespasian annulled this decree, believing that Galba had sent assassins from Spain to Judaea, to take his life.

---

[1] *Iliad,* 5, 254; *Odyssey,* 21, 426.

[2] These pieces, *aurei,* were equivalent to about $4.00 each.

[3] He ate so much that the remains were enough to feed the attendants.

OTHO

THE ancestors of Otho came from an old and illustrious family in the town of Ferentium and were descended from the princes of Etruria. His grandfather Marcus Salvius Otho, whose father was a Roman Knight but whose mother was of lowly origin and perhaps not even free-born, became a Senator through the influence of Livia Augusta, in whose house he was reared, but did not advance beyond the grade of Praetor.

His father Lucius Otho was of a distinguished family on his mother's side, with many powerful connections, and was so beloved by Tiberius and so like him in appearance, that he was believed by many to be the Emperor's son. In the regular offices at Rome, the Proconsulate of Africa, and several special military commands he conducted himself with extreme severity. In Illyricum he even had the courage to punish some soldiers with death, because in the rebellion of Camillus,[1] repenting of their defection, they had killed their officers on the ground that they were the ringleaders in the revolt against Claudius. And they were executed in his presence before his headquarters, although he knew that they had been promoted to higher positions by Claudius because of that very act. By this deed, while he increased his reputation, he lost favor at court. But he speedily regained it by detecting the treachery of a Roman Knight, whose slaves betrayed their master's design of killing the Emperor. For in consequence of this, the Senate conferred a very unusual honor on him by setting up his statue in the Palace, and Claudius also enrolled him among the patricians, and after praising him in the highest terms, added these words: "Such a man I do not wish my children may surpass." By Albia Terentia, a woman of an illustrious line, he had two sons, Lucius Titianus and a younger called Marcus, who had the

---

[1] Mentioned in *Claudius*.

same surname as himself; also a daughter, whom he betrothed to Drusus, son of Germanicus, almost before she was of marriageable age.

The Emperor Otho was born on the fourth day before the Kalends of May in the consulate of Camillus Arruntius and Domitius Ahenobarbus. From earliest youth he was so extravagant and wild that his father often flogged him. And they say that he used to rove about at night and lay hands on any one whom he met who was feeble or drunk and toss him in a blanket.

After his father's death he pretended love for an influential freedwoman of the court, although she was an old woman and almost decrepit, that he might more effectually win her favor. Having through her wormed his way into Nero's good graces, he easily held the first place among the Emperor's friends because of the similarity of their characters, but according to some, also through immoral relations. At any rate his influence was such, that when he had bargained for a huge sum of money to procure the pardon of an ex-consul who had been condemned for extortion, he had no hesitation in bringing him into the Senate to give thanks, before he had fully secured his restoration.

He was privy to all the Emperor's plans and secrets, and on the day which Nero had chosen for the murder of his mother he gave both of them a most elaborate banquet, in order to avert suspicion. Also when Poppaea Sabina, who up to that time had been Nero's mistress, was separated from her husband and turned over for the time being to Otho, he pretended marriage with her.[1] But not content with seducing her he became so devoted that he could not endure the thought of having Nero even as a rival. At all events it is believed that he not only would not admit those whom Nero sent to fetch her, but that on one occasion he even shut out the Emperor himself, who stood before his door, vainly mingling threats and entreaties and demanding the return of his trust. Therefore Nero annulled the marriage and under color of an appointment as Governor banished Otho to Lusitania, contenting himself

---

[1] Tacitus writes, *Annals* XIII, 45, the marriage was real, which may also be inferred from below.

with this through fear that by inflicting a severer punishment he would make the whole farce public. But even as it was, it was published abroad in this couplet:

"You ask why Otho's banished? Know the cause
Comes not within the scope of vulgar laws.
Against all rules of fashionable life
The rogue had dared to sleep with his own wife."

With the rank of Quaestor [1] Otho governed the province for ten years with remarkable moderation and integrity.

When at last an opportunity for revenge was given him, Otho was the first to espouse Galba's cause, at the same time conceiving on his own account high hopes of imperial power, because of the state of the times, but still more because of a declaration of the astrologer Seleucus.[2] For he had not only promised Otho some time before that he would survive Nero, but had at this time unexpectedly appeared unsought and made the further promise, that he would soon become Emperor as well.

Accordingly Otho let slip no opportunity for flattery or attention to any one. Whenever he entertained Galba at dinner, he gave a gold piece to each man of the cohort on guard, and put all the soldiers under obligation in one form or another. Chosen arbiter by a man who was at law with his neighbor about a part of his estate, he bought the whole property and presented it to him. As a result there was hardly any one who did not both think and openly declare that he alone was worthy to succeed to the empire.

Now he had hoped to be adopted by Galba, and looked forward to it from day to day. But when Piso was preferred and he at last lost that hope, he resorted to force, spurred on not merely by feelings of resentment, but also by the greatness of his debts. For he flatly declared that he could not keep on his feet unless he became Emperor, and that it made no difference whether he fell at the hands of the enemy in battle or at those of his creditors in the Forum.

---

[1] As a rule only those who had been Consuls or Praetors were appointed provincial governors.

[2] Ptolemaeus, according to Tacitus and Plutarch.

He had extorted a million sesterces [1] from one of the Emperor's slaves a few days before for getting him a stewardship. This was the entire capital for his great undertaking. At first the enterprise was entrusted to five of his body-guard, then to ten others, two being chosen by each of the first five. To all of them ten thousand sesterces [2] were paid at once and they were promised fifty thousand [3] more. Through these others were won over, but not so very many, since he had full confidence more would join him when the business was afoot.

He had been inclined to seize the camp immediately after the adoption, and set upon Galba as he was dining in the palace, but had been prevented by consideration for the cohort which was on guard at the time, and a reluctance to increase its ill repute. For it was while that same cohort was at its post that both Gaius had been slain and Nero had been forsaken. The intervening time [4] was lost owing to bad omens and the warnings of Seleucus.

Accordingly, when the day was set, after admonishing his confederates to await him at the golden mile-post [5] under the temple of Saturn in the Forum, he called upon Galba in the morning and was welcomed as usual with a kiss. He also attended the Emperor as he was offering sacrifice, and heard the predictions of the soothsayer. Then a freedman announced that the architects had come, which was the signal agreed on, and going off as if to inspect a house which was for sale, he rushed from the palace by a back door and hastened to the appointed place. Others say that he feigned an attack of fever and asked those who stood near him to give that excuse, in case he should be missed. Then hurriedly entering a closed sedan, such as women use, he hurried to the camp, but got out when the bearers' strength flagged, and started to run. His shoe came untied and he stopped, whereupon without delay he was at once taken up on the shoulders of his

[1] $41,000.00.

[2] $410.00.

[3] $2,050.00.

[4] Between the adoption and the death of Galba, a space of five days.

[5] The gilded pillar at which all the great military roads of Italy converged. On it were marked the distances to the principal towns. It was erected by Augustus in 20 B.C.

companions and hailed as Emperor. In this way he arrived
at headquarters, amid acclamations and drawn swords, while
every one whom he met fell in, just as though he were an
accomplice and a participator in the plot. He then sent emissaries to kill Galba and Piso, and made no further promises
in the assembly to win the loyalty of the soldiers than to declare that he would have that, and only that, which they
should leave to him.

Next, as the day was drawing to its close, he entered the
Senate and after giving a brief account of himself, alleging
that he had been carried off in the streets and forced to undertake the rule, which he would exercise in accordance with the
general will, he went to the palace. When in the midst of the
other adulations of those who congratulated and flattered
him, he was hailed by the common herd as Nero, he made
no sign of dissent. On the contrary, according to some writers,
he even made use of that surname in his commissions and his
first letters to some of the Governors of the provinces. Certain it is that he suffered Nero's busts and statues to be set
up again, and reinstated his procurators and freedmen in
their former posts, while the first grant that he signed as
Emperor was one of fifty million sesterces [1] for finishing the
Golden House.

It is said that he had a fearful dream that night, uttered
loud groans, and was found by those who ran to nis aid lying on the bare floor beside his couch; that he tried by every
kind of expiatory rite to propitiate the shade of Galba, by
whom he dreamt that he was ousted and thrown out; and that
next day, as he was taking the auspices, a great storm arose
and he had a bad fall, whereat he muttered from time to time:

With long pipes what concern have I? [2]

Now at about this same time the armies in Germany swore
allegiance to Vitellius. When Otho learned of this, he persuaded the Senate to send a deputation, to say that an Emperor had already been chosen and to counsel peace and harmony. In spite of this he offered Vitellius by messengers and

---

[1] $2,050,000.00.

[2] A proverbial expression meaning to undertake something beyond
one's powers.

letters a share in the imperial dignity and proposed to become his son-in-law. But when it became clear that war was inevitable, and the generals and troops which Vitellius had sent in advance were already drawing near, he was given a proof of the affection and loyalty of the praetorians towards himself which almost resulted in the destruction of the Senate. It had been resolved that some arms should be removed and carried back [1] on shipboard by the marines. But as these were being taken out of the camp armory towards nightfall, some suspected treachery and started a riot. Then on a sudden all the soldiers hastened to the palace without any particular leader, demanding the death of the Senators. After putting to flight some of the Tribunes who attempted to stop them, and killing others, just as they were, all blood-stained, they burst right into the dining-room, demanding to know where the Emperor was. And they could not be quieted until they had seen him.

He began his expedition with energy and in fact too hastily, without any regard even for the omens, and in spite of the fact that the sacred shields had been taken out,[2] but not yet put back, which for ages has been considered unlucky. This was on the very day, too, when the worshipers of the Mother of the Gods [3] begin their wailing and lamentation, and also with most unfavorable auspices. For having offered up a victim to father Dis, he had good omens, whereas in such a sacrifice adverse indications are more favorable. And when he first left the city, he was delayed by floods of the Tiber, while at the twentieth milestone he found the road blocked by fallen buildings.

With like rashness, although no one doubted that the proper course was to protract the war, since the enemy were hard pressed by hunger and by the narrowness of their quarters, he decided to fight a decisive battle as soon as possible, either because he could not endure the continued worry and hoped that the war could be ended before the arrival of Vitellius, or from inability to resist the impetuosity of his

---

[1] To Ostia.

[2] Of the temple of Mars to be carried through the streets in the sacred procession customary before leaving for military operations.

[3] Cybele, whose festival was from March 24 to 30. Her priests were castrates, and in her rites sexual elements predominated.

soldiers, who clamored for the fight. He himself did not take part in any of the battles, but remained behind at Brixellum.[1]

He was victorious in three contests, but they were of little moment: in the Alps, near Placentia, and "at Castor's," as the place is called. In the final and decisive struggle at Betriacum he was defeated, but through treachery. For hope of a conference was offered, and when his soldiers were led out in the belief that they were to discuss terms of peace, a battle was forced upon them unexpectedly, just as they were exchanging greetings with the foe. After the defeat, Otho at once resolved to take his own life, rather from a feeling of shame, as many have thought with good reason, and an unwillingness to persist in a struggle for imperial power at the expense of such danger to life and property, than from any despair of success or distrust of his troops. For even then he had a fresh and strong force which he had held in reserve for a second attempt, while others were on their way from Dalmatia, Pannonia, and Moesia. Even the defeated troops were not so crushed as not to be ready to undergo any danger, and even without support undertake to avenge their disgrace.

My father Suetonius Laetus took part in that war, as a Tribune of the equestrian order in the thirteenth legion. He used often to declare afterwards that Otho, even when he was a private citizen, so loathed civil strife, that at the mere mention of the fate of Brutus and Cassius at a banquet he shuddered; that he would not have engaged with Galba, if he had not felt confident that the affair could be settled peacefully; further, that he was led to hold his life cheap at that time by the example of a common soldier. This man on bringing news of the defeat of the army was believed by no one, but was charged by the soldiers now with falsehood and now with cowardice, and accused of running away. Whereupon he fell on his sword at the Emperor's feet. My father used to say that at this sight Otho cried out that he would no longer endanger the lives of such brave men, who had deserved so well.

Having therefore advised his brother, his nephew, and his friends one by one to look out each for his own safety as best

---

[1] Between Mantua and Cremona.

they could, he embraced and kissed them all and sent them off. Then going to a retired place he wrote two notes, one of consolation to his sister, and one to Nero's widow Messalina, whom he had intended to marry, commending to her his corpse and his memory. Then he burned all his letters, to prevent them from bringing danger or harm to any one at the hands of the victor. He also distributed what money he had with him among his servants.

When he had thus made his preparations and was now resolved upon death, learning from a disturbance which meantime arose that those who were beginning to depart and leave the camp were being seized and detained as deserters, he said "Let us add this one more night to our life" (these were his very words), and he forbade the offering of violence to any one. Leaving the door of his bedroom open until a late hour, he gave the privilege of speaking with him to all who wished to come in. After that quenching his thirst with a draught of cold water, he took up two daggers, and having tried the point of both of them, put one under his pillow. Then closing the doors, he slept very soundly. When he at last woke up at about daylight, he stabbed himself with a single stroke under the left breast. Alternately concealing the wound and exposing it to those who rushed in at his first groan, he breathed his last and was hastily buried (for such were his orders) in the thirty-eighth year of his age and on the ninety-fifth day of his reign.

Neither Otho's person nor his bearing suggested such great courage. He is said to have been of moderate height, splay-footed and bandy-legged, but almost feminine in his care of his person. He had the hair of his body plucked out, and because of the thinness of his locks wore a wig so carefully fashioned and fitted to his head, that no one suspected it. Moreover, they say that he used to shave every day and smear his face with moist bread, beginning the practice with the appearance of the first down, so as never to have a beard; also that he used to celebrate the rites of Isis publicly in the linen garment prescribed by the cult. I am inclined to think that it was because of these habits that a death so little in harmony with his life excited the greater marvel.[1] Many of

---

[1] A saying persisted for many years that "none ever died like Otho."

the soldiers who were present kissed his hands and feet as he lay dead, weeping bitterly and calling him the bravest of men and an incomparable Emperor, and then at once slew them-selves beside his bier. Many of those who were absent too, on receiving the news attacked and killed one another from sheer grief. In short the greater part of those who had hated him most bitterly while he lived lauded him to the skies when he was dead. It was even commonly declared that he had put an end to Galba, not so much for the sake of ruling, as of restoring the republic and liberty.

VITELLIUS

OF the origin of the Vitellian family different and widely varying accounts are given, some saying that the family was ancient and noble, others that it was new and obscure, if not of mean extraction. I should believe that these came respectively from the flatterers and detractors of the Emperor, were it not for a difference of opinion about the standing of the family at a considerably earlier date.

We have a book of Quintus Elogius addressed to Quintus Vitellius, Quaestor of the Deified Augustus, in which it is written that the Vitellii were sprung from Faunus,[1] King of the Aborigines, and Vitellia, who was worshiped as a Goddess in many places; and that they ruled in all Latium. That the surviving members of the family moved from the Sabine district to Rome and were enrolled among the patricians. That traces of this stock endured long afterwards in the Vitellian Road, running from the Janiculum all the way to the sea, as well as in a colony of the same name, which in ancient days the family had asked the privilege of defending against the Aequicoli with troops raised from their own family. That when afterwards a force was sent into Apulia at the time of the Samnite war, some of the Vitellii settled at Nuceria, and that after a long time their descendants returned to the city and resumed their place in the senatorial order.

On the other hand several have written that the founder of the family was a freedman, while Cassius Severus and others as well say further that he was a cobbler, and that his son, after making a considerable fortune from the sale of confiscated estates and the profession of informer, married a common strumpet, daughter of one Antiochus who kept a bakery, and became the father of a Roman Knight. But this difference of opinion may be left unsettled.

---

[1] Third legendary King of Italy, identified with the Greek Pan.

In any event Publius Vitellius of Nuceria,[1] whether of ancient stock or of parents and forefathers in whom he could take no pride, was unquestionably a Roman Knight and a steward of Augustus' property. He left four sons of high rank with the same name and differing only in their forenames: Aulus, Quintus, Publius and Lucius. Aulus, who was given to luxury and especially notorious for the magnificence of his feasts, died a Consul, appointed to the office with Domitius, father of the Emperor Nero. Quintus lost his rank at the time when it was resolved, at the suggestion of Tiberius, to depose and get rid of undesirable Senators. Publius, a member of Germanicus' staff, arraigned Gnaeus Piso, the enemy and murderer of his commander, and secured his condemnation. Arrested among the accomplices of Sejanus, after holding the praetorship, and handed over to his own brother to be kept in confinement, he opened his veins with a penknife, but allowed himself to be bandaged and restored, not so much from unwillingness to die, as because of the entreaties of his friends; and he met a natural death while still in confinement. Lucius attained the consulate and then was made Governor of Syria,[2] where with supreme diplomacy he not only induced Artabanus, King of the Parthians, to hold a conference with him, but even to do obeisance to the standards of the legion. Later he held, with the Emperor Claudius, two more regular consulships and the censorship. He also bore the charge of the empire while Claudius was away on his expedition to Britain. He was an honest and active man, but of very ill repute because of his passion for a freedwoman, which went so far that he used her spittle mixed with honey to rub on his throat and jaws as a medicine, not secretly nor seldom, but openly and every day. He had also a wonderful gift for flattery and was the first to begin to worship Gaius Caesar [3] as a God. For on his return from Syria he did not presume to approach the Emperor except with veiled head, turning himself about and then prostrating himself. To neglect no means of gaining the favor of Claudius, who was a slave to his wives and freed-

---

1 Modern Nocera, near Salerno.
2 Josephus frequently commends him for his kindness to the Jews.
3 Caligula.

men, he begged of Messalina as the highest possible favor
that she would allow him to take off her shoes. When he
had done this he took her right slipper and constantly carried it about between his toga and his tunic, and sometimes
kissed it. Narcissus also and Pallas he honored by cherish-
ing their images among his household Gods. It was he who
made the famous remark, "May you often do it," when he
was congratulating Claudius at the celebration of the Secular
games.[1]

He died of a paralytic stroke on the second day after he
was seized, leaving two sons, begotten of Sestilia, a most
worthy woman and of no mean family, and having lived to
see them Consuls both in the same year, and for the whole
year, since the younger succeeded the elder for six months.
On his decease the Senate honored him with a public funeral
and with a statue on the rostra with this inscription: "Of
unwavering loyalty to his Emperor."

The Emperor Aulus Vitellius, son of Lucius, was born on
the eighth day before the Kalends of October, or according
to some, on the seventh day before the Ides of September,
in the consulship of Drusus Caesar and Norbanus Flaccus.[2]
His parents were so aghast at his horoscope as announced by
the astrologers, that his father tried his utmost, while he
lived, to prevent the assignment of any province to his son,
and when he was sent to the legions and hailed as Emperor,
his mother immediately mourned over him as lost. He spent
his boyhood and early youth at Capri among the pathics
of Tiberius, being branded for all time with the nickname
Spintria[3] and suspected of having been the means of his
father's first advancement at the expense of his own chastity.

Stained by every sort of baseness as he advanced in years,
he held a prominent place at court, winning the intimacy of
Gaius[4] by his devotion to chariot-driving and of Claudius

---

[1] Everybody else was amused on this occasion (related in *Claudius,*)
because Claudius announced a new series of entertainments whereas
people remembered Augustus had given the same sort before.

[2] The year after Augustus' death. Vitellius was thus seventeen years
older than Otho.

[3] Concerning whom see *Tiberius.*

[4] Caligula.

by his passion for dice. But he was still dearer to Nero, not only because of these same qualities, but because of a special service besides. For when he was presiding at the contests of the Neronia and Nero wished to compete among the lyre-players, but did not venture to do so although there was a general demand for him and accordingly left the theater, Vitellius called him back, alleging that he came as an envoy from the insistent people, and thus gave Nero a chance to yield to their entreaties.

Having in this way through the favor of three Emperors been honored not only with political positions but with distinguished priesthoods as well, he afterwards governed Africa as Proconsul and served as curator of public works, but with varying purpose and reputation. In his province he showed exceptional integrity for two successive years, for he served as deputy to his brother, who succeeded him. But in his city offices he was said to have stolen some of the offerings and ornaments from the temples and changed others, substituting tin and brass for gold and silver.

He had to wife Petronia, daughter of an ex-consul, and by her a son Petronianus, who was blind in one eye. Since this son was named as his mother's heir on condition of being freed from his father's authority, he manumitted him, but shortly afterwards killed him, according to the general belief, charging him besides with attempted parricide, and alleging that he had, from consciousness of his guilt, drunk the poison which he had mixed for his father. Soon afterwards he married Galeria Fundana, daughter of an ex-praetor, and from her too he had a son and a daughter, but the former stammered so, that he was all but dumb and tongue-tied.

Galba surprised every one by sending him to Lower Germany. Some think that it was due to Titus Vinius, who had great influence at the time, and whose friendship Vitellius had long since won through their common support of the Blues.[1] But since Galba openly declared that no men were less to be feared than those who thought of nothing but eating, and that Vitellius's bottomless gullet might be filled

---

[1] A faction in the Circus.

from the resources of the province, it is clear to any one that he was chosen rather through contempt than favor. It is notorious that when he was about to start, he lacked means for his traveling expenses, and that his need of funds was such, that after consigning his wife and children, whom he left in Rome, to a hired garret, he let his house for the rest of the year; and that he took a valuable pearl from his mother's ear and pawned it, to defray the expenses of his journey. He had to resort to false accusation to get rid of the throng of creditors that lay in wait for him and tried to detain him. Among them were the people of Sinuessa and of Formiae, whose public revenues he had embezzled. These he terrified with false accusations. Against one of them, a freedman who was somewhat persistent in demanding what was due to him, he brought an action for damages, alleging that he had been kicked by him, and would not let him off until he had squeezed him to the tune of fifty thousand sesterces.[1]

On his arrival the army, which was disaffected towards the Emperor and inclined to mutiny, received him gladly with open arms, as if he had come to them as a gift from the Gods; since he was the son of a man who had thrice been Consul, in the prime of life, and of an easy-going and lavish disposition. This earlier good opinion Vitellius had also strengthened by recent acts, for throughout the march he kissed even the common soldiers whom he met, and at the posthouses and inns he was unusually affable to the mule drivers and travelers, asking each of them in the morning whether they had breakfasted and even showing by belching that he had done so.

As soon as he entered the camp, he granted every request that any one made and even of his own accord freed those in disgrace from their penalties, defendants of suits from their mourning,[2] and the convicted from punishment. Therefore hardly a month had passed, when the soldiers, regardless of the hour, for it was already evening, hastily took him from his bedroom, just as he was, in his common houseclothes, and hailed him as Emperor. Then he was carried about the most

----

[1] $2,050.00.

[2] Defendants in law suits had to wear mourning in public.

populous villages, holding a drawn sword of the Deified Julius, which some one had taken from a shrine of Mars and handed him during the first congratulations. He did not return to headquarters until the dining-room caught fire from the stove and was ablaze. And then, when all were shocked and troubled at what seemed a bad omen, he said: "Be of good cheer; to us light is given." This was his only address to the soldiers. When he presently received the support of the army of the upper province too, which had previously transferred its allegiance from Galba to the Senate, he eagerly accepted the surname of Germanicus, which was unanimously offered him, put off accepting the title of Augustus, and forever refused that of Caesar.

Then hearing of the murder of Galba, he settled affairs in Germany and made two divisions of his forces, one to send on against Otho, and the other to lead in person. The former was greeted with a lucky omen at the start, for an eagle suddenly flew towards them from the right and after hovering about the standards, slowly preceded their line of march. But, on the contrary, when he himself began his advance, the equestrian statues which were being set up everywhere in his honor on a sudden all collapsed with broken legs, and the laurel crown which he had put on with due ceremony fell into a running stream. Later, as he was sitting in judgment on the tribunal at Vienna,[1] a cock perched on his shoulder and then on his head. And the outcome corresponded with these omens, for he was not by his own efforts able to retain the power which his lieutenants secured for him.

He heard of the victory at Betriacum and of the death of Otho when he was still in Gaul, and without delay by a single edict he disbanded all the praetorian cohorts, as having set a pernicious example,[2] and bade them hand over their arms to their Tribunes. Furthermore, he gave orders that one hundred and twenty of them should be hunted up and punished, having found petitions which they had written to Otho, asking for a reward for services rendered in connection with Galba's murder. These acts were altogether admirable and

---

[1] Modern Vienne, near Lyons, in France.
[2] In deserting Galba for Otho.

noble, and such as to give hope that he would be a great prince, had it not been that the rest of his conduct was more in harmony with his natural disposition and his former habits of life than with imperial dignity. For when he had begun his march, he rode through the middle of the cities like a triumphing general, and on the rivers he sailed in most exquisite craft wreathed with various kinds of garlands, amid lavish entertainments, with no discipline among his household or the soldiers, making a jest of the pillage and wantonness of all his followers. For not content with the banquets which were furnished them everywhere at public expense, they set free whatever slaves they pleased, promptly paying those who remonstrated with blows and stripes, often with wounds, and sometimes with death. When he came to the plains where the battle was fought and some shuddered with horror at the moldering corpses, he had the audacity to encourage them by the abominable saying, that the odor of a dead enemy was sweet and that of a fellow-citizen sweeter still. But nevertheless, the better to bear the awful stench, he openly drained a great draught of unmixed wine and distributed some among the troops. With equal bad taste and arrogance, gazing upon the stone inscribed to the memory of Otho, he declared that he deserved such a Mausoleum, and sent the dagger with which his rival had killed himself to the Colony of Agrippina,[1] to be dedicated to Mars. He also held an all-night festival on the heights of the Apennines.

Finally he entered the city to the sound of the trumpet, wearing a general's mantle and a sword at his side, amid standards and banners, with his staff in military cloaks and his troops with drawn swords.

Then showing greater and greater disregard for the laws of Gods and men, he assumed the office of high priest on the day of Allia,[2] held elections for ten years to come, and made himself Consul for life. And to leave no doubt in any one's mind what model he chose for the government of the State,

---

[1] Modern Cologne, birthplace of Agrippina, daughter of Germanicus, wife of Nero.

[2] July 17, an especially unlucky day because it was the annivarsary of the great victory of the Gauls near the river Allia in 390 B.C., after which they sacked Rome.

he made funerary offerings to Nero in the middle of the
Campus Martius, attended by a great throng of the official
priests. When at the accompanying banquet a flute-player
was received with applause, he openly urged him "to render
something from the Master's Book [1] as well." And when he
began the songs of Nero, Vitellius was the first to applaud
him and even jumped for joy.

Beginning in this way, he regulated the greater part of his
rule wholly according to the advice and whims of the com-
monest of actors and chariot-drivers, and in particular of
his freedman Asiaticus. This fellow had immoral relations with
Vitellius in his youth, but later grew weary of him and ran
away. When Vitellius came upon him selling *posca* [2] at
Puteoli, he put him in irons, but at once freed him again
and made him his favorite. His vexation was renewed by the
man's excessive insolence and thievishness, and he sold him
to an itinerant keeper of gladiators. When, however, he was
once reserved for the end of a gladiatorial show, Vitellius
suddenly spirited him away, and finally, when the man had
reached his province, set him free. On the first day of his
reign he presented him with the golden ring at a banquet,
although in the morning, when there was a general demand
that Asiaticus be given that honor, he had deprecated in the
strongest terms such a blot on the equestrian order.

But his besetting sins were luxury and cruelty. He divided
his feasts into three, sometimes into four a day, breakfast,[3]
luncheon, dinner, and a drinking bout. And he was readily
able to do justice to all of them through his habit of taking
emetics. Moreover, he had himself invited to each of these
meals by different men on the same day, and the materials
for any one of them never cost less than four hundred thousand
sesterces.[4] Most notorious of all was the dinner given by his
brother to celebrate the Emperor's arrival in Rome, at which
two thousand of the choicest fishes and seven thousand birds
are said to have been served. He himself eclipsed even this

---

[1] The name applied to a collection of Nero's compositions.

[2] Sour wine or vinegar mixed with water. The common drink of the
Roman soldier.

[3] Ordinarily a very light meal.

[4] $16,400.00.

at the dedication of a platter, which on account of its enormous size he called the "Shield of Minerva, Defender of the City." In this he mingled the livers of pike, the brains of pheasants and peacocks, the tongues of flamingoes and the milt of lampreys, brought by his captains and triremes from the whole empire, from Parthia to the Spanish Strait. Being besides a man of an appetite that was not only boundless, but also regardless of time or decency, he could never refrain, even when he was sacrificing or making a journey, from snatching bits of meat and cakes amid the altars, almost from the very fire, and devouring them on the spot; and in the cookshops along the road, viands smoking hot or even those left over from the day before and partly consumed.

He delighted in inflicting death and torture on any one whatsoever and for any cause whatever, putting to death several men of rank, fellow students and comrades of his, whom he had solicited to come to court by every kind of deception, all but offering them a share in the rule. This he did in various treacherous ways, even giving poison to one of them with his own hand in a glass of cold water, for which the man had called when ill of a fever. Besides he spared hardly one of the money-lenders, contractors, and tax-gatherers who had ever demanded of him the payment of a debt at Rome or of a toll on a journey. One of these, while in the very act of saluting him, he sent off to be executed, but immediately recalled, and, as all were praising his mercy, gave orders to have him killed in his presence, saying that he wished to feast his eyes. In another case he had two sons who attempted to intercede for their father put to death with him. A Roman Knight also, who cried as he was being taken off to execution, "You are my heir," he compelled to show his will. Reading that one of the man's freedmen was put down as joint-heir with himself, he ordered the death both of the Knight and the freedman. He even killed some of the common people, merely because they had openly spoken ill of the Blue faction, thinking that they had ventured to do this from contempt of himself and in anticipation of a change of rulers. But he was especially hostile to writers of lampoons and to astrologers, and whenever any one of them was accused, he put him to death without trial, particularly incensed because after a proclamation of his in which he ordered the astrologers to leave the city and Italy before the Kalends of October, a placard was at once posted, reading: "By proclamation of the Chaldeans, God bless the State! Before the same day and date Vitellius Germanicus shall not be living anywhere." Moreover, when his mother died, he was suspected of having forbidden her being given food when she was ill, because a woman of the Chatti,[1] in whom he believed as he would in an oracle, prophesied that he would rule securely and for a long time, but only if he should survive his parent. Others say that through weariness of present evils and fear of those which threatened, she asked poison of her son, and obtained it with no great difficulty.

In the eighth month of his reign the armies of the Moesian provinces and Pannonia revolted from him, and also in the provinces beyond the seas those of Judaea and Syria, the former swearing allegiance to Vespasian in his absence and the latter in his presence. Therefore, to retain the devotion and favor of the rest of the people, there was nothing that he did not lavish publicly and privately, without any limit whatever. He also held a levy in the city, promising those who volunteered not only their discharge upon his victory but also the rewards and privileges given to veterans after their regular term of service. Later, when his enemies were pressing him hard by land and sea, he opposed to them in one quarter his brother with a fleet manned by raw recruits and a band of gladiators, and in another the forces and leaders who had fought at Betriacum. And after he was everywhere either worsted or betrayed, he made a bargain with Flavius Sabinus, the brother of Vespasian, that he should have his own life and a hundred million sesterces.[1] Thereupon he immediately declared from the steps of the palace before his assembled soldiers, that he withdrew from the rule which had been given him against his will. But when all cried out against this, he postponed the matter, and after a night had passed, went at daybreak to the rostra in mourning garb and with

---

[1] The Chatti were a German tribe inhabiting what is now Hesse. The Germans had great confidence in the prophetical utterances of the women of this tribe.

[1] $4,100,000.00.

many tears made the same declaration, but from a written document. When the people and soldiers again interrupted him and besought him not to lose heart, vying with one another in promising him all their efforts in his behalf, he again took courage and by a sudden onslaught drove Sabinus and the rest of the Flavians, who no longer feared an attack, into the Capitol. Then he set fire to the temple of Jupiter Optimus Maximus and destroyed them, viewing the battle and the fire from the house of Tiberius, where he was feasting. Not long afterwards he repented of his action and, throwing the blame upon others, called an assembly and took oath, compelling the rest to do the same, that there was nothing for which he would strive more earnestly than for the public peace. Then he took a dagger from his side and offered it first to the Consul, and when he refused it, to the magistrates, and then to the Senators, one by one.[1] When no one would take it, he went off as if he would place it in the temple of Concord but when some cried out that he himself was Concord, he returned and declared that he would not only retain the steel but would also adopt the surname Concordia.

He also persuaded the Senate to send envoys with the Vestal Virgins, to sue for peace or at least to gain time for conference.

The following day, as he was waiting for a reply, word was brought by a scout that the enemy was drawing near. Then he was at once hurried into a sedan with only two companions, a baker and a cook, and secretly went to his father's house on the Aventine, intending to flee from there to Campania. Presently, on a slight and dubious rumor that peace had been granted, he allowed himself to be taken back to the palace. Finding everything abandoned there, and that even those who were with him were stealing away, he put on a girdle filled wtih gold pieces and took refuge in the lodge of the door-keeper, tying a dog before the door and putting a couch and a mattress against it.

The foremost of the army had now forced their way in, and since no one opposed them, were ransacking everything in

---

[1] As though he were willing to renounce the power of life and death over the people.

the usual way. They dragged Vitellius from his hiding-place and when they asked him his name (for they did not know him) and if he knew where Vitellius was, he attempted to escape them by a lie. Being soon recognized, he did not cease to beg that he be confined for a time, even in the prison, alle_ging that he had something to say of importance to the safety of Vespasian. But they bound his arms behind his back, put a noose about his neck, and dragged him with rent garments and half-naked to the Forum. All along the Sacred Way he was greeted with mockery and abuse, his head held back by the hair, as is common with criminals, and even the point of a sword placed under his chin, so that he could not look down but must let his face be seen. Some pelted him with dung and ordure, others called him incendiary and glutton, and some of the mob even taunted him with his bodily defects. He was in fact abnormally tall, with a face usually flushed from hard drinking, a huge belly, and one thigh crippled from being struck once upon a time by a four-horse chariot, when he was in attendance on Gaius [1] as he was driving. At last on the Stairs of Wailing he was tortured for a long time and then dispatched and dragged off with a hook to the Tiber.

He met his death, along with his brother and his son,[2] in the fifty-seventh year of his age, fulfilling the prediction of those who had declared from an omen which befell him at Vienna, as we have stated,[3] that he was destined to fall into the power of some man of Gaul. For he was slain by Antonius Primus, a leader of the opposing faction, who was born at Tolosa and in his youth bore the surname Becco, which means a rooster's beak.

---

[1] Caligula.

[2] Lucius and Germanicus were slain near Terracina. Lucius was marching to his brother's relief.

[3] Suetonius earlier told of the cock, *gallus* in Latin, which perched on his head.

BOOK VIII

THE DEIFIED VESPASIAN, THE DEIFIED TITUS, DOMITIAN

THE DEIFIED VESPASIAN

THE empire, which for a long time had been unsettled and,
as it were, drifting, through the usurpation and violent death
of three Emperors, was at last taken in hand and given
stability by the Flavian family. This house was, it is true,
obscure and without family portraits, yet it was one of
which our country had no reason whatever to be ashamed,
even though it is the general opinion that the penalty which
Domitian paid for his avarice and cruelty was fully merited.

Titus Flavius Petro, a burgher of Reate and during the
civil war a Centurion or a volunteer veteran on Pompey's side,
fled from the field of Pharsalus and went home, where after at
last obtaining pardon and an honorable discharge, he carried
on the business of a collector of moneys. His son, surnamed
Sabinus (although some say that he was an ex-centurion of
the first grade, others that while still in command of a cohort
he was retired because of ill-health), took no part in military
life, but was a common collector in Asia of the two and a
half per cent tax on imports and exports. And there existed
for some time statues erected in his honor by the cities of
Asia, inscribed "To an honest tax-gatherer." Later he carried on a banking business in the Helvetian country and
there he died, survived by his wife, Vespasia Polla, and by
two of her children, of whom the elder, Sabinus, rose to the
rank of Prefect of Rome and the younger, Vespasian, even
to that of Emperor. Polla, who was born of an honorable
family at Nursia, had for father Vespasius Pollio, thrice
Tribune of the soldiers and Prefect of the camp, while her
brother became a Senator with the rank of Praetor. There is
moreover on the top of a mountain, near the sixth milestone
on the road from Nursia to Spoletium, a place called Ves-
pasiae, where many monuments of the Vespasii are to be
seen, affording strong proof of the renown and antiquity of

the house. I ought to add that some have bandied about the report, that Petro's father came from the region beyond the Po and was a contractor for the day-laborers who come regularly every year from Umbria to the Sabine district, to till the fields; but that he settled in the town of Reate and there married. Personally I have found no evidence whatever of this, in spite of rather careful investigation.

Vespasian was born in the Sabine country, in a small village beyond Reate, called Falacrina, on the evening of the fifteenth day before the Kalends of December, in the consulate of Quintus Sulpicius Camerinus and Gaius Poppaeus Sabinus, five years before the death of Augustus. He was brought up under the care of his paternal grandmother Tertulla on her estates at Cosa. Therefore even after he became Emperor he used constantly to visit the home of his infancy, where the manor house was kept in its original condition, since he did not wish to miss anything which he was wont to see there. And he was so devoted to his grandmother's memory, that on religious and festival days he always drank from a little silver cup that had belonged to her.

After assuming the garb of manhood he for a long time made no attempt to win the broad stripe of Senator, though his brother had gained it, and only his mother could finally induce him to sue for it. She at length drove him to it, but rather by sarcasm than by entreaties or parental authority, since she constantly taunted him with being his brother's footman.

He served in Thrace as Tribune of the soldiers. As Quaestor he was assigned by lot the province of Crete and Cyrene. He became a candidate for the aedileship and then for the praetorship, attaining the former only after one defeat and then barely landing in the sixth place, but the latter on his first canvass and among the foremost. In his praetorship, to lose no opportunity of winning the favor of Caligula, who was at odds with the Senate, he asked for special games because of the Emperor's victory in Germany and recommended as an additional punishment of the conspirators [1] that they be cast out unburied. He also thanked the Emperor be-

---

[1] Lepidus and Gaetulicus.

fore that illustrious body because he had deigned to honor him with an invitation to dinner.

Meanwhile he took to wife Flavia Domitilla, formerly the mistress of Statilius Capella, a Roman Knight of Sabrata in Africa, a woman who at first had only partial citizenship but was afterwards declared a freeborn citizen of Rome in a suit before arbiters, brought by her father Flavius Liberalis, a native of Ferentum and merely a Quaestor's clerk. By her he had three children, Titus, Domitian, and Domitilla. He outlived his wife and daughter; in fact lost them both before he became Emperor. After the death of his wife he resumed his relations with Caenis, freedwoman and amanuensis of Antonia, and formerly his mistress; and even after he became Emperor he treated her almost as a lawful wife.

In the reign of Claudius he was sent in command of a legion to Germany, through the influence of Narcissus. From there he was transferred to Britain, where he fought thirty battles with the enemy. He reduced to subjection two powerful nations, more than twenty towns, and the island of Vectis,[1] near Britain, partly under the leadership of Aulus Plautius, the Consular Governor, and partly under that of Claudius himself. For this he received the triumphal regalia, and shortly after two priesthoods, besides the consulship, which he held for the last two months of the year. The rest of the time up to his proconsulate he spent in rest and retirement, through fear of Agrippina, who still had a strong influence over her son and hated any friend of Narcissus, even after the latter's death.

The chance of the lot then gave him Africa, which he governed with great justice and high honor, save that in a riot at Hadrumetum he was pelted with turnips. Certain it is that he came back none the richer, for his credit was so nearly gone that he mortgaged all his estates to his brother, and had to resort to trading in mules to keep up his position; whence he was commonly known as "the Muleteer." He is also said to have been found guilty of squeezing two hundred thousand sesterces [2] out of a young man for whom he obtained the

---

[1] The Isle of Wight.
[2] $8,200.00.

broad stripe [1] against his father's wish, and to have been severely rebuked in consequence.

On the tour through Greece, among the companions of Nero, he bitterly offended the Emperor by either going out often while Nero was singing, or falling asleep, if he remained. Being in consequence banished, not only from intimacy with the Emperor but even from his public receptions, he withdrew to a little out-of-the-way town, hiding in fear of his life till a province and an army were offered him.

There had spread over all the Orient an old and established belief, that it was fated at that time for men coming from Judaea to rule the world.[2] This prediction, referring to the Emperor of Rome, as afterwards appeared from the event, the people of Judaea took to themselves. Accordingly, they revolted, and, after killing their Governor, they routed the consular ruler of Syria as well, when he came to the rescue, and took one of his eagles. Since to put down this rebellion required a considerable army with a leader of no little enterprise, yet one to whom so great power could be entrusted without risk, Vespasian was chosen for the task, both as a man of tried energy and as one in no wise to be feared because of the obscurity of his family and name. Therefore there were added to the forces in Judaea two legions with eight divisions of cavalry and ten cohorts. He took his elder son as one of his lieutenants, and as soon as he reached his province he attracted the attention of the neighboring provinces also. For he at once reformed the discipline of the army and fought one or two battles with such daring, that in the storming of a fortress he was wounded in the knee with a stone and received several arrows in his shield.

While Otho and Vitellius were fighting for the throne after the death of Nero and Galba, he began to cherish the hope of imperial dignity, which he had long since conceived because of the following portents:

On the suburban estate of the Flavii an old oak tree, which was sacred to Mars, on each of the three occasions when Vespasia was delivered suddenly put forth a branch

---

1 Symbol of the senatorial order.

2 Tacitus (*Histories* V, 13) mentions this prediction in nearly the same terms, referring also in the plural number to the coming power.

from its trunk, obvious indications of the destiny of each child. The first was slender and quickly withered, and so too the girl that was born died within the year. The second was very strong and long and portended great success. But the third was the image of a tree. Therefore their father, Sabinus, so they say, being further encouraged by an inspection of victims, announced to his mother that a grandson had been born to her who would be a Caesar. But she only laughed, marveling that her son should already be in his dotage, while she was still of strong mind.

Later, when Vespasian was Aedile, Gaius Caesar, incensed at his neglect of his duty of cleaning the streets, ordered that he be covered with mud, which the soldiers accordingly heaped into the bosom of his purple-bordered toga. This some interpreted as an omen that one day in some civil commotion his country, trampled under foot and forsaken, would come under his protection and as it were into his embrace.

Once when he was taking breakfast, a stray dog brought in a human hand from the cross-roads and dropped it under the table. Again, when he was dining, an ox that was plowing shook off its yoke, burst into the dining-room, and after scattering the servants, fell at the very feet of Vespasian as he reclined at table, and bowed its neck as if suddenly tired out. A cypress tree, also, on his grandfather's farm was torn up by the roots, without the agency of any violent storm, and thrown down, and on the following day rose again greener and stronger than before.

He dreamed in Greece that the beginning of good fortune for himself and his family would come as soon as Nero had a tooth extracted. And on the next day it came to pass that a physician walked into the hall and showed him a tooth which he had just then taken out.

When he consulted the oracle of the God of Carmel in Judaea, the lots were highly encouraging, promising that whatever he planned or wished, however great it might be, would come to pass. And one of his high-born prisoners, Josephus [1]

---

[1] The famous Pharisean historian who was an important and romantic figure in Vespasian's and Titus's struggles with the Jews. He describes Jesus as "a wise man, if indeed one should call him a man," asserting "This was the Christ." This is the most definite reference we have to the founder of Christianity.

by name, as he was being put in chains, declared most confidently that he would soon be released by the same man, who would then, however, be Emperor. Omens were also reported from Rome: Nero in his latter days was admonished in a dream to take the sacred chariot of Jupiter Optimus Maximus from its shrine to the house of Vespasian and from there to the Circus. Not long after this, too, when Galba was on his way to the elections which gave him his second consulship, a statue of the Deified Julius of its own accord turned towards the East. And on the field of Betriacum, before the battle began, two eagles fought in the sight of all, and when one was vanquished, a third came from the direction of the rising sun and drove off the victor.

Yet he made no move, although his followers were quite ready and even urgent, until he was roused to it by the accidental support of men unknown to him and at a distance. Two thousand soldiers of the three legions that made up the army in Moesia had been sent to help Otho. When word came to them after they had begun their march that he had been defeated and had taken his own life, they none the less kept on as far as Aquileia, because they did not believe the report. There, taking advantage of the lawless state of the times, they indulged in every kind of pillage. Then, fearing that if they went back, they would have to give an account and suffer punishment, they took it into their heads to select and appoint an Emperor, saying that they were just as good as the Spanish army which had appointed Galba, or the praetorian guard which had elected Otho, or the German army which had chosen Vitellius. Accordingly the names of all the Consular Governors who were serving anywhere were taken up, and since objection was made to the rest for one reason or another, while some members of the third legion, which had been transferred from Syria to Moesia just before the death of Nero, highly commended Vespasian, they unanimously agreed on him and forthwith inscribed his name on all their banners. At the time, however, the movement was checked and the soldiers recalled to their allegiance for a season. But when their action became known, Tiberius Alexander, Prefect of Egypt, was the first to compel his legions to take the oath for Vespasian on the Kalends of July, the day which was afterwards celebrated as that of his accession. Then the army in Judaea swore allegiance to him personally on the fifth day before the Ides of July.

The enterprise was greatly forwarded by the circulation of a copy of a letter of the late Emperor Otho to Vespasian, whether genuine or forged, urging him with the utmost earnestness to vengeance and expressing the hope that he would come to the aid of his country; further, by a rumor which spread abroad that Vitellius had planned, after his victory, to change the winter quarters of the legions and to transfer those in Germany to the Orient, to a safer and milder service; and finally, by the support of Licinius Mucianus,[1] among the Governors of the provinces, and among the Kings, by that of Vologaesus, the Parthian. The former, laying aside the hostility with which up to that time jealousy had obviously inspired him, promised the Syrian army, and the latter forty thousand bowmen.

Therefore beginning a civil war and sending ahead generals with troops to Italy, he crossed meanwhile to Alexandria, to take possession of the key to Egypt. There he dismissed all his attendants and entered the temple of Serapis alone, to consult the auspices as to the duration of his power. And when after many propitiatory offerings to the God he at length turned about, it seemed to him that his freedman Basilides offered him sacred boughs, garlands and loaves, as is the custom there. And yet he knew well that no one had let him in, and that for some time he had been hardly able to walk by reason of rheumatism, and was besides far away. And immediately letters came with the news that Vitellius had been routed at Cremona and the Emperor himself slain at Rome.

Vespasian as yet lacked prestige and a certain divinity, so to speak, since he was an unexpected and still new-made Emperor. But these also were given him. A man of the people who was blind, and another who was lame, came to him together as he sat on the tribunal, begging for the help for their disorders which Serapis had promised in a dream. For the God declared that Vespasian would restore the eyes, if he would spit upon them, and give strength to the leg, if he would deign to touch it with his heel. Though he had hardly any faith that this could possibly succeed, and therefore shrank

---

[1] Governor of the neighboring province of Syria.

even from making the attempt, he was at last prevailed upon by his friends and tried both things in public before a large crowd; and with success. At this same time, by the direction of certain soothsayers, some vases of antique workmanship were dug up in a consecrated spot at Tegea in Arcadia and among them was an image very like Vespasian.

Returning to Rome under such auspices and attended by so great renown, after celebrating a triumph over the Jews, he added eight consulships to his former one, and also assumed the censorship. During the whole period of his rule he considered nothing more essential than first to strengthen the State, which was tottering and almost overthrown, and then to embellish it as well.

The soldiery, some emboldened by their victory and some resenting their humiliating defeat, had abandoned themselves to every form of license and recklessness. The provinces, too, and the free cities, as well as some of the kingdoms, were in a state of internal dissension. Therefore he discharged many of the soldiers of Vitellius and punished many. But so far from showing any special indulgence to those who had shared in his victory, he was even tardy in paying them their lawful rewards. To let slip no opportunity of improving military discipline, when a young man reeking with perfumes came to thank him for a commission which had been given him, Vespasian drew back his head in disgust, adding the stern reprimand: "I would rather you had smelt of garlic"; and he revoked the appointment. When the marines who march on foot by turns from Ostia and Puteoli to Rome, asked that an allowance be made them under the head of shoe money, not content with sending them away without a reply, he ordered that in future they should make the run barefooted. And they have done so ever since.

He made provinces of Achaia, Lycia, Rhodes, Byzantium and Samos, taking away their freedom, and likewise of Trachian Cilicia and Commagene, which up to that time had been ruled by Kings. He sent legions to Cappadocia because of the constant inroads of the barbarians, and gave it a consular Governor in place of a Roman Knight.

As the city was unsightly from former fires and fallen buildings, he allowed any one to take possession of vacant sites and build upon them, in case the owners failed to do so. He began the restoration of the Capitol in person, was the first to lend a hand in clearing away the débris, and carried some of it off on his own head. He undertook to restore the three thousand bronze tablets which were destroyed with the temple, making a thorough search for copies: priceless and most ancient records of the empire, containing the decrees of the Senate and the acts of the commons almost from the foundation of the city, regarding alliances, treaties, and special privileges granted to individuals.

He also undertook new works, the temple of Peace hard by the Forum and one to the Deified Claudius on the Caelian mount, which was begun by Agrippina, but almost utterly destroyed by Nero; also an amphitheater [1] in the heart of the city, a plan which he learned that Augustus had cherished.

He reorganized, augmented and reviewed, the great orders of Senators and Knights, which had been reduced by a series of murders and fallen into disrepute by long neglect. He expelled those who least deserved the honor and enrolled the most distinguished of the Italians and provincials. Furthermore, to let it be known that the two orders differed from each other not so much in their privileges as in their rank, in the case of an altercation between a Senator and a Roman Knight, he rendered the decision that "unseemly language should not be used toward Senators, but if they were the aggressors, it was proper and lawful to return their insults in kind."

Lawsuit upon lawsuit had accumulated in all the courts to an excessive degree, since those of long standing were left unsettled though the interruption of court business and new ones had arisen through the disorder of the times. He therefore chose commissioners by lot to restore what had been seized in time of war, and to make special decisions in the court of the Hundred, reducing the cases to the smallest possible number, since it was clear that the lifetime of the litigants would not suffice for the regular proceedings.

Licentiousness and extravagance had flourished without

---

[1] The Coliseum, known until the Middle Ages as the Flavian amphitheater.

restraint. He therefore induced the Senate to vote that any woman who formed a connection with the slave of another person should herself be treated as a bond-woman; and that those who lend money to young men still under the control of their father should never have a legal right to enforce payment, that is to say, not even after the death of the fathers.

In other matters he was unassuming and lenient from the very beginning of his reign until its end, never trying to conceal his former lowly condition, but often even parading it. Indeed, when certain men tried to trace the origin of the Flavian family to the founders of Reate and a companion of Hercules whose tomb still stands on the Salarian Road, he laughed at them for their pains. So far was he from a desire for pomp and show, that on the day of his triumph,[1] exhausted by the slow and tiresome procession, he did not hesitate to say: "It serves me right for being such a fool as to want a triumph in my old age, as if it were due to my ancestors or had ever been among my own ambitions." He did not even assume the tribunicial power at once nor the title of Father of his Country until late. As for the custom of searching[2] for those who came to pay their morning calls, he gave that up before the civil war was over.

He bore the frank language of his friends, the quips of pleaders, and the impudence of the philosophers with the greatest patience. Though Licinius Mucianus, a notorious pathic, presumed upon his services to treat Vespasian with scant respect,[3] he never had the heart to criticize him except privately and then only to the extent of adding to a complaint made to a common friend, the significant words: "I at least am a man." When Salvius Liberalis ventured to say while defending a rich client, "What is it to Caesar if Hipparchus has a hundred millions," he personally commended him. When the Cynic Demetrius met him abroad after being condemned to banishment, and without deigning to rise in his presence or

---

[1] Vespasian and his son Titus had a joint triumph for the conquest of Judaea.

[2] For murderous weapons.

[3] He boasted that the rule had been at his disposal and that he had given it to Vespasian.

to salute him, even snarled out some insult, he merely called him "cur."

He was not inclined to remember or to avenge affronts or enmities, but made a brilliant match for the daughter of his enemy Vitellius, and even provided her with a dowry and a house-keeping outfit. When he was in terror at being forbidden Nero's court, and asked what on earth he was to do or where he was to go, one of the ushers put him out and told him to "go to hell." Yet when the man later begged for forgiveness, Vespasian confined his resentment to words, and those of about the same number and purport. Indeed, so far was he from being led by any suspicion or fear to cause any one's death, that when his friends warned him that he must keep an eye on Mettius Pompusianus, since it was commonly believed that he had an imperial horoscope, he even made him Consul, guaranteeing that he would one day be mindful of the favor.

It cannot readily be shown that any innocent person was punished save in Vespasian's absence and without his knowledge, or at any rate against his will and by misrepresentation. Although Helvidius Priscus was the only one who greeted him on his return from Syria by his private name of "Vespasian," and moreover in his praetorship left the Emperor unhonored and unmentioned in all his edicts, he did not show anger until by the extravagance of his railing Helvidius had made him out as little better than an ordinary person. But even in his case, though he did banish him and later order his death, he was most anxious for any means of saving him, and sent messengers to recall those who were to slay him. And he would have saved him, but for a false report that Helvidius had already been done to death. Certainly he never took pleasure in the death of any one, but even wept and sighed over those who suffered merited punishment.

The only thing for which he can fairly be censured was his love of money. For not content with reviving the imposts which had been repealed under Galba, he added new and heavy burdens, increasing the amount of tribute paid by the provinces, in some cases actually doubling it, and quite openly carrying on traffic which would be shameful even for a man in private life. For he would buy up certain commodities merely in order to distribute them at a profit. He did not scruple to sell offices to candidates and acquittals to men under prosecution, whether innocent or guilty. He is even believed to have had the habit of designedly advancing the most rapacious of his procurators to higher posts, that they might be the richer when he later condemned them. In fact, it was common talk that he used these men as sponges, because he, so to speak, soaked them when they were dry and squeezed them when they were wet.

Some say that he was naturally covetous and was taunted with it by an old herdsman of his, who on being forced to pay for the freedom for which he earnestly begged Vespasian when he became Emperor, cried: "The fox changes his fur, but not his nature." Others on the contrary believe that he was driven by necessity to raise money by spoliation and robbery because of the desperate state of the treasury and the privy purse, to which he bore witness at the very beginning of his reign by declaring that forty thousand millions [1] were needed to set the State upright. This latter view seems the more probable, since he made the best use of his gains, ill-gotten though they were.

He was most generous to all classes, making up the requisite estate for Senators,[2] giving needy ex-consuls an annual stipend of five hundred thousand sesterces,[3] restoring to a better condition many cities throughout the empire which had suffered from earthquakes or fires, and in particular encouraging men of talent and the arts.

He was the first to establish a regular salary of a hundred thousand sesterces [4] for Latin and Greek teachers of rhetoric, paid from the privy purse. He also presented eminent poets with princely largess and great rewards, and artists, too, such as the restorer of the Venus of Cos and of the Colossus.[5] To a mechanical engineer, who promised to transport some heavy columns to the Capitol at small expense, he gave no mean reward for his invention, but refused to make use of it, saying

---

[1] $1,640,000,000.00.
[2] Increased to $49,200.00 by Augustus.
[3] $20,500.00.
[4] $4,100.00.
[5] A statue of Nero.

that he should not be forced to take from the poor commons the work that fed them.

At the plays with which he dedicated the new stage of the theater of Marcellus he revived the old musical entertainments. To Apelles, the tragic actor, he gave four hundred thousand sesterces [1]; to Terpnus and Diodorus, the lyre-players, two hundred thousand each; to several a hundred thousand; while those who received least were paid forty thousand, and numerous golden crowns were awarded besides. He gave constant dinner-parties, too, usually with many sumptuous courses, to help the marketmen. He gave dinner gifts to women on the first of March,[2] as he did to the men on the Saturnalia.

Yet even so he could not be rid of his former ill-repute for covetousness. The Alexandrians persisted in calling him Cybiosactes,[3] the surname of one of their Kings who was scandalously stingy. Even at his funeral, Favor, a leading actor of mimes, who wore his mask and, according to the usual custom, imitated the actions and words of the deceased during his lifetime, having asked the procurators in a loud voice how much his funeral procession would cost, and hearing the reply "Ten million sesterces," cried out: "Give me a hundred thousand and fling me even into the Tiber."

He was well built, with strong, sturdy limbs, and the expression of one who was straining at stool. Apropos of which a witty fellow, when Vespasian asked him to make a joke on him also, replied rather cleverly: "I will, when you have finished relieving your bowels." He enjoyed excellent health, though he did nothing to preserve it except to rub his throat and the other parts of his body a certain number of times in the exercise grounds attached to the baths, and to fast one day in every month.

This was in general his manner of life. While Emperor, he always rose very early, in fact before daylight. After reading

---

[1] $16,400.00.

[2] The Matronalia or feast of married women. At this the matrons served their female attendants, as at the feast of the men's Saturnalia in December the masters served their slaves.

[3] A transliterated Greek word meaning "a dealer in square pieces of salt fish."

his letters and the reports of all the officials, he admitted his friends, and while he was receiving their greetings, he put on his own shoes and dressed himself. After dispatching any business that came up, he took time for a drive and then for a nap, lying with one of his mistresses, of whom he had taken several after the death of Caenis. After his siesta he went to the bath and the dining-room. And it is said that at no time was he more good-natured or indulgent, so that the members of his household eagerly watched for these opportunities of making requests.

Not only at dinner but on all other occasions he was most affable, and he turned off many matters with a jest. For he was very ready with sharp sayings, albeit of a low and buffoonish kind, so that he did not even refrain from ribald expressions. Yet many of his remarks are still remembered which are full of fine wit, and among them the following. When an ex-consul called Mestrius Florus called his attention to the fact that the proper pronunciation was *plaustra* rather than *plostra*, he greeted him next day as "Flaurus." [1] When he was importuned by a woman, who said that she was dying with love for him, he took her to his bed and, after he had gratified her desires, gave her four hundred thousand sesterces.[2] Being asked by his steward how he would have the sum entered in his accounts, he replied: "To a passion for Vespasian."

He also quoted Greek verses with great timeliness, saying of a man of tall stature and monstrous members:

"Striding along and waving a lance that casts a long shadow," [3]

and of the freedman Cerylus, who was very rich, and, to cheat the privy purse of its dues at his death had begun to give himself out as freeborn, changing his name to Laches:

"Laches, O Laches, once you are dead
Back to Cerylus you'll have it instead." [4]

---

[1] *Plaustra* was the urban form for "wagons." Rustics pronounced it *plostra*. Vespasian had either never entirely discarded the dialect of his Sabine countrymen or he still affected it. His retort was happy, since Flaurus was derived from a Greek word meaning "worthless."

[2] $16,400.00.

[3] *Iliad*, VII, 213.

[4] From Menander's θεοφορουμένη.

But he particularly resorted to witticisms about his unseemly means of gain, seeking to diminish their odium by some jocose saying and to turn them into a jest.

Having put off one of his favorite attendants, who asked for a stewardship for a pretended brother, he summoned the candidate himself, and after compelling him to pay him as much money as he had agreed to give his lawyer, appointed him to the position without delay. On his attendant's taking up the matter again, he said: "Find yourself another brother; the man that you thought was yours is mine." On a journey, suspecting that his muleteer had got down to shoe the mules merely to make delay and give time for a man with a lawsuit to approach the Emperor, he asked how much he was paid for shoeing the mules and insisted on a share of the money. When Titus found fault with him for contriving a tax upon public toilets, he held a piece of money from the first payment to his son's nose, asking whether its odor was offensive to him. When Titus said "No," he replied, "Yet it comes from urine." On the report of a deputation that a colossal statue of great cost had been voted him at public expense, he demanded to have it set up at once, and holding out his open hand, said that the base was ready. He did not cease his jokes even when in apprehension of death and in extreme danger. For when, among other portents, the Mausoleum opened on a sudden and a comet appeared in the heavens, he declared that the former applied to Junia Calvina of the family of Augustus,[1] and the latter to the King of the Parthians, who wore his hair long. And as death drew near, he said: "Woe's me. Methinks I'm turning into a God."

In his ninth consulship he had a slight illness in Campania, and returning at once to the city, he left for Cutilae and the country about Reate, where he spent the summer every year. There, in addition to an increase in his illness, having contracted a bowel complaint by too free use of the cold waters, he nevertheless continued to perform his duties as Emperor, even receiving embassies as he lay in bed. Taken on a sudden with such an attack of diarrhœa that he all but swooned, he

---

[1] The Flavian family had their own tomb. Therefore it did not concern him if the Mausoleum, the tomb of Augustus and his descendants, flew open.

said: "An Emperor ought to die standing," and while he was struggling to get on his feet, he died in the arms of those who tried to help him, on the ninth day before the Kalends of July, at the age of sixty-nine years, one month and seven days.

All agree that he had so much faith in his own horoscope and those of his family, that even after constant conspiracies were made against him he had the assurance to say to the Senate that either his sons would succeed him or he would have no successor. It is also said that he once dreamed that he saw a balance with its beam on a level placed in the middle of the vestibule of the palace, in one pan of which stood Claudius and Nero and in the other himself and his sons. And the dream came true, since both houses reigned for the same space of time and the same term of years.

THE DEIFIED TITUS

Titus, of the same surname as his father, was the delight and darling of the human race; such surpassing ability had he, by nature, art, or good fortune, to win the affections of all men, and that, too, which is no easy task, while he was Emperor. For as a private citizen and even during his father's rule, he did not escape hatred, much less public criticism.

He was born on the third day before the Kalends of January, in the year memorable for the death of Caligula in a mean house near the Septizonium and in a very small dark room besides; for it still remains and is shown to the curious.

He was brought up at court in company with Britannicus and taught the same subjects by the same masters. At that time, so they say, a physiognomist was brought in by Narcissus, the freedman of Claudius, to examine Britannicus and declared most positively that he would never become Em peror, but that Titus, who was standing near by at the time, would surely rule. The boys were so intimate too, that it is believed that when Britannicus drained the fatal draught, Titus, who was reclining at his side, also tasted of the potion and for a long time suffered from an obstinate disorder. Titus did not forget all this, but later set up a golden statue of his friend in the palace, and dedicated another equestrian statue of ivory, which is to this day carried in the procession in the Circus, and attended it on its first appearance.

Even in boyhood his bodily and mental gifts were conspicuous and they became more and more so as he advanced in years. He had a handsome person, in which there was no less dignity than grace, and was uncommonly strong, although he was not tall of stature and had a rather protruding belly. His memory was extraordinary and he had an aptitude for almost all the arts, both of war and of peace, Skillful in arms and horsemanship, he made speeches and wrote verses in Latin and Greek with ease and readiness, and even off-hand. He was besides not unacquainted with music, but sang and played the harp agreeably and skillfully. I have heard from many sources that he used also to write shorthand with great speed and would amuse himself by playful contests with his secretaries; also that he could imitate any handwriting that he had ever seen and often declared that he might have been the prince of forgers.

He served as military Tribune both in Germany and in Britain, winning a high reputation for energy and no less for integrity, as is evident from the great number of his statues and busts in both those provinces and from the inscriptions they bear.

After his military service he pleaded in the Forum, rather 'or glory than as a profession, and at the same time took to wife Arrecina Tertulla, whose father, though only a Roman Knight, had once been Prefect of the praetorian cohorts. On her death he replaced her by Marcia Furnilla, a lady of a very distinguished family, but divorced her after he had acknowledged a daughter which she bore him.

Then, after holding the office of Quaestor, as commander of a legion he subjugated the two strong cities of Tarichaeae and Gamala in Judaea, having his horse killed under him in one battle and mounting another, whose rider had fallen fighting by his side.

Presently he was sent to congratulate Galba on becoming ruler of the state, and attracted attention wherever he went, through the belief that he had been sent for to be adopted. But observing that everything was once more in a state of turmoil, he turned back, and visiting the oracle of the Paphian Venus, to consult it about his voyage, he was also encouraged to hope for imperial power. Soon realizing his hope [1] and left behind to complete the conquest of Judaea, in the final attack on Jerusalem he slew twelve of the defenders with as many arrows. He took the city on his daughter's birthday,[2] so delighting the soldiers and winning their devotion that they

[1] By the elevation of his father to the throne.

[2] Jerusalem was taken, sacked, and burned, by Titus, after a two years' siege, September 8, 70, in the second year of Vespasian's reign. Vespasian was 60. Titus 30. Pompey had taken it in 65 B.C. after a three months' siege.

hailed him as Imperator and detained him from time to time
when he would leave the province, urging him with prayers
and even with threats either to stay or to take them all with
him. This aroused the suspicion that he had tried to revolt
from his father and make himself King of the East. He
strengthened this suspicion on his way to Alexandria by wearing a diadem at the consecration of the bull Apis in Memphis,
an act quite in accord with the usual ceremonial of that ancient religion, but unfavorably interpreted by some. Because
of this he hastened to Italy, and putting in at Regium and
then at Puteoli in a transport ship, he went with all speed
from there to Rome, where, as if to show that the reports
about him were groundless, he surprised his father with the
greeting, "I am here, father; I am here."

From that time on he never ceased to act as the Emperor's
partner and even as his protector. He took part in his father's
triumph [1] and was Censor with him. He was also his colleague
in the tribunicial power and in seven consulships. He took
upon himself the discharge of almost all duties, personally
dictated letters and wrote edicts in his father's name, and even
read his speeches in the Senate in lieu of a Quaestor. He also
assumed the command of the praetorian guard, which before
that time had never been held except by a Roman Knight,
and in this office conducted himself in a somewhat arrogant
and tyrannical fashion. For whenever he himself regarded any
one with suspicion, he would secretly send some of the guard
to the various theaters and camps, to demand their punishment, as if by consent of all who were present. He would then
put them out of the way without delay. Among these was
Aulus Caecina, an ex-consul, whom he invited to dinner and
then ordered to be stabbed almost before he left the dining-
room. But in this case he was led by a pressing danger, having
got possession of an autograph copy of an harangue which
Caecina had prepared to deliver to the soldiers. Although by
such conduct he provided for his safety in the future, he incurred such odium at the time that hardly any one ever came

---

[1] Commemorated by the triumphal monument called the Arch of
Titus, erected by the Senate and people of Rome after his death. It is
still standing, and is one of the most beautiful and interesting models
of Roman architecture.

to the throne with so evil a reputation or so much against the desires of all.

Besides cruelty, he was also suspected of riotous living, since he protracted his revels until the middle of the night with the most prodigal of his friends; likewise of unchastity because of his troops of catamites and eunuchs, and his notorious passion for Queen Berenice, to whom it was even said that he promised marriage. He was suspected of greed as well, for it was well known that in cases which came before his father he put a price on his influence and accepted bribes. In short, people not only thought, but openly declared, that he would be a second Nero. But this reputation turned out to his advantage and gave place to the highest praise, when no fault was discovered in him, but on the contrary the highest virtues.

His banquets were pleasant rather than extravagant. He chose as his friends men whom succeeding Emperors also retained as indispensable alike to themselves and to the State, and of whose services they made special use. Berenice he sent from Rome at once, against her will and against his own. Some of his most beloved paramours, although they were such skillful dancers that they later became stage favorites, he not only ceased to cherish any longer, but even to witness their public performances.

He took away nothing from any citizen. He respected others' property, if any one ever did. In fact, he would not accept even proper and customary presents. And yet he was second to none of his predecessors in munificence. At the dedication of the amphitheater [1] and of the baths which were hastily built near it he gave a most magnificent and costly gladiatorial show. He presented a sham sea-fight too in the old Naumachia, and in the same place a combat of gladiators,[2] exhibiting in one day five thousand wild beasts of every kind.

He was most kindly by nature, and whereas in accordance with a custom established by Tiberius, all the Caesars who followed him refused to regard favors granted by previous Emperors as valid, unless they had themselves conferred the same ones on the same individuals, Titus was the first to

---

[1] The Coliseum, which had been in construction for four years.
[2] After the water had been let out.

ratify them all in a single edict, without allowing himself to be asked. Moreover, in the case of other requests made of him, it was his fixed rule not to let any one go away without hope. Even when his household officials warned him that he was promising more than he could perform, he said that it was not right for any one to go away sorrowful from an interview with his Emperor. On another occasion, remembering at dinner that he had done nothing for anybody all that day, he gave utterance to that memorable and praiseworthy remark: "Friends, I have lost a day."

The whole body of the people in particular he treated with such indulgence on all occasions, that once at a gladiatorial show he declared that he would give it, "not after his own inclinations, but those of the spectators"; and what is more, he kept his word. For he refused nothing which any one asked, and even urged them to ask for what they wished. Furthermore, he openly displayed his partiality for Thracian gladiators and bantered the people about it by words and gestures, always, however, preserving his dignity, as well as observing justice. Not to omit any act of condescension, he sometimes bathed in the baths which he had built, in company with the common people.

There were some dreadful disasters during his reign, such as the eruption of Mount Vesuvius in Campania, a fire at Rome which continued three days and as many nights, and a plague the like of which had hardly ever been known before.[1] In these many great calamities he showed not merely the concern of an Emperor, but even a father's surpassing love, now offering consolation in edicts, and now lending aid so far as his means allowed. He chose commissioners by lot from among the ex-consuls for the relief of Campania, and the property of those who lost their lives by Vesuvius and had no heirs left alive he applied to the rebuilding of the buried cities. During the fire in Rome he made no remark except "I am ruined,"[2] and he set aside all the ornaments of his villas for the public buildings and temples, and put several men of the equestrian order in charge of the work, that everything might be done

---

[1] Eusebius (*Chronicon* II) says the dead numbered as high as ten thousand a day.

[2] Implying that it was his personal loss, which he would make good.

with the greater dispatch. For curing the plague and diminish·
ing the force of the epidemic there was no aid, human or
divine, which he did not employ, searching for every kind of
sacrifice and all kinds of medicines.

Among the evils of the times were the informers and their
instigators, who had enjoyed a long standing license. After
these had been soundly beaten in the Forum with scourges
and cudgels, and finally led in procession across the arena of
the amphitheater, he had some of them put up and sold, and
others deported to the wildest of the islands. Further to dis-
courage for all time any who might think of venturing on
similar practices, among other precautions he made it unlawful for any one to be tried under several laws for the same offense, or for any inquiry to be made as to the legal status of
any deceased person after a stated number of years.

Having declared that he would accept the office of Pontifex
Maximus for the purpose of keeping his hands unstained, he
was true to his promise. For, after that he neither caused nor
connived at the death of any man, although he sometimes had
no lack of reasons for taking vengeance; but he swore that he
would rather be killed than kill. When two men of patrician
family were found guilty of aspiring to the throne, he satisfied
himself with warning them to abandon their attempt, saying
that imperial power was the gift of fate, and promising that if
there was anything else they desired, he himself would bestow
it. Then he sent his couriers with all speed to the mother of
one of them, for she was some distance off, to relieve her
anxiety by reporting that her son was safe. And he not only
invited the men themselves to dinner among his friends, but
on the following day at a gladiatorial show he purposely placed
them near him, and when the swords of the contestants were
offered him,[1] handed them over for their inspection. It is even
said that he inquired into the horoscope of each of them, and
declared that danger threatened them both, but at some future
time and from another, as turned out to be the case.

Although his brother [2] never ceased plotting against him,
but almost openly stirred up the armies to revolt and meditated

---

[1] The weapons of gladiators were regularly examined by the giver
of the games to see if they were sharp enough.

[2] Domitian.

flight to them, he had not the heart to put him to death or banish him from the court, or even to hold him in less honor than before. On the contrary, as he had done from the very first day of his rule, he continued to declare that he was his partner and successor, and sometimes he privately begged him with tears and prayers to be willing at least to return his affection.

In the meantime he was cut off by death, to the loss of mankind rather than to his own. After finishing the public games, at the close of which he wept bitterly in the presence of the people, he went to the Sabine territory, somewhat cast down because a victim had escaped as he was sacrificing and because it had thundered from a clear sky. Then at the very first stopping place he was seized with a fever, and as he was being carried on from there in a litter, it is said that he pushed back the curtains, looked up to heaven, and lamented bitterly that his life was being taken from him contrary to his deserts. For he said that there was no act of his life of which he had cause to repent, save one only. What this was he did not himself disclose at the time, nor could any one easily divine.[1] Some think that he recalled the intimacy which he had with his brother's wife. But Domitia swore most solemnly that this did not exist, although she would not have denied it if it had been in the least true, but on the contrary would have boasted of it, as she was most ready to do of all her scandalous actions.

He died in the same farmhouse as his father, on the Ides of September, two years two months and twenty days after succeeding Vespasian, in the forty-second year of his age. When his death was made known, the whole populace mourned as they would for a loss in their own families, the Senate hastened to the House before it was summoned by proclamation, and with the doors still shut, and then with them open, rendered such thanks to him and heaped such praise on him after death as they had never done even when he was alive and present.

---

[1] Perhaps Domitian's charge that Titus had tampered with Vespasian's will was true. See *Domitian*.

DOMITIAN

DOMITIAN was born on the ninth day before the Kalends of November of the year when his father was Consul-elect and was about to enter on the office in the following month, in a street of the sixth region called "the Pomegranate," in a house which he afterwards converted into a temple of the Flavian family. He is said to have passed the period of his boyhood and his early youth in great poverty and infamy. For he did not possess a single piece of plate and it is a well known fact that Claudius Pollio, a man of praetorian rank, against whom Nero's poem entitled "The One-eyed Man" is directed, preserved a letter in Domitian's handwriting and sometimes exhibited it, in which the future Emperor promised him an assignation; and there have not been wanting those who declared that Domitian was also debauched by Nerva, who succeeded him. In the war with Vitellius he took refuge in the Capitol with his paternal uncle Sabinus and a part of the forces under him. When the enemy forced an entrance and the temple was fired, he hid during the night with the guardian of the shrine, and in the morning, disguised in the garb of a follower of Isis and mingling with the priests of that fickle superstition, he went across the Tiber with a single companion to the mother of one of his school-fellows. There he was so effectually concealed, that though he was closely followed, he could not be found, in spite of a thorough search. It was only after the victory that he ventured forth and after being hailed as Caesar,[1] he assumed the office of City Praetor with consular powers, but only in name, turning over all the judicial business to his next colleague. But he exercised all the tyranny of his high position so lawlessly, that it was even then apparent what sort of a man he was going to be. Not to mention all details, after making free with the wives of many men, he

---

[1] He governed the city till his father arrived.

went so far as to marry Domitia Longina, who was the wife of Aelius Lamia, and in a single day he assigned more than twenty positions in the city and abroad, which led Vespasian to say more than once that he was surprised that he did not appoint the Emperor's successors with the rest.

He began an expedition against Gaul and the Germanies, which was uncalled for and from which his father's friends dissuaded him, merely that he might make himself equal to his brother in power and rank. For this he was reprimanded, and to give him a better realization of his youth [1] and position, he had to live with his father, and when they appeared in public he followed the Emperor's chair and that of his brother in a litter, while he also attended their triumph over Judaea riding on a white horse.[2] Moreover, of his six consul ships only one was a regular one, and he obtained that only because his brother gave place to him and recommended his appointment.

He himself too made a remarkable pretense of modesty and especially of an interest in poetry, an art which had previously been as unfamiliar to him as it was later despised and rejected, and he even gave readings in public. Yet in spite of all this, when Vologaesus, King of the Parthians, had asked for auxiliaries against the Alani and for one of Vespasian's sons as their leader, Domitian used every effort to have himself sent rather than Titus. And because the affair came to nothing, he tried by gifts and promises to induce other eastern kings to make the same request.

On the death of his father he hesitated for some time whether to offer a double largess [3] to the soldiers, and he never had any compunction about saying that he had been left a partner in the imperial power, but that the will had been tampered with. And from that time on he never ceased to plot against his brother secretly and openly, until Titus was seized with a dangerous illness, when Domitian ordered that he be left for dead, before he had actually drawn his last breath. And after his death he bestowed no honor upon him, save that of deification, and he often assailed his memory

---

[1] He was eighteen at the time.
[2] The usual procedure for a youthful prince.
[3] Double his brother's in order to sway them to support him.

in ambiguous phrases, both in his speeches and in his edicts. At the beginning of his reign he used to spend hours in seclusion every day, doing nothing but catch flies and stab them with a keenly-sharpened stylus. Consequently when some one once asked whether any one was in there with Caesar, Vibius Crispus made the witty reply: "Not even a fly."

Soon after his advancement he bestowed the name of Augusta on his wife Domitia. He had had a son by her in his second consulship, and in the following year a daughter. He divorced her because of her love for the actor Paris, but could not bear the separation and soon took her back, alleging that the people demanded it.

In his administration of the government he for some time showed himself inconsistent, with about an equal number of virtues and vices, but finally he turned the virtues also into vices. For, so far as one may guess, it was contrary to his natural disposition that he was made rapacious through need and cruel through fear.

He constantly gave grand and costly entertainments, both in the amphitheater and in the Circus, where in addition to the usual races between two-horse and four-horse chariots, he also exhibited two battles, one between forces of infantry and the other by horsemen. And he even gave a naval battle in the amphitheater. Besides he gave hunts of wild beasts, gladiatorial shows at night by the light of torches, and not only combats between men but between women as well. He was always present too at the games given by the Quaestors, which he revived after they had been abandoned for some time, and invariably granted the people the privilege of calling for two pairs of gladiators from his own school, and brought them in last in all the splendor of the court. During the whole of every gladiatorial show there always stood at his feet a small boy clad in scarlet, with an abnormally small head, with whom he used to talk a great deal, and sometimes seriously. At any rate, he was overheard to ask him if he knew why he had decided at the last appointment day to make Mettius Rufus Prefect of Egypt. He often gave sea-fights almost with regular fleets, having dug a pool near the

Tiber and surrounded it with seats; and he continued to witness the contests amid heavy rains.

He also celebrated Secular games, reckoning the time, not according to the year when Claudius had last given them, but by the previous calculation of Augustus. In the course of these, to make it possible to finish a hundred races on the day of the contests in the Circus, he diminished the number of laps from seven to five.

He also established a quinquennial contest in honor of Jupiter Capitolinus of a threefold character, comprising music, riding, and gymnastics, and with considerably more prizes than are awarded nowadays. For there were competitions in prose declamation [1] both in Greek and in Latin. And in addition to contests of the lyre-players, there were others of several playing together as well as singly but without singing, while in the stadium there were races even between maidens. He presided at the competitions in half-boots, clad in a purple toga in the Greek fashion, and wearing upon his head a golden crown with figures of Jupiter, Juno, and Minerva, while by his side sat the Priest of Jupiter and the college of the Flaviales,[2] similarly dressed, except that their crowns bore his image as well. He celebrated the Quinquatria too every year in honor of Minerva at his Alban villa, and established for her a college of priests, from which men were chosen by lot to act as officers and give splendid shows of wild beasts and stage plays, besides holding contests in oratory and poetry.

He made a present to the people of three hundred sesterces [3] each on three occasions, and in the course of one of his shows in celebration of the feast of the Seven Hills gave a plentiful banquet, distributing large baskets of victuals to the Senate and Knights, and smaller ones to the Commons. And he himself was the first to begin to eat. On the following day he scattered gifts of all sorts of things to be scrambled for, and since the greater part of these fell where the people

---

[1] As well as in poetry.

[2] Established for the worship of the deified Emperors of the Flavian line after the manner of the Augustan.

[3] $12.30.

sat, he had five hundred tickets thrown into each section occupied by the senatorial and equestrian orders.

He restored many splendid buildings which had been destroyed by fire, among them the Capitolium, which had again been burned,[1] but in all cases with the inscription of his own name only, and with no mention of the original builder. Furthermore, he built a new temple on the Capitoline hill in honor of Jupiter Custos and the Forum which now bears the name of Nerva;[2] likewise a temple to the Flavian family, a stadium, an Odeum,[3] and a pool for sea-fights. From the stone used in this last the Circus Maximus was afterwards rebuilt, when both sides of it had been destroyed by fire.

His campaigns he undertook partly without provocation and partly of necessity. That against the Chatti was uncalled for, while the one against the Sarmatians was justified by the destruction of a legion with its commander. He made two against the Dacians, the first when Oppius Sabinus an exconsul was defeated, and the second on the overthrow of Cornelius Fuscus, Prefect of the praetorian guard, to whom he had entrusted the conduct of the war. After several battles of varying success he celebrated a double triumph over the Chatti and the Dacians.[4] His victories over the Sarmatians he commemorated merely by the offering of a laurel crown to Jupiter of the Capitol.

A civil war which was set on foot by Lucius Antonius, Governor of Upper Germany, was put down in the Emperor's absence by a remarkable stroke of good fortune, for at the very hour of the battle the Rhine suddenly thawed and prevented his barbarian allies from crossing over to Antonius. Domitian learned of this victory through omens before he actually had news of it, for on the very day when the decisive battle was fought a magnificent eagle enfolded his statue at Rome with its wings, uttering exultant shrieks, and soon afterwards a report of the death of Antonius became so cur-

---

[1] For the third time: first in the Marian war, and rebuilt by Pompey; second in 69, during the reign of Vitellius; third in 80 in the fire mentioned in *Titus*.

[2] Who finished and dedicated it.

[3] The first Music Hall in Rome.

[4] This triumph Tacitus in *Agricola* XXXIX calls a farce.

rent, that several went so far as to assert positively that they had seen his head brought to Rome.

He made many innovations also in common customs. He did away with the dole of food distributed in baskets to the people and revived the old custom of regular public dinners. He added two factions of drivers in the Circus, with gold and purple as their colors, to the four former ones. He forbade the appearance of actors on the stage, but allowed the practice of their art in private houses. He prohibited the castration of males, and kept down the price of the eunuchs that remained in the hands of the slave dealers. Once upon the occasion of a plentiful wine crop, attended with a scarcity of grain, thinking that the fields were neglected through too much attention to the vineyards, he made an edict forbidding any one to plant more vines in Italy and ordering that the vineyards in the provinces be cut down, or but half of them at most be left standing. But he did not persist in carrying out the measure. He divided some of the most important offices of the court [1] between the freedmen and Roman Knights. He prohibited the uniting of two legions in one camp and the deposit of more than a thousand sesterces [2] by any one soldier at headquarters,[3] because it was clear that Lucius Antonius had been especially led to attempt a revolution by the amount of such deposits in the combined winter quarters of two legions. He increased the pay of the soldiers one-fourth, by the addition of three gold pieces each year.[4]

He administered justice scrupulously and conscientiously, frequently holding special sittings on the tribunal in the Forum. He rescinded such decisions of the Hundred Judges as had been made through favor or interest. He often warned the arbiters not to grant claims for freedom made under false pretenses. He degraded jurors who accepted bribes, together with all their associates. He also induced the Tribunes of the Commons to prosecute a corrupt Aedile for extortion, and to

[1] Formerly held by freedmen. Hadrian restricted them to Knights.
[2] $41.00.
[3] Soldiers had been encouraged to deposit all they could save with the general in command. They would then have ready money at the end of the term of their service. In the meantime they would fight better.
[4] That is, he raised the amount from $36.9 to $41.20.

ask the Senate to appoint jurors in the case. He took such care to exercise restraint over the city officials and the Governors of the provinces, that at no time were they more honest or just, whereas after his time we have seen many of them charged with all manner of offenses.

Having undertaken the correction of public morals, he put an end to the license at the theaters, where the general public occupied the seats reserved for the Knights. He did away with the prevailing publication of scurrilous lampoons, in which distinguished men and women were attacked, and imposed ignominious penalties on their authors. He expelled an ex-quaestor from the Senate, because he was given to acting and dancing. He deprived notorious women of the use of litters, as well as of the right to receive inheritances and legacies. He struck the name of a Roman Knight from the list of jurors, because he had taken back his wife after divorcing her and charging her with adultery. He condemned several men of both orders, offenders against the Scantinian law.[1] And the incest of Vestal Virgins, condoned even by his father and his brother, he punished severely in divers ways, at first by capital punishment, and afterwards in the ancient fashion. For while he allowed the sisters Oculata and also Varronilla free choice of the manner of their deaths, and banished their paramours, he later ordered that Cornelia, a chief-Vestal who had been acquitted once but after a long interval again arraigned and found guilty, be buried alive; and her lovers were beaten to death with rods in the Comitium, with the exception of an ex-praetor, whom he allowed to go into exile, because he admitted his guilt while the case was still unsettled and the examination and torture of the witnesses had led to no result. To protect the Gods from being dishonored with impunity by any sacrilege, he caused a tomb which one of his freedmen had built for his son from stones intended for the temple of Jupiter of the Capitol to be destroyed by the soldiers and the bones and ashes contained in it thrown into the sea.

In the earlier part of his reign he so shrank from any form of bloodshed, that while his father was still absent from the

---

[1] Against sodomy.

city, he planned to issue an edict that no oxen should be offered in sacrifice, recalling the line of Vergil,

> "Ere godless men, restrained from blood in vain,
>   Began to feast on flesh of bullocks slain." [1]

He was equally free from any suspicion of love of gain or
of avarice, both in private life and for some time after becoming Emperor. On the contrary, he often gave strong proofs
not merely of integrity, but even of liberality. He treated all
his intimates most generously, and there was nothing which
he urged them more frequently, or with greater insistence,
than that they should not be niggardly in any of their acts.
He would not accept inheritances left him by those who had
children. He even annulled a legacy in the will of Rustus
Caepio, who had provided that his heir should yearly pay a
specified sum to each of the Senators on his entrance into the
House.[2] He canceled the suits against those who had been
posted as debtors to the public treasury for more than five
years, and would not allow a renewal except within a year
and on the condition that an accuser who did not win his suit
should be punished with exile. Scribes of the Quaestors who
carried on business, which had become usual although contrary to the Clodian law, he pardoned for past offenses. Par-
cels of land which were left unoccupied here and there after
the assignment of lands to the veterans he granted to their
old-time owners as by right of possession. He checked false
accusations designed for the profit of the privy purse and inflicted severe penalties on offenders. And a saying of his was
current, that an Emperor who does not punish informers
hounds them on.

But he did not continue this course of mercy or integrity,
although he turned to cruelty somewhat more speedily than
to avarice. He put to death a pupil of the pantomimic actor
Paris, who was still a beardless boy and ill at the time, because in his skill and his appearance he seemed not unlike
his master; also Hermogenes of Tarsus because of some al-
lusions in his History, besides crucifying even the slaves who

---

[1] *Georgics* II, 537.
[2] On his first entrance, Suetonius probably meant.

had written it out. A householder who said that a Thracian gladiator was a match for the *murmillo,* but not for the giver of the games, he caused to be dragged from his seat and thrown into the arena to dogs, with this placard: "A favorer of the Thracians who spoke impiously." [1]

He put to death many Senators, among them several ex-consuls, including Civica Cerealis, at the very time when he was Proconsul in Asia, Salvidienus Orfitus, and Acilius Glabrio while he was in exile, under the pretense they were plotting revolution. For the rest, any charge served, no matter how trivial. He slew Aelius Lamia for joking remarks, which were reflections on him, it is true, but made long before and harmless. For when Domitian had taken away Lamia's wife, the latter replied to some one who praised his voice: "I practice continence"; [2] and when Titus urged him to marry again, he replied: "Are you too looking for a wife?" He put to death Salvius Cocceianus, because he had kept the birthday of the Emperor Otho, his paternal uncle; Mettius Pompusianus, because it was commonly reported that he had an imperial nativity and carried about a map of the world on parchment and speeches of the Kings and Generals from Titus Livius, besides giving two of his slaves the names of Mago and Hannibal. He put Sallustius Lucullus, Governor of Britain, to death for allowing some lances of a new pattern to be called "Lucullean," after his own name; Junius Rusticus, because he had published eulogies of Paetus Thrasea and Helvidius Priscus and called them the most upright of men, banishing, on the occasion of this charge, all the philosophers from the city and from Italy. He executed the younger Helvidius, alleging that in a farce composed for the stage he had under the characters of Paris and Oenone censured Domitian's divorce from his wife; also Flavius Sabinus, one of his cousins, because on the day of the consular elections the crier had inadvertently announced him to the people as Emperor-elect, instead of Consul.

---

[1] Domitian favored the *murmillos,* the gladiators who fought with Gallic arms. The spirit of partisanship ran so high at the gladiatorial combats that it was almost treason to speak against the Emperor's favorites.

[2] Part of the method of voice training then practiced.

After his victory in the civil war he became even more cruel, and to discover any conspirators who were in hiding, tortured many of the opposite party by a new form of inquisition, inserting fire in their privates; and he cut off the hands of some of them. It is certain that of the more conspicuous only two were pardoned, a Tribune of senatorial rank and a Centurion, who the more clearly to prove their freedom from guilt, showed that they were of shameless unchastity and could therefore have had no influence with the general or with the soldiers.

His savage cruelty was not only excessive, but also cunning and sudden. He invited one of his stewards to his bedchamber the day before crucifying him, made him sit beside him on his couch, and dismissed him in a secure and gay frame of mind, even deigning to send him a share of his dinner. When he was on the point of condemning the ex-consul Arrecinius Clemens, one of his intimates and tools, he treated him with as great favor as before, if not greater, and finally, as he was taking a drive with him, catching sight of his accuser he said: "Pray, shall we hear this base slave tomorrow?"

To abuse men's patience the more insolently, he never pronounced an unusually dreadful sentence without a preliminary declaration of clemency, so that there came to be no more certain indication of a cruel death than the leniency of his preamble. He had brought some men charged with treason into the Senate, and when he had introduced the matter by saying that he would find out that day how dear he was to the members, he had no difficulty in causing them to be condemned to suffer the ancient method of punishment.[1] Then appalled at the cruelty of the penalty, he interposed a veto, to lessen the odium, in these words (for it will be of interest to know his exact language): "Allow me, Fathers of the Senate, to prevail on you by your love for me to grant a favor which I know I shall obtain with difficulty, namely that you allow the condemned free choice of the manner of their death; for thus you will spare your own eyes and all men will know that I was present at the meeting of the Senate."

---

[1] Necks locked in a pillory, then beaten to death.

Reduced to financial straits by the cost of his buildings and shows, as well as by the additions which he had made to the pay of the soldiers, he tried to lighten the military expenses by diminishing the number of his troops. But perceiving that in this way he exposed himself to the attacks of the barbarians, and nevertheless had difficulty in easing his burdens, he had no hesitation in resorting to every sort of robbery. The property of the living and the dead was seized everywhere on any charge brought by any accuser. It was enough to allege any action or word derogatory to the majesty of the prince. Estates of those in no way connected with him were confiscated, if but one man came forward to declare that he had heard from the deceased during his lifetime that Caesar was his heir. Besides other taxes, that on the Jews [1] was levied with the utmost rigor, and those were prosecuted who without publicly acknowledging that faith yet lived as Jews, as well as those who concealed their nationality and did not pay the tribute levied upon their people.[2] I recall being present in my youth when the person of a man ninety years old was examined before the Procurator and a very crowded court, to see whether he was circumcised.

From his youth he was far from being of an affable disposition, but was on the contrary presumptuous and unbridled both in act and in word. When his father's concubine Caenis returned from Histria and offered to kiss him as usual, he held out his hand to her. He was vexed that his brother's son-in-law had attendants clad in white, as well as he, and uttered the words

"Not good is a number of rulers." [3]

When he became Emperor, he did not hesitate to boast in the Senate that he had conferred their power on both his father and his brother, and that they had but returned him his own; nor on taking back his wife after their divorce, that

---

[1] A tax of $0.38 per head, imposed by Titus, in return for permission to practice their religion.

[2] Christians doubtless, whom the Romans commonly confounded with the Jews.

[3] *Iliad,* II, 204.

he had "recalled her to his divine couch." [1] He delighted to
hear the people in the amphitheater shout on his feast day:
"Good Fortune attend our Lord [2] and Mistress." Even more,
in the Capitoline competition when Palfurius Sura received
the prize for oratory and all the people begged with concerted
unanimity that he be restored to his place in the Senate from
which he had been banished some time before, Domitian
deigned no reply, but merely had a crier bid them be silent.
With no less arrogance he began as follows in issuing a circular letter in the name of his procurators, "Our Master and
our God bids that this be done." And so the custom arose of
henceforth addressing him in no other way even in writing or
in conversation. He suffered no statues to be set up in his
honor in the Capitol, except of gold and silver and of a fixed
weight. He erected so many and such huge vaulted passage-
ways and arches in the various regions of the city, adorned
with chariots and triumphal emblems, that on one of them
some one wrote in Greek: "It is enough." [3]

He held the consulship seventeen times, more often than
any of his predecessors. Of these the seven middle ones were
in successive years, but all of them he filled in name only,
continuing none beyond the first of May and few after the
Ides of January. Having assumed the surname Germanicus
after his two triumphs, he renamed the months of September
and October from his own names, calling them "Germanicus"
and "Domitianus," because in the former he had come to the
throne and was born in the latter.

In this way he became an object of terror and hatred to
all, but he was overthrown at last by a conspiracy of his
friends and favorite freedmen, to which his wife was also
privy. He had long since had a premonition of the last year
and day of his life, and even of the very hour and manner of
his death. In his youth astrologers had predicted all this to
him, and his father once even openly ridiculed him at dinner

---

[1] As if he were God, for the word here translated as couch means
specifically the dais on which the images of the gods rested.

[2] Augustus shrank from the salutation of *dominus*, lord, as implying
a slave master.

[3] The pun turns on the similar sound of the Greek word for "enough"
and the Latin for "arch."

for refusing mushrooms, saying that he showed himself unaware of his destiny in not rather fearing the sword. Therefore he was at all times timorous and worried, and was disquieted beyond measure by even the slightest suspicions. It is thought that nothing had more effect in inducing him to ignore his proclamation about cutting down the vineyards than the circulation of notes containing the following lines:

"Gnaw me to my root, O goat, yet shall my juice suffice
  To wet your head when you are led to sacrifice." [1]

It was because of this same timorousness that although he was most eager for all such honors, he refused a new one which the Senate had devised and offered to him, a decree, namely, that whenever he held the consulship Roman Knights selected by lot should precede him among his Lictors and attendants, clad in the trabea [2] and bearing lances.

As the time when he anticipated danger drew near, becoming still more anxious every day, he lined the walls of the colonnades in which he used to walk with phengite stone, to be able to see in its brilliant surface the reflection of all that went on behind his back. And he did not give a hearing to any prisoners except in private and alone, even holding their chains in his hands. Further, to convince his household that one must not venture to kill a patron even on good grounds, he condemned Epaphroditus, his confidential secretary, to death, because it was believed that after Nero was abandoned the freedman's hand had aided him in taking his life.

Finally he put to death his own cousin Flavius Clemens, suddenly and on a very slight suspicion, almost before the end of his consulship. And yet Flavius was a man of most contemptible laziness and Domitian had besides openly named his sons, who were then very young, as his successors, changing their former names and calling the one Vespasian and the other Domitian. And it was by this deed in particular that he hastened his own destruction.

---

[1] From the Greek poet Evenus. Some of the Suetonius texts read "Caesar" instead of "goat."

[2] A toga ornamented with horizontal purple stripes worn by the Knights on public occasions, as well as by the early Kings and Consuls.

For eight successive months so many strokes of lightning occurred and were reported, that at last he cried: "Well, let him now strike whom he will." The temple of Jupiter of the Capitol was struck and that of the Flavian family, as well as the palace and the Emperor's own bedroom. The inscription too on the base of a triumphal statue of his was torn off in a violent tempest and fell upon a neighboring tomb. The tree which had been overthrown when Vespasian was still a private citizen but had sprung up anew, then on a sudden fell down again. Fortune of Praeneste had throughout his whole reign, when he commended the new year to her protection, given him a favorable omen and always in the same words. Now at last she returned a most direful one, not without the mention of bloodshed.

He dreamed that Minerva, whom he worshiped with superstitious veneration, came forth from her shrine and declared that she could no longer protect him, since she had been disarmed by Jupiter. Yet there was nothing by which he was so much disturbed as a prediction of the astrologer Ascletarion and what befell him. When this man was accused before the Emperor and did not deny that he had spoken of certain things which he had foreseen through his art, he was asked what his own end would be. When he replied that he would shortly be rent by dogs, Domitian ordered him killed at once, but to prove the fallibility of his art, he ordered besides that his funeral be attended to with the greatest care. While this was being done, it chanced that the pyre was overset by a sudden storm and dogs mangled the corpse, which was only partly consumed, and that an actor of farces called Latinus, who happened to pass by and see the incident, told it to Domitian at the dinner table, with the rest of the day's gossip.

The day before he was killed he gave orders to have some apples which were offered him kept until the following day, and added: "If only I am spared to eat them." Then turning to his companions, he declared that on the following day the moon would be stained with blood in Aquarius, and that a deed would be done of which men would talk all over the world. At about midnight he was so terrified that he leaped from his bed. The next morning he conducted the trial of a soothsayer sent from Germany, who when consulted about the lightning strokes had foretold a change of rulers, and condemned him to death. While he was vigorously scratching a festered wart on his forehead, and had drawn blood, he said: "May this be all." Then he asked the time, and by prearrangement the sixth hour was announced to him, instead of the fifth, which he feared. Filled with joy at this, and believing all danger now past, he was hastening to the bath, when his head chamberlain Parthenius changed his purpose by announcing that some one had called about a matter of great moment and would not be put off. Then he dismissed all his attendants and went to his bedroom, where he was slain.

Concerning the nature of the plot and the manner of his death, this is about all that became known. As the conspirators were deliberating when and how to attack him, whether at the bath or at dinner, Stephanus, Domitilla's [1] steward, at the time under accusation for embezzlement, offered his aid and counsel. To avoid suspicion, he wrapped up his left arm in woollen bandages for some days, pretending that he had injured it, and concealed in them a dagger. Then pretending to betray a conspiracy and for that reason being given an audience, he stabbed the Emperor in the groin as he was reading a paper which the assassin handed him, and stood in a state of amazement. As the wounded prince attempted to resist, he was slain with seven wounds by Clodianus, a subaltern, Maximus, a freedman of Parthenius, Satur, head chamberlain, and a gladiator from the imperial school. A boy who was engaged in his usual duty of attending to the images of the household Gods in the bedroom, and so was a witness of the murder, gave this additional information. He was bidden by Domitian, immediately after he was dealt the first blow, to hand him the dagger hidden under his pillow and to call the servants. But he found nothing at the head of the bed save the hilt, and besides all the doors were closed. Meanwhile the Emperor grappled with Stephanus and bore him to the ground, where they struggled for a long time, Domitian trying now to wrest the dagger from his assailant's

---

[1] Domitian's niece.

hands and now to gouge out his eyes with his lacerated fingers.

He was slain on the fourteenth day before the Kalends of October in the forty-fifth year of his age and the fifteenth of his reign. His corpse was carried out on a common bier by those who bury the poor, and his nurse Phyllis cremated it at her suburban estate on the Via Latina. But his ashes she secretly carried to the temple of the Flavian family and mingled them with those of Julia, daughter of Titus, whom she had also reared.

He was tall of stature, with a modest expression and a high color. His eyes were large, but his sight was somewhat weak. He was handsome and graceful too, especially when a young man, and indeed in his whole body with the exception of his feet, the toes of which were somewhat cramped. In later life he had the further disfigurement of baldness, a protruding belly, and spindle legs, though the latter had become thin from a long illness. He was so conscious that the modesty of his expression was in his favor, that he once made this boast in the Senate: "So far, at any rate, you have approved my heart and my countenance." He was so sensitive about his baldness, that he regarded it as a personal insult if any one else was twitted with that defect in jest or in earnest, though in a book "On the Care of the Hair," which he published and dedicated to a friend, he wrote the following by way of consolation to the man and himself:

" 'Do you not see that I am comely, too, and tall?' [1]

And yet the same fate awaits my hair, and I bear with resignation the aging of my locks in youth. Be assured that nothing is more pleasing than beauty, but nothing shorter-lived."

He was incapable of exertion and seldom went about the city on foot, while on his campaigns and journeys he rarely rode on horseback, but was regularly carried in a litter. He took no interest in arms, but was particularly devoted to archery. There are many who have more than once seen him slay a hundred wild beasts of different kinds on his Alban estate, and purposely kill some of them with two successive

---

[1] *Iliad*, **XXI**, 108.

shots in such a way that the arrows gave the effect of horns. Sometimes he would have a slave stand at a distance and hold out the palm of his right hand for a mark, with the fingers spread. Then he directed his arrows with such accuracy that they passed harmlessly between the fingers.

At the beginning of his rule he neglected liberal studies, although he provided for having the libraries, which were destroyed by fire, renewed at very great expense, seeking everywhere for copies of the lost works, and sending scribes to Alexandria to transcribe and correct them. Yet he never took any pains to become acquainted with history or poetry, or even to acquiring an ordinarily good style. He read nothing except the memoirs and transactions of Tiberius Caesar. For his letters, speeches and proclamations he relied on others' talents. Yet his conversation was not inelegant, and some of his sayings were even noteworthy. "How I wish," said he, "that I were as fine looking as Maecius thinks he is." He declared too that the head of a certain man, whose hair had changed color in such a way that it was partly reddish and partly gray, was like "snow on which mead had been poured."

He used to say that the lot of princes was most unhappy, since when they discovered a conspiracy, no one believed them unless they had been killed.

Whenever he had leisure he amused himself with playing at dice, even on working days and in the morning hours. He went to the bath before the end of the forenoon and lunched to the point of satiety, so that at dinner he rarely took anything except a Matian apple [1] and a moderate amount of wine from a jug. He gave numerous and generous banquets, but usually ended them early. In no case did he protract them beyond sunset, or follow them by a drinking bout. In fact, he did nothing until the hour for retiring except walk alone in a retired place.

He was excessively lustful. His constant sexual intercourse he called bed-wrestling, as if it were a kind of exercise. It was reported that he depilated his concubines with his own hand and swam with common prostitutes. After persistently

---

[1] A famous variety named after C. Matius, friend of Augustus and writer on cookery and gardening.

refusing his niece,[1] who was offered him in marriage when she was still a maid, because he was entangled in an intrigue with Domitia, he seduced her shortly afterwards when she became the wife of another, and that too during the litetime of Titus. Later, when she was bereft of father and husband, he loved her ardently and without disguise, and even became the cause of her death by compelling her to get rid of a child of his by abortion.

The people received the news of his death with indifference, but the soldiers were greatly grieved and at once attempted to call him the Deified Domitian, while they were prepared also to avenge him, had they not lacked leaders. This, however, they did accomplish a little later by most insistently demanding the execution of his murderers. The Senators on the contrary were so overjoyed, that they raced to fill the House, where they did not refrain from assailing the dead Emperor with the most insulting and stinging kind of outcries. They even had ladders brought and his shields and images torn down before their eyes and dashed upon the ground. Finally they passed a decree that his inscriptions should everywhere be erased, and all record of him obliterated.

A few months before he was killed, a raven perched on the Capitolium [2] and cried "All will be well," an omen which some interpreted as follows:

> "Late croaked a raven from Tarpeia's height,
> 'All is not yet, but shortly will be, right.' "

Domitian himself, it is said, dreamed that a golden hump grew out on his back, and he regarded this as an infallible sign that the condition of the empire would be happier and more prosperous after his time. And this was shortly shown to be true through the uprightness and moderate rule of the succeeding Emperors.

---

[1] Julia, daughter of Titus.
[2] Sometimes called the Tarpeian Hill from the Tarpeian Rock at its southwest corner.

MODERN LIBRARY GIANTS

A series of sturdily bound and handsomely printed, full-sized library editions of books formerly available only in expensive sets. These volumes contain from 600 to 1,400 pages each.

THE MODERN LIBRARY GIANTS REPRESENT A SELECTION OF THE WORLD'S GREATEST BOOKS

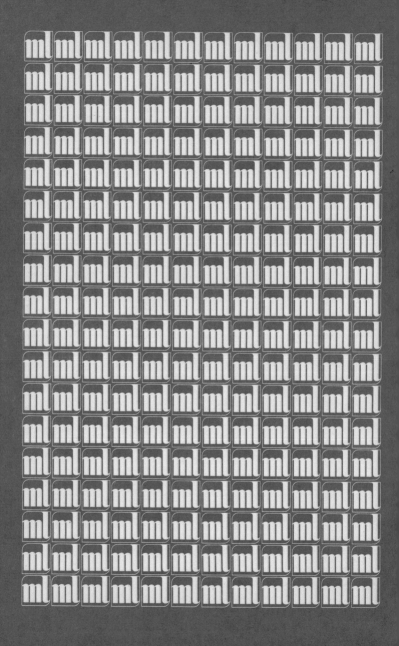